# BASEBALL ON THE BORDER

# BASEBALL ON THE BORDER

A TALE OF TWO LAREDOS

*Alan M. Klein*

PRINCETON UNIVERSITY PRESS     PRINCETON, NEW JERSEY

Copyright © 1997 by Princeton University Press
Published by Princeton University Press, 41 William Street,
Princeton, New Jersey 08540
In the United Kingdom: Princeton University Press,
Chichester, West Sussex
All Rights Reserved

*Library of Congress Cataloging-in-Publication Data*
Klein, Alan M., 1946–
Baseball on the border : a tale of two Laredos / Alan M. Klein.
   p.   cm.
Includes bibliographic references and index.
ISBN 0-691-01198-2 (alk. paper)
1. Baseball—Social aspects—Texas—Laredo—Case studies.
2. Baseball—Social aspects—Mexico—Nuevo Laredo—Case studies.
3. Nationalism and sports—Texas—Laredo—Case studies.
4. Nationalism and sports—Mexico—Nuevo Laredo—Case studies.
5. Cities and towns—Mexican-American Border Region—Social
conditions—Case studies.   I. Title.
GV867.64.K54   1997
796.357'09764'462—dc21   96-46301   CIP

This book has been composed in Janson

Princeton University Press books are printed
on acid-free paper and meet the guidelines
for permanence and durability of the Committee
on Production Guidelines for Book Longevity
of the Council on Library Resources

Printed in the United States of America
by Princeton Academic Press

10   9   8   7   6   5   4   3   2   1

FOR MILTON MY COMPASS, AND MARY MY LIGHT,

WITH LOVE AND GRATITUDE

*AND* ——————————————————————————

IN MEMORY OF ISMAEL MONTALVO (1913–1996),

A BRIGHT STAR IN LAREDO'S BASEBALL FIRMAMENT

# Contents

# *Preface* ———————————————————————

## Teco Time: A Night at La Junta

D AN F IROVA bolts out of the front door carrying the top of his Tecos uniform and hat in one hand, his duffel bag in the other. If he doesn't hurry
he'll get caught in the Laredo bridge traffic heading into Mexico. Jumping
into the family 1988 Ford pickup, he catches himself just as he is about to
fling the clean white Teco baseball uniform onto a melted mass of Revlon
lipstick that his wife Esther has inadvertently left on the seat. The 104
degree heat liquefies most things in less time than it takes to go through
the drive-through window at Taco Bell. "God damn it!" shouts Firova,
slowing down only long enough to delicately shove the caked lipstick pud-
dle to the floor. That's all Dan's south Texas taciturnity will allow on the
matter. The brevity is needed so he can better figure out which street to go
down the wrong way, pick up his batting coach, Ricardo Cuevas, and shave
a precious minute or two off of his ride to Parque La Junta just across the
border. Four U.S. ballplayers, as well as one Mexican national married to
a local Laredoan, all of whom play for the Tecos (short for the *Tecolotes de
los dos Laredos*, the Owls of the Two Laredos), also head for the bridge
hoping for a fast crossing. A simple "no" or a "*No traigo nada*" [I'm not
bringing anything in] suffices to get you through customs going into
Nuevo Laredo, but the volume of cars and trucks on the bridge can take
forever.

Batting practice is called for 5 P.M., and that's when the rest of the team
will show up, not before. Nobody gets to the park early in order to flow
easily into the 8 P.M. contest. No one shows up early to get their game face
on, either. The ballpark, Parque La Junta, is a decrepit old concrete affair
more in need of a wrecker's ball than another makeover. Paint won't help
the forty years that went into ignoring its needs. Despite the aversion that
almost everyone feels toward the place, Firova and Cuevas want to get
there punctually. The amount of heat the thirty-six-year-old manager has
been taking from the Nuevo Laredo press only makes him more obsessive
about time and efficiency, but you wouldn't know it to look at his tanned
and rested bearing. His impassive demeanor and clean good looks never
betray his tumultuous rookie season as manager. A forty-minute stint of
pitching batting practice in the northern Mexican desert environment,
however, will have him looking drenched and spent. Cuevas, on the other
hand, never seems to break a sweat, even after spending an hour hitting

grounders to the infield and barking instructions in the late afternoon heat. Cuevas, a third-generation Mexican ballplayer, is a study in economy of movement, and a well-chosen word or signal from his soft ex-infielder's hands suffices to get his meaning across.

The Tecos appear at the park like the intermittent glowing of fireflies, in groups of twos and threes. Though straggling in as they do, everyone somehow is ready for the scheduled batting practice at 5 P.M. Each knot of hitters has its time in the batting cage, where they are cycled through a string of required hitting exercises (e.g., bunting, hitting behind the runner, swinging away). The scene could be enacted in any ballpark: the batter in the cage moves through his repertoire while another three stand around taking shadow swings in anticipation of their turns or potshots at the fellow in the cage. Just now twenty-three-year-old Eduardo Salgado, the Teco mime who doubles as a speedy reserve outfielder, is exaggerating his teammates' batting moves: butt out, elbows splayed, front foot pointing toward the pitcher, clownish smirk on his face.

The group of high-status veterans moves to take their turn at the cage. Andrés Mora, a home run legend with almost twenty years of baseball behind him, is joined by two more sluggers, Alejandro Ortiz and Marco Antonio Romero. Mora delights in hitting high arching balls that clear the fence by fifty feet, while Ortiz's line shots clear the fence by only four feet but never seem to come down. Mora pauses to watch his, puffing a bit from repetition of swings. Ortiz whistles as his projectiles sear the top of the wall. Mora, Ortiz, and Romero pride themselves on being latter-day Mexican versions of the legendary Cincinnati slugger Ted Kluszewski, who had to cut off his shirt sleeves to accommodate his massive arms. This mustachioed burly trio lives for power, rarely attempting to leg out a wall-banging hit for a double. There is the big bang, and everything else. "*Chinga* [fuck], [I] thought it was gone," growls Mora, missing a home run by a half a foot.

The beef in the batting cage is counterpoised by the long-legged grace of the pitchers running easy laps along the outfield fence. Teco mainstays Ernesto Barraza (a Mexican Bill Lee), Enrique Couoh (so pensive and delicate that he looks more like a young professor than a devastatingly good forkballer), and Juan Jesus Alvarez (a Yaqui Indian who looks as if he were called by central casting at Paramount Pictures) try to run three miles a night. It matters little if the temperature is 103; they walk easily back toward the dugout for a casual drink of water.

Before the last Teco batter has successfully lined a ball into the left field gap, tonight's opponents, the Sultanes of Monterrey, arrive at the park. Because of their comparatively lengthy careers, Mexican League players are remarkably familiar with each other. Warm greetings and hugs between members of these teams abound. The "*Como estas*" [How are you] and "*Oye Indio* [Hey Indian], where's that carburetor I asked you to get for my Chevy?" [in Spanish] is mixed with an occasional English "Hey dude! They told me you were down here. When was it? Spring training '92?" Imports, mostly refugees from the ranks of American AAA teams, form together tightly like elderly emigrés pulling their afghans snugly around them in a foreign world. They search eagerly for warmth in a strange, new place. For them, coming to play in the Mexican League is a betrayal full of incredulity mixed with pain. And no one typifies this more than a young blond Teco Import, pitcher Willie Waite.

From a distance there is nothing to suggest his socially dyslexic character. His WASPish good looks and intelligent brow seem to point to the opposite. Yet in almost any interaction there is some misfiring of neurons that seems to botch even the most innocent conversation. Only three days earlier, after being relieved in the eighth, he entered the dugout to be attended to by the Tecos trainer, a wonderfully jovial older man with a disarming smile. As the trainer went about ministering an ice pack to Waite's arm, the pitcher peered down at the little man busily working on him and sneered, "Shit man, I thought you were supposed to be the best." Not understanding the slight, the trainer smilingly tried to communicate to Waite—flashing his hand three times—that he should wear the ice wrap for fifteen minutes. Waite didn't understand, and the trainer gently patted Waite on the back, laughing at the communication breakdown. The Anglo pitcher turned, scowled, and gritted a "Fuck you." At this, Cuevas turned to me and said, "And, he pitched good tonight. Can you imagine [if he'd been bad]?" Ortiz would brook none of this. He understood enough English to know that Waite had acted disrespectfully to this older man, and he bellowed in Spanish, "Gringo prick, you have something to say?" Waite was already off to the bullpen and acted as if he hadn't heard a thing.

Tonight, however, Waite is uncharacteristically warm and friendly because he has discovered that a television crew from across the river in Laredo is on tap to do a segment on him and the touching binational camaraderie of the Tecos. Thankfully, no one outside of the team seems to sense the antagonism between Mexicans and this group of Americans. A young Anglo television producer is on hand to put the piece together. He knows nothing about baseball or the Tecos, wanting only to get the minimum coverage and interview material. Constantly patting down the long wisps of his balding pate, the television producer spies Waite and directs the cameraman to him. He asks Waite how he likes it here, and the pitcher confides off the record to his compatriots, "Dude, it's a nightmare." Sensing a story, the producer quickly asks him to elaborate. The Anglo pitcher first looks around, responding, "Jesus, you wanna get me killed?"—this in front of fellow pitchers Barraza, Moreno, and Couoh, who all speak English. The three Mexicans impassively look at Waite and the Anglo film

crew, making eye contact with each other only fleetingly. Couoh disdain-
fully turns and begins to help fellow pitcher Alvarez to stretch out his
lower back. Expectations of gringos are not very high, and Mexican Leaguers have little time to engage their ignorance or even to try to educate
them.

Despite these very real schisms when the Tecos take the field, they are as
one. The pageantry and ritual of the game aid the impression that binational harmony is at work. Wearing the same uniforms and playing a sport
that fosters mutual dependency for success, as well as raising the flags and
playing the anthems of both nations, help too. Moments when a gringo
teammate does something positive are (with the exception of Waite) met
with public congratulations. To the naive eye the Tecos appear so cohesive.

It's about an hour before game time and the Tecos are all back in the
dugout replacing the fluids they lost out on the field with buckets of water.
They file through the tunnel to the clubhouse, sounding like a herd of deer
wearing taps as their cleats echo across the concrete floor. A large cooler
filled with soft drinks and ice sits in the center of the clubhouse. There is
nothing unusual about the place. Full-length lockers line three walls. Most
everything is painted in a Caribbean blue that has long since let the grey of
concrete through. No moldings, carpets, or wood to soften the glare from
the industrial lights above. The smell of urinals is never far. This is the
minor leagues, and everyone has played in at least one such stadium. There
are much better places in the Mexican League than the Tecos' park, whose
owners have been fighting with state and local officials for a new facility.
The Tecos have been together so long, however, that it no longer occurs
to them to comment on the subject. Surroundings and heat pale by comparison to the anticipation of taking over first place tonight.

Game time. A trio of young military cadets marches out to center field
carrying both a Mexican and an American flag as the loudspeaker plays first
one and then the other national anthem. Because of its length the Mexican
anthem has to be cut short, and everyone is eager to get the game started,
especially the four thousand "Teco Maniacs" that paid to get in. They're
cranking their *sonejos* (wooden noisemakers) and yodeling, Mexican style.
In the dugout the players either hold hat over heart American style, or
salute hands over heart Mexican style, but many distractedly go through
the motions, and some, like outfielder Luís Fernando Díaz, practice English phrases, such as "This is very nice. That was very nice." Pitcher Rene
Rodríguez is making kissing sounds in the ear of Eduardo Salgado, who
absentmindedly flicks him away.

The Tecos take the field and third baseman Ortiz is shouting for everyone to talk it up. He can't be heard above the din the players are making,
however. The Yaqui Indian, Juan Jesús Alvarez, is pitching, and his back
woes seem apparent as he struggles with his control early on. The Sultanes

quickly strike for two runs, and the Tecos return to the dugout slightly disgusted. Romero, as always, places his glove gently but compulsively on the white chalk line around the perimeter of the dugout, then seeks something to pound. There is a corner of the dugout I call the "time out" zone that shifts location from one game to the next. You go there to vent: to swear, kick, throw something; and just then one hears two or three "fuuuck"s and a kick of the wall. It passes, though, as first Gerardo Sánchez homers, and then doubles by Luís Fernando Díaz and Pedro Meré and a single by Marco Antonio Cruz bring in three runs. Alvarez gives up only one more run in his gritty, pain-filled six-plus innings of work, while the Tecos rack up another two runs for a 5–3 lead.

The magician Enrique Couoh enters to close out the seventh with two strikeouts on pitches that just slide into the red earth around home plate. "Tenedor" is what they call a forkball, but "tender" is how the batters seem to swing at it, as if it actually hurts to make contact. In the eighth Couoh runs into trouble, momentarily struggling with control. A Sultanes single, followed by a double, brings Monterrey to within one run, 5–4. The Tecos bring in the "refuerzos" (reinforcements), which is what, among other things, imports are called. Six-foot six-inch Jay Baller, an ex-Chicago Cub pitcher, comes in to stifle the rally and promptly—in five pitches—pops up the first batter and strikes out the second. The fans and Tecos get a surge of energy and shout their approval as they move back to the dugout. Bobby Moore, import outfielder, mumbles, "I can't see shit out there," while Romero, who is scheduled up second in the inning, asks Mora, "What did he start you off with last time?" Baseball conversations, often in stark contrast to the lengthy indolence of the game itself, are usually short blasts like this. Someone in the far corner is talking to no one in particular, "*Chinga su madre* [fuck his mother], he threw me change, change, then fastball!" Although they are in need of insurance runs, the Tecos in the eighth inning manage only two weak groundouts and a fly out deep to center, taking a nervous one-run lead to the ninth inning. Baller strikes out the first man. The next batter hits the first pitch over the right field wall . . . foul (although he argued that it was fair). Baller tries hard to keep the next pitch outside so that it can't be pulled, but the pitch drifts over the heart of the plate, and leaves the park in a hurry . . . fair. It's a new ball game! The score is tied 5–5. The big righthander, however, retains his composure, striking out the last two batters. He walks quickly back to the dugout where, predictably, he vents in the time-out zone. As always, the others look over, under, around, through, but never at, their distraught compadre.

Blowing a lead like this late in the season is dispiriting. No matter what spin you attempt to put on it, it is a failure. Locals, however, view it as a wake-up call, a familiar challenge. "Stay, and see what we will do," they reminded me on one occasion. They become even more jubilant and raucous when the opponent jumps out to a lead, or as in this case, pulls into a tie. The team is riding a six-game winning streak, and for those in attendance, confidence, rather than trepidation, seems to well up. Díaz obliges in the bottom of the ninth by promptly singling the first pitch up the middle. Third baseman Alejandro Ortiz comes to the plate, pushing his cut-off sleeves up and clanging the bat handle off his cup. With a threat to steal on first base, manager Firova gives Ortiz a "show" bunt sign, to give the impression of intent to move the runner along. Ortiz obliges, and the infield charges in. Strike one. Assuming bunt on the second pitch, the Sultanes pitcher falls for the ruse and tries to throw a fastball for an unambiguous strike (so that they might be able to throw the lead runner out at second base). Firova, however, has taken off the bunt sign, giving Ortiz the green light to swing away. Baseball drama is cross-cultural in this regard. There is a sense of anticipation all over the stadium that this is the instant—the pitch, the hit that will deliver them. The fans begin to press against the first rows of the park, while the Tecos themselves all come to stand in front of the dugout. Ortiz cocks his bat, then reacts with an explosive swing that sends the ball somewhere deep into Nuevo Laredo. Ortiz is so much in a "zone" that from the moment he is in the on-deck circle everything is hyper-remote: "I couldn't even hear the fans. Nothing but me and the pitch." He comes to at the instant of contact and uncharacteristically—for him—punches the night air. The Tecos rush out with a shout that is like a bursting dam, swarming home plate to welcome the game winner. Let off the hook, pitcher Baller breathes a sigh of relief. The others, however, are euphoric, playing as if they simultaneously expected and are surprised by this ending. "Somehow, someway God is watching over us. We get the runs and the pitching when we need them. Look how many times we've gone to the playoffs," comments Couoh. Each night seems to produce the needed hero, and most nights it is someone different; and the antagonism between players is momentarily swept away as all join in triumph and cold cans of Tecate in that big cooler with the ice in it. This was, indeed, "Teco time."

After everyone has had their share of beer in the clubhouse and left, Firova and Cuevas want one more before returning to Laredo. No hurry now at midnight. It has cooled down to 92 degrees and one could breathe a little.

Tomorrow night's game is in Laredo, Texas, the Tecos' other home field. It is this novel arrangement of having a binational team with two home parks and a mixed staff and players that has made the Tecos a mild pop-culture curiosity, focusing increasing national and international attention on this stretch of the border.

# BASEBALL ON THE BORDER

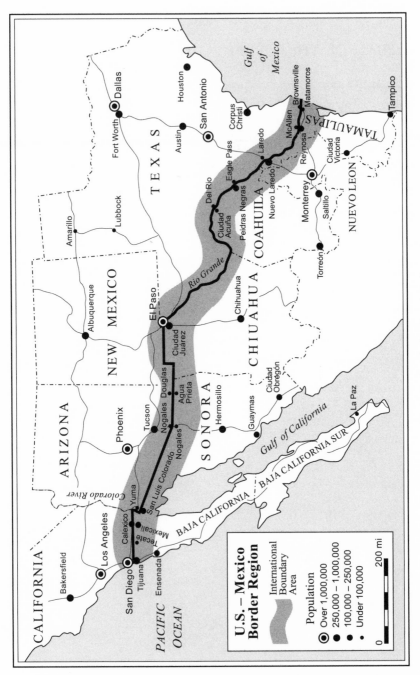

United States–Mexico border with shaded area depicting borderlands cultural area.

# Introduction _____

ODDLY ENOUGH, in first driving down Interstate 35 toward Laredo, Texas, and the U.S.-Mexican border, I felt as I did upon first approaching Niagara Falls many years before. Back then, the river road I followed propelled me forward until, without warning, the explosion of mist and thundering water rushed up to overwhelm me. You can't prepare for something that grand and terrifying. And similarly, as I approached the outskirts of Laredo, Texas, I felt that the highway was that river, nearing what would be, I felt, an enormous rift in the earth. At the bottom of the chasm would churn the Rio Grande River, and across it two large and very different nations would eye each other. Large, green, suspended signs over the pin-straight interstate, which had grown to six lanes, underscored this impression. Imagine my surprise at encountering the border: a foot-dragging river barely 200 yards across, cut between two very hot and tired-looking towns.

Since it was only a stop-over, I really didn't feel the need to think of the border in any informed way. Unfortunately, travelers have been treating the area that way for two centuries. So just as New York has become the "Big Apple" and Seattle the "Emerald City," Laredo, from the mile-long backup of trucks that daily snake along the river waiting to clear customs, is the "Stop Over Capital." In spite of this, Laredo, like the tree near my house that persevered and grew right through the unsightly chainlink fence that sought to confine it, the city actually prospered. The ubiquitous fast-food chains, cheap motels, and businesses selling "Mexico insurance" line the highway as so many pit-stops for travelers. Even the better hotels, distinguished from Motel 6 by their elegance and an identity fashioned out of traditional border stucco and beautiful tile, have their share of truckers, bikers, and an assortment of late-twentieth-century road warriors.

My friend and colleague, Milton Jamail of the University of Texas, was to meet me at the hotel. He had arranged an introduction for me with the general manager of Leones de Mérida (Mérida Lions), a Mexican League baseball team from the far southern reaches of the country. The Leones were on the northern border to play the Tecos. Jamail, a Texan and expert in Latin American baseball (and border relations), had convinced me to come here, joining me because this was the closest the Mérida team would get to me. In this short four-day visit I hoped to make contact with some of the gatekeepers of the Leones by meeting with their manager and any members of the front office that might have accompanied them to Laredo.

My previous fieldwork on baseball in the Dominican Republic whetted my appetite for merging social science and the study of sport.[1] What I wanted now was a new site that would be culturally intriguing and physically beautiful, with a substantial history of baseball linked to social and cultural factors. Mexico in general and Mérida in particular seemed to fill the bill. A wonderful study of Yucatecan baseball at the turn of the century by historian Gil Joseph convinced me that baseball in the Yucatan had political significance, and I thought I might carry some of his ideas forward.[2] The close proximity of the Yucatan peninsula to baseball-rich countries such as Cuba, the Dominican Republic, and Puerto Rico was also a draw. So, too, was the lure of Mayan communities on the peninsula and exquisite archaeological sites such as Chichen Itza. Mérida, according to colleagues and friends who had visited the city, was a beautiful colonial treasure.

The Tecos, Jamail assured me, were an unusual team in their own right. They represented both Nuevo Laredo, Tamaulipas, and Laredo, Texas. They had two home parks, in two countries! We would attend our Saturday game in the United States and jump across the river to Mexico the following night. By the time we got to Laredo's West Martin Field, I had already begun to ask questions of this dusty urban crossing. It paled by comparison with Mérida in every respect but one: the link between baseball and society (in this case, nationalism) was, I felt, riveting. How does the team mediate their different followings, nations, cultures? Without fully realizing it at the time, I was getting caught up with the border.

We arrived at West Martin Field just before game time. Stopping at the concession stand for a Coke, I asked the young man working the booth why there weren't any pennants or other souvenirs. This young Mexican American responded by wrinkling his nose slightly, and derisively jerking his thumb behind him (toward the border). "Ever since *they* took it over [the concessions business], we don't have that stuff anymore." "They" were the "Mexicans on the other side," and the condescension in this young Chicano's demeanor struck me as odd. I had expected more of an identity with his "kinsmen" across the way.

The game was very much a well-played minor league affair, which of course is what Mexican League baseball is. The league has the distinction of being the only foreign league with AAA status in the United States. Nothing unique or anthropologically noteworthy occurred. Baseball-wise, however, we spied an Import (U.S. player) who looked vaguely familiar to us. Checking the scorecard, we found he was who we suspected him to be: Mickey Pina, a minor leaguer in the Boston Red Sox organization who, many had thought, was a "can't miss" prospect. He was voted the Most Valuable Player in the Carolina League in 1988, became a major contributor when promoted to the Red Sox AAA affiliate in Pawtucket, Rhode Island, in 1989, and had a great spring training with the parent club in 1990.

He didn't make the Red Sox that year and somehow degenerated back in Pawtucket. That led to a trade and injuries, and the flushing sound could be heard. Whatever the reasons for his demise, Pina was in Laredo playing for the Mérida team now and munching on a ham sandwich. He had been picked up at the tail-end of the season and, like most Imports, was expected to deliver. It was clear that he was pressing, again perhaps, and trying too hard to make up too much ground in a hurry. Because he spoke only English, Pina's private hell was made worse by not knowing what those around him were saying, thinking, feeling. When we approached him for an interview between games in the double-header, he latched onto us with the gratitude of a shipwrecked survivor. At that time, in the summer of 1992, Mickey Pina looked hot, tired, and lost. As we spoke with him he wanted very much to conjure up better times, or at least to conjure up home.

In subsequent years I would see other, even more accomplished players, such as ex–Red Sox pitcher Oil Can Boyd, Cy Young winner Fernando Valenzuela, and his one-time Dodger teammate Pedro Guerrero, players who had made their mark in the majors but who had disappeared from sight. They may have vanished, but they were not gone. From a mainstream American perspective these men were playing in baseball's Bermuda Triangle, a parallel universe to the one we know located just beyond our view. From a Mexican perspective this league had been home to some of the game's giants: Cuban legend Martín Dihigo, Negro Leaguers Satchel Paige, Josh Gibson, and Cool Papa Bell, and established major leaguers of the 1940s such as Sal Maglie and Vern Stephens, who had temporarily jumped ship. Mexican baseball tradition resonates in places that have ranged from state-of-the-art stadiums to quirky parks with trains running through the outfield, with teams that have played the sport for over a century. And while this book views the border as porous, in at least one sense the border has been impermeable: the border has been able to prevent Americans from ever realizing the rich tapestry of baseball that has been woven in the country to the south. The Border Patrol could not have done a better job. Mexican League baseball has never really been thought of as anything but an elephant's graveyard, where ballplayers who can't quit on their own (with dignity) go to die. Jamail maintains that Mexican (and all Latin American) baseball is not so much invisible as it is inaudible. For Mickey Pina and others who are toiling to get out, it probably seems like both.

The following day I was introduced to Larry Dovalina, a city official whose family had deep roots in the area and was responsible for the handling of the Tecos' games on the U.S. side. We mentioned the young employee's comments to him, noting how odd they were in the light of the binational arrangement enjoyed between the cities. "Not at all [odd]," responded Dovalina. "We say, 'The river joins, and the river divides.' People here spend as much time at each other's throats as they do at each other's weddings." The view of outsiders who think of relations between the two sides as either one of accord or tension is simply wrong. I had just been given my first, and most important, lesson on border relations and nationalism.

Each of us, as social scientists, fashions both paradigms and perspectives that we feel are so natural and yielding of truths that they actually help to psychologically center us as individuals. We approach everything with our tool kit at the ready and wield our analytical implements with ease and comfort. These models and methods become our ways of seeing life. For me, sport, and particularly the study of baseball, has become a lens through which I can view social life even more clearly than more conventional institutions. This book looks at a century of baseball played on the Texas-Mexican border, specifically in the two cities of Laredo, Texas, and Nuevo Laredo, Tamaulipas. Through the sport, I was able to look at the history of the region and the relations between people on either side of the international boundary. The Tecos are a Mexican League team, until 1985 officially the representative of Nuevo Laredo, with deep roots in the history of baseball in this area. In 1985 the team formally took on the mantle of the two Laredos, becoming the first and only binational sports franchise. In becoming an official representative and emblem of two cooperating national constituencies, the Tecos, I would find, were encoded with information that might help me understand larger international relations and identities. The Tecos' baseball team played dramatically during the two seasons (1993 and 1994) that I followed them. As a group they struggled impressively to succeed one year and fail the next; coming within a few wins of the national crown in 1993, then failing in the following year to even get into the post-season. Outside of the white lines, however, there was acrimony. This was not an alienated team like the 1991 Boston Red Sox, a team so alienated that it was often said of them that they were twenty-six players taking twenty-six separate cabs home following a game. Rather, the Tecos were split by resentment and distrust born of a jealous nationalism. The presence of such an Anglo-irritant only reinforced the sense of Mexicanness of the *mexicanos*, which in turn fueled the Anglos' sense of isolation and their national identity. But such antagonisms are only one layer of borderland identity and international relations.

## The Three Faces of Laredo's Nationalism

Underscoring the nationalism fostered through baseball, A. J. Spalding, the sport's first pitching ace and profit maker, declared that the function of the sport was "to follow the Flag."[3] On the Texas-Mexican border, and particularly along the stretch that includes the two Laredos, both nationalism and baseball are tempered by the perception that the borderlands constitute something more unique. The result is that nationalism is more variegated, at once conventionally enacted yet completely novel. One of the border's foremost historians, Oscar Martínez, used the poetry of Gloria Anzaldúa to get at the quasi-distinct sense of the region in his social examination of the border:[4]

> To live in the borderlands means
> the mill with the razor white teeth wants to shred off
> your olive-red skin, crush out the kernel, your heart
> pound you pinch you roll you out
> smelling like white bread but dead;
> To survive in the borderlands you must live *sin fronteras* [without borders],
> be a crossroads.[5]

Most border inhabitants and border scholars understand the way national identity along the U.S.-Mexican border is fragmented and layered. For these individuals the idea that the border is not fixed and impenetrable is nothing new. Neither is the view that border relations between Americans, Mexican Americans, and Mexicans on the border is an ambivalent one: bonding at points, divisive at other points. But for the other 220,000,000 or so nonborder-dwelling Americans, the idea that the international boundary is complex, porous, and consists of a cultural corridor some three hundred miles wide on both sides of the boundary is somewhat novel. Understanding how the concept of nationalism operates on the border is what drives this book. Nationalism is a concept that crosses disciplinary borders as easily, and often as informally, as do the young drug peddlers daily floating across the river from Nuevo Laredo on inner tubes, trailing duffel bags full of marijuana for sale in Laredo's neighborhoods. As a result, the concept defies easy classification, taking on the protective coloration of the interdisciplinary environment. Still there have been several studies of nationalism that reconfigure some of the traditional perceptions of nationalism into new, more layered interpretations.

Nineteen eighty-three was a somewhat journeyman year in major league baseball. No team or individual performance stuck out. LaMarr Hoyt and John Denny won Cy Young awards with good but mortal years. Cal Ripken, Jr., was voted the Most Valuable Player in the American League with solid, unpretentious numbers: a .318 batting average, 27 home runs, and 102 runs batted in, with 19 errors in the field. His Baltimore team went on to beat Philadelphia in the World Series, four games to one.

For the Tecolotes of Nuevo Laredo, 1983 was a rare off year. It was one of only three seasons since returning to the border in 1976 that the team failed to get into the playoffs, and one of the few times that slugger Andres Mora failed to hit twenty or more home runs in a season. Fans of the "border birds," as they are sometimes called, were disappointed.

But 1983 was a "monster" year for scholars writing on the subject of nationalism. In that year three books, all destined to make their marks, were published. Eric Hobsbawm and Terrence Ranger edited a collection of historical studies exploring Hobsbawm's intriguing concept of "invented tradition."[6] Within his contribution to the volume, Hobsbawm loosely linked the study of sport to attempts on the part of social historians to chronicle the rise of nationalism in Europe. He argued that certain institutions, rituals, and spectacles of recent origin, such as sport, have ancient trappings and wind up linking something new to something quite a bit older. No concrete study of sport was offered, however, leaving it to others to use the concept in one way or another.[7] *Baseball on the Border* attempts to deepen our understanding of sport as an invented tradition.

Benedict Anderson's acclaimed *Imagined Communities* is an anthropological and historical study of the emergence of national cultural forms that aid in the establishment of a national consciousness through looking at large-scale cultural forms.[8] Since actual face-to-face familiarity is impossible among members of the nation-state, more circuitous cultural routes (such as the cultural implications of publishing books and newspapers) for achieving a general sense of belonging to a community are created.

Finally, Ernest Gellner's *Nations and Nationalism* also appeared that year.[9] He too informed the study of nationalism with an anthropological sensibility. Gellner's book provided a thorough-going assessment of the social and ideological roles behind the emergence of nationalism out of agrarian societies.

So, while Baltimore and Ripken impressed but underwhelmed us, and while the Tecos disappointed, "nationalism" had a career year. Baseball and nationalism meet in the study of popular culture, and there is little doubt that the two play off each other. They are not equal partners, though. Spalding's nationalist pronouncement about the role of baseball has gone unchallenged, and reading any of the smattering of writers on international baseball continues to show the disproportionate weight of nationalism.[10] People may die because of baseball, but not for it. Nationalism, on the other hand, is a consequence of political programs and sociocultural forms that have garnered more than its share of canon fodder,[11] and is considerably more critical to the functioning of the modern nation-state than any game. What then is the role of sport in the study of nationalism? What can sport tell us about nationalism that other institutions can't or don't?

As defined by Ernest Gellner, nationalism strives "to make culture and polity congruent, to endow a culture with its own political roof."[12] Used in a broad sense, we can join Gellner's definition with those of others so that nationalism is seen as made up of political positions and cultural properties such as rituals, sentiments, and perceived history, in addition to broad-based social institutions such as education and media. All of these are designed to foster a sense of political sovereignty and identity within some political entity, typically the nation-state. On the U.S.-Mexican border the ideal conditions discussed in works like Gellner's are not met, with the result that nationalism is fractured in such a way as to enable people on both sides of the border to claim a variety of structural relations and identities. I have targeted three of these faces of nationalism, which I refer to as autonationalism, binationalism, and transnationalism. All three are based on the particular kinds of structural and behavioral relations that characterize the border. If living on the border demands a constant and structured exchange and interaction of one sort or another, there is bound to be a set of identities that reflects this.[13] I simply isolated three (there may be more) forms of nationalism, two of which may not be present further in the interior of either country, and hence are somewhat unique to the border.

Autonationalism consists of what most scholars have viewed as nationalism: namely, political and social relations that foster an identity with the nation-state. To avoid confusion with conventional use of nationalism, and to emphasize its "quality of self reference,"[14] I use *autonationalism*. Autonationalism fosters collective identification both through the inclusion of those living within fixed borders and the exclusion of neighboring entities and others. Nations divide social/national reality into idyllic "we" and demonic "they."[15] At best, these international relations allow for interludes of alliance and assistance, reserving most of their energy for quickly recasting the "other" as an enemy.[16]

Promoting national identity through the state's apparatus, its sociocultural institutions, is a twofold proposition: either directly inducing a sense of pride in one's nation through its accomplishments (e.g., a gold medal at the Olympics, viewing a national treasure), or fomenting and channeling anger at an enemy and thereby promoting internal cohesion.

Mexican nationalism, which has proceeded in fits and starts for over a century and a half, used both mechanisms of autonationalism. Certainly the presidency of Porfirio Díaz is linked with the largest advance in nationalism.[17] The economic modernization Díaz orchestrated between 1876 and 1910, while further impoverishing the majority, also managed to push the cause of economic development. The volume of manufactured goods doubled during his thirty-four years in office.[18] Albeit with foreign capital, Díaz built the railroad system, which in turn spurred on the growth of mining, textiles, and oil industries, while encouraging the growth of industrial centers such as Monterrey.

The Porfiriato (as the Díaz presidency was known), the revolution, and the period after it all furthered the development of Mexican nationalism through a growing sense of regional integration, a national art movement (e.g., Diego Rivera), and a new-found pride in the Indian culture from which the country sprang. These sources of positive national pride came from the nationalist movement that Díaz worked tirelessly to initiate. Pride in things Mexican was the ideological word of the day.

If positive and direct forms of autonationalism were emerging, they worked in tandem with the anti-imperialism and resentment toward Americans that was never far away. When American troops invaded the port of Veracruz in 1914, the Mexican outrage was so intense and far-flung that it almost served to make the political factions (Huerta and the Constitutionalists) at each other's throat align against the *yanquis*.[19] Likewise, when in 1962 President López Mateos nationalized the U.S. and Canadian electric companies and boldly declared with electric lights that *La electricidad es nuestra* (the electricity is ours!), there was an edge to the declaration that could only be tapped by referring to the U.S. role in fueling Mexican nationalism.

A much more direct and a more contemporary form of anti-imperial autonationalism is found in the cultural interplay that is part of tourism along the border. Arreola and Curtis's examination of tourism in Mexican border cities sheds new light on the roles and functions of U.S-Mexican relations.[20] Exploring the sights and meeting the people of Mexico are not objectives for the American border tourists who, parenthetically, make up the brunt of tourists to Mexico.[21] The authors isolated two primary poles around which tourism on the border revolves: escaping the drudgery of their lives, and validating their social and cultural self-worth. The purchase of artifacts or speciality items such as liquor and leather goods, or the entertainment that American tourists pay for, translates into fleeting cultural voyeurism that enables them to feel as if they have experienced stereotypic "old Mexico." In this tourist pattern, the visitor along Nuevo Laredo's Avenida Guerrero or infamous bordello district ("Boy's Town") can safely (i.e., without being encumbered by Mexican reality) engage a contrivance as a genuine cultural experience.

The second function of tourism in border cities works off the invidious comparisons tourists and those in developing nations typically make.[22] Here, autonationalism makes real cultural use of imagined communities. The Mexican, for his/her part, earns a living from their presence and reinforces his/her disdain for U.S. tourists by exploiting their cultural ignorance. As one border scholar pointed out, "Anglos often comment on the worthlessness of border crafts and curios, but it's only Gringos, not the Mexicans, who buy the crap sold in tourist areas."[23] Anglos living on the U.S. side of the border also get to make invidious comparisons since life on the U.S. side is so much better.

Mexicans visit U.S. cities for work and to consume goods that they cannot get, or get as cheaply, in Mexico. The vast majority of Mexicans who visit U.S. border cities are Norteños or recent emigrés to the northern Mexican states. Their experiences in U.S. cities only reinforce their perception as being less fortunate, and indirectly fuel the mindset of "haves and have nots" replete with resentment, arrogance, and inferiority.[24] Less well known is the presence of small numbers of affluent Mexicans who visit the U.S. side of the border to buy whatever they fancy. These Mexican tourists do not share the mindset of their compatriots as wanting and underdeveloped. In border tourism, each side learns disdain, and through it they validate their national selves.

It is not out of a sense of international altruism that *binationalism* is forged, but rather out of enlightened self-interest. Sharing common resources, hence destinies, makes for a particularly compelling set of reasons for the establishment of binational traditions and practices along the border. For communities along the Rio Grande pollution of the river has become increasingly problematical.[25] Where once the two nations mostly negotiated access to water for arid communities,[26] they now regularly discuss health hazards stemming from the large-scale dumping of toxins by the *maquiladoras* (foreign, typically U.S.-owned factories operating on the Mexican side of the border) along the river. Reports of the alarming rise in cancer rates among border dwellers, particularly on the Mexican side,[27] has begun to focus attention on lack of adequate environmental policies that can safeguard the health of the region's residents. Nevertheless, despite a common interest, geographer Lawrence Herzog points out that one of the problems hampering progress in these areas is that the Mexican prioritizing of problems is quite different from the American view.[28] Environmental safeguards are distinctly secondary to employment and increased manufacturing for Mexican authorities.

In the stretch of river passing through the two Laredos these problems also exist. The summer of 1994 recorded the first confirmed death from contact with bacteria in the Rio Grande in the vicinity of Laredo.[29] Further confirming what locals already know, a Washington D.C.–based environmental research group, American Rivers, has concluded that the Rio Grande is among the ten most threatened rivers in the world. While the *maquiladoras* of Nuevo Laredo are among the major culprits in dumping of toxins locally, it is the combined efforts of los dos Laredos that resulted in a binationally financed water treatment plant completed in 1994.[30] Of longer-range impact and equally promising is the sociocultural way in which the two cities are going about trying to meet the problem. "Project del Rio" is a binational educational program that pulls together high school students from both sides of the river in an effort to teach them how to test for pollution, inform them of the severity of the rivers problems, and work with them on how to develop environmental solutions. The program exists in cities all along the border, and in time could begin to compete with the more widespread perception of pursuing economic growth at all costs. This particular example illustrates the ways in which the binational relations are forged to face issues of common interest. For the two Laredos binationalism is just as much a precondition as it is a consequence of these problems. Long before there was ever a water hazard along the Rio Grande, the inhabitants of the two Laredos were exhibiting forms of binational identities (see below). The border is a shared space in which sovereign nations are forced to confront each other's existences and find ways of relating to each other, not simply in the conduction of commerce, but in solving problems. In the Laredo area this binationalism is mutated, an outgrowth of an earlier tradition of unity that became fractured and was forced to face itself as binationalism.

The Laredos' binational relations are social and cultural as well. During the impending destruction of Nuevo Laredo in the bloody fighting of 1916, for instance, it was a team of doctors and nurses from Laredo who came to the aid of wounded Mexican fighters, just as now the local heads of the Laredo fire departments are sharing their training in hazardous waste cleanup with their Nuevo Laredo counterparts. Culturally, there are a number of events that fuse the two cities. Some of these events—the Washington's Birthday Celebration discussed in Chapter 1, for instance—involve sharing in the celebrations of one city by their cross-river neighbor.

With nonstop movement (legal or illegal) of goods and people along the border comes the potential for the development of a *transnationalism*, a cultural identity forged out of each country's autonationalism and binational links. In time, the approach-avoidance so characteristic of autonationalism and binationalism is parlayed in a distinct set of traditions that identifies the two as more identified with each other than they are with their national points of origin. Operating out of the clash of traditions, this new identity is intensified or ameliorated by other factors, most notably by the distance from centers of each country. In the case of the two Laredos this fused identity preceded the border, and dates to a time when Laredoans were Mexican citizens who happened to live on one side or another of the Rio Grande (see Chapter 1). Their sense of common identity was further fueled by their distance from either Mexican or U.S. centers of power. Viewed from the centers of each nation these developments can, at times, take on the appearance of a fugitive construct, as in the 1840 attempt at nationalist cessation by an amalgam of people on both sides of the river in the short-lived Republic of the Rio Grande.

Most U.S.-Mexican border scholars, regardless of their disciplines, have long ago promoted the notion of the border as a quasi-independent identity. While some hedge a bit on the extent of this transcendent identity, feeling more on solid ground with the notion of binationalism, most agree that the border has a unique set of qualities not found in the interior of either nation. Likewise most scholars are acutely aware of the differences that rest principally on economics. But even though there are qualitative differences in the urban couplings found along the border and the extent of economic development found on each side, the continued interaction between the two carries forth the border tradition that began centuries ago.

All three forms of nationalism exist as structural relations, behavior, and sentiment (identity), and all of them have analogs in the realm of baseball on the border. While present within the context of baseball and the border, these three nationalistic forms are not present in equal proportions, however. One has to see them as more or less present at different times and in differing ways. With this caution in mind, I would argue that in some respects an examination of the sport and subculture of baseball in this region illustrates these nationalisms as well or better than other kinds of studies. In this context sport is a reflection of international relations and politics, and more. Told from the perspective of the people on the border, the examination of baseball becomes a story of families who celebrate and cry together, who seethe and scream at one another, but who are bound together by a common past and future. In looking at baseball we can glimpse the way in which local social relations can obscure and at times are obscured by larger national considerations. As poorly outlined as they are, the North American Free Trade Agreement (NAFTA) and other binational enterprises such as Europe's European Union (EU) might benefit from small-scale studies such as this by keying in on how local relations work in relation to the larger picture. An equally important motive in writing this book has to do with presenting back to the people of the two Laredos a piece of their own history, one which I came to realize they had never before seen compiled.

The book is divided into three parts, describing the origins of the region and the sport of baseball, the team itself, and finally the issues and crises Laredoans in both cities faced over a period of two years. The region and its history is presented in Chapter 1. Through two and a half centuries the Laredo borderlands struggled with a range of natural and manmade problems, in the course of which they fashioned the three forms of nationalism discussed in this book. Several very important local cultural institutions are also examined as forms of popular culture that also reflect nationalism. The sport of baseball arrived with the railroads and modernization, and Chapter 2 examines the first decades of the sport of baseball up to the 1930s. This was an era of semi-professional sport marked by a high degree of local control. Questions of origins of baseball in the region (including Mexico) are answered through archival material. Once the game was established in this region, a tradition of baseball excellence emerged that produced some of the finest semi-pro teams in either country, culminating in the La Junta teams of the mid-to-late 1930s.

As the decade of the 1940s dawned, the Mexican League had become professionally established and was headed by its most famous commissioner, the flamboyant Jorge Pasquel. Chapter 3 chronicles how Pasquel and his brothers grew to control the league, own its most powerful teams, and dominate Mexican baseball for over a decade. Pasquel's nationalism was quite antagonistic to U.S. baseball interests and their patronizing attitudes directed at Latin America. In response, Pasquel embarked on an ambitious—some would say instigated—project of recruiting major league players for his league, thereby ushering in what has become known as the "baseball wars." The chapter then goes on to more briefly chronicle the last half-century of baseball for the Tecos.

Chapters 4–7 feature the ethnographic study of the team. Likening the Tecos to a modern city with a historic center and suburban ring, Chapter 4 is my structural description of the team. Relations between different parts of the team are made to resemble different interactions between parts of contemporary cities. In an effort to develop a sense of familiarity with key individuals that appear over and other again in the ethnographic material, eleven mini-biographies are presented.

In Chapter 5 I link the institution of machismo with dimensions of nationalism. Using ethnographic observations and interviews, I look at the way Mexican players reflect and depart from traditional Mexican forms of machismo, as well as how they differ from gringos. These contrasts wind up indirectly fueling nationalist resentment.

Chapter 6 is the heart of the Teco ethnography, a look at the 1993 season. As with all the chapters, issues of nationalism emerge, but this micro-examination takes the reader through what anthropologists refer to as the "annual round" of activities that give us a sense of yearly cycle that encompasses life and also structures behavior.

The final chapter chronicles the demise of the binational experiment in 1994. The crisis that led to the rupture is discussed in terms of the trinational model. Again, ethnography lies at the heart of this chapter. In the course of the events up to and after this breakup, other components of the local baseball scene are also examined as they respond to the Teco predicament.

The appendixes include a brief explication of the methods employed in this study, as well as a somewhat longer bibliographic essay that discusses pertinent definitions of nationalism and how they have been employed by border scholars seeking to look at the complexities of border identity.

# Part One

ORIGINS

# One

## A Brief History of the Two Laredos

WHILE THE Tecos are being presented as the crown jewel of border events along this stretch of the river, they are only one part of a much larger array of binational events that bring both sides of the border together. They include sports ventures such as the "Border Olympics" (begun in 1933), which preceded the Tecos. Most recently the Juegos de la Amistad (Peace Games) were started in hopes of bringing even closer ties between the two cities, with a one-day event featuring competition in baseball, basketball, soccer, and softball.[1] Binational cultural events are also part of the arts. The Orquestra de Cámara de los dos Laredos (the Chamber Orchestra of the two Laredos) was begun in 1994 and features musicians from both cities. The Tecos are certainly not the oldest such phenomenon either. Nor are they the most widely attended, but because of the length of the baseball season, stretching some six to seven months, the Tecos occupy the longest period of time in the consciousness of the people of the Laredos. Because of this, the team has more potential to weave itself into the daily life of the communities.

There is an impressive sense of social reciprocity to all these binational celebrations. When one city holds an event it is assumed that celebrants will be drawn from the other side. Thus, when Nuevo Laredo celebrated its 146th anniversary in 1994, a festival that included a wide range of arts and music from not only northern Mexico but other Mexican States as well, the media in Laredo featured it prominently, and thousands from the Laredo area attended. The same is true of the "Borderfest," a Laredo area (south Texas) cultural event that takes place over the July fourth weekend, in which Nuevo Laredoans flock to taste and take part in the cultural events. With Laredo being approximately 93 percent Hispanic, even purely national Mexican holidays such as Cinco de Mayo (May 5) and Independence Day (September 16) are celebrated in Laredo. Since 1983 the city of Laredo has intensified these binational efforts by having representatives from Nuevo Laredo come into local schools and take part in educating young Laredoans about the importance of the holidays.

### Washington's Birthday Celebration

No border tradition in Laredo, however, is quite as binational, culturally curious, or as contested as is Washington's birthday. Begun in 1898, as an

attempt to inject an Anglo element into Laredo's Mexican-dominated culture, the Washington's Birthday Celebration (WBC) has become the
granddaddy of binational events on this stretch of the border. It has grown
into a ten-day-long event that includes parades, festivals, and lavish balls in
which Laredo's most distinguished families concoct versions of eighteenth-
century New England colonial attire. Parades featuring many of these cos-
tumes, which have been exaggerated somewhat, are also part of the festivities. Here we see a mixture of Anglo and Mexican elements, whether it be
in the elaborate brocade so much a reflection of Mexican dress or the laps-
ing into Spanish on the part of the periwigged Washingtons.[2]

The irony, as Hinojosa points out,[3] is that the original motive on the
part of the Anglos was to counter the *mexicano* emphasis on *las fiestas patrias*
with a celebration of one of the biggest American icons. In the course of its
development, this event has gone from reenacting the Boston Tea Party,
to a Pocahontas dress competition, back again to the formation of the Fiesta Mexicana (begun in 1925). Whatever the original Anglo intent, the
WBC has been partially coopted by Laredo's Mexican Americans, who
have always maintained a degree of cultural control in the Laredo region
and, in true binational spirit, not only attend these celebrations, but take
on key roles in them. The *fiesta mexicana* culturally corrected the over-
whelmingly Anglo content of this event, making it more an event beholden
to two cultures. In the first Fiesta, workmen converted the city's central
plaza into a replica of a Mexican village, offsetting the culturally irrelevant
Boston Tea Party motif.[4] Looked at over time, this festival is certainly
amenable to Limón's metaphor of *mexicanos* "dancing with the devil," the
view held of Texans.[5] The dance may be with the devil, indicating the
cultural tensions between the races, but it is nevertheless—or more importantly—a dance.

From the first, officials of Nuevo Laredo were part of the festivities, but
more importantly, so were thousands of ordinary Mexican citizens, and not
simply from Nuevo Laredo. It was reported that there was even a trainload
of visitors from Saltillo, Mexico, at the first celebration.[6] The most direct
and important political moment occurs in the "*abrazos*" (embraces) ritual in
which leaders of both cities (and sometimes, as in 1995, the governors of
Texas and Tamaulipas) meet at the midway point of the international
bridge to exchange embraces and the promise of continued cooperation
and goodwill between countries.

Is this level of mutual interest and involvement equally true of other metropolitan border couples? Not according to local civic leaders such as the
head of Laredo's Civic Center, Larry Dovalina, who, as I mentioned earlier,
first presented me with the river as a joining and dividing image. Looking at
the history of the Laredos shows us that the Tecos, as an enterprise linking
people on both sides of the river, are nothing at all unusual, nor are the
tensions that somehow or other seem to exist alongside these linkages.

## Social History of the Laredos

Little known and unsettled by eighteenth century Spanish colonists, Nuevo Santander was a vast stretch of territory along the lower Rio Grande in what was part of the northern reaches of Spain's Mexican colony. Apaches and Comanches, both of whom considered this area home and often raided along this stretch, considerably cooled colonization ardors. Despite the potential for attack, the Spanish felt forced to settle the area in response to inroads made by the French, who had already colonized the areas of east Texas and parts of the Mississippi River valley. Suddenly, the Spanish wanted a presence to anchor the area, and so called on Colonel Jose de Escandón to start a string of settlements and missions along the Rio Grande in Nuevo Santander. Escandón responded by commissioning the founding of Dolores, Revilla, and eighteen other locations, and granted to don Tomás Sánchez the opportunity to found Laredo in 1755.[7] The fordability of the river made it ideal in Sánchez' eyes. Indeed, ease of crossing was the factor in most of the settlements on the river. Settlers in this region lived "hard by water,"[8] making the river a social magnet and the wellspring for economic life. With its steep banks, the river did not allow settlers to divert its water into an irrigation system; consequently farming of the bottom lands was not effective. Ranching, on the other hand, was. Vaquero culture and the Anglo imitation of it, later termed "cowboy" culture, was to evolve as people raised sheep and cattle on the arid grasslands along the river.

On May 15, 1755, Sánchez and three families arrived at their destination (named for the Spanish town of Laredo on the Bay of Biscayne) on the north shore of the Rio Grande. Two years later, the hamlet had grown to eleven families and some eighty-five people, mostly immigrants from downriver at Revilla. The new immigrants were, at first, welcomed as they set up households on the southern bank of the river. The easily forded location made movement back and forth easy for the community's ranching population: "The Rio Grande in those years was not only the commercial artery, but the link of the townspeople with each other. There they drew their water, the women washed clothes and chatted, and lovers met after dark."[9]

The prickly exteriors of the men and women of *la frontera* that fostered regional identity, brooking neither Mexican or American interference, also fostered bitter factionalism.[10] At the outset, the major source of rancor in the newly formed community involved the refusal of the most recent arrivals to move across the river to the main settlement.[11] Don Tomás saw this as a threat to his political authority. When, in 1767, Sánchez distributed *porciones* (land titles) among the heads of households in the steadily growing community, forty-four out of ninety were awarded to families on the south side of the river.[12] Try as he might, however, Sánchez could not successfully get all of the south-bank inhabitants to move across the river until, later in the nineteenth century, Indian raids forced the issue.[13] While serious, these factional disputes did not completely disrupt the life of early Laredo, which continued attracting settlers. Within ten years of its founding Laredo became incorporated as a villa (town) "of 60 huts which straddled the Rio Grande."[14] The growth of the villa of Laredo, in spite of Indian depredations and internal squabbling, speaks volumes for the way in which conflict and cooperation seemed to mutually reinforce each other.

Through the nineteenth century three factors combined to forge the unique character of this region: the vaquero/ranching culture, the remoteness of the Rio Grande from centers of Américan and Mexican power, and the chronic depredations from hostile Indian groups. These conditions made for a social/cultural life that promoted a local sense of autonomy, and a perception elsewhere that these people were significantly different.

This area of New Spain was notorious for its deserts, rugged mountain chains, and lack of river systems. Agriculture, certainly along the Rio Grande, was a frustrating undertaking, but the climate and terrain was well suited to ranching. The settlers of the Laredo area found that their sheep herds proliferated quickly, while attempts to raise corn were so pathetic that they resorted to importing it from the neighboring state of Coahuila.[15]

The culture that grew up around raising sheep, horses, and cattle was as hard-bitten as the environment in which it grew up: "Frontier Laredo was not the classical romantic Spanish colonial society of gallant dons and gracious donas, but a rough and, at times, bloody ranching society," writes Laredo historian Stanley Green.[16] The conditions of ranching life were difficult enough to prompt some families to abandon the free and open land that lured them to the Laredo area in the first place.[17] There is an old Navajo Indian saying: "It is only when you've lost some toenails to frostbite that your sheep belong to you."[18] This willingness to endure hardships was just as characteristic of the vaquero tradition that evolved in Texas-Tamaulipas as of their Native American neighbors to the west.

*Transnationalism.* In his classic work *The Great Plains*, Walter Prescott Webb first put forward the argument that cowboy culture's origins could be traced to the "cattle culture" in the Texas-Tamaulipas area.[19] The success of this tradition led to its diffusion throughout the west. His view of *"ranchero"* culture involved the fusion of Mexican vaquero techniques for raising herds with American innovations (e.g., barbed wire, revolvers, and new view on land ownership). Folklorist-anthropologist Américo Paredes,[20] looking at *vaquero* tradition in the borderlands area, was more intrigued by the cultural implications and trajectory of this northern Mexican institution: "Mexicans lent the image of the *vaquero* to their neighbors to the north, and the image returned to Mexico wearing a six-shooter and a Stetson hat."[21] Both authors convey the sense of the cultural evolution of the cowboy as conceived in the earlier horseback-riding *vaquero* of the Texas-Tamaulipas region.

The distance of Nuevo Santander from Mexico City posed administrative problems for the central government, as did all of the northern provinces.[22] Combined with a desert environment and sealed off by rugged mountains, the northern provinces of Mexico were culturally and bureaucratically isolated from the central valley of Mexico. Until the railroad system was brought into Mexico in the late nineteenth century, California, New Mexico, and Texas (also Nuevo Leon, Tamaulipas, Coahuila) were hard to govern. In the earliest days this was of little consequence since only Native American tribes and a trickle of explorers were to be found there. But from the late eighteenth century on, when there was a concerted effort to colonize the area, problems arose between the northern area and the central government.

The distance of the Laredo region from Anglo centers of power, while of more recent vintage, also fostered the independence. When the Republic of Texas declared its political autonomy in 1835, Anglo-dominated Austin became the dominant sphere of influence on Laredo, yet could do little for the new republic's most southern community. The *alcalde* (mayor) of the village of Laredo beseeched first the Mexican government, then the Texans, for relief from the chronic raiding by Comanches but received little support. Yet when Santa Anna drove to Goliad he expected to be quartered and serviced at Laredo. So it was too with the Texas troops that later entered Laredo. The feeling of abandonment by both Mexicans and Americans along the border was palpable by the late 1830s.[23]

*Indian Presence.* In the histories of the region, attention is invariably focused on Spanish colonization, the development of the border, and the intersection of Anglo, Mexican, and Mexican American groups. With rare exception, Native Americans are treated as a preface or an afterthought to the drama of Mexico, Texas, and the United States.[24] Overlooked are the consequences of colonization and the expansion accompanying nation-building, which took their toll first on these Native American groups.

Resistance to the Spanish was forthcoming almost immediately. Their missionizing efforts were a combination of condescension, callousness, and brutality.[25] Physical abuse in the form of attacks against native populations, or corporeal punishment such as flogging and mutilation for those populations already presumed to have become civilized, were mixed in with policies that advocated dependency on alcohol and playing groups off against one another.[26] Significant armed resistance against these colonial efforts was documented in 1616 by the Tepehuan in Durango; in 1640 by the

Tarahumara in Chihuahua; and the Pueblos of New Mexico in 1860. The response on the part of New Spain was to institute *presidios* (armed forts) throughout the vast expanses of the territories it hoped to effectively colonize. This worked little better than to divert attacks by Indian groups from one area to another. The missionary and colonial efforts essentially stagnated from the eighteenth century on as Spain's inability to control so vast a domain in the Western hemisphere became ever more apparent. One result was the hiving off of Mexico, which successfully claimed its independence in 1821; another was the gradual encroachment from the east of France and American trappers, traders, and would be settler-colonists.

Facing "seemingly endless civil strife,"[27] Mexico was also unable to establish a successful Indian policy. The result was, if anything, an increased scope of Indian attack against all representatives of Mexico. For the *norteño*, this meant chronic threat to life and limb as bands of Yaquis, Lipan Apaches, Kiowas, and predominantly Comanche roamed far and wide across the border raiding and frequently capturing and killing their targets.

With the establishment of the Republic of Texas in 1836 and twelve years later the U.S.-Mexican border, the creation of an international boundary along the Rio Grande only intensified Indian attacks. The impact of all this geopolitical shifting was to further disrupt the economic systems of a range of Native American groups living close to the border. A domino effect was created because in order to establish the border, Texas intensified its essentially genocidal policy toward Indians.[28]

By the late eighteenth century the Comanche had become the most powerful Indian group in Texas. As the nineteenth century progressed, however, they found themselves pushed further and further west and south by increased pressure from Anglo settlements. The Texans' policy toward Indian groups differed little if at all from that of Mexican Americans; that is, it was intolerant of them culturally yet determined to dispossess them of their lands.[29] Ironically, relations between native groups and Anglos began peaceably. Even in their early dealings with Austin and Houston, founder and first president of the Republic, respectively, there were attempts to act in a conciliatory way with natives, particularly the Comanche.[30]

When, in 1838, Mirabeau Lamar succeeded Houston as president of the Republic of Texas, Indian policy took an aggressive turn.[31] Lamar's tenure as president coincided with increased Comanche attacks on San Antonio, which led to both the establishment of military posts throughout the southern Texas region along with a series of aggressive campaigns against the Comanche. The wholesale killing of hundreds of innocents on both sides worked to foster a vicious cycle throughout the nineteenth century. Because of the mistrust engendered by Lamar's tenure as president, Sam Houston's efforts to develop peaceful relations with Indian groups failed after he regained the presidency in 1841.

The aboriginal inhabitants of the area around Laredo were not maraud-
ing Lipans or Comanches, but rather peaceful bands of gatherers and
hunters called "Carrizos," also known as Coahuiltecans.[32] These people
posed no problem for the early settlers of the region, often being mission-
ized or otherwise assimilated.[33]

Laredo historian Stanley Green notes that Lipan and Comanche raids
on Laredo began roughly about the time the hamlet was established,[34]
which makes the peaceful comportment of local indigenous groups pretty
much a moot point. These raids were a direct outgrowth of the displace-
ment of these groups from areas further north. Certainly that was the reason that a garrison was first placed on the hamlet's outskirts in 1775.[35] By
at least 1786, "it became viceregal policy to pay tribute to the Apaches in
order to keep them peaceful."[36] So vulnerable was the area between the
Nueces and Rio Grande rivers that Indian raids were the number one reason for periodic declines in population. "Hostile Indians" caused the with-
drawal of Mexican settlers from the Bruni, Texas, area in 1813,[37] and the
abandonment of settlers around Dolores (across the river) in 1815.[38]

Even earlier, in 1790, raiding Indian groups (identification not known)
occupied Laredo's central plaza where they held a *mitote*, a dance cere-
mony, leaving only after they cleaned out the garrison's powder and rattled
the nerves of every settler in the hamlet.[39] Four of Sánchez's sons were
captured by Comanches in 1825 (later released),[40] and in what was the
single worst period for the town (1835–36), twenty-six people were killed
by Indians,[41] contributing both directly and indirectly to the population
decline that occurred in 1835. Even with the establishment in Laredo of
Fort McIntosh in 1849, Indian raids fluctuated seasonally and yearly, never
completely ceasing until 1879.[42]

*Common Identity and Division on the Border.* The overall effect of Indian
raids, the lack of protection received from other quarters, and the "despo-
liation" at the hands of troops from the central governments predisposed
these border dwellers to seek to control their own destiny. This effort was
most dramatically illustrated in the establishment and brief existence of the
Republic of the Rio Grande (1840). With the creation of Mexico in 1821
a debate emerged between political factions that wanted to see control
concentrated in the central government (Centralists) and those who
wanted states' rights (Federalists). Because they felt alienated from both
the United States and Mexico, the northern states of Tamaulipas, Nuevo
León, Coahuila, and Texas were advocates of the Federalist's position.
When in the 1830s Santa Anna assumed the presidency and moved the
government further away from a Federalist position, most people in the
north objected strenuously. Political debate gave way to force, and Santa
Anna directly interceded to put an end to the revolt brewing in the Tamau-

lipas area in 1836. Thus, the Alamo fell and a month later Santa Anna was defeated and the Republic of Texas born.

The northern Mexican states continued to express their autonomy even afterward. While Texas and Mexico argued over the area between the Nueces and Rio Grande Rivers, the northern Mexican states and southern Texas continued to push the Federalist cause. In 1838 Antonio Canales issued a call and wound up receiving support from both sides of the Rio Grande. Antonio Zapata (above) became the de facto military leader for what was emerging as a secessionary movement. The Mexican government sent forces to suppress this latest uprising in 1839. All that year the tide swung back and forth across the river. On the north bank of the River at Dolores on January 1, 1840, a call to found the "Republic of the Rio Grande" was issued by Canales. It was to include southern Texas (below the Nueces) and the states of Tamaulipas, Nuevo León, and Coahuila, with Laredo serving as its capital. The chickens were clearly coming home to roost. Having been ignored or ungratefully used for decades, the people of the north and in particular of Laredo were joining the Federalists because, as the Alcalde wrote in 1839, "at present the administration does not merit our confidence."[43] A truly transcultural phenomenon, Texans and Mexicans on both sides of the river were joining the cause. Laredo, and other Texas towns, sent numbers of *rancheros* in service to the newly formed army.[44] In July 1840, Texas Colonel Samuel Jordan codirected a force of fifty Texans and one hundred Mexicans that seized Laredo from the Centralists who had taken it a few months earlier.[45] The Republic of the Rio Grande lasted a mere 285 days before it was crushed by Mexican troops, but it clearly demonstrated the political and cultural autonomy of the region that straddles the border. The political division promulgated by Washington, D.C., and Mexico City had less effect on the border cities of Laredo and Nuevo Laredo than was hoped. Faced with outsiders, these border dwellers generally came together.

The ability of this northern region to act in its collective interests and through its own identity did not, however, rule out the potential for factional splits. If the Republic of the Rio Grande reflected the ability of people on both sides of the river to rally around transcultural political issues, then the events that followed flushed out the divisive qualities (autonationalism) always just beneath the surface.

Stephen F. Austin was awarded the contract by Mexican authorities to recruit 1,200 Anglo families on a 300,000 acre tract of land in Texas in 1821, thereby protecting Mexican interests against possible French intrusion. He had ensured the Mexican government of his political allegiance and of efforts to see to it that the new emigrants would learn Spanish and become followers of the Roman Catholic Church, conditions that were only nominally met. Yet the ranks of these immigrants swelled so that within a decade Anglos outnumbered Mexicans in the Texas region (*tejanos*) six to one.[46]

Even in the bicultural push to establish the Republic of Texas against Mexican authority, a regional cast bonding Texas's Mexicans and Anglos was at points very thin.[47] Nowhere is this as dramatically and sadly presented as it is in the case of Juan Seguin. Being a Federalist, Seguin took up the cause of the Republic of Texas against Santa Anna and his Mexican Centralists. Seguin, mistakenly it turns out, "believed it possible to be both a proud *mexicano* and a loyal *tejano*."[48] The cooperation between *mexicanos* (native Mexicans) and Anglos in Texas lasted only so long as unity against Mexico was needed, and soon after, the racial and cultural divisions rose to the surface with Anglos dispossessing *mexicanos* of their lands and political rights.[49]

Anglo distrust of *mexicanos* was economic at root. *Mexicano* control of land, especially around San Antonio, was the prize to be taken. Culture and race were attributes that became politically loaded. Able to "demonize" the Mexican population on the basis both of racial or cultural affinities with Mexico aided the Texan cause by inflating their sense of common cause. The defeat of the Texans at the Alamo and Goliad in 1836 and the martyrdom that resulted perfectly served this end. Mexicans too seized on race and culture as a tool of nationalism. Seguin was chastised for aiding the gringos in the Texas Republic War, and it was only when he repudiated his connection to them, fighting against them in the Mexican War of 1846 that he was reintegrated as a Mexican.[50]

Historians on both sides of the river grant that the war with Mexico in 1846 was engineered to satiate U.S. thirst for territory.[51] The speedy victory of the United States initiated discussion as to just how much land Mexico would cede, but with the Treaty of Guadalupe Hidalgo (1847), what had been an ambiguous border zone between Texas and Mexico for a decade was finally determined to be the Rio Grande. With this treaty, a river that once flowed through a singular Laredo, now served as a division into two Laredos.

Despite a generally neutral political position during the Mexican War, Laredoans had for cultural and racial reasons emotionally sided with the Mexicans.[52] The occupation of Laredo by noted expansionist and racist Mirabeau Lamar in 1847 brought the consequences of the war home for people along the river. Lamar is credited with dividing Laredo in two. On September 15, 1847, some five and a half months before the Treaty of Guadalupe-Hidalgo, Lamar ordered the town of Nuevo Laredo into existence and appointed Andrés Martinez its *alcalde*.[53] It was up to Laredo's border dwellers to choose which nation they would become part of, and a significant number opted for the Mexican fatherland.[54] Most stayed on, not simply because of their loyalty to the United States or Texas, but rather

because of their landholdings. Some, like one branch of the Laredo Dovalinas, initially chose to relocate to the Mexican side of the river, only to
return in a few years.[55] Historians of Nuevo Laredo have concluded that
the claim of many Laredoans crossing the river is more a product of the
"romantic imagination" than historic fact.[56] Some, like the first appointed
*alcalde* of Nuevo Laredo, Andrés Martínez, actually did cross over, but
Mexican historians emphasize that the south bank was already in existence,
not a function of the Treaty of Guadalupe-Hidalgo.[57] Laredo, had, as a
function of the war, become the "American" version of the Mexican town
it had previously been, staring at its twin across an international boundary.
What had been one (one town, one people) now became two exhibiting a
muted antagonism.

The resentment of Nuevo Laredoans can be found in the ideology and
myth surrounding the establishment of their town. Celebrating the town's
centennial in 1948, Nuevo Laredo fashioned a new official shield depicting
an event that, more than any other, dramatically evokes Mexican sentiment
about the war with the United States. Those leaving the Texas side of the
river to remain Mexican so deeply felt their decision "that they disinterred
their dead, moved their remains across the river, and reinterred them in
Nuevo Laredo so they would not lie in a foreign country."[58] The official
shield of the city depicts this legendary event. While most historians[59]
would assign the rise of nationalism in Mexico to the era of Presidents
Juárez and Díaz in the final quarter of the nineteenth century, the humiliation suffered at the hands of Texas and the United States did much to
promote a sense of common identity at the hands of rapacious gringos
from the north. The civic monument dedicated to the founders also recalls
this event and bears the following inscription: "A city as patriotic and Mexican in its very essence as Nuevo Laredo knows that a city is not only a
present and a future, but also a past; in order to settle in this site they
brought the revered remains of their ancestors, making them part of Mexican history."[60] The extent of the repudiation of the "lost Laredo" is clearly
referred to in this act, and that it should become an official part of the city's
identity speaks volumes about the antagonistic essence of autonationalism
in the two Laredos.

The unequal economies of border communities grew sharply as a result
of the formation of the border. Martínez points out that by the mid-1850s,
the American cities had the benefit of low tariffs, free internal trade, and a
rapidly expanding capitalist sector that would usher in the railroads.[61] The
Mexican communities seemed cursed by underdevelopment, "oppressive
taxes imposed on the country's internal trade,"[62] plus the additional tariffs
on goods brought in from the other side now generated by the border. To
alleviate the crushing burden, the Mexican government and Tamaulipas
officials, in 1849 and 1858, respectively, first lowered and then exempted

border communities from tariffs forming a free trade zone. Mexican border communities blossomed as repatriating countrymen infused their local economies with capital and life.[63] Mexican historian Salinas Domínguez finds the year 1855 to be one of Nuevo Laredo's most important.[64] The economic boom in Nuevo Laredo came at the expense of their U.S. neighbors across the river, and the latter began to lobby for an end to the "free zone." After almost a half century of pushing their cause, U.S. merchants in 1909 managed to dismantle the free zone.

During the years of the Mexican Revolution in the first three decades of the twentieth century, the Laredo area periodically found itself playing a role in the course of events. From roughly 1890 on, Laredo served as a repository for anti-Díaz elements.[65] So outraged was Díaz about his enemies being allowed to work against him in the safety of the U.S. border that on one occasion, in 1891, he had a prominent foe (Dr. Ignacio Martínez) gunned down in the streets of Laredo.[66] The exiles continued to publish diatribes against Díaz, however, eventually backing Díaz rival Francisco Madero, who successfully revolted in 1910. It appeared to Díaz that the provocateurs were able to function freely because they had U.S. backing, which may or may not have been true. This in turn fueled another round of antagonism between Americans and Mexicans.

Laredo Judge John Valls offers yet another illustration of this principle. As district attorney, Valls attempted to arrest the president of Mexico, Plutarco Elías Calles.[67] In a series of events reminiscent of the high level political culpability over assassinations in Mexico in 1994, the Mexican leadership seventy-two years earlier was also implicated in the 1922 assassination of a Carrancista, Lucio Blanco, living in San Antonio; he had been talked into meeting with Mexican officials in Laredo. Blanco and his friend, another Carrancista, were fished out of the Rio Grande handcuffed. While suspecting a political assassination, nothing conclusive was uncovered and the case lingered through the decade. Finally, in October 1929, based on information Valls gathered, he was able to link Elías Calles (then home secretary) to the murder. It just so happened that Elías Calles was returning from a visit to Washington, a train trip that would take him through Laredo. The State Department tried to warn the independent-minded Valls not to impede Elías Calles's journey, but he was outraged that the Mexican president would commit such an act in his jurisdiction. Consequently he was bent on taking the Mexican president off the train at the Webb County stop with a warrant for his arrest on the charge of conspiracy to commit murder.[68] The U.S. government placed a military contingent on board the train and ordered it straight through to Nuevo Laredo. The Mexicans, meanwhile, retaliated by denying their citizens permission to cross into Laredo. This had an immediate impact on the merchants of Laredo, who have always been heavily dependent on Mexican trade.

Further, the Mexican Consulate was closed and formal statements to the effect that Valls was an enemy of Mexico were made. Relations were normalized once Elías Calles gave way to the presidency of Cárdenas in the 1930s.[69] Once again we see that *los dos Laredos* operate in a sphere that is distinct from international relations.

As stated, the border as a geopolitical fact of life necessitates formal agreements between residents of Laredo and Nuevo Laredo where once they had no need to do so: "When the Rio Grande became a border, friends and relatives who had been near neighbors—within shouting distance across a few hundred feet of water—now were legally in different countries."[70] The river was converted into what officials hoped would be a state-controlled barrier permeable only with a license. Day-to-day border issues and problems have always remained the responsibility of the local government, calling into play networks and relationships between officials and citizens of the border cities.

The necessity of working together was a function of the river at that time, and it is more so now. The need to lend a hand in time of crisis was understood by both cities. Hence, when Nuevo Laredo was the scene of bloody fighting in the Mexican Revolution, assistance in the form of medical aid was sent from its neighbor. During periods of flooding or other disasters residents of the two cities would work together to get through the crisis.

Most recently, this has been seen in the rise of the *maquiladora*,[71] and the serious pollution that has resulted in the training (by U.S. federal agencies) of environmental specialists from both cities to reduce pollution and handle toxic cleanups.[72] Crime, which moves easily between the two cities, necessitates the close cooperation of each city's police agencies.[73] Similarly, in areas that can benefit both communities, such as tourism, there have been binational efforts. Los Caminos del Rio is a binational group of civic-minded citizens and leaders seeking to restore the historic sites all along both sides of the river in the hopes of attracting visitors.

There is a second dimension to the binationalism of the border cities that is purely informal. In a real sense, the impenetrable border envisioned that would regulate the movement of goods and people on the border was faulty from the start (see Appendix B). Paredes, cited above, points to this:

> If they (locals on both sides of the river) wanted to visit each other, the law required that they travel many miles up or down stream, to the nearest official crossing place, instead of swimming or boating directly across as they used to do before. It goes without saying that they paid little attention to the requirements of the law. When they went visiting, they crossed at the most convenient spot on the river; and, as is ancient custom when one goes visiting loved ones, they took gifts with them: farm products from Mexico to Texas, textiles and other manufactured goods from Texas to Mexico. Legally, of course, this was smuggling, differing from contraband for profit in volume only.[74]

Social relations, it can be seen, continued despite formal governmental attempts to legislate all such movements. People in the two Laredos have continued to work and carry on business in each other's cities, and socialize in either place legally and illegally. An odd example, but one nevertheless illustrative of this, comes from Gonzáles's gleaning of newspapers from Nuevo Laredo.[75] He makes mention of an American, Richard Bechetel Davis, who marries a woman, Elisa Méndez, from Nuevo Laredo in 1951. The wedding made the news on September 5 because at their wedding reception presided over by the bride's father, a certain Epifanio Salazar became outraged at the two and a half pesos charged by Mr. Méndez who, in turn, shot and killed the unhappy wedding guest. Intermarriage continues as it has since before the demarcation, and at all levels: from working poor, to Tecos like Alejandro Ortiz and his Laredo wife, to well-to-do businessmen like Moi Goldberg and his Nuevo Laredo socialite wife Laura. In a real sense, despite their differing levels of economic development and belonging to different and sometimes antagonistic nations, the two Laredos have paid the border very little heed. People in both cities work out their relations as they need to, using national regulations judiciously, relying heavily on local traditions worked out between them over two centuries. The Tecos, too, are a part of this legacy.

## Integrating the Border into the Nation-State

With the arrival of the railroads in 1881, the two Laredos became structurally integrated into the socioeconomic mainstream of both countries. The Texas-Mexican "Tex Mex" Railroad was the first to arrive in Laredo via Corpus Christi in September of that year, but by 1883 the International and Great Northern was in town as well. On the Nuevo Laredo side, the Mexican government was working feverishly to build a railroad from Mexico City to its northern border. Historians Meyer and Sherman maintain that the Mexican National Railroad Company (chartered under Colorado law and eventually bought by British and French interests) built a line from the Mexican capital to Nuevo Laredo-Laredo in 1888.[76]

The upshot of much of the march of political-economic expansion to the border from Mexico City was to promote a sense of nationalism, albeit in fits and starts. This most certainly began with Porfirio Díaz's presidency, which encompasses the last quarter of the nineteenth century,[77] and continues to the present day. The economic programs Díaz orchestrated between 1878 and 1910, while further impoverishing the majority, managed nevertheless to push development. The volume of manufactured goods doubled during his thirty-four-year tenure.[78] He built the railroad system, which spurred on the growth of mining, textiles, and oil, while encouraging the growth of northern industrial centers like Monterrey.

While the price paid for this expansion (e.g., the dispossessing of most of Mexico's small farmers, and wholesale encouragement of foreign colonialism) ultimately led to his demise, Díaz's presidency most certainly fostered Mexican nationalism. Once started, the process of building nationalist sentiment continued through the Mexican Revolution of 1910–1917 and on to the present, primarily through a growing sense of regional integration, a national culture fostered in art (e.g., José Clemente Orozco and Diego Rivera and the Indianist themes of their work), as well as through heroes such as Emiliano Zapata. Mexican nationalism is regularly constructed in combining an internally devised sense of nationhood and a willingness to stand up to *norteamericanos*. Being a northern representative of the Mexican nation, Nuevo Laredo prospered through the Díaz presidency, through the free zone, through the establishment of the railroad, and Monterrey, the emergence of a powerful regional center only 140 miles to the south. Nothing more concretely established the emergence of the two Laredos' modern period than the railroad.

An article in the *Laredo Times* of January 1, 1883, however, indicates the presence of all three railroads in the twin cities area, including the Mexican National Railroad. The Mexican National Railroad may not have been formally completed until 1888, there being "gaps" just south of the two Laredos, but it was present in the area. The railroad built a huge machine shop tagged as "the largest west of the Mississippi,"[79] indicating a physical presence in the area long before it was ready for service. Hence, as far as influencing the area, the railroad's presence was felt in advance of its formal completion and without much concern for international boundaries. In the two Laredos the arrival of these railroads ushered in a building boom during the decade of the 1880s. In Laredo the new courthouse, opera house, marketplace, and a new infrastructure (including streets and sewers) accompanied the population explosion that saw the city swell from 3,500 to 11,319 by 1890.[80] Nuevo Laredo's majestic new hotels in the town center and other public works were all constructed through this period.[81] The railroad facilitated the entrance of mainstream American cultural traits, but even before it formally arrived in Laredo, the railroad was, through supervisors and work crews, spreading the game of baseball in its wake.

Traversing the far west proved to be financially risky for many of the railroad lines.[82] Unlike their eastern counterparts that followed population growth, western railroads often preceded population in the hopes that people and towns would make them viable. South Texas got the railroads late enough to avoid the financial pitfalls attendant to many of these endeavors. The railroad line coming from San Antonio (1883) and Corpus Christi (1881) to Laredo was needed and quickly proved worthy of the effort. In a separate endeavor, Mexico's Díaz government, backed by

French and British investors, completed a line from Mexico City to Nuevo Laredo by 1888. The goals in both cases, to bring the frontier into a more functional relationship to the state, were partially accomplished.[83]

Both Laredo and Nuevo Laredo experienced population and building booms.[84] Part of this development included a newfound sense of connectedness with popular culture from both mainstream Mexico and the United States. Historian William Beezley has documented the spread of American and British forms of sport and leisure into Mexican life (primarily in Mexico City).[85] Baseball was a major component of this diffusion.

# Two

## Early Baseball on the Border

BECAUSE it is a game rather than an important economic or political institution, hence less subject to chronicling, baseball's origins and the route it took through various countries are often mere speculation. For instance, it has long been accepted that baseball was introduced into Cuba in the 1860s through the presence of U.S. Marines. In recent important corrective studies, however, Wagner[1] and Pérez[2] have shown that it was Cuban students studying in the United States who first brought the sport to their homeland. The absence of recorded material on sports subjects means that in chronicling its earliest days, one may chance upon a windfall of data rather than systematically tap available sources. Certainly this is the case with Mexico.

Writing in the most recent edition of the *Enciclopedia del Beisbol Mexicano*,[3] Tomás Morales begins his history of Mexican baseball by underscoring this point: "It is impossible to assure with scientific certainty where the first game of baseball was played in Mexico. Various cities claim the honor and in spite of the efforts to discover the exact place, none of the historians agree."[4] For Morales, four places might have been first: Guaymas in Sonora; Cadereyta Jiménez in Nuevo León; Mérida, Yucatan; and Nuevo Laredo in Tamaulipas. As bibliographic sources of any sort are not provided, the Morales account must be read more as a popular guide than a serious inquiry. Still, it is among the few accounts of the origins of the sport in Mexico.

Morales's earliest date comes from Guaymas where, sometime in 1877, U.S. Marines disembarked from the USS *Montana* and, among other things, played a game of baseball among themselves.[5] In short order, Morales asserts, a local team was formed, though no date is provided. An exact date is provided, on the other hand, in Cadereyta Jiménez where, on 4 July 1889, Colonel Treadwell Robertson initiated a game between his employees and those of the locals working the Monterrey-Tampico railroad. Also mentioned as a distant possibility is Mérida, Yucatan, which, because of its proximity to Cuba, got the game quite early. There, according to Gil Joseph,[6] Cubans visiting Yucatecan beaches introduced the game to local families in 1890. Much of this portrait of early baseball is circumstantial. In most cases we are not certain when these games were played, whether Mexicans played (or even watched) these early games, or how long it took to for the sport to root in Mexico.

More precise is historian William Beezley's seminal article entitled, "The Rise of Baseball in Mexico and the First Valenzuela," which documents the sport's institutionalization in the Republic's Capital.[7] Beezley's "hook" is a game that took place in 1903, in which a player for the Mexico City team singlehandedly won a game and was carried off the field by his teammates. Information on the hero is limited to his last name, Valenzuela, and so, writing in the era of Fernando Valenzuela, major league star of the Los Angeles Dodgers in the 1980s, Beezley brackets his article between the "first Valenzuela" and the one we are more familiar with today. Beezley notes the presence of American baseball exhibitions as early as 1882. Such contests were played before Anglo crowds, although some Mexican elite attended. There followed a period of about six years in which efforts to get the sport going were haphazard and unsuccessful. The sport finally began to take root in 1887, and following another attempt to generate interest, a three-team circuit (including one all-Mexican club) was formed. By 1888 baseball was established in Mexico City.[8]

## The Origins of Baseball in the Two Laredos

The imprecision of the dates suggested for the origins of baseball in Mexico does not prevent Morales from assigning 1877 as the appearance of baseball in Nuevo Laredo.[9] Despite the absence of sources, there can be little doubt that he took that date from the Nuevo Laredo sports journalist and self-styled baseball historian Fiacro Díaz Corpuz. Díaz wrote two histories of baseball in Mexico, one devoted purely to Nuevo Laredo,[10] the other a more general history of the game.[11] Historical work of this kind is quite unusual in Mexico where serious work on sports topics is rarely carried out. For his discussion of the origins of the sport in Nuevo Laredo, Díaz relied on first-person narratives taken in the early 1950s of several surviving players and fans of the earliest periods. In this way Díaz was able to get eyewitness accounts of the last decades of the nineteenth century. In particular, it was the narratives of a ninety-year-old retired plumber, don Cipriano Pedraza, and seventy-four-year old don Procopio Herrera on which Díaz relied most heavily.

Don Cipriano was born in 1865 in Matamoros and came to Nuevo Laredo in 1880 to work on the railroad line coming north from Mexico City. He claimed a date of 1893 for the first game in the region:

> In 1893 an assistant supervisor of the station, a North American very fond of baseball named Johnny Tayson, formed a team made up of Mr. Tayson, Felix Mass, Pedro Garcia, Cecilio Herrera Quintana, and others whose names I can't remember. I played second base. It was already known that Manuel Bocanegra, Lucas and Catarino Juárez, Eulalio Solís, "El Chamuco" [local players] had gone

to play baseball in the Capital [Mexico City].

I am certain that baseball entered precisely through Nuevo Laredo when the railroad arrived from the Capital. As always we railroad men went and we loved to practice this sport. And for their part, the North American supervisors always tried to raise teams from the lower ranks [of Mexican employees].

In the year 1893, the team we ended up with played locally against other nines, but at the same time concentrated our games against San Antonio, Corpus Christi, Cotulla, Brownsville.[12]

Don Cipriano's account claims Tayson introduced the game in 1893, putting it at odds with Morales's 1877 date. All accounts, however, agree that the game was spread through the railroads, which would have brought it to the Laredo area in approximately 1881 (the Texas-Mexican Railroad was extended to Nuevo Laredo in 1882). This, too, furthers doubt on the 1877 date Morales used. No direct accounts of baseball being played in either Laredo as early as 1881 exist, but for baseball to have been so well formed locally by the Tayson date of 1893, it would had to have been played for some time before. This is suggested in don Cipriano's account, when he asserts that local standout Manuel Bocanegra had already left the area to play in Mexico City (probably by 1888).

A second oral history of the period collected by Corpus also points to this conclusion as well. Procopio Herrera, Sr., was seventy-four years of age at the time of his 1953 interview. A retired city employee in Nuevo Laredo, he was father to Procopio Herrera, Jr., the "Pride of the Laredo," who played for the Nuevo Laredo Tecolotes in the 1940s and 1950s. The elder Herrera's earliest memories of baseball go back to the watershed year of 1890, but also suggest an earlier date of origin:

> My brother Natividad Herrera Quintana played baseball in the year 1890, and by his account to me the King of Sports [baseball] was practiced in this city [Nuevo Laredo] before that date. In the above-mentioned year, 1890, my brother formed part of a baseball team on which Pedro Palacios, Antonio Valdez, los 'cuates' Hernández[,] who formed a magnificent battery[,] played. One was a pitcher and the other catcher. He [Natividad] related to me also that at that time they [people] already talked about the names of Lucas y Catarino Juárez, Eulalio Solís, and Manuel Bocanegra. [These men] already walked [played] in distant parts of the Republic principally Veracruz and in Mexico [City] in which they did very well; but it was in Nuevo Laredo and Laredo, Texas[,] in which these teams were formed and learned to play baseball. The diamond for playing baseball was situated precisely where the border customs building now stands, and this place was the scene of the magnificent heroics and feats of the first Nuevo Laredo baseball players.[13]

Living cheek-by-jowl with Laredo might also have accounted for an earlier introduction to the game in Nuevo Laredo. If the game really did arrive via the railroad, then it must have entered the borderlands area (in Laredo) not long after 1881 with the arrival of the Tex Mex Railroad and in 1883 with the International and Great Northern. Montejano describes the "Americanization," the cultural impact of the railroads in southern Texas, and though no one seems to have conducted a detailed study of the cultural impact of the railroad on the Laredo area, there is little doubt that the almost threefold population increase experienced in the area between 1880 and 1890 was significantly made up of Americans of one stripe or another.[14] Cultural traits did not, of course, stop at the border waiting for customs officials to allow entry. If baseball was practiced in the Laredo area in the early 1880s, it is reasonable to assume that it was played in Nuevo Laredo as well.

## Laredo's View of the Game in the Two Laredos

While Díaz focused on Nuevo Laredo, the game entered Mexico through Laredo. The fluid nature of transnational border relations was as evident with baseball as it was with any other area. This is important for establishing both when the game arrived and how it developed. If we extend our search for baseball origins to Laredo we see that the earliest game reported by the *Laredo Times* was on September 23, 1884. No doubt there were earlier games, because the paper, while giving it a full description, made no mention that the game being played was unusual or the first. Reporting on sports of any sort was spotty in newspapers of the time, as were the games themselves, and coverage of sporting events were given less attention than they later received. Surprisingly, the first game reported was described at some length. The following is excerpted from the lengthy article:

> During the early part of last week the Laredo Base Ball club received a challenge from the Sunsets of San Antonio, to play a match game in the latter city on September 21. Accompanying the challenge was an offer of a certain portion of the gate money, the proposition was agreed to, and a readiness expressed to play the game was stipulated by the Sunsets. . . . Below is given a recapitulation of the score, as owing to unavoidable circumstances it is impossible to publish a detailed tabular statement, and in comparing the results the reader must not forget the disadvantages which the Laredo club experienced in keeping their appointment—as exceedingly tiresome and enervating railroad trip, and not the least, a captain with a broken finger.[15]

With an opening like that, it comes as no surprise that Laredo lost, by a score of 13 to 6. From the article, however, the Anglo makeup of the team, or at least those mentioned by name (Elstner, Sturgeon, Smith, Flynn, Maxwell, and Connon), is quite apparent. The following day the Laredo paper announced a meeting to form the "Laredo Base Ball Association."

These men may have come from the ranks of railroad employees or from the nearby military installation, Fort McIntosh, but there were no *mexicanos* among them.[16] Three years later, in 1887, "Laredo's crack nine" was still made up of Anglos Flynn and Connon, as well as Wilson and Porter.

Fourth of July festivities seemed to spawn a whole range of institutions, including an annual event involving baseball between Laredo and Corpus Christi on the Texas coast. This baseball competition involved hundreds of Laredoans who annually chartered a train for the holiday on the coast where the games were played. For these events Laredoans began to prepare early. By 1888 these reports begin to list *mexicanos* in small numbers playing alongside Anglos. In early June of 1888, for instance, the Laredo papers announced a planning meeting to organize the ball team.[17] By June 10 a team previously called "the Kids" was preparing for the new 1888 season by changing their names to the Laredo Reds and recruiting local talent. At least two of their numbers were *mexicanos*, not yet available to play: "Messrs. R. Sanchez and Johnny Orfila, the club's battery[,] are still away at school, one in San Antonio and the other at Austin, but they will return this month, and then the boys will be ready for business."[18] In the following July 4 weekend, the lineup included a third *mexicano*, "S. Benavides."[19] Laredo won that tournament, which included teams from San Antonio as well as Corpus Christi. The *Corpus Christi Caller*, however, expressed disapproval of the Laredo team trashing its hotel room. The *Laredo Times* defended the action by claiming that their players were being gouged by local merchants.[20]

The following year the paper was reporting games between "the Kids" and Fort McIntosh with lineups composed solely of Anglos. That there were a number of clubs operating in Laredo was mentioned in the paper,[21] and we know that local *mexicanos* could be found among their ranks. Their names were not mentioned as frequently, which forces the question of whether or not Mexican Americans in Laredo were playing the game as frequently as Anglos or whether the earliest editors of the Laredo newspapers were simply not predisposed to covering *mexicano* events in the same way as Anglo events.

Anglo culture at the time was certainly being showcased in national rites such as the July 4 events, which, by 1889, had come to include the annual baseball game replete with marching band, grandstand, and awning.[22] Similar reportage was found for July 4 in 1892 and 1893. In the light of such a nationalistic spectacle it is hard to imagine that *mexicano* culture and social relations, predicated on sharing of cultural space, would take place.

The local military installation, Fort McIntosh, had regularly fielded teams that had been covered by the local press almost since the inception of the newspaper. Rivalry between the town and the base was generally friendly, although close ties with the Mexican American majority were generally kept to a minimum. When in 1914 a three team military league from the nearby base was formed, it was claimed in the local press that every effort was being put forth to field a group of "locals" to compete against the base. *Mexicano* players were rarely mentioned in these contests, however, though it may be assumed that through the first decade of the twentieth century they were deeply embedded in the baseball scene and often recruited to play against the military teams. Playing against one of these "base teams" in the 1930s (long after the period of *mexicano* exclusion), Fernando Dovalina recalls an occasion on which he was hired to play for Hebbronville, Texas, against Fort McIntosh. After accepting the offer, don Fernando was approached by the local base to see if he'd play for them; but feeling uncomfortable with them he begged off. Needing a ride to Hebbronville, however, don Fernando asked to accompany the team without telling the base team that he was to pitch against them. It was arranged that he be picked up by the personnel carrier used to carry the team on the day of the game. No one seemed unduly suspicious to see him in uniform. When they arrived at Hebbronville, don Fernando popped out of the back of the transport and proceeded to go over to the opponent's side. He pitched effectively that day, beating the boys from Fort McIntosh. Following the last pitch he jumped back into the transport, hoping that no one would be too angry. As the team approached the vehicle, he heard someone say, "What do you wanna do with this guy?" He just smiled, letting the soldier grumble a bit, and acted as if nothing much had happened. He got the ride home.

This strikingly Anglo bent in cultural events began to even out after the turn of the century. We have already indicated that the Washington's Birthday Celebration was culturally reclaimed by Laredo's Mexican Americans in the first quarter of the twentieth century. Something similar seemed to have occurred in the coverage of baseball by the Laredo paper. The city managed to place a team, the Laredo Bermudas, in the Southwest Texas League, a short-lived professional league operating for a few years between 1910 and 1913. Many of the players were professionals hired from other towns and brought in on a seasonal basis, including two Cubans: a first baseman named Hernández, and a pitcher named Ramos (first names not mentioned).[23]

A much more significant set of events had already been transpiring from the actual turn of the century. Four Laredo ballplayers—two *mexicanos* and two Anglos—transformed the level of play from haphazard to acclaimed. These men were Manuel Bocanegra, Tomás Valenzuela, Charlie Pierce, and Chester Burbank. Bocanegra and Valenzuela first appear in local print in 1903 in a vaunted July 4 contest.[24] This seems to mark a watershed of sorts in reporting *mexicano* play. While baseball games remained irregularly reported, *mexicanos* were increasingly being mentioned alongside

Anglos. By 1915, the Laredo press even makes mention for the first time of a "Mexican team of this city" playing a contest against the local military installation.[25] Reporting on a September 28, 1918, game between Laredo and Kelly Field, the paper listed the lineup, which was predominantly *mexicano*. This same lineup or a facsimile thereof was reported in action a week later as well. In both games we see Bocanegra and Tomás Valenzuela present. In the 1920s the strong Milmo teams regularly featured Latinos playing alongside Anglos, a situation that had long taken place but was only then mentioned in the press.

Mexican Americans had been involved with the sport since its appearance in the Laredos. They had played alongside Anglos in the late 1880s, and with Pierce and Burbank since at least the turn of the century, becoming more frequently mentioned as time went on. It would be tempting to think of this as an issue of ethnicity or race, but in the Laredo area class comes to count for more. Montejano[26] and Limón[27] have both discussed the powerful role of class relations in south Texas, and in the Laredos in particular. With this in mind, it might also be argued that finding Sánchez and Orfila playing alongside Anglos in 1888 counts for less than finding Bocanegra and Valenzuela playing alongside their Anglo teammates twenty years later. While all were Mexican American, the first two, by virtue of attending school in Austin and San Antonio[28] were probably of that sector of Mexican American society that represented the old elite, while the latter were from the working class. Beezley's[29] trajectory of sport, diffusing down from the elite to other classes, seems applicable here and helps us account for the time it seems to have taken for working class *mexicanos* to locally assert themselves in baseball.

Nowadays, every Friday at the small deli area of a local H.E.B. supermarket, the baseball old-timers gather in ever dwindling numbers to sip coffee and recount games played fifty, sixty, and seventy years ago. In my last encounter with them I revealed that the early *Laredo Times* newspaper reported few *mexicano* or Mexican players. Lázaro Dovalina looked at me incredulously and concluded, "How can that be? We're over 90 percent *mexicano* here." He's right, of course, but viewed from a class perspective the gradually increased reportage of *mexicanos* may reflect the trickling of the game down to the general public.

## The Transnational and Autonational Nature of the Sport

With its free movement of goods and services and the sharing of resources between the cities, the nature of baseball and other institutions along the border continued to deny the political boundary that was designed to separate them. That these "sister cities" are joined at the hip, particularly against outsiders, is manifest in the forms of baseball competition. While they often engage in contests against each other, all distinctions disappear when faced with external competitors. This was certainly the case in the recruitment of players across the border. Don Procopio's narrative claimed that even in the late nineteenth century, the two Laredos routinely combined the best talent when playing outsiders. The presence of Anglos such as Chester Burbank and Charlie Pierce on the teams mentioned by don Procopio suggests that not only was the relationship transnational but multiracial as well.

While Díaz's history documents a transnational quality to baseball, he simultaneously sought to write a history of the game for *his city*, Nuevo Laredo, and in doing so he at times expressed his anti-American nationalism. Thus, in concluding one section of his book, on the origins of the sport in Nuevo Laredo, he felt the need to affix the "historic refusal" of the founders of Nuevo Laredo (Chapter 1). At this point, Díaz perceives of the two cities as separate, temporarily denying the sport and historic link between them: "And what is settled in our small arena [Nuevo Laredo]? We hope to serve those who want to affirm the exact place where baseball entered our Republic: Nuevo Laredo, the city first founded as a loss, in the annexation of Texas to the United States in 1848, and which vigorously prided itself in those early inhabitants who didn't want to leave their ancestors to rest in Laredo and brought them to the city they founded."[30]

The tone of Díaz's account contains the same ambivalence that is found in all sectors of the border relationship: at times joined, at times divided. The players in the two Laredos would, throughout the history of the game, form teams along national lines and play heated contests against each other. Don Procopio Herrera mentions one such typical alignment in his narrative:

> In the year 1900 the Nuevo Laredo Club was formed, made up of my brother Natividad, don Cecelio and don Zenobio Archiga, the Lázaro brothers. . . . This Nuevo Laredo baseball club confronted the other team from Laredo, Texas[,] performing with don Manuel Bocanegra, don Tomás Valenzuela, . . . and others most of whom were born in Laredo, Texas. The series was hard fought. Sometimes the Texans won and other times we did, but sport supremacy in these contests was never clear.[31]

When facing teams from outside the Laredo area, however, the political distinctions between the two cities seemed to spontaneously melt as they joined forces. If the dates given by Díaz can be believed, this was the case as early as 1893 when Tayson was trying to form teams: "In order for Mister Tayson's team to get more power and do well against the teams of these cities a good team formed, reinforced with players of the quality of Manuel Bocanegra, one of the best pitchers that existed in both Laredos."[32]

This was also the case in 1900, as well with the Nuevo Laredo Baseball Club, when "on many occasions teams from San Diego, Alice, Cotulla, Corpus Christi, San Antonio and Robstown, Texas[,] came here to play. . . . On these occasions we reinforced our teams with Bocanegra, Valenzuela, the Juarezes, Chester Burbank, and Charlie Pierce [Laredoans all]."[33] The city of Nuevo Laredo fielded a wide variety of teams, but by the turn of the century it was the governmental teams, such as the Customs Agency that put up the best teams. In 1909 Nuevo Laredo fielded a team called "White Cross" that played locally and against Laredo.[34] At the same time, however, when a series of games against Tampico, Mexico, had been slated, Nuevo Laredo put together a team made up of the best local players. In what was early on a strategy for recruitment when playing important teams from elsewhere in Texas or Mexico, the border cities fused their talent.

When the competition was international, as in this case, teams often played for a prize: two huge barrels of beer, one made in the United States, the other in Mexico. At times, in a fashion reminiscent of collegiate Crew competitions, they played for uniforms as well:

> Generally they made wagers of a barrel of North American beer named "Budweiser," against one of "Kloster," made and sold by the famous "Cuauhtemoc" brewery of Monterrey, Nuevo León. At the end of the encounter both of the teams tasted that liquid, one to celebrate the victory and the other to ease the pain of defeat. . . . But the nicest thing was the bet they made to hand over their uniforms, which is to say that the team that lost was dispossessed of their uniforms and delivered them to the team that won. This was a ceremony at the end of the game in which the local public hotly applauded whenever we won and lamented when we lost. Many times the teams that visited us were without uniforms.[35]

During the worst fighting in the Mexican Revolution (1910–17), baseball was suspended in Nuevo Laredo. Laredo, then, picked up the slack, hosting games with players from both sides throughout the struggle. When the sport returned across the river in 1917, it did so in Nuevo Laredo's first park built by don Francisco Barrero Argilleles, a devoted sportsman.[36] He put together a team that played against other outfits from Monterrey to San Antonio, and included talent from wherever he could find it. At least one of his players, a star pitcher by the name of José "The German" Rivier, was said to have come to Nuevo Laredo to evade military service in World War I.[37]

During the First World War, Laredo's military installation was home to a number of soldiers who had professional baseball experience, and local players on both sides of the border were able to play with and against some of these men. It was also during this time (1918) that the Almendares, the famous Cuban team, visited and played on the border as part of their Mexican American tour. Those who saw that game recall it as a sobering lesson for the highly touted local team: "I must confess it was a sound thrashing," noted one spectator.[38]

## The Legend of Manuel Bocanegra

What is impressive at so early a time in the sport's local development is the stature of Laredoans Manuel Bocanegra and Tomás Valenzuela on both sides of the border. These men are touted as having dominated the baseball scene from at least 1890 to as late as 1924, some thirty-four years. The stories of their range and prowess have become legendary. More importantly, these two, along with others such as Lucas Juárez, Charlie Pierce, and Chester Burbank, were gifted players that Díaz claimed formed the core of baseball teams from the border that helped institutionalize baseball throughout Mexico. When Beezley writes of the development of the sport in the capital in 1887–88,[39] he writes of the formation of a Mexican team that played against American squads. According to the oral histories taken by Díaz, at least three players from the Laredo–Nuevo Laredo area could have been among the players forming those first all-Mexican teams.[40] What then is the truth? Could these two Laredoans have been responsible for helping the game become established in Mexico's capital?

While both Bocanegra and Valenzuela were lionized, little is known of them outside of the stories of their baseball feats; and here most of it pertains to Bocanegra. Those who knew the latter recalled both his love of the game and his upbeat and amiable character off the field.[41] While Bocanegra is remembered for his pitching prowess, he also had a lifetime batting average over .300 and could play any position. Detailing a bit of their history further underscores the transnational character of baseball on the border.

Bocanegra is reputed to have held a particularly strong attachment to the Laredo area. In a career studded with opportunities to play for teams in cities that would offer him much more than he could have ever received in Laredo, he rarely accepted the offers, preferring instead to remain a streetcar conductor! Perhaps it was because of his unassuming manner and loyalty to the border that he was nicknamed "Honest John" by the men who played against him at the local military installation.

It was typical of the earliest days of baseball in this region that the caliber of teams varied widely. Bocanegra and other talented players might find themselves playing against local military men one week, and traveling semi-pro teams from Corpus Christi or San Antonio the next. The haphazard range of visiting teams would come to include the famous Cuban team Almendares (1918) or even a contingent of the Chicago White Sox (1906). When border pride was at stake, Bocanegra and Valenzuela were always the battery (later they would play first base and second base, respectively). It wouldn't matter who they played for, since when one pitched the other caught. One old timer recalled a contest in 1900 between Corpus

Christi and Laredo:

> The Kids [Corpus Christi] had Clarence Morris, a sensational young lefty, on
> the hill. Valenzuela was Bocanegra's catcher and Joe Mireur was [catching] for
> the Kids. There were 5,000 fans in the seats to see this game in Corpus Christi.
> The game turned out to be one of the best ever seen in this port. For 17
> weighty innings an emotional challenge was offered the fans. With the score tied
> 1–1 since the ninth inning, no one could score. Meanwhile, Morris had to be
> relieved at the end of the 12th inning. Bocanegra continued pitching the ball as
> freshly as when he began the game, and Valenzuela caught everything that was
> thrown. Finally, when they arrived at the 17th inning, the sun had almost com-
> pletely set, and night commenced. The game was called for night, and Bocane-
> gra vigorously protested saying that his arm felt fine.
> The next day Valenzuela warmed up his arm to pitch . . . and Bocanegra was
> the catcher. The Kids won 2–1. On the third day, however, Bocanegra returned
> to the mound. Not so Morris, who was too fatigued to oppose him. Bocanegra
> managed to win for his team by a score of 1–0.[42]

Pitching twenty-six innings of one-run ball in two outings over three
days was the stuff of the iron-man Bocanegra legend. Combined with
Valenzuela's superb pitching performance (one run in a complete game),
the two Laredoans were understandably respected by teams everywhere.

Despite his travels, the provincialism of Bocanegra was often evident.
The following anecdote concerns Bocanegra playing in Houston for the
first time (date unknown) and his astonishment at encountering a fellow
*mexicano* who could not speak the language. It also illustrates the cultural
prominence of *mexicanos* in the Laredo area:

> We arrived in Houston, Texas, for one of a number of games in which my
> brother in-law Tomás Valenzuela and I formed the battery. If he pitched, I
> caught, or when he received, I pitched. I [became] separated from the team. I
> didn't know the people of Houston, being my first time visiting, and I did not
> know the way to the hotel in which we were staying.
> At that moment it seemed very odd for I did not see any familiar faces. And
> when I saw someone who looked Mexican I asked him, when I was close to him,
> if he knew of the hotel and the directions to it. The answer of this man who
> resembles an authentic resident of central Mexico was the following: "I don't
> speak Spanish."
> I was left frightened [shaken] to see this dark-skinned man with pear-shaped
> eyes that couldn't speak the language of Cervantes, but I didn't put up with it and
> asked someone else who spoke Spanish about directions back to the hotel.
> The following day I was assigned to pitch and won the game in a pitchers' duel
> with my opponent and his American teammates by a 1–0 score in fourteen in-
> nings. The thousands of Mexican fans who were present at the Houston ballpark

rushed the field at the end of the game and raised me up on their shoulders, they were so jubilant and happy.

And to my surprise while carrying me around the field on their shoulders I noticed that one of those that hoisted me up on their shoulders was none less than the "Mexican" of the previous day that could not speak Spanish! It's something I'll never forget, that when the Mexican in question saw me on his shoulder, instead of giving me the courage to take revenge on him, I felt proud to have him as a donkey taking me to the hotel whose address he had ignored by saying he didn't speak Spanish. . . . and during the entire march from the park to the hotel he did nothing but shout, "Viva mi paisano Manuel Bocanegra. [Long live my countryman Manuel Bocanegra]."[43]

Bocanegra's lengthy career was studded with impressive invitations and letters of thanks for having played on both sides of the border. In appreciation for having lent his talents to a team from Mexico City in 1904, Mexican president Porfirio Díaz wrote Bocanegra a personal note. And equally in recognition of the role Bocanegra played in helping to establish the game in southern Texas, the vice president of the highly regarded San Antonio Missions baseball team gave him a lifetime pass to all Mission games.

## The Historiography of Bocanegra

Hall of Famer Satchel Paige was legendary for having a career spanning five decades, a mind-boggling feat of stamina and endurance that few ever achieve. Yet it is exactly that sort of longevity that Díaz claims for Bocanegra in his book. Díaz includes Bocanegra among the first ballplayers to visit Mexico City, as the capital began to take to the sport in 1887. Along with Valenzuela and Juárez, Bocanegra's purpose was to exhibit and teach the sport as played by the best Mexicans of the time.[44] Bocanegra's career takes on Bunyanesque stature in the pages of Díaz's history of the sport in Nuevo Laredo. Most importantly, Bocanegra is also central to Díaz's efforts to claim that the game entered via Nuevo Laredo.

I accepted the dates provided by Díaz's first person accounts until, in reading his second book, I became aware of the change in the dates of events. Using the same quotes from Pedraza and Herrera, Díaz, in his second book, set the dates back ten years. Compare the two entries for Pedraza and the two for Herrera, two that are typical of the discrepancies throughout:

Pedraza 1955: "Already by this date, the year 1890, baseball was played in this city of Nuevo Laredo and Laredo."[45]

Pedraza 1979: "Already by this date, the year 1880, baseball was played in this city of Nuevo Laredo and Laredo."[46]

Herrera 1955: "My brother Natividad Herrera Quintana played baseball in the
year 1890."[47]

Herrera 1979: "My brother Natividad Herrera Quintana played baseball in the
year 1880."[48]

It appears that Díaz was eager to make the case for Nuevo Laredo being
the original source of Mexican baseball. Clearly the discrepancies between
the two books raised a problem of credibility and would require corrobora-
tion of these dates. I waded through those same years of the *Laredo Times*
to see if they mentioned any of the early events or even the individuals
most often named as playing with Bocanegra: Valenzuela, Burbank, Pierce.
As Laredo stars, these men would have to appear in lineups as they periodically appeared in the newspaper. Even if in the earliest years the *Laredo
Times* tended not to mention *mexicanos* as often as it should have, this was
not so strictly the case by the turn of the century. And, assuming the paper
systematically avoided mentioning *mexicanos*, the presence of Anglos Burbank and Pierce would be documented. There is no mention of Bocanegra
or Valenzuela or Burbank (Pierce is first mentioned in 1909 in a Nuevo
Laredo paper) until 1900 when they are listed as part of the lineup that was
to travel to Corpus Christi for the annual July 4 event.[49] While it might be
wrong to think that this was the first year in which these men established
themselves in the local baseball scene, it is likewise not very likely that
these men had been playing in complete obscurity for over twenty years.
Díaz has at least three accounts that place them considerably earlier
(Pedraza, Herrera, and Favella). What do we make of these accounts? How
do we account for the time gap of over a decade between Díaz's assertion
and the first mention in the local papers?

While Díaz was, it appears, overly ambitious in his interpretation of the
data, and maybe given to juggling the dates somewhat, once the arguments
for the earliest dates of baseball in Nuevo Laredo are discounted, his account of baseball history in Nuevo Laredo nevertheless remains valuable
for its presentation of first person narratives that hold up fairly well. Perhaps the most important piece of his book is the picture of the 1903–1904
*el Club Mexico* team that graces the beginning of the Díaz volume on baseball in Nuevo Laredo. In the picture we see Bocanegra, Valenzuela, and
Lucas Juárez situated in time. It also forces us to recognize that these men
may have played for a time without any newspaper coverage, because for
these men of Laredo to have been recruited to Mexico City, they would
have had to have considerable reputation and skill, both of which take time
to develop. This picture is important for a variety of reasons, one of which
is that it explains more clearly the handwritten note of thanks Bocanegra
received from Mexican president Díaz in 1904 for helping the capital out.
Yet the argument must also fit into the confines of their actual lives.

I attempted to get the dates of Bocanegra's birth (as well as those of Valenzuela, Pierce, and Burbank) to determine if the actual dates would allow a match with Díaz's account. Manuel Bocanegra, it turns out, was born in 1880 and died in 1942, both in Laredo. Given these dates he would have had to have played for Johnny Tayson's 1893 team of railroad employees at the tender age of thirteen, and even younger when, according to some of Díaz's informants, he was asked to come to Mexico City to help establish the game.

Bocanegra and Valenzuela are almost always listed together, but their careers are also bracketed by Pierce and Burbank. Checking on the birth dates of Valenzuela, Pierce, and Burbank shows that, like Bocanegra, Díaz's dates for their earliest play is not feasible given their recorded birthdates. Tomás Valenzuela was born in 1887, and Pierce in 1876 (I was unable to find Burbank's birth or death record). Chronologically, Pierce could have played for Tayson's team, but Valenzuela would have been a six-year-old. It seems pretty clear that the tantalizingly early dates of Díaz for the play of Bocanegra and friends are incorrect, so the argument that baseball began in the Laredos might not be as strong as Díaz suggests.

The earliest confirmable date for Bocanegra, Valenzuela, and Juárez is 1899, when they played for the brewery Cuauhtemoc de Monterrey against a team in Mexico City. It would be safe to argue that by the late 1890s these men were playing regularly. If we posit a date of 1896 for Bocanegra, that would make him sixteen. For Valenzuela that date would be too early, and it seems more likely that he played for Club Mexico as a youthful star of fifteen.

According to their chronicler, Bocanegra and Valenzuela preferred playing locally, and they were regularly mentioned in the press from about 1903 on. This decision was no doubt influenced by the Mexican Revolution, which disrupted all of Mexico's institutions, focusing baseball more in distant Laredo. Playing alongside Bocanegra in 1900 were Burbank, Pierce, and brother-in-law Valenzuela on a powerful Laredo team that regularly challenged their rivals across the river. While the two brothers-in-laws often played against teams from Fort McIntosh, on occasion they might play for the local military base as they did against teams from Nuevo Laredo in 1918.[50]

Even if there was a bias on the part of Díaz regarding the origins of the game, the narratives of Pedraza and Herrera and others nevertheless constitute an important document about the game's earliest years. If they are chronologically inaccurate, being off by a decade (taking the 1955 account), they are otherwise internally consistent with each other and with other narratives as well as newspaper accounts. Inaccuracies such as these are common for people trying to recollect events that occurred a half century before. At worst, we can say that Bocanegra and his associates were playing later than previously thought. The arrival of baseball in the area, however, still seems to have taken place around the mid-1880s on the Laredo side, and there is no reason to think that it would have been prevented from crossing over at that point in time as well. It just didn't come via Manuel Bocanegra.

The following is the chronology of play by Bocanegra and Valenzuela (and where applicable Pierce and Burbank) that can be confirmed by reliable sources:

| | |
|---|---|
| 1899: | with Cuauhtemoc de Monterrey against the capital team (Bocanegra, Valenzuela, and Juárez). |
| 1900: | with Laredo against Nuevo Laredo, and the Corpus Christi Kids (Bocanegra and Valenzuela). |
| 1903–1905: | with Club Mexico (Bocanegra, Valenzuela, Juárez); with a Laredo team going to Corpus Christi for July 4. |
| 1911: | with Laredo (Pierce). |
| 1912: | with Laredo (Bocanegra, Valenzuela, Burbank, Juárez). |
| 1917: | with Fort McIntosh (Bocanegra and Valenzuela). |
| 1918: | with Laredo (Bocanegra, Burbank). |
| 1922: | with Milmos (Valenzuela, Pierce, Burbank). |
| 1924: | with Laredo (Bocanegra, Burbank). |

## The Decade of the 1920s

Between 1920 and 1930, baseball remained local with small amateur and semi-pro teams playing irregularly. Fans in Laredo were forever admonished by the press "to go out to the Legion Park Sunday and support the local club as the boys are playing for the love of the game and receive no compensation for their services."[51] Sporadic contests between Nuevo Laredo and Laredo dotted this period, and locals could count on at least one series a year between *los dos Laredos*. By the late 1920s teams from Monterrey and San Antonio would regularly play against nines from either of the two Laredos, as when in 1929 Monterrey's Vidriera team, "one of the strongest in northern Mexico . . . will be encountered by The Central Power and Light Co." of Laredo.[52] The wider attention brought to the sport and region by the likes of Bocanegra and Valenzuela, among others, however, was gone by the mid-1920s. Professional baseball in Texas was then being played by the Texas League, but this found no representation on the border where leagues and teams would form, fail, disband, and reform. It wasn't until the 1930s that a new talent base was established that could rival the level of play found in these pioneers of baseball in the two Laredos.

While Nuevo Laredo was caught up with purely local baseball, the game was becoming more organized in Mexico. Beginning in 1925, and lasting for a decade, the Mexican League was slowly taking its modern (1938) form. Most chroniclers describe this early period as an "antecedent" to the modern Mexican League.[53] Alejandro Aguilar Reyes, also known as "Frey Nano," founded the league, intending to field teams from throughout the Republic. "He shared his ideas with his friend don Ernesto Carmona V. who loved baseball and sponsored teams and competitions, but also managed, played, and owned Franco Inglés Park."[54] Between the two, the league was formed and began play in June 1925 with five teams: Agrario, Dicho, Guanajuato, Nacional de Bixler, and 74 Regimiento de la ciudad de Puebla.

Erratic play, schedules, and teams characterized this period of Mexican baseball. In the inaugural season, the entire franchise of the 74 Regimiento de la ciudad de Puebla had to be moved to San Lu FE/ s Potosi.[55] Whole slates of games that had been scheduled were abandoned and only occasionally replaced; games were played on Sundays only, and when not changing locations, teams changed their names. The league was mostly focused on Mexico City, where it was best organized, and where it fielded as many as four teams. Despite the unorganized nature of this period, many characteristics that presaged the modern era were introduced. The first All-Star team was formed in 1929, and the first championship series was held in 1933. Delta Park, Mexico's premier facility for years to come, opened in 1930. And throughout this period the presence of foreign players, primarily Cubans, became a regular feature of Mexican baseball, a feature that would continue to the present.

## The La Junta Era: 1930–1935

Laredo dominated the baseball scene through Bocanegra and Valenzuela et al. until almost 1920, but thereafter Nuevo Laredo took over the mantle of border baseball preeminence. In particular, the establishment of the La Junta team focused baseball attention on the Mexican side of the river. Much of the perception of which side predominated was, in reality, undercut by the transnationalism that regularly took place. The collaborative-local baseball theme deepens throughout the La Junta Era.

As early as 1900, the role of political officials in aiding the development of baseball had been noted in the high visibility of customs officials and generals. In 1932, General Luís Horcasitas, president of the *La Junta Federal de Mejoras Materiales* in Nuevo Laredo, along with General Leopoldo Dorantes and Pablo Peña, both stockholders in the venture, commissioned Erasmo Flores to form a team named after the enterprise, known by most as simply "La Junta." At first, the La Junta team, like its predecessors, seemed to use the best talent in Nuevo Laredo, supplementing itself with Laredoans when needed. But in 1934, after a highly successful season the previous year, the plans don Erasmo began to envision grew more grandiose.

### The 1934 Season

Border baseball begins in earnest each February when plans are drawn up for a season that often begins three or four weeks later. The year 1934 opened with the announcement in the *Laredo Times* that a new league would be forming that would include the city. Harry Wanderling, a baseball entrepreneur/promoter and outsider to the Laredos, declared that he intended to open a baseball academy in Nuevo Laredo in which he hoped to train as many as two hundred young ballplayers for a league he was beginning.[56] "I'm opening the school to cater principally to ball players of Spanish descent. . . . I have been told for the past several years that baseball is coming along fast in this section and decided to come here and open a training school and organize a league later."[57] It was Wanderling's goal to fashion a league that was binational, made up of players from Laredo, Corpus Christi, Nuevo Laredo, Mission, Monterrey, Tampico, and Torreon. February gave way to March and nothing yet materialized on this proposed league—indeed nothing ever would—but the intentions remain noteworthy from a binational perspective and foreshadow later such attempts.

Meanwhile in Laredo, plans were being put forth to field a competitive team for the coming year. The team would ride on the arms of a core of excellent young pitchers: Ismael "Oso" Montalvo, Fernando "Big" Dovalina, and his brother "Lefty." La Junta, for its part, had already raised its standing as a powerful semi-pro team the previous year, and the traditional inter-city rivalry was more intense than ever: "Reports were flocking fast back and forth across the Rio Grande as to which city had the best team."[58] They would find out by opening the 1934 season with a three-game series (two more such series would follow through the summer) between the two clubs: "Scheduling of the series at the start of the season will probably make rivalry between the two cities even stronger than it was last year. During 1933, a game between Laredo and La Junta brought out as much ballyhoo as any political campaign that has ever been staged here."[59]

Laredo swept a doubleheader on that first Sunday of the season 9–4 and 4–2 with Fernando Dovalina and Ismael Montalvo each going the distance. The two also chipped in at the plate with Dovalina going 1 for 2 (a triple) and Montalvo 2 for 4. Comparisons of these pitchers to Bocanegra and Valenzuela were quickly made as the La Junta team returned to Nuevo

Laredo somewhat shocked that their highly touted season had begun so poorly. Laredo, on the other hand, went on to ring up fourteen straight victories. These were not throwaway contests, either. Following the opener, a very strong Sabinas Baseball Club from San Antonio came in for a hard-fought doubleheader, Laredo winning both games by one run. It was becoming clear that team pitching was superb, but the club was also capable of hitting. Honneyman, Kelo, and Durán were all hitting above .300.

Despite having a strong club and an impressive record early on, the Laredo team ran into managerial problems, changing their administration midway through the season. Although the team had been regularly shifting people from one week to the next, the new management promised substantial changes in personnel. The early season chemistry could not be recovered, however, and Laredo continued to slide downward in both performance and popularity. La Junta, on the other hand, had performed as well as expected. Following the opening-day losses to Laredo, La Junta augmented their club with the important addition of Cuban pitching ace Ramón Bragaña, his countryman Santos Amaro, as well as Laredo's star pitcher Ismael "Oso [bear]" Montalvo. Laredo's first baseman, Durán, had also come over. The second meeting between the two clearly demonstrated the trajectories that they were taking. Montalvo shut out his former teammates 4–0 in the first game of the series, and Palma and Bragaña beat Laredo in the Sunday doubleheader 4–2 and 8–5.

What was telling during the 1934 season was the steady shift of interest on the part of the press and fans of Laredo away from their own club and to the La Junta team. This was further underscored by the fact that the La Junta team began to play its games against non-Laredo competition *in* Laredo as well as in their home stadium, foreshadowing the binationalism of the Tecos of the future. There was no proprietary sense on the part of either the fans or media in all of this. Laredoans identified easily with La Junta. The Laredo press heralded the upcoming series of La Junta against Sabinas (in Laredo) as "one of the classics of the season."[60] Having grown disinterested in their own team, Laredo fans were neither apathetic nor resentful toward their "rivals" across the river. Quite the contrary. Officials of the La Junta club were making arrangements for the capacity crowds of the season at the Laredo park and additional chairs were being added to the reserve seat section.[61]

The Sabinas series would showcase some of the talent that La Junta had assembled for their 1935 season. Amaro homered; "It was one of the hardest hit balls of the season here," said the *Laredo Times* on August 4.[62] Even with a sub-par pitching performance by Montalvo, the La Junta team had so much power that they could pull out an 11–9 win. The next day the La Junta team played a doubleheader in front of 2,000 Laredoans, the largest crowd in the city's history; they swept the Sabinas Brewery of San Antonio

8–0 and 7–5, behind Bragaña's pitching in the opener (the only time that year the San Antonio team was shut out) and continued steady hitting in the second game.

Tellingly, the *Laredo Times* prominently featured the La Junta–Sabinas series, while only briefly mentioning on the same page that Laredo was playing across the river in Rosita. Indeed, from roughly mid-August on, as far as the Laredo press was concerned La Junta was the local team. Announcing an upcoming game in Nuevo Laredo, the *Laredo Times* announced, "Local baseball fans have a good three game series scheduled for the week-end when La Junta meets the Austin Black Senators starting Saturday and continuing with two games Sunday. The games will be played at the brand new 'Nuevo Laredo' ball park on kilometer 3 on the Pan-American highway."[63] And La Junta continued to schedule games on both sides of the border through the season. When, at the end of September, La Junta played an all-star team from the highly respected Texas League, it did so in both Laredos, cementing its status as the team of the two Laredos. This was repeated when La Junta played the famous House of David team the following month. Yet, while it appeared that Laredo's team had all but disappeared from the baseball scene, when it came time for the final three-game series between the two cities, Laredo fielded a very strong club and the rivalry was suddenly rekindled. In true transnational fashion, Montalvo had hopped back to Laredo to pitch against his sometime teammates, while Durán and the others stayed with La Junta. The constant shuffling of players from one side to another, the playing of La Junta in Laredo's park as well as in their own, the easy adoption of La Junta by the Laredo media, and the readiness of fans to attend games on either side of the river gave true meaning to the term transnationalism. There was no purely Nuevo Laredoan or Laredoan team or fans or media. There was only los dos Laredos.

This relatively unknown team from Nuevo Laredo had, in the course of one season, shown that it was capable of competing against good professional and the best semi-pro teams around. Morris Koplan, business manager of the Texas League's San Antonio Missions, noted in the *Laredo Times* that "the La Junta Baseball Club could win today in the Texas baseball league, they are a fast aggregation; they hustle all of the time and are no set-up for any ball team."[64]

## The 1935 La Junta Barnstorming Tour

The idea of "barnstorming," setting up a tour comprised of paid playing dates in a string of cities and towns, was very popular in the United States during the 1930s. The Harlem Globetrotters basketball team is the last real barnstorming sports team. Sixty years ago, however, such enterprises were common. In baseball the most famous of these was the House of David team.

Founded by Benjamin Purnell as the Israelite House of David Colony in Benton Harbor, Michigan, in 1903, this colony preached collective Christianity and egalitarianism. They also preached sexual abstinence, sobriety, and growing their beards. The collective underpinnings of the colony enabled it to become economically successful in selling its large stores of fruit crops.[65] Branching out into the restaurant business, the colony ran a string of eateries. By 1910 the colony was attracting visitors who wanted to observe this odd collection of Christian believers. Purnell built an amusement park to make money off the many visitors from Kalamazoo and Chicago.[66] It was in that year that the team was established as part of the entertainment complex fashioned by the colony. By 1920 the House of David team realized how profitable barnstorming might be when it played in New York: "In just one of the matched affairs that mark every large institution's baseball season, the House of David nine met such a rousing welcome from the ticket-buying customers the club stayed two months—incidentally clearing the staggering sum of $23,000! The idea of maintaining a traveling club was not born—it was shoved at the IHD [Israelite House of David]."[67]

According to Doc Tally, who managed the club in 1935 and had played with it for twenty years, they also developed the "Pepper Game," a highly entertaining pregame ritual in which a ball is quickly tossed among players without giving the impression of it being held and without the ball touching the ground.[68] So successful was this operation that it spawned many imitators (nine by the House of David's account) and much litigation.

Of course, to be so sought after required more than just an entertaining gimmick; it also required skill. The House of David team was considered by most observers to be the best semi-pro team in the country, rivaled only by the best of the Negro League teams. In 1934 the House of David assembled a record of 142 wins and 50 losses, while covering over 25,000 miles in Mexico, the United States, and Canada. The following year they won 139 games against 32 losses.[69]

Being on the border, the two Laredos were often asked for playing dates by other teams from the United States or Mexico. The House of David played there often. The following excerpted proposal to the Laredo Chamber of Commerce from the famous Cuauhtemoc Brewery in Monterrey, Mexico, was typical of such inquiries:

February 14, 1935

I wish to notify you that we have the best organized baseball team in this locality, called the "Carta Blanca" club. Therefore I wish to play with any team there is or with any formed in Laredo during the 22nd, 23rd, or 24th of February during the Washington Birthday Celebration. . . .

Yours truly

Jesus Ma. Garza[70]

Oftentimes these requests were made on behalf of American teams preparing itineraries for tours into Mexico. Playing dates in the two Laredos were ideal stopovers into and out of Mexico. Mexican teams touring deep into the United States, on the other hand, never occurred. The 1935 La Junta tour changed all of that. La Junta was an assemblage of the greatest ballplayers in the history of border baseball, a team that took to the road for three months through the heartland of the United States as far north as North Dakota. They toured through ten states, playing eighty-three games against some of the finest semi-pro teams in the country and ringing up an impressive record of 62 wins, 18 losses, and 3 ties.

La Junta's manager Erasmo Flores may have conceived of the idea of touring after watching so many teams come through the twin border towns, but he could never have undertaken the planning and execution of it. As barnstormers, these border people were provincials, rarely traveling much beyond the Monterrey–San Antonio borderlands area. Flores, however, got the House of David's business manager to assemble the trip.[71] Fernando Dovalina, the strong-armed righthander who was a standout on that La Junta team, concurred: "The idea [for the tour] came from the House of David team and the manager who scheduled the games for them. He talked to Erasmo Flores, the manager for La Junta, and told him it was a good idea to do a tour in the United States."[72] A core of forty-three games were scheduled in advance,[73] with the remainder to unfold as the tour progressed. Indeed, the preliminary road trip included games through June 25, but more games were added so that the team did not return until early July.

### The Social Makeup of Semi-Pro Teams

La Junta had shown the previous year that it could play with anybody. They had Mexican standout Agustín Bejerano in the outfield, and they already had two Cubans stars, Santos Amaro and Ramón Bragaña. In 1935 they added Chile Gómez at shortstop (Gómez would sign with the Philadelphia Phillies before the end of the season,) Barrada and Cháves at first and second base, and Arjona and Cabal. From Laredo they hired on pitcher-outfielder Ismael Montalvo, pitcher Fernando Dovalina, and Pelón Rodríguez. All told, manager Flores had the strongest team ever assembled on the border. By the mid-1930s baseball in Mexico was beginning to go international, as it had in the Dominican Republic,[74] Cuba, and Venezuela.[75] On the Laredo–Nuevo Laredo border it had always been so. The transnational quality of the relations between the cities assumed that they would use each other's resources. Hiring Montalvo, Dovalina, Rodríguez, and later Kelo García from Laredo teams, was done without any thought.

In one respect La Junta's 1935 season was a first. Exceptional foreign players traveling from team to team had become commonplace in Mexico, as had the competition between the country's better teams, but long-term trips by Mexican teams abroad were unheard of. The oral histories of two Laredo stars—Fernando Dovalina and Ismael Montalvo—provide a certain amount of insight into the nature of baseball in the area. Through them we can piece together the social history of this momentous trip.

Fernando Dovalina was born in 1913 in Laredo. By the time he was about sixteen he was already one of the local stars, being asked to play by Laredo and Nuevo Laredo teams. Semi-pro baseball was, for him, a game-to-game proposition, and playing for many teams within a single season was the norm:

> When you played semi-pro you didn't have a contract. If a guy asks you, "How much are you making over there?" You might say, "Ten dollars." He would say, "Okay, I'll give you 15." And you would go with him. I used to pitch for La Junta back in the 1930s, and they laid me off. They said they couldn't afford to pay me anymore. The next Sunday, a team from Laredo went over there and I pitched for Laredo after I had been pitching for La Junta all year. That's the way it was.[76]

Even today ballplayers in this region are recruited while quite young. Long careers in baseball were and are fairly common in Mexico by comparison with the United States, and contracts were for short periods ranging from a single game (or even part of it) to a season. Owners of teams were generally military men and other top governmental officials.

Ismael Montalvo, born in 1913 in San Benito, Texas (in the Rio Grande Valley), narrates his first years as an itinerant in semi-pro Mexican ball:

> I started playin' [semi-pro] in 1930. I was eighteen when I dropped out of school. A Yankee scout came over. In those days it was hard to get into professional ball, even in Class D: many ballplayers, hungry ballplayers. Then, when I was eighteen, I went to play ball in this town close to Monterrey: Linares. They had a team owned by a general. In those days only generals had baseball teams. All the players had to put on soldier's uniforms [join the army]. I told him I'm not gonna put on no uniform. There were two of us, both pitchers. In those days they paid a hundred dollars a month and expenses in gold. . . . The general called me to play around Christmas, just for a series. We played a team from Mexico City and

beat them 4–0. It was an important series and that game was Saturday. I said, "If we play Sunday, I'm not gonna play both games. I'm gonna leave." I wanted to go home and see my mother. I didn't tell anybody I was leaving. I just went to the train station. Got my ticket. Two soldiers came over out of nowhere and said, "The general wants to talk to you." The general was in a big ol' Lincoln, sittin' in the back. He asked me, "Where you goin', Montalvo?" I told him. He shook his head slowly. "You're not goin' anywhere. Give me your ticket." He gave it to the soldiers and said, "Go get his money back." I got into the car and he took me to Boy's Town [the area of town with bars and prostitutes] over there. I was going there to help him for only one week. You know when I got outta there? 'Bout two months later. You couldn't mess with those guys.

In 1931, I went with the Aztecas in Mexico City. It was the number one semi-pro team in Mexico then. . . . We used to draw 10,000 people in those days. There were Mexicans, Cubans. We had a helluva good club. Then in 1932 I went to San Antonio to play with the Mexican Nationals, a very good semi-pro team. In 1933 I moved to Laredo.[77]

Many semi-pro players had to juggle lives at home and work with base-ball, and that was a major reason why most stayed close to home. Fernando Dovalina had these sorts of responsibilities, so when the offer to join La Junta on a tour of the United States came, he had to deliberate. "They offered me the chance to play for La Junta, but I was working for a whole-sale grocery store. I was the foreman of the warehouse. The president of the company, he liked baseball, and he said, 'Go ahead, Dovalina. When you come back you'll have your job back.' So I went, otherwise I wouldn't have gone. We were supposed to be back in two months, but we were gone longer so I had to write him for an extension."[78]

It wasn't even a one-time act of juggling work and play, as don Fer-nando pointed out. For many of these better ballplayers the daily grind of a job, often a hard job, competed for their energy and time. Lázaro Dovalina, younger brother of Fernando and himself a player with the 1949 Laredo Apaches, astutely points this out in discussing his brother's accomplishments:

You know, this guy [pointing to his older brother Fernando] worked hard ever since he was fifteen years old. And you know, at that time they worked from sunup to sundown. He didn't have time to practice. By the time he got home from work, changed, and went to the ball park it was dark. And this guy would grab a mitt and say, "Let me throw some." He could throw hard all right, but when he came back from that [1935 La Junta] tour he said, "Put the glove on." And he threw harder than I ever saw him throw because those two months on tour, *that's all he did*! Over here, he'd be working all week long. It's like "Lalo" Hernández. He was a carpenter. Can you imagine? He's with a hammer all week long and then he'd go out and pitch on Sunday.[79]

In any event, once the opportunity came virtually all of the players manager Flores asked to play eagerly agreed, and the first tour of a Mexican team into the United States commenced in May 1935.

## Life on the Tour

Some teams, like the House of David, toured in large, well appointed cars, but the vast majority of barnstorming teams, La Junta included, went the bus route. Recalled Montalvo:

> We had an old bus, one of those "Pee Wee's," we used to call them. It was a good bus, though, and we had a good driver too. We had to play in St. Joseph, Missouri, I remember, a whole week because he had to take the motor off and overhaul it. He did too. Good driver. The longest trip we had was about 250 miles. After a night game we got on the bus, get a big ol' seat there, and take off. We had a lot of fun. We picked on each other, but we got along pretty good. Oh, sometimes we had fights, but we really respected each other.[80]

Pay was negligible, but still considered better than most border dwellers made (about $100 a month). Playing ball conferred its own rewards on players. Being the best team was nice, but so was traveling and the ever present opportunity of finding women. The parks and sometimes the after-game spots were natural places where ballplayers would socialize with women, as Dovalina noted:

> I never asked for much pay while on the tour (saved it for the end). Others did and sent it home. They didn't want to give us a lotta money in our packs because then we might play poker. We couldn't even go look for women cuz we didn't have much money. We'd drink a beer or two and that was it. We went to a whorehouse, Cabal and myself, and we had a dollar each [laughs]. The lady looked at us and shook her head no, not enough money, so I said, "Let's flip for it."
>
> Lots of girls at the ballpark, though. They went to see us, talk to us. They'd ask each other, "Which one do you like the best?" There was one girl in Chicago, and she would play catch with us. I have pictures of her. She was the wife of the clerk at the hotel we stayed at. Very beautiful. When we played in Chicago there were a lotta people who knew about us, a lotta people from Laredo.[81]

No matter how well they meshed, long tours invariably tested the tempers of players. A team like La Junta that had players of different nationalities and races, not to mention the more obvious personality differences, contained the potential for strife. There were the long hours on the bus, followed by long hours of finding accommodations or running from one game to another, or simply fatigue, but the interviews reveal that team solidarity remained high. In part, this must have been because even though there were racial differences among them (e.g., Hispanic, black), the team as a whole was foreign while traveling in the U.S. heartland. For nonwhites to travel in the United States in the 1930s was often difficult. Dovalina and Montalvo both mention incidents of this nature:

> We'd come into town and we'd pull up to a hotel and find out if they'd take the Black players like Bragaña and Amaro. If they said no, we'd go and look for another place. Sometimes we had to take them to the Black section, to people's houses. When we went to eat, sometimes we ate together and sometimes they wouldn't take the Blacks. Sometimes, instead of being separated from them, and so they wouldn't feel bad, we'd all eat in the kitchen.[82]

While racism such as this occurred often enough, the Cuban blacks were by no means obsequious about it. Montalvo relates one incident:

> We stopped in a hotel in Wichita Falls, Texas, and the manager of the hotel came out. We were getting off the bus after a long hot ride. We had Bragaña and Amaro, and the hotel manager says, "Those two niggers ain't gonna stay in my hotel." Bragaña turned to him and shouted, "Mister, this hotel ain't shit" and started goin' after him. Anyway, after we separated them, I don't know how, but he [hotel manager] kinda began to like Bragaña and they gave him a room on the fifth floor. They became good buddies because Bragaña was a good domino player.[83]

Hispanic players also felt discrimination, especially in Texas towns, recalled Dovalina:

> It was hard for the blacks to play in Austin. When we were returning from the tour we played there, but they wouldn't let the blacks play and they beat us. When they came down here to play later, we played with Bragaña and Amaro. We beat them and they said we weren't the same team.[84]
>
> In German towns [like New Braunfels, or San Marcos, Texas] there was discrimination. The players had a tough time staying in hotels, and they would yell things at us on the field. . . . Up north in places like Chicago most of the time we went straight to the game. No hanging around hotel lobbies like they do now. At the ballparks sometimes the people or the police would come over to me asking about Mexico [laughs]. I didn't know very much. "How are the Catholics doing in Mexico? Are they still throwin' them out? How is the Church down in Mexico?" I didn't know what to say.[85]

Montalvo also recalls discrimination:

> We were playing in Devil's Lake, North Dakota. And we play at night there, and I walked into a bar there. Have beer around 11 o'clock at night. They had a long bar there, one block [long] owned by the city. They open sections of the bar

according to the time of the day. I walk in and think, "fuck it's long [bar]." And there was Amaro down at one end of the bar havin' a beer and I couldn't see him. And I walk into the place. And I say to the bartender, "How bout a beer." And he say, "No. We don't serve Injuns." He thought I was an Indian. The Cuban wasn't sayin' anything, then he come up to me and said, "God damn, son of a bitch. You an American and they don't serve you in the United States." Then the bartender heard me talkin' Spanish and came back and he said, "Oh, you're with the team," and he gave me a beer. Then he laughed and told everybody that he didn't want to serve me cuz he thought I was an Indian.[86]

Racism worked to promote the team's cohesiveness, but the travails of the road would eat away at this, and at times the players would get testy. Perhaps this was more so because oftentimes in small towns the La Junta team did not feel comfortable enough to split up and go out. The nightly poker games might occasion a fight, or the game situations might act as triggering mechanisms:

> Sometimes we used to say things to each other, but we didn't have serious prob-lems. We didn't have guys like Deion Sanders on our club. Everybody was seri-ous about playing ball. You know, like everybody, we sometimes used to have fights among the ballplayers. We didn't fool around too much. We weren't makin' that kind of money, but sometimes fights would happen. Chile Gómez fought with Bragaña in Battle Creek, Michigan, one time. What the hell, we were fourteen guys and we never really saw eye-to-eye, there were some differ-ences, but it was fun, a lotta fun.[87]
>
> One time we were playing in Battle Creek, Michigan. They beat us there and Bragaña was pitching. Cabal dropped a fly ball and when we went to take a shower after the game Bragaña told Cabal about it. He got real mad with Cabal and Chile Gómez somehow got in the way of those two, and Gómez wound up fighting with Cabal. They didn't have clothes on, no shoes, nothin'. And we were right next to the White club. Just a door divided the whole shower. And they came to watch the fight. We couldn't stop it because if we tried to hold Chile, Bragaña would hit him or Amaro might get mad. And then we would have a big fight, so we let em fight for about ten or fifteen minutes. That's a long fight! A bottle broke on the cement floor and they were stepping on it, but no one stopped them.[88]

## Barnstorming and Entertainment

Having the House of David's manager help set up the tour for the La Junta club necessitated their entertainment of the crowds with more than just their baseball skills. The tour was being labeled as a "Good Will Tour" of the United States by Mexicans, so it was decided that the ballplayers should take on the *Charro* (Mexican cowboy) look. Pictures of them in sombreros and sarapes, smoking cigars or holding bats were used in promotional literature. In fact the team was periodically referred to as the *Charros* by local American newspapers.[89] While serious ball clubs did not normally do the entertaining before and during the games themselves, they were often accompanied by individuals who did.

One amusing story told of don Fernando Dovalina illustrates the use of such entertainers and also points up how culturally removed the border was from Mexico City–based culture. Don Fernando's son Ramón, former editor of *El Noticiario Nacional*, published his account of the story that bears quoting at length. I append some of don Fernando's comments as well. In this story a young talented Dovalina, unaware of much of life and culture away from the border, is being recruited by the manager of a Mexican team:

> The manager needed a pitcher for his team in Nueva Rosita, Coahuila, Mexico. It seems that the team was playing a barnstorming Negro team from the United States and the Mexican team was in need of a good pitcher.
>
> The manager found my father's home and asked my grandmother for permission to borrow her son for the weekend to play baseball. The manager assured my grandmother that my father would be in good hands and would stay in the manager's home overnight. . . . My father packed a little bag with his change of clothing, his glove, and his spikes. He got in the back seat of the car since another ballplayer from Mexico was already in the front. The player was introduced to my father as Mario Reyes, an outfielder perhaps a year or two older. . . . at the ballpark the next afternoon. It was quickly evident that Reyes was the star of the team since the crowd was relatively large for such a small town, and it seemed that all the young women mingled around him as if he were a matinee star.
>
> My father took his warm ups but paused occasionally to see *el tim de negros americanos* [the American negro team] hit towering flyballs to the outfield and beyond the fence. They looked like too strong an opponent for the smaller built Mexican team. . . . The game started and the Mexicans took the field as the first visitor came to bat. My father threw two inside fast balls to brush him away from the plate. Then he threw a little curve just below the letters. The player swung and hit a shot to right field beyond where Reyes was playing. Reyes took off after it but before he took three steps, his baggy baseball pants began to fall off his waist. Two steps later his pants were down to his knees and Reyes was no longer running. Rather, he was taking that funny walk that is customary with long distance walkers. The fans broke out in laughter as Reyes proceeded to catch up with the ball. Neither my father nor the opposing team understood that Reyes was not a ballplayer; he had been added on as a special attraction to draw the

crowd. He was in fact a comedian who was quickly becoming known throughout Mexico for his antics. . . . The ballplayer became better known later as Mario Reyes Moreno "Cantinflas."[90]

He [Cantinflas] came to bat too, and then the black guys from Austin said, "This is not a ballplayer." They didn't know who he was, but they knew he wasn't a ballplayer because he was checking his bat like this [imitating the clowning movements of Cantinflas]. I was thinking about the ballgame. These guys can beat me with one run and I was angry.[91]

The 1935 La Junta team had its share of such entertainers as well. The Dovalina brothers recall a baseball clown who traveled with the team:

I don't know if he was given to us by the House of David or what. He was from Austin, an Anglo. Happy Fitzhugh. Happy had no arms, just stumps. He would sit at home plate and open up his suitcase, pull out a dinner setting, a plate and all. He'd sit down to a meal. He'd shave himself. Great guy. We had a lotta fun with him. He'd stand up on a corner where the hotel was on the other side of the street and make signs at the hotel. People would stop and wonder what he was doing. In the mornings when we didn't have nothing to do sometimes we played pool and Happy played with us. He put the cue like this [strapped to his stump], held with the other one and break like this [a slap shot]. He could do everything except button his shirt. Well, he couldn't wash his armpits either.[92]

## The Tour

Reyes Ortiz, secretary for the club, whose real job was at the post office, would get the wires every day with the bare-bones reports of the most recently completed game. He would call the *Laredo Times* with the news, but the reports were rarely very detailed. The quality of the teams played ranged widely. H. Witte, the advance agent for the team (affiliated with the House of David also), did not control the quality of the clubs, but as the team began to amass an enviable record, offers to play better teams came in on their own. La Junta's overall record was 62 wins, 18 losses, and 3 ties. Some of those wins, such as those over Waco, Texas, seemed easy. In Waco, Dovalina and Bragaña shut out the locals on two hits, winning 9–0. This was also the case in Jamestown, North Dakota, on July 6 when Dovalina won 7–3, pitching shutout ball until the ninth inning, when he gave up three runs; but the game had long since been determined by the power-hitting of Santos Amaro, who had homered and doubled.

Wherever they went, La Junta was depicted as an exciting and danger-ous team. Some of this was typical of the publicity that leads up to the games in the hopes of luring more fans, but by their record it was clear that few teams could beat them. The press understood them as legitimate competitors:

> *Pampa* (Texas) *Daily*: "the peppery little Mexicans have had better luck with Panhandle teams than did the House of David."

> *Wisconsin State Journal*: "The La Junta boys got a sweet ball club. They hit that ball on the nose, no pop flies in the bag. . . . They had a beautiful crowd at the game. Over 2,000 saw the game. . . . They got stars galore. One is Gonzáles, the shortstop. That baby can field and is a pretty nice hitter. And Gómez at second can rap that apple. . . . That centerfielder, Bejerano, is the fastest man ever to step into this ball park. On a perfect hit ball he ran over first base four feet before the ball ever got there."[93]

Not only did this team have speed and defense, but Montalvo remembered the balanced hitting of La Junta as well. "We were playing in Belleville, Illinois, just across from St. Louis. About 10,000 people there in that small park. People all over the place. First inning Bragaña was off that day, they got 6 runs. We come right back and beat them 20 to 8. Home runs all over the place. People didn't believe it! Amaro, me, Rodríguez, bam, bam, bam."[94] Dovalina added, "One guy standing behind the fence was saying, 'Hey, those Mexicans can't do anything but eat beans.' But after we started hitting home runs and we had about three double steals and we were beating them badly, he started hollering, 'Hey get those Mexicans out of here before they steal the park.'"[95] For the tour Amaro led the team in home runs with twelve and seemed to regularly generate extra base hits. La Junta batters were hitting for average as well, with six players batting over .300.

Pitching was their strong suit, however. The pitching staff compiled the following records over the tour:

|          | Won | Lost | Tied |
|----------|-----|------|------|
| Montalvo | 13  | 2    | 0    |
| Cabal    | 13  | 3    | 1    |
| Dovalina | 12  | 3    | 0    |
| Barradas | 3   | 1    | 0    |
| Salazar  | 10  | 4    | 2    |
| Bragaña  | 11  | 5    | 0    |

Montalvo also led the team with three shutouts, and both he and Dovalina pitched a team-leading nine complete games. Dovalina was somewhat surprised at his success during the tour:

> I was having troubles with my curve. For me that [curve] was important. One year [1934] Montalvo and myself we won thirteen games straight. . . . That year

I had a good curve ball and a good fast ball. I learned the curve from a book. I had faith that if somebody got on base I could strike out the next guy, that they wouldn't get three hits in succession. On the tour I went with my fastball because I saw Bragaña getting away with a fastball. So I started throwing like Bragaña. He was older than me and had played in Mexico before he came to Nuevo Laredo in '32.[96]

As strong as this team was, there were some that seemed to dominate them. The Overton, Texas, Oilers had La Junta's number. On the initial run out of Texas, Overton won both ends of their doubleheader, 2–1 and 5–2. The Oilers were often used as a benchmark by which teams could declare their strength, as when the *Laredo Times* indicated that Nu Icy (an Austin team) would be a hard contest because they had beaten Overton twice that year.[97] No one seems to have remembered Overton, however. Bismark, North Dakota, was another story.

While we have come to think of baseball's race barrier as substantial, unilaterally in place between the 1880s and 1946, there existed pockets of integration where black and white athletes played together. North Dakota was one such place. By most accounts, North Dakota has not been considered a source of baseball talent in the way that the south or far west has been. Yet during the decades of the 1920s and 1930s semi-pro teams such as Bismark and Jamestown were competing in the prestigious Denver Post Tournament, and doing so with integrated teams.[98] When, in 1932, rival Jamestown hired three Negro League standouts to play for its team, the manager of Bismark's semi-pro team (and mayor of the city) contacted Negro League promoter Abe Saperstein to sign the best pitcher that the league offered. Satchel Paige signed with the 1933 Bismark team and won the state baseball championship.[99] Paige re-signed with Bismark in 1935. That year a touring House of David team studded with ringers such as Grover Cleveland Alexander and Elmer Dean, as well as its regulars, appeared in Bismark. Paige pitched both ends of a doubleheader against them and won. According to Roper, Paige had thirty-one wins that season for Bismark, against only two losses. It was into this Bismark maelstrom that an unsuspecting La Junta team walked on July 4, 1935.[100]

Paige's signature was style. Everything he did was dramatic. He would often send the outfielders back to the bench and retire the side. Fans loved this sort of showmanship and Paige is rumored to have been paid $300 a game in the 1930s, a handsome sum during the Depression. Don Ismael Montalvo smiled when asked about the first time he saw Paige. He recalled that the long black Cadillac in which Paige traveled pulled up to the grandstand chauffeured not by a man, but a weary, sensuous-looking black woman. She pulled to a stop and stared ahead, fatigued from the two-hundred-mile trek to Chicago, while the back door opened to discharge a tall, lanky young figure. Montalvo continued:

> It was ten minutes before the game when he came in that big ol' car of his. He
> got out of the car, play[ed] pepper 'bout ten minutes, then pitched. He threw
> fastballs, I think, over a hundred miles an hour. He didn't mess around with a
> curveball, nothin'. One, two, three, vamonos. He wanted to get out of there
> quick. He pitched against us three games, two in a row and we didn't score a
> run.[101]

Don Fernando Dovalina also recalls those games and the overpowering
presence of Paige:

> We got to Bismark, North Dakota. When we got there the Cubans got sick.
> Amaro, Bragaña, they knew Paige was warming up. They knew him from Mex-
> ico, but our guys, we never heard of him. He played for anybody who'd pay him.
> Gee, I don't know, $200, $500 whatever. He had his car and he had his satchel
> and he'd go from one place to another. Some of the people in the crowd were
> telling us that this guy Satchel Paige was the best pitcher in the world. Bragaña
> and Amaro said to me, "You have no chance." The Cubans all knew him so they
> got sick. "Let somebody else pitch," said Bragaña. He beat us easy. The next day
> we played against them again, and found out that Satchel Paige was gonna pitch
> again. He could pitch every day. We all got sick this time. When he warmed up,
> he'd go over to first base and throw like anybody, like a first baseman. Then he'd
> warm up like a pitcher, and then we couldn't see it [his pitches]. Some guys
> would come back to the bench and say, "I was lucky, I got a foul off him." He'd
> keep the ball low all the time. Hitters knew he was comin' right there, they just
> couldn't hit it. They couldn't see it.[102]

The pages of the *Bismark Tribune* report that Paige pitched against the
"Mexican Charros" on July 4 in a rain-shortened game of five innings that
ended in a scoreless tie. Paige gave up two singles and no runs, striking out
nine. A week later the two teams met again.[103] Paige won, pitching a complete game and giving up one run and three singles and fanning thirteen.
(Although Montalvo claimed that they never scored off Paige, it may just
have felt like they never did.) A third game was reported in the *Bismark
Tribune*, but the results were not published. Montalvo's recollection was
that La Junta failed to score.

Paige was so impressive and dominating a pitcher that any team to face
him held the memory of it long afterward, and La Junta teammates, whose
memories might blur on other aspects of the tour, were able to vividly
recall events having to do with Paige decades after the games had been
played. Encountering Paige was, in the larger picture of the 1935 season,
a high point. Simply facing a legend—a future Hall of Famer and major
league player—was awesome enough for the border team, and the losses

they suffered were buffered by the winning record that La Junta compiled in their northern swing.

Major league lightning was to strike even more directly before the tour was done. Philadelphia Phillies scouts had come to hear of the "crack" Mexican team that was beating some of the best teams in the heartland. After watching La Junta for weeks, the scouts were most impressed by second baseman Chile Gómez. He was granted a tryout with the team and signed in early July. The payoff was immediate, and the Laredo paper eagerly reported the results of his first series: Gómez fielded flawlessly and collected five hits in eight at-bats.[104] Underscoring the transnational self-identity of the Laredos was the fact that whenever players were lost to injury or, in this case, to another team, La Junta would look home to find replacements; new players were as often as not from Laredo as they were from Nuevo Laredo.

Upon returning to Nuevo Laredo in early August, the owners of the team in conjunction with city officials from both Laredos arranged a border version of a "ticker-tape parade" for La Junta:

> Ball fans are going to greet the players on their arrival today at 2:00 p.m. with the municipal band. . . . members of the Nuevo Laredo Chamber of Commerce and officials of the La Junta Federal de Mejoras Materiales will be among the reception committee which will be waiting to parade down Guerrero Avenue. . . . Music will be played throughout the down town section and everything will be done to show Nuevo Laredo's appreciation for the only team which has ever traveled the northern states in a successful tour.[105]

On September 27, 1935, the House of David arrived in the Laredos from a series of games played in Mexico. All three games were played under the lights at La Junta park, with the "bearded beauties" (as House of David players were often called) winning two of three seesaw contests. Gonzáles reports that 6,300 fans watched one game.[106] The presence of this legendary team in the Laredos had become something of an eagerly anticipated annual event in the 1930s. The House of David had regularly made Mexico a part of their annual 40,000 mile treks, and stopping at Nuevo Laredo or Laredo was a natural jumping off point.

The spectacular 1935 season culminated in the appearance of the American League All-Star team, which toured in Mexico in October of that year. A three-game series was arranged between La Junta and the American League team. La Junta managed a 2–1 win in the rubber game of that series, but the local paper opined that the La Junta win was as much a result of the American League All-Stars' "inclination to clown and over-confidence" as to Cabal's excellent pitching performance.[107] The box scores suggest a series of closely fought contests with La Junta roughly matching the All-Stars in hits and overall play. Whatever the outcome, the presence in Nuevo Laredo of this august body—"The biggest affair in the annals of baseball around here"[108]—seemed to cap a heady season. In the winter of 1995, Fernando Dovalina and Ismael Montalvo, along with a few other old players, were still "pitching" every Friday and Saturday at Margarita's Restaurant. Among the games they pitch, those from the 1935 season still get the lion's share of attention.

## Conclusion

Baseball in the Laredos was, from its inception through the 1930s, a regional affair, more appropriately termed "borderland ball." Local parties both north and south of the international line organized teams, scheduled contests, and recruited for the region. Don Ismael Montalvo was one of those Laredoans, who, because of his prowess, traveled far and wide, but in recalling his beginnings in the Rio Grande Valley, he characterized the game as regional:

> I was raised in the [Rio Grande] Valley, in San Benito. My older brother played, and two other brothers. We were twelve children. In those days there were a few teams in the Valley, 'bout four or five. I stayed home to help with the family and played for the highest bidder and they paid me fifteen dollars a game. Was a lotta money. I played for the .30/.30s. There was another team in Brownsville. Call them the Hatmakers. Semi-pro. They were very good ball clubs, but no competition except with each other.[109]

Between the twin cities were shared players, scheduled contests, fans, and reportage. When teams from other cities within the sphere that included San Antonio to the north and Monterrey to the south came to town, there was but a single identity. At other times the cities competed—sometimes bitterly—with each other: "We used to play against each other, we were rivals. In those days there wasn't much to do. They used to charge twenty-five or thirty-five cents for the bleachers. So baseball was a big thing with fans. But even then we would switch sides, play for one side one week, the other the next."[110] For many players, this made it difficult to generate an absolute sense of identity, though it was not necessary to do so.

As the 1930s progressed Laredo saw the emergence of more powerful clubs increasingly staffed with foreign (mostly Cuban) players who were relatively well paid. This shift in semi-pro baseball, of course, was a transition to the fully professional Mexican League that would emerge at the end of the decade. Historian Allen Guttmann's typology is appropriate here in that the differences between borderland baseball of the 1930s and the period that followed is vaguely reminiscent of Guttmann's distinctions between capitalist/industrial sport and the medieval period.[111] The semi-pro teams like La Junta were much more egalitarian, much less bureau-cratic, rationalized, specialized, and record-oriented than were the teams that came in the wake of the Mexican League of the 1940s. As a profes-sional league, the Mexican League centralized baseball operations, either severely reducing or curtailing altogether local control and autonomy. In the same way that the capital exerts its political and cultural power over the margins of a state, Mexico City would come to dominate the sport of base-ball, first through Pasquel and later in the 1950s through Alejo Peralta.

# *Three*

## Nationalizing the Game[1]

SPREADING OUT cold cash on a beautiful antique mahogany desk is a little like having comedienne Roseanne Barr sit down to dine with Katharine Hepburn; the simple juxtaposition of the two exaggerates the coarseness of the former. That was precisely what Jorge Pasquel did when, in 1946, Pasquel brought Tom Gorman into his plush Mexico City office. The manner in which Pasquel pulled out that huge wad of thousand-dollar bills from the desk drawer, spreading twenty of them out on the beautifully burnished desktop like so much raw meat, was a vulgar move, just as was his stuffing the bills into a brown paper bag and handing it to Gorman.

Much of this was lost on a young gringo pitcher, however. He was newly married, nursing an injury, and broke: "We were on velvet. I thought I was. Twenty thousand was more money than I'd ever had before, and more than I was to have for a long time in the future. And there it was, right there before me on the desk, waiting for me to pick it up. Jorge put all that money into a paper sack, a little grocery bag, and handed it to me. So I had twenty grand and I hadn't thrown a ball."[2]

When asked by Pasquel which method of payment he preferred, Gorman had opted for cash, a move that probably confirmed Pasquel's low view of employees in general. The quasi-feudal social world that continues to color so much of the Mexican elite's relations contains a generous dose of benevolent disdain for subordinates. Let the underling attempt to step outside of these social bounds and, for instance, demand better pay or changed conditions, and the benevolence turns into cold-blooded ruthlessness, as it did with the Mexican baseball players' *Asociación Nacional de Beisbolistas* (ANABE) strike of 1981. But this could hardly have occurred to Gorman and his wife Margery, as they were being wined and dined by Pasquel that evening.

These aspects of Pasquel's personality could be glimpsed in his surroundings. His office was decorated in early macho-posh. The walls were filled with trophies of the chase, both four-legged and two-legged. There were heads of animals and heads of state spread around. Pictures of Miguel Alemán, soon-to-be president of Mexico, in the company of Jorge Pasquel were in abundance as were other narcissistic extensions such as sports mementos. The pelt of a large grey mountain lion, for instance, replete with snarling teeth, lay spread on the highly polished blue-tile floor. Gorman recalls that Pasquel named it "Ted Williams." And, in strict Hemingway literary fashion, Pasquel liked to keep a loaded .45 caliber automatic pistol on his desk just for talking with visitors.

Why would a Mexican multimillionaire, an astute businessman with a keen sense for value, pay out $20,000 to a "virtual rookie" with a "dubious future"[3] to play in *La Liga Mexicana*? Tom Gorman was, by 1946, washed up as a major leaguer after a career of only five innings (all back in 1939). He had spent four years in the U.S. Army during the Second World War, winding up his tour of duty with calcium deposits in his throwing arm, which made pitching painful and his future cloudy. Nevertheless, like almost all ballplayers who had had a taste of the "big time," Gorman showed up at the New York Giants' Winterhaven, Florida, spring training camp in February of 1946. Almost immediately traded to the Boston Braves and shipped over to Ft. Lauderdale, Florida, Gorman pitched seven shutout innings against his old team. Fortuitously, some of Pasquel's scouts were in attendance, reconnoitering for *el Jefe*, and recommended Gorman for the Mexican League.

The push to get American players for the Mexican League was seen by American baseball interests as a naked act of aggression, unprovoked and without justification. It ushered in what has become known as the "baseball war" of 1946. The process by which this unfolded illustrates several features of the use and medium of sport in promoting nationalism. Just as the 1935 tour of the United States by La Junta was emblematic of the highest point achieved by border baseball, the subsequent period of professionalization of Mexican baseball was most dramatically illustrated in the 1946 season. This chapter examines a unique year in the annals of baseball, and the man who orchestrated the events of that year.

## The Mexican Baseball League of 1940

The Mexican League began in earnest in 1940, and Nuevo Laredo's entry was, predictably, La Junta. Most Mexican chroniclers of the sport consider the Mexican League to have begun in 1925,[4] but such histories also distinguish between a period roughly between 1925–1938 and what follows. The latter marks the emergence of organized leagues throughout the republic, while the earlier period is more akin to the semi-pro baseball played by La Junta in the 1930s. When don Ismael Montalvo mentioned playing for the Aztecas of Mexico City in 1931, he characterized the organization of baseball as loose with no overarching structure tying teams together or orchestrating play or a season. The caliber of baseball was good and getting better, but cohesion and integration was absent. Teams started and folded in the same season, the schedules were erratic, and rosters chaotic.

Certainly by the late 1930s Mexican teams had begun to attract Negro League stars. Playing for Tampico in 1939, Montalvo was on a team with James "Cool Papa" Bell. Foreign players, especially from Cuba, had been part of Mexican baseball since at least the early 1930s. Santos Amaro and Ramón Bragaña were with La Junta by then, and the legendary Martín Dihigo was playing in the south, but the numbers of these foreigners and Negro Leaguers reached a critical threshold by the late 1930s. The entrance of the Pasquel brothers into Mexican baseball in 1940 accelerated this process and ushered in an era of organization that made effective use of the increasingly talented players in that country. While exciting to see talent from different countries, local players felt uneasy. Don Ismael explains, "When I went away [from Laredo] in 1939 [to Tampico] they had six foreigners, most of them Black. Pasquel took over in 1940 and he raised it to twelve. Sometimes you'd see only one Mexican player; all the others were foreign."[5]

For the Mexican League, reinventing itself in a more modern context entailed a more structured format and schedule, as well as finding owners who were committed to regularly fielding established teams that would be profitable. More modern facilities, such as Mexico City's Delta Park (built in 1930) were needed. The outcome, however, remained checkered with some teams able to meet the new, more professional standards and others less so. Tampico's stadium, for instance, never completely shed its past:

> The railroad went right through centerfield in Tampico. There'd be around five thousand people there, [and the] game'd stop for about ten minutes because behind the grandstand was the railroad depot. When the train'd come in, they'd open gates in centerfield to let it in, stop a game because when the train was switching cars at the depot the cars would trail into the stadium. We'd wait. . . .
> I had a catcher over there, and he was also an engineer on a train too. And when the railroad would go through the ballpark full of people he would stop the train and talk with his friends on the train. The fans would scream, "Sale la madre!" [Get the mother out!], and he would holler back, "tu tambien!" [Same to you!][6]

Nuevo Laredo entered the league partly on the basis of having had one of the more successful teams of the 1930s, although the La Junta team that entered the league bore no resemblance to the team that defined 1930s baseball in the area. The stars of the mid-1930s—Amaro, Bragaña, Cabal, Montalvo—were all playing elsewhere in the league that year. Despite using twenty foreigners, more than twice what most other teams were using that year, they still finished twenty-four and a half games behind Veracruz. Still, the 1940 Nuevo Laredo team had talent. Pitcher Edward "Pullman" Porter, a veteran of the Negro Leagues, was their top starter. His devastating fastball enabled him to set a Mexican League record that would stand for a dozen years. He struck out 232 batters that year and compiled a 21–14 record. There seemed to be an ineptitude on the field that cost most of the other pitchers games and hid their accomplishments. Tom "Lefty" Glover's record was 8–13, but would periodically show flashes of brilliance as when, on more than one occasion, he would strike out the side in the ninth inning with the bases loaded and a one run lead. These high points were relatively rare, however.

After dropping out for three seasons (1941–43), La Junta became the Tecolotes when they returned to the Mexican League in 1944. They took their name because Nuevo Laredo was the first team to play night games. They reentered the league boasting the likes of Dihigo and Cabal and the border's own Montalvo, but all of these players were now past their prime. Dihigo batted only .249, while Cabal was 0–2 with a bloated 9.09 earned run average. Montalvo had his best year at the plate with a .317 batting average. On the mound he managed only a 1–1 record with a 3.38 ERA. The entire decade was not one that Nuevo Laredo could be particularly proud of. They twice left the league, in 1941–43 and 1947–48. When they fielded a team they did poorly, coming in second once, as well as fourth, sixth, and eighth (last) in other years. This was not a stellar franchise in the 1940s, but the events taking place within the league swept the Tecolotes into a current that involved international intrigue and drama. Just as 1935 marked the year that defined the decade for baseball in the Laredos, so 1946 branded the decade of the 1940s.

## An Overview of 1946

It was in 1946 that major league baseball was attacked from both flanks by a combination of forces bent on undoing the grip that owners had over the fortunes of their players. In that year, Mexican baseball impresario Jorge Pasquel and his brothers launched an effort to bring the quality of the Mexican League up to that of something like major league baseball and began signing American (and other foreign) players (some right under the noses of the owners)—a move that directly stepped on the toes of American baseball owners and seemed to them a declaration of war. The entire season took on an aura of international conflict with accusations and charges flying between Pasquel and major league baseball commissioner A. B. "Happy" Chandler. Even the Mexican government and the U.S. State Department were forced to take positions on the matter. At the core of the conflict was the dual issue of a foreign competitor operating in an American market, and a test of baseball's reserve system. An equally unexpected assault came with the formation of the American Baseball Guild (ABG) by Robert Murphy, a Boston lawyer. This bold move sought to unionize the players at all levels of professional play. Coming as it did against baseball owners, the ABG was seen as particularly audacious and, in conjunction with foreign interference, besieged owners from two directions at once.

Because all of America was waiting for their heroes to return, little attention was initially paid to Pasquel by major league baseball, and Murphy's union was, as of February 1946, not in existence. World War II had decimated the ranks of major league baseball, so the new season would mark the first time in years that teams would be able to return to full force. Other currents, however, were also about to surface. With the Brooklyn Dodgers' signing of Jackie Robinson, a half century of racial segregation in professional baseball was about to end. And, unbeknownst to anyone in baseball, labor challenges were looming on the horizon. But with the arrival of the drab days of February 1946, all of America was heady in anticipation of baseball.

However timeless and pastoral it may appear to those who love the game, it is important to remember that the sport of baseball was and is a branch of the entertainment industry. The structural relations between labor and management that characterize most sectors of the economy were strangely absent from baseball in that era. The strong union movement that was flexing its negotiating muscle in other industries had been aborted in baseball, which remained locked in the feudal-like "reserve system." No less an august body than the Supreme Court aided the monopolistic grip that owners had at the time by ruling in 1922 that baseball was exempt from antitrust legislation.[7] Against this backdrop, and for very different reasons, the impending 1946 season was eagerly awaited by owners, players, and fans alike. Owners anticipated big gate receipts in the first post-war season. Players' ranks were realigning, reflecting the return of major leaguers to their teams and the demotion of the stop-gap minor leaguers used on major league rosters during the war. Fans were, as already indicated, eager to see a return to halcyon days. John Morrissey, ticket manager for the Washington Senators, beamed, "We're all set with the best ticket sales in history. It's far better than pre-war, and 100 percent better than 1945."[8]

## Early Family History

By the time Jorge Pasquel was born in 1907, his father had already begun establishing the family fortune. What started as a "little cigar factory" in the 1890s grew quickly into Mexico's largest factory, and spread laterally to include a railroad and customhouse brokerage.[9] As the eldest of eight children, Jorge declared himself head of the family to direct the family fortunes following the father's retirement. Jorge would later boast, "My family is in everything. We have banks, ranches, real estate, ships. We are agents for General Motors. We are customs brokers for the Mexican Government."[10]

Pasquel's panache and sense of entitlement was ever present. His aesthetics and actions, everything about him, bespoke of his position in Mexican society. This was capped by the 1940s male macho so characteristic in Ernest Hemingway and actor Errol Flynn. Pictures of Pasquel show him as a rakish man with a black Clark Gable mustache and slicked-back hair. Atypically however, in an era of cigarette-smoking men, Pasquel was a militant nonsmoker and nondrinker and worked out daily.

He married Ernestina Calles in July 1932, a marriage born of political and economic expedience. Because Ernestina was the daughter of former Mexican president Plutarco Elías Calles, Pasquel stood to benefit directly and indirectly from the union. Gerald Vaughn, who pulled together an excellent portrait of Pasquel, points out how rewarding Pasquel's ability to exploit his affinal ties to the Calles family was in establishing his customs house: "The Pasquel firm eventually handled more government shipping than any competitor and benefited greatly from trade with the U.S. The company reportedly was the largest liquor importer in Mexico."[11] Pasquel family holdings grew from an estimated $1 million at the time of his father's death to somewhere in the vicinity of $60 million by the time Jorge and his brothers ventured into the game of baseball. The Pasquels naturally enough hobnobbed with Mexico's elite, and his closest friends included several presidents of the country, a fact not lost on those who have followed his life and his effect on baseball in Mexico.

As with many politically influential Mexicans, nationalism, particularly as an expression of resentment toward the United States, is a central element in the story of Jorge Pasquel. Growing up in Veracruz in 1914, a young Pasquel experienced the bombing and eventual occupation of his hometown by U.S. military forces. He recalled how he cowered in his basement, certain he and his family would be killed by these gringos. This invasion alone provided a generation of Mexicans with a wellspring of resentment toward the United States, which they could readily tap into. The imperialism of the United States was certainly not confined to Mexico. Haiti, the Dominican Republic, Nicaragua, and Cuba were all countries that experienced something similar during that period. My own research into the Dominican Republic,[12] and even more so the work of Bruce Calder,[13] examines the anger that such intrusions foster: anger not easily or perhaps never quelled. This was most certainly the case for the people of Mexico, and Veracruz in particular.

Another youngster to witness this outrage was Pasquel's childhood friend, Miguel Alemán, who also grew up in Veracruz. Alemán would eventually embark on a career in politics that would end with his election as president of Mexico (1946–52). As governor of Veracruz in 1938, Alemán played a key role in the movement that sought to nationalize the U.S.-owned oil companies in Mexico. Through this action he quickly became a popular nationalist figure who could express, and therefore tap into, the resentment many felt toward American economic and political policy in Latin America. The Roosevelt administration was forced to begin lengthy deliberations with Mexico to seek fair compensation for their holdings, and through it all glimpsed the depth of Mexican resolve and nationalism. Alemán's role in all this was rewarded in his appointment as minister of the interior in President Avila Camacho's 1940 cabinet. It would be a scant six years before he would mount his own successful bid for presidency. Pasquel and Alemán would grow up to become business partners as well.[14] At Alemán's inauguration, Pasquel was found close at hand, which led Vaughn to conclude that Pasquel lobbied actively on behalf of his close friend's bid for presidency.

## The 1946 Mexican League

While the facilities might have continued to be less than acceptable by U.S. standards, by 1946 the league would evolve. Teams in Torreón and San Luís Potosí were added to Mexico City, Veracruz (also housed in Mexico City), Nuevo Laredo, Tampico, Puebla, and Monterrey. The upgraded caliber of play was most in evidence, however. To ensure parity among teams the league intended to place all Imports into the same hopper to be redistributed among the teams. For a time it appeared as if the flood of Imports would make it impossible for Mexicans to play. An amendment limiting the number of Imports per team to eight and thereby "sav[ing] the game for Mexicans"[15] was made on March 20, 1946. Thus the seventeen former major leaguers, along with the forty-five stars of Latino baseball (e.g., Cuba and Venezuela) were theoretically parcelled out evenly throughout the league. The season, going from mid-March for twenty-eight weeks, was split into two rounds with each team playing a weekly three-game slate. The top four teams would, at season's end, vie for the championship. At the helm of the league sat don Jorge, who decided on all matters of importance. It was he and his brothers who recruited and signed all talent, who waged the war with major league baseball, who were responsible for the image of the league at home and abroad, and who, at times, even managed his personal favorite team, the Veracruz Blues. Alfonso was primarily responsible for making initial contact with players in the United States, in the hopes of interesting them. Once signed, Bernardo would take over all legal and fiscal dealings, making sure to bring the players into Mexico. Upon arrival in Mexico City Jorge took over and saw that they were paid, assigned to a team, and generally handled throughout the season.[16]

If the league made efforts to formalize its existence through structuring itself along Major League lines, it still lacked the wherewithal to moderate the behavior of fans, umpires, and players. The Mexican League has always been a bastion of fervor. Commenting on this, ex–Mexican Leaguers never fail to mention the capability of fans to alter a game:

> They could be very nasty. They'd holler at you and a lotta personal things too. And, sometimes they'd jump on the field. There were soldiers there for that kind of thing. We were playing Torreón one time, and the umpire was so terrible that the manager told our pitcher, "Walk everybody so they can win the game and we can get the hell outta here." We were six or seven runs ahead at the time. He walked everybody and then after the game all the fans jumped on the field. The soldiers had to get in there quick. We had a hard time getting to the bus. The soldiers cocked their rifles and their officer said, "Anybody touch a player, shoot'em." Then we got back to the hotel and the police picked up the blacks and took them off to jail. They used some excuse that they had failed to play as well as expected. And to get these guys out of jail we had to get the governor— nice fellow, I think he was from Chihuahua, but he lived in Coahuila. Spoke good English too—but he had to come down to get these guys outta jail.[17]

Despite these local adventures, the caliber of the league, according to most observers, rivaled the best AAA team in the United States.

## Blacks and Cubans in the League

While nationalist resentment may have played a significant role in Pasquel's "raiding" of major league baseball, there were other motives exerting at least as much force, and predating the fateful 1946 season. The Anglo major leaguers were not the first *extranjeros* (foreigners) to be hired by the Mexican League. Before Gorman and the others there were Satchel Paige and Ray Dandridge, and before them the Cubans such as Santos Amaro. "All those blacks and Cubans were major leaguers in my book. They made the Mexican League five times better than it is now. When they started usin' blacks in the United States, the Mexican League went down."[18]

Jorge Pasquel was a devoted fan, a player in his youth, a spot-manager of the Veracruz team, and given completely to upgrading the level of play in his country. This is interpreted as a constructive form of nationalism, taking no part of its identity from the presence of outside influences or the expression of resentment. Importantly, upgrading Mexican baseball was a program effectively carried out long before he trampled on the toes of major league owners. Stars in the Negro Leagues and Latin Americans (e.g., Cubans, Venezuelans) had been playing in Mexico since the 1920s.[19] With the formal establishment of the Mexican League, however, the sport evolved and efforts to bring even more talented foreigners were increased.

For barnstorming Negro Leaguers such as Satchel Paige playing in Mexico was a real opportunity to increase their often meager earnings:

> I guess it was because I only thought of old number one in those days that I jumped to Mexico before the season was over. . . So, when a guy down there put a few bucks in my pocket—a few more than Gus Greenlee'd give me—I walked down to Mexico. . . I was running up and down that country. And everywhere I went in Mexico I ran into Negro League players.[20]
>
> I went to Mexico when Jorge Pasquel was giving all that money away. I jumped and went too.[21]

Ray Dandridge was a standout Negro Leaguer who also starred in the Mexican League. His experiences over eight years in Mexico illustrates both the money that African-American players earned, as well as the culturally and racially more benevolent climate south of the border. Dandridge threatened Pasquel with quitting if he didn't get a raise in the heady days of spring 1946:

> Lanier [one of the Anglo major leaguers that Pasquel had signed], all those guys were coming down, making all that money, getting $5,000 bonuses. We were making nothing, we were making chicken feed, $350 a month. I told Pasquel, "I want more money." I went to his office. "Look, I'm getting my family up and going back home if I don't get some more money." He said he couldn't give me more money, so we packed up our things and were down at the station ready to get on the train. All of a sudden, here comes the chauffeur—oh man, a lot of people.[22]

Pasquel's agents whisked Dandridge away to his office where they quickly settled on his new $10,000 contract. Herein lies a critical difference between the United States and Latin America, a difference not lost on African-Americans of the time: earning power and social mobility were not restricted by race. In the Mexican League it was common for Negro Leaguers to live in fashionable neighborhoods in Mexico City, hobnob with men of distinction, and even have their children tutored. Willie Wells, a stand out for the Pittsburgh Crawfords, observed: "We are heroes here [in Mexico] . . . while in the United States everything I did was regulated by color. Well, here in Mexico I am a man."[23] The Pasquel treatment was extended to athletes black and white, but the player who was probably closest to him was Ray Dandridge. He was enlisted to be Pasquel's agent to the Negro Leagues, entrusted with large sums of money, and given authority and responsibility to work on his own.[24] Of all those who played in the heyday of the Mexican League, Dandridge was treated with special consideration, as the following account shows. After playing winter ball in Cuba, Dandridge was flown back to Mexico City and met at the airport:

His [Pasquel's] other brother met the plane, game me $100 pocket money, put me in a hotel. The next morning Pasquel's chauffeur came, and I went to his house. I said, "Look, if you want me to come back, you have to give me a bonus. What I want to do is buy me a house. I want some money in advance." I was talking about $10,000. A two-family house cost $7,500 back during that time.

He said, "How you going to pay me back?"

I said, "How you want to be paid?"

He called his secretary up, said, "Make out a certified check for Ray for $10,000 and put him on the plane to Newark." He game me another $100 for my pocket. I never got to spend nothing of it, because they paid all the expenses in Mexico. So that was pretty good: I still had $2500 profit and $300 pocket money too.

He took out money for two pay days and then told his secretary to forget it. I was Pasquel's number-one boy.[25]

It seemed that there were no ends to which Pasquel would not go to get and keep the talented black players of the period. Quincy Trouppe and Theolic Smith were two Negro Leaguers who were contacted by Pasquel to play in Mexico during the 1943 season. Because of the war, however, they had to declare their intentions to their local Los Angeles draft boards, who turned them down. They were needed in their Los Angeles defense plant. No sooner had they been denied and written to Pasquel informing him of the board's decision than the Mexican consulate contacted them at their homes. Trouppe recalled, "The representative from Mexico told me that they had loaned the United States 80,000 workers to fill the manpower shortage caused by the war and [that] all they wanted in return was two ballplayers by the name of Quincy Trouppe and Theolic Smith."[26] There is little question that Pasquel treated black players well. Still, among other nonblack Latinos Pasquel might express racist thinking. After visiting Pasquel's posh Mexico City office, Ismael Montalvo described an incident revealing Pasquel's personal style as well as a hint of racism. Entering Pasquel's office, Montalvo encountered the Paul Bunyun of the Negro Leagues, Josh Gibson:

> One day I went to [Pasquel's] office. He had a big office in Mexico City, and I used to live in a *colonia* nearby. . . . They got those big ol' doors and I knock on the door. They open them from some kinda connection and these big dogs [Great Danes] were standing there, so I walk real slow to the office in the back. They had Josh Gibson there in the office. Next to the office was a vacant lot and from the window, I think it was forty or fifty yards to a big wall. Brick. He was shooting at a target with a .45 from the window. One of his *pistoleros* would load [it], hand the gun back to him. He'd shoot some more. He turned to me and said, "Montalvo, come on, ask this *negro hijo de puta* [black son of a whore], Josh

Gibson, why he hasn't hit a home run lately." . . . Gibson knew Spanish and he says back, "*Jorge, yo no soy un hijo de puta* [I'm not a son of a whore]." Later Gibson said to me, "You think I'm gonna say anything to get him mad? Shit no!"[27]

Personal comments like this aside, Pasquel regarded these black players as worthy of playing alongside others and treated them well; in addition, he had the political wherewithal to indirectly influence the American government on issues as described above. This is where his ties to Alemán (who in 1943 was minister of the interior) enabled Pasquel to wield such widespread influence. With an infusion of black talent that was not wanted in the United States, the Mexican League quickly became a highly competitive league and had by 1942 already shown a respectable profit.

## Nationalism and Baseball

It is difficult to say just when Pasquel decided to take on American baseball or exactly what his motives were. Most agree that it was fueled by his nationalism.[28] But of what type? Nationalism as a constructive, collective sense of self, or nationalism as a collective demonizing of an enemy? Vaughn, for instance, precluded any anti-Americanism on Pasquel's part.[29] Rogosin, on the other hand, intimated that Pasquel's actions were informed by a willingness to challenge American hegemony. Tom Gorman, the pitcher introduced at the beginning of this chapter, leaned in the direction of Pasquel's anti-imperialist nationalism. Whether or not he really understood Pasquel's nationalism, Gorman imputed conscious resistance to him: "He was a genuine patriot, a Mexican chauvinist. The people he hurt were the major-league moguls, but his real target, I suspect, was the entire United States of America. Like many other people, the Mexicans love to see a little man defeat a big man."[30] I conclude that Pasquel's efforts were a blend of resentment directed against American baseball interests and the desire to promote a form of Mexican baseball that was admired internationally. Viewed from America, Pasquel's actions appeared as unjustified, naked aggression. The view from Mexico, however, saw Pasquel as someone who was reciprocating the Americans' arrogant imperialism. Of particular interest is the way in which Pasquel was able to manipulate the media to justify his position and garner support. This he did not only in Mexico but in the United States as well; and his success speaks to his capacity to function as a binational-bicultural actor.

In his effort to develop Mexican baseball Pasquel a priori incurred the wrath of major league baseball commissioner Happy Chandler and many of the owners by signing American players. Events spiraled so that with each move to improve Mexican baseball, Pasquel further angered U.S. baseball interests, which in turn inflamed Pasquel and pushed him into an ever more antagonistic stance. In this way, one can view Pasquel's actions as reactive rather than proactive.

One could also claim that Pasquel was merely operating within the norms established by successful businessmen anywhere. The aggressiveness that Pasquel displayed as commissioner of the league was in keeping with successful bourgeois practices: using wealth and political power to organize, centralize, and otherwise turn the enterprise into a monopoly (or as close to one as he could make it). While Pasquel was not elected president of the league until 1946, he was the real power behind the league from the beginning. As early as the inaugural season, Pasquel was already majority owner of the Veracruz Blues (a team named after his hometown but located in Mexico City) and a second team in the capital, in addition to Delta Park, the premier facility in the country. Owning the state-of-the-art facility and the capital's teams, Pasquel was bent on stocking his holdings with the best players.

A related but little known event that might have acted as a tripwire in Pasquel's decision to take on U.S. baseball was his determination to make the Mexican League the only serious league in Mexico. The Mexican National Baseball League, a rival of Pasquel's Mexican League, had been making a bid to become affiliated with the U.S. minor league system since 1944.[31] It appears that this rival was also being used by U.S. baseball interests as a beachhead in Mexico. The periodical *Current Biography 1946* argued that U.S. baseball sought to recognize this rival league in response to Pasquel's raiding of U.S. players.[32] The January 26 edition of the *Laredo Times* makes brief, but telling, mention of these events: "Bob Ingram, Mexican league [i.e., the rival Mexican National Baseball League] commissioner, learned yesterday from NAPBL [National Association of Professional Baseball Leagues, or the U.S. minor leagues] President W. G. Bramham that the Mexican loop would be admitted on a probation membership thus giving Mexico teams their first play under the rules of organized baseball."[33]

By late April 1946, the Mexican National Baseball League was essentially finished, however, and the only discussions from that point forward were if, how, and when Pasquel's Mexican League would enter in place of its rival. At least one observer noted that Pasquel "won the war between his 'league' and the other by the simple expedient of buying Delta Park, Mexico City's only place to play. The rival faction folded."[34] There is little doubt that Pasquel and other Mexican baseball promoters knew of the relations between the Mexican National Baseball League and U.S. interests, and that the willingness of the two to work against Pasquel and the Mexican League further inflamed the situation. This may have been a baseball intrigue, but it was also very reminiscent of international relations between the countries.

Pasquel's actions have always been interpreted as naked aggression, "a raid on the major leagues."[35] But for the record, it should be shown that the United States fired the first salvo in this international baseball war. As large numbers of players left to serve the nation's armed forces, their ranks were partially filled by minor leaguers.[36] Just as often, the effort to replenish the talent pool led some major league owners (such as Clark Griffith of the Washington Senators) to places like Cuba and Mexico to sign players.[37] It was the U.S. baseball intervention into Latin America—the signing or "raiding" of players out of the Mexican League—that occurred first. When Latin American owners complained to Commissioner Chandler about these raids on their players, the Chandler barely slapped the hands of the offending owners.[38]

Chandler's insult to Latin American owners was certainly a contributing factor in Pasquel's brazen response. The conflict with the major leagues, however, seemed to evolve by degrees rather than all at once. In keeping with the political and cultural hegemony of foreigners in the Third World, U.S. baseball was always judged to be the standard by which Latin baseball measured itself. Conversely, the United States always assumed its supremacy in the sport and took any interest in Third World talent as a special show of compassion for their nonwhite subordinates—until their own stock of players temporarily dwindled during the war, that is. Then major league teams roamed through Cuba and Mexico, picking up players as if they were stocking private wine cellars. For nationalists and *beisbolistas* this was as naked a form of imperialism as the Marine invasions; and it was this that built up the reservoir of anger and resentment that Pasquel could tap into at any time. It could be as diffuse as the resentment learned growing up—in school, for instance—that many Mexicans felt and continue to feel toward *norteamericanos*. Or, it could have been more specific, such as the bombing of his hometown that terrified Pasquel as a child. The rebuff he felt at the hands of Chandler could simply have been a button that pushed these feelings.

Pasquel was also responding to a string of successes that reinforced him at every turn. His league was solvent and seemed to be making profits in direct relationship to the numbers of quality Imports he was bringing in. By 1945 the league claimed gross profits of $800,000 and a net profit of $400,000. Its payroll for the year was $300,000.[39]

In 1944 Hall of Famer Rogers Hornsby was hired to play for and manage the Veracruz team. While this baseball legend had fallen on hard times, his presence in Mexico served a vital symbolic function, coming as it did on the heels of financial success and increased signings of top flight players. According to *Current Biography 1946*,[40] the Hornsby signing precipitated the first time many Anglo Americans ever heard of the Mexican League. That year also saw the league signing their first player directly off a major league roster: Chico Hernández, a catcher for the Chicago Cubs. The fact that he was Latino probably smoothed over any ruffled feathers in the U.S. baseball establishment, on the assumption that Hernández was predisposed to go to a Latin country.

For eight months in 1944 Pasquel actually traveled in the United States. The entourage he brought with him must have looked like yet another Latin American high roller indulging his fancies, but Pasquel was earnestly studying the game's organization. This scouting mission would provide him with many of the ideas that he would use when he finally decided to take on U.S. major league baseball. While the events of 1946 have become known as the year Pasquel "invaded" or "raided" the United States, it was certainly not the first time that international politics and baseball were fused.

## Ichiko School Takes on the United States

The manner in which baseball was used to symbolize late nineteenth-century Meiji Japan's rising nationalism has been chronicled by Rhoden.[41] To my knowledge it was the first concrete instance of baseball and nationalism. A. G. Spalding, the sport's first powerful entrepreneur and one of its earliest superstars, had already understood the political value of baseball abroad. At the turn of the century Spalding argued that the manifest function of baseball was to culturally support America's sense of Manifest Destiny, that baseball was to "follow the flag."[42] Whether or not he was aware of the events going on half way around the world in Yokohama is not known, but the small drama of the diamond turned into a national incident in 1896. The First Higher School of Tokyo (Ichiko) was one of ten or so schools to develop reputable baseball programs in the 1890s. They quickly became the preeminent youth team in Japan, sustaining an almost unblemished string of victories against other schools that stretched through the mid-1890s. These young men were part of the Japanese elite class that would eventually form Japan's ruling strata.

As the country began to emerge from an entrenched feudalism that lasted until late in the nineteenth century—a process hastened by U.S. imperialism of the period—the more forward-looking segments of Japanese society began taking on American cultural notions. One of these had to do with American notions of leisure and physical conditioning. British and American notions of Social Darwinism extended to include other civilizations maintaining a moral and physical readiness to demonstrate their superiority.[43] This was certainly the attitude of Americans in foreign countries. The Ichiko School too adopted this notion and intended it to be proof that American standards for modernity could be incorporated without violating the Japanese sense of cultural identity. Baseball, then, had become an innocent party to a larger cultural battle.

When intercollegiate competition was no longer challenging, the young men of Ichiko sought out the Americans living in their exclusive Yokohama enclave to play against. The Yokohama Athletic Club rejected this first invitation in 1891 and all subsequent invitations until 1896. Initially, the Americans rejected the Japanese because it was felt that a nation of kite flyers and flower arrangers could never really offer a sufficiently virile challenge to Americans playing the American game. Eventually the Japanese request was condescendingly taken up. Playing on their home turf (the Yokohama Athletic Club team would have never considered attending a game on Japanese turf), the Americans treated the high school boys from Ichiko dismissively, even jeering at them during the warmups. Once underway, however, the game turned into a Japanese rout. Ichiko won handily 29–4, as the Americans and their supporters were stunned into silence. The fans and press of the Ichiko, who were made to stay at the Athletic Club's gates, greeted their team as they would a victorious army. Three return matches followed, with the next two equally one-sided. On both occasions the Americans conscripted ballplayers from the Navy ships docked in the harbor, but the boys of Ichiko still won convincingly. Finally, pulling in a complete team of experienced players from a freshly docked boat, the Americans eked out a 14–12 victory. The date of this rematch—July 4—was, not surprisingly, an emotionally charged one, and may have aided the American team; although they had been trounced three straight times, the Yokohama Athletic Club was taking the risk of being defeated on the most important American holiday of the year. Despite losing the fourth game, the boys of Ichiko had become genuine national heroes, inspiring an outpouring of public hosannas, including a song that became the school's fight song. It is one of the most succinct statements on nationalism and baseball that one is likely to run across:

> The valorous sailors from the Detroit, Kentucky, and Yokohama
> Whose furious batting can intimidate a cyclone
> Threw off their helmets, their energies depleted
> Behold how pathetically they run away defeated.
> Courageously, we marched twenty miles south
> To fight the Americans in Yokohama
> Though they boast of the game as their national sport
> Behold the games they have left with no score.[44]

## Trujillo's Team

In 1937, the Dominican Republic dictator Rafael Trujillo was approaching the height of his power.[45] Trujillo was born a poor mulatto who overcame his humble roots, rising up through the ranks of the National Police (a military force fashioned by the United States during its occupation of the island between 1916 and 1923) to become the country's leader. He eventually controlled much of the country's wealth and ruthlessly dominated its politics and culture until he was assassinated in 1961. He was so self-obsessed and megalomaniacal that he renamed the capital city of Santo Domingo after himself.

While he was not as fanatical about baseball as many other Dominicans,[46] Trujillo was nevertheless a patron of the sport. Baseball was enjoying increased formal organization during the 1930s. Three teams, representing Santo Domingo, Ciudad Trujillo, and the cities of San Pedro de Macorís and Santiago emerged as the premier teams of 1937. Licey and Escogido were the capital's two teams. The former was the country's oldest organized team and its most widely followed, having played continuously since 1907. Escogido, on the other hand, was formed in 1921 and immediately established a rivalry with Licey. These two teams also came to represent political parties. Trujillo took to the Escogido team. Some claim that the team's name, which means "the chosen," originated when Trujillo's son could not make Licey's squad, prompting his father to conscript—to "choose"—players from other teams onto a new team just for him. This folklore is valuable but not accurate. Trujillo did not become the Dominican head of state until 1930, nine years after Escogido was started.

Everything about the 1937 season was odd. The configuration of the teams was aberrant. Licey and Escogido merged their rosters in a historic move. The season was thirty-six games long and had only three teams, but each owner was determined to take home bragging rights. The frenzy for a championship had been building steadily through the mid-1930s as each team sought to sign the best foreign talent it could find. In the 1936 season, the owner of the San Pedro de Macorís club spent lavishly to sign four of the best Cuban players of the period as well as local super heroes like Tetelo Vargas. That year's championship was won loudly and "in the face" of Ciudad Trujillo, prompting the increased interest of Trujillo in seeing that the title came back to the capital where he felt it belonged.

What followed rivaled anything that Pasquel could conjure up. Trujillo's agents were sent into the United States and Cuba to sign the best Negro Leaguers and Cubans they could find. Naturally, interest centered on Satchel Paige, perhaps the best pitcher of his time. He was signed for a salary in excess of a thousand dollars a month, and along with him came other African-American stars of the period, such as Josh Gibson and Cool Papa Bell. There were few games, making the emotional buildup to them pressure-packed. There was political intrigue and incidents involving riotous fans that resulted in forfeits, but all accounts agree that the season was the most dramatic and powerful in the history of baseball on that island.

Trujillo was facing an upcoming election, and he wanted attention drawn to himself.[47] A baseball championship would help focus the popu-

lace back on the capital city after the Antun family of San Pedro de Macorís
had turned the nation's gaze to the eastern part of the island by amassing
talented teams. The money spent was astronomical by standards of the day,
and the collective result of this outlay was that it exhausted the owners and
league. "The 1937 championship stopped baseball. All our money was
gone. We were exhausted financially and in enthusiasm also."[48] The financial exhaustion did not extend to Trujillo, whose worth was estimated at a
half billion dollars. For him, 1937 was merely a plume in his political cap,
further evidence that his destiny was to rule the island.

There are, in both the Japanese and Dominican cases, precedence for
Pasquel's use of baseball as a political tool, and with each, the direct or
indirect use of American notions of the role of baseball in their culture.
Since it is a part of the cultural inventory of a country, baseball is a mem-
brane through which influences may pass, an instrument of popular culture
that political institutions can utilize for their own ends.

## Pasquel's Use of Baseball as Nationalism

In a typical display of cultural arrogance, the major and minor leagues in
the United States labeled themselves "organized baseball," implying that
baseball outside of white America was disorganized, chaotic, and of poorer
qualify. Major league condescension, little more than rank ethnocentrism,
was easily detected by Pasquel in some of his facetious remarks about the
sport north of the border. Responding to a report of major league baseball's willingness to grant amnesty to banned American players who had
"jumped" to the Mexican League, Pasquel rhetorically asked, "What kind
of organization do those *señors* have that is called organized baseball?"[49]
Commenting on the "outlaw" label applied to his league, Pasquel responded, "I resent being referred to as an 'outlaw' operator because we
operate completely within Mexican laws."[50] The legal and cultural relativ-
ity is neatly expressed in the forgoing statement, but was lost on Commissioner Chandler's office. Once Pasquel began signing players in earnest,
the season would increasingly take on the look of a battle between Pasquel
and Chandler, a contest that necessitated monopolizing the press of both
countries.

## Playing the Press

To gain his larger objectives, Pasquel needed a medium with which to
attack major league baseball. The Mexican press would back him, of
course, but its message would stop at the Rio Grande. The U.S. press, it
was supposed, would automatically support the "national pastime" and its

agents. The anti-Mexican sentiment of certain members of the press, as well as certain regions of the United States, was easily tapped once Pasquel began taking players away, as this United Press piece indicates: "Pancho Villa's raids over the border looked like pale stuff Thursday night compared to the antics of a peso-happy caballero who is promoting big-time baseball in Mexico and using bonafide Brooklyn Dodgers for bait."[51]

Other members of the American press were also quick to paint Pasquel and his brothers as "raiders," using such culturally insensitive language as "Peso Pains" to describe the unwillingness of U.S. owners to pay their players more, or "Pancho Villa" to describe Pasquel's signing of players, attributing to them "a master spy system."

Despite the anti-Mexican sentiment, Pasquel was able to gain reasonable access to the U.S. print media. Jorge Pasquel was, after all, no uncouth bandit. Whether on safari in Africa or out and about in Mexico City, he always cut a stylishly rakish figure, an image much appreciated by the U.S. press. The references to Jorge in the press describe him as "dapper," "silk-shirted," "a dapper diamond mogul," "a gold-plated president." With his social charm and panache, Pasquel effortlessly projected a cosmopolitan image, easily overcoming much of the American media resistance to him as a "raider." As we shall see below, major league baseball was not able to rely on the loyalty of the American press, and, Pasquel's image aside, there were other problems faced by those who controlled the "national game." A brief chronology of the season will illustrate the variables at work in this piece of international intrigue.

## A Chronology of 1946

By February, press reports were regularly coming out detailing Pasquel's intention to or actual signings of professional U.S. players. In Nuevo Laredo, manager Arturo Garcia of the La Junta team was scouting players on the Mexican west coast as well as those in the U.S. Pacific Coast League. The *Laredo Times* reported on February 7 that former Red Sox players Bob Lemon and James Steiner "have been offered contracts with La Junta and are expected to come into the fold."[52] A United Press story from Havana on that same day first disclosed the massive infusion of money that the Pasquel brothers were ready to provide.[53] Jorge's brother Bernardo was scouting in Havana with other Mexican baseball owners and revealed that they "were ready to spend $20,000,000 to improve standards of the sport" in their homeland. He simultaneously boasted of having signed forty-five players from Cuba and Puerto Rico and eight from American professional leagues, yet declared his subordinance by claiming that "he had no intention of competing with American Major Leagues."[54] Sensing that his signings of U.S. ballplayers might anger the major league owners, Pasquel noted, "The big league owners in American shouldn't worry about me too much. . . . They have material among 125 million inhabitants in the whole United States. I'm just trying to get a fair share where I can."[55]

Less than two weeks later Pasquel more clearly revealed his goals, as a United Press story from New York printed his "vow that he not only will keep it [the Mexican League] going but develop it to the point where American organized baseball will have to accept it as a member. His supreme goal is a Pan-American series between the Mexican League champion and the Pacific Coast League winner."[56] This promise marked an escalation of the tension. Clearly Pasquel was determined that his league, not the rival Mexican National Baseball League, would be the one recognized by U.S. baseball's minor league system, and the shortest path to this end came about through posing a direct threat to major league baseball. Quickly signing players such as Luís Olmo of the Brooklyn Dodgers and other holdouts gave him immediate credibility.

Irked, but unruffled by Pasquel's move, major league owners predicted record ticket sales in the upcoming, first post-war season.[57] After Dodger owner Branch Rickey lost his hard-hitting outfielder, Luis Olmo, to the Mexican League, however, he began to urge Commissioner Chandler "to take strong action against major league players who jump from organized baseball to the Mexican League."[58] In so doing Rickey became the first voice to push for banishment of players who violated their American contracts. Other owners of teams hard-hit by such events included Clark Griffith of the Washington Senators and Horace Stoneham of the New York Giants. On February 28, Alejandro Carrasquel, a Venezuelan pitcher formerly of the Senators but now traded to the White Sox, became the ninth major leaguer to "jump" to the Mexican League. Pressure was beginning to mount on the commissioner to act.[59] At first, Chandler, who was new to the position, declared that there was no ruling about such matters: "One thing I can tell you for sure is that there is no rule of organized baseball which automatically suspends a man for competing against ineligible players. I've seen it written that such player is automatically suspended for five years or even for life, but I've read the rules and I can't find anything like that."[60]

Against this neutral position Pasquel pressed his position with the U.S. media with a string of releases and interviews that showed him to be absolutely fearless in his attempts to gain U.S. players, even willing to use his personal fortune to bring in the best. On March 7 Pasquel elevated his war of words when he outlined to eager reporters a series of elaborate schemes for his rapidly evolving Mexican League. Hitherto, the players who entered his league were essentially Latino and/or journeymen, but on this day the papers reported that Cleveland Indians' pitcher Bob Feller, one of baseball's highest-paid stars, had been offered a three-year contract by Pasquel in the range of $300,000, more than twice his U.S. salary. Going after established players marked a definite escalation of hostilities, but it was Pasquel's attitude that must have angered the major league owners even more. The *Laredo Times* story quoted him as follows: "'That is nothing,' smiled the head of the so-called 'outlaw' league. Next season he said he hopes to get sluggers Hank Greenberg and Ted Williams of the Detroit Tigers and Boston Red Sox, respectively."[61] The U.S. baseball world was predictably aghast at these declarations. Feller, Williams, and Greenberg were baseball icons. The combative tones were not simply from the way the story was written but in Pasquel's responses as well. Answering the criticism of his league and its tactics, Pasquel said, "We are ready to fight with them in any way that may be necessary. If they want to come and scrap it out they'll have to put out $30,000,000."[62] Furthering the millenarian nature of his league, he declared that a two million dollar, 52,000-seat "baseball city, excelling any baseball park in the United States" would soon be built with cushioned seats. Ironically, while later rejecting Pasquel's contract offer, Bob Feller added credibility to Pasquel's millenarian baseball movement by confirming the possibility of "America's pastime" truly becoming international. Feller, a veteran of Latin American baseball, was interviewed in the March 8 *Laredo Times*:

"Regular international Baseball competition is only a couple of years away." Feller proclaimed that when it finally happened he would be playing for the United States. Denying any offer from Pasquel to him, Feller continued to ruminate on the prospects for Latin American baseball, ". . . international competition is just around the corner. They're playing it in a great number of countries now and our armies have carried it around the world. It wouldn't surprise me if a city like Mexico City was in some major league some time."[63]

The commissioner's office was not idle during these final weeks before the start of the season. Chandler traveled to Havana to establish an agreement with Cuban and Mexican baseball that would bring these countries into accord with major league plans. The Cubans were the only ones in place, however, and Chandler's accord with them, among other things, prevented Cubans from signing "ineligibles" to play in that country. Pushing the Cubans to this position was a hard-nosed effort by major league baseball to force Mexican compliance by restricting opportunities for ballplayers who used winter ball in Cuba as an economic supplement. He also brought Cuba into a closer relationship with U.S. baseball by initiating the entry of the Havana franchise into the International League (a U.S. minor league). While offering "outlaw" players an opportunity to return before the onset of the season, Chandler held the threat of a five-year banishment over their heads.

Responding to the olive branch offered by the commissioner, Pasquel said that he might consider the proposal of a United States-Mexico-Cuba agreement; "If they want to make an agreement giving us treatment like the really big league we are, we're ready to enter into it. Otherwise we are ready to give them a terrific fight they never expected to have."[64] Brother Bernardo was busy issuing press statements that were even more uncompromising and inflammatory. Speaking from Havana he declared, "If the U.S. baseball officials want a war, they will have it. Mexico is out to destroy the United States monopoly on baseball."[65] Clearly the Pasquels had no intention of backing down. To the contrary, they seemed more bellicose the closer the 1946 season loomed. In Bernardo's line lies the core issue for what was emerging as major league baseball's toughest test: a challenge to it as an unregulated monopoly both within and outside of the United States.

The attacks and counterattacks occurred on a regular basis with each side depicting the other as contemptible. The Mexicans saw U.S. baseball as monopolistic oppressors, while the major leagues saw the Mexicans as low grade. As the season opener neared Pasquel continued his encroachments. He announced his signing of unattached, professional umpires from the United States for his upcoming season.[66] The first round of this rapidly escalating battle ended on March 12 when Commissioner Chandler announced the five-year suspension of players who had signed with the Mexican League if they failed to return before the beginning of the Major League season, effective one month from that day.

## The Season Begins and the Signing War Continues

The sun shone brightly on March 21, 1946 for Opening Day in Mexico City. It did likewise in Puebla, Tampico, and Torreon, all of which hosted the first games of the season. In the capital, Mexican President Manuel Avila Camacho threw out the first ball in a sold-out stadium of 30,000 for a game between Veracruz and the Mexico City.

Even as the season opened, Americans were still being actively recruited to play for the "Peso-curcuit," as the American press referred to the Mexican League. Contract disputes between players and owners contributed mightily to the recruitment efforts of the Pasquel brothers. Probably the biggest major leaguers to sign on were Mickey Owen, catcher for the Brooklyn Dodgers, and St. Louis Browns' shortstop Vern Stephens.

On March 29 a small article appeared in the *Laredo Times* indicating that, in light of the refusal of the Dodgers to tender him a new contract, Owen might consider the generous five-year offer with a $12,500 signing bonus made by Pasquel. Vern Stephens traveled to Laredo the following day to meet with Alfonso Pasquel and discuss the terms of the offer. Stephens and Owen were both given three-year contracts that vastly exceeded any they would have received in the U.S. Vern Stephens, 1945 home run leader in the American League, signed a particularly generous contract that called for him to be paid $25,000 a year for three years.

Pasquel was able to take particular advantage of teams with parsimonious owners, most notably the Dodgers. An April 8 Laredo Times editorial chastised the Brooklyn owner: "Branch Rickey's penny-pinching tactics kicked back in the latter two cases [a reference to Olmo and Owen]. The trouble with the Mahatma of Montague Street is that he can't get himself out of St. Louis. Although now in the rich field that is Brooklyn, he quibbled with Owen and Olmo until they took wings in self-defense."[67]

Early season drama revolved around Owen and Stephens. The press bristled with reports of these men, their dealings with the owners of the Dodgers and Browns, and the Pasquels. Overshadowed in all this were the signings of at least fifteen other major leaguers, among them Sal Maglie, Max Lanier, and George Zimmerman. What made the cases of Owen and Stephens newsworthy was their established major league credentials, and their willingness to act against baseball's reserve system in which players were tied to their clubs in perpetuity.

Arriving in Mexico City with his signing bonus in hand, Stephens, however, lasted only one week before bolting back to the U.S. on April 6, amid threats from Pasquel that he would sue for $100,000. The U.S. press elaborated on Stephens's disillusionment with both Mexico and the Mexican League. Much of what he declared as intolerable rings of the entitlement of a spoiled athlete, but the press made sure to pick up Stephens's negative imagery: "It was like a concentration camp in Mexico," he was quoted as saying. "Everyone with six-shooters on the hip. Mr. Pasquel is the nicest guy in the world, but I want to play baseball. The low caliber play and the high altitudes in Mexico got me down. So did the *no spika da English*." In his interview with the *New York Times*, Stephens elaborated on his adjustment problems:

> Most players from the United States are bothered by the language. They don't know what's being said to them. . . . "After two days you start talking to yourself," said Stephens. . . . The ball parks themselves are a far cry from major league diamonds, and to this too the players object. . . . "There is no grass on the infields. The ground is hard and rocky. . . ." No park has a shower or dressing facilities for the players. They must do all this at the hotel and sometimes there is little or no water in the hotels. . . . The dugouts are small, dingy and with no semblance of air. . . . "When you do find a shower," Stephens growled, "you have to be careful. The tap marched 'C' doesn't mean 'cold,' it means 'hot.'" The Mexican word for hot is "caliente."[68]

In the light of difficulties in language and culture experienced by Latino players coming to the United States, showering and playing field conditions seem to pale as reasons for leaving. Stephens obviously had never played much in the U.S. minor leagues or barnstormed around the country, where he might have complained of the same things. As we shall see in Chapter 6, American players today continue to have difficulties with cultural adjustments in Mexico.

Other news reports, however, contradicted Stephens's view of the Mexican League. Veteran sportswriter Rud Rennie, traveling to Mexico City to examine the situation American players were facing there, filed this report: "American players getting in at the beginning of this program are falling into a gold mine. And Vern Stephens ran out on all this. He's crazy. . . . Stephens is strictly a sucker. He should have fulfilled the contract and bought the Browns. . . . As things are, all Junior Stephens has to look forward to is additional years of underprivileged slavery."[69]

Other players in Mexico characterized their conditions positively. Mickey Owen, for instance, beamed, "I'm perfectly happy here. My wife likes Mexico and we moved into this super-modern apartment today and everything is just dandy."[70] Ex–New York Giant Danny Gardella concurred. Walking down a peaceful street in Mexico City, he felt happy to be in Mexico. Alejandro Carrasquel was also glad to be rid of his former team, the Chicago White Sox. Many felt that Mexican owners were more fair than their American counterparts. Commented Owen, "The Mexican League is, perhaps, the most democratic in the world. Here they pool 75 percent of the gate receipts for a common fund."[71]

The flight of Stephens back to the St. Louis Browns angered Jorge Pasquel. His league could ill afford a desertion so early, especially of one of their genuine stars. While Stephens was in Houston awaiting an opportunity to rejoin the Browns, Pasquel's people upped their offer to him: $25,000 a year for five years with $50,000 deposited into a New York bank as a guarantee. Stephens, however, declined and Pasquel quickly marshaled his legal staff to sue Stephens for breach of contract. The latter claimed that he had called Pasquel and informed him by phone that he was "as of now resigning from your league, under the provisions of our contract," which Stephens claimed allowed for it to be terminated "at any time by either party." To finalize the walkout, Stephens announced, "I am returning the $5,000 bonus they gave me when I signed a three-year contract."[72]

Pasquel formally complained to the Mexican Embassy and even went to the American Embassy to inquire about bringing Stephens to trial in Mexico for breach of contract. There was also a discrepancy between the $25,000 advance Pasquel said he had given Stephens and the $5,000 advance Stephens was prepared to return. Said Pasquel, "I am going to get even with him if it is the last thing I do. I am going to spend every cent I have to have him extradited to Mexico so that he can be tried here."[73]

But just as quickly as the story spilled onto the sports pages, the lawsuit threatened by Pasquel seemed to vanish. What originally proved so vexing for Pasquel (and contributed to the level of legal threats) was the potential defection of his other star attraction, Mickey Owen, on the heels of Stephens. That would have proven devastating for the fledgling league and its grand experiment. As it turned out, Owen did not jump back to the major leagues, and Pasquel did not act on this threat to sue Stephens.

When he left for the Navy in 1945, Owen was considered the future catcher for the Dodgers. Contract negotiations with Rickey began just before he was slated to be discharged in the spring of 1946, but not before Owen had contacted Pasquel indicating he was interested in an offer. Pasquel's agents quickly responded with an offer of $12,500 for signing, $15,000 a year for five years, transportation to and from Torreón, and living expenses, including a modern apartment for both him and his wife. In return Owen would be the player/manager for the Torreón team in the Mexican League until 1951. Owen let Rickey know what the Pasquel package was and, receiving no response, decided to take the offer. He was to be in Mexico on April 5. Three days later, however, following the desertion of Vern Stephens, Owen began to waffle as well. "Mickey Owen Rides Fence and Waits," shrieked the *Laredo Times* headline.[74] Halting in San Antonio, Owen made contact with Rickey in an attempt to find some middleground that might enable him to return.

On April 12, six days after Stephens rejoined "organized baseball," Owen announced to the press that he would indeed play in the Mexican League. The reasons varied depending on whom one spoke with. Owen claimed that when he found out that Rickey "intended to make him the whipping boy, he changed his mind. Rickey, he added, had asked him to go back and play with the Dodgers at the old salary of $14,500."[75] Branch Rickey told a different story. Owen called him from San Antonio intent upon returning to the Dodgers, claimed Rickey. "I told him at the time to apply for reinstatement, but that I thought it would be in the best interests of my club if he played with some other major league team."[76]

Although it is impossible to determine for certain who said what, a case could be made that Pasquel exploited the rift between Owen and Rickey. Three days before the Owen-Rickey conflict was decided, Pasquel announced to the press that Rickey had made a lucrative offer to Owen: "Rickey promised Owen a three-year contract at $20,000 tax free. . . . Well, it's the first time Rickey ever paid a player what he was worth. A Mexican taught him the value of his men."[77] Anyone dealing with Rickey knew that he had a history of letting people go rather than succumbing to a bidding war, all of which points to Pasquel's planting of the story to exacerbate the differences between Owen and Rickey. Pasquel then came back to Owen with a slightly better offer than originally given because to lose Owen would harm his efforts at league building. "I've won the greatest battle of my Mexican League career," crowed Pasquel as he met Owen at the airport in Mexico City.[78] If true, this masterful use of the press epitomized Pasquel's skills as a strategist.

Pasquel went on trying to sign players throughout the season. The big stars he went after with open checkbook turned him down, though not without mentioning the generosity of the offer. Bob Feller, Stan Musial, and Ted Williams all were courted and let the press know that, while not accepted, the offers were serious. Pasquel even tried to sign Jackie Robinson in his inaugural season in "organized baseball," further angering Branch Rickey.[79] Much of this had the effect of keeping major league baseball off balance by convincing owners that Pasquel might try anything, and served the players as public acknowledgment of their real worth.

## The Mexican League as Catalyst for the Players' Union

One of the most poignant criticisms leveled against major league baseball by Pasquel had to do with the collective inability of players to get salary increases from owners. Pasquel had been making the argument that the owner's monopoly had acted to suppress the players wages and that only in Mexico could these athletes get what they deserved: "Anybody who thinks we're throwing money away is wrong. The league is paying fairly for its players. The boys who run the baseball monopoly in the U.S. are scared because they pay starvation salaries to good men. The Mexican League is paying the players what they're worth and that's why they are coming to Mexico."[80]

Pasquel's framing of the argument as one of capitalist versus worker gave Pasquel the moral high ground, and was well received by various members of the U.S. press. This is somewhat ironic in light of Pasquel's generally anti-labor position, but it shows that his anti-imperialist position subsumed his views on labor.[81] The antimonopolist argument gained unexpected momentum with the emergence of the American Baseball Guild (ABG) on April 17.

Spearheaded by Boston lawyer Robert Murphy, the independently registered union sought to become the collective bargaining agent for all professional players. As news of the ABG spread, Murphy claimed that he had a "substantial membership" in at least ten major league clubs.[82] He also quickly outlined the guild's goals in a didactic tone that reflects the labor struggles of the times: "Organized baseball no longer can rule with the iron hand of an absolute dictator. From now on it must deal with organized baseball players in the form of the baseball guild. The guild's purpose is to right the injustices of professional baseball and to give a square deal to the players, the men who make possible big dividends and high salaries for stockholders and club executives."[83]

Murphy, a former examiner for the National Labor Relations Board, intended to have a team petition for labor board recognition whenever the ABG had sufficient presence with it, and announced that several "big name players" were already organizing on its behalf. The specific aims of the ABG were outlined by Murphy in an eight-point program: "(1) 50% of purchase price to go to player if sold; (2) arbitration; (3) no maximum salary; (4) minimum salary of $7,500 in big leagues; (5) greater freedom of contracts; (6) peaceful settlement of disputes with no-strike pledge; (7) bonuses, insurance, etc.; (8) all officers from players ranks." Comparing the baseball player to the Medieval serf, Murphy went on to predict that "the days of baseball serfdom will soon be over":

> Today when a player signs up with any professional club he must go where he is sent without regard for home and family ties. He must work for the club that is his master, whether he likes it or not, or as an alternative be barred forever from playing in what is called organized baseball. A laborer, an electrician, an actor can work wherever or for whomever he pleases. This is true of almost any working man or professional man except a baseball player. . . . The Poohbahs of baseball and Commissioner Chandler, their stooge lord, high executioner, could teach even a Hitler something about methods of despotism."[84]

Interestingly, while Pasquel's and Murphy's actions fed off of each other, as if they held the same views on labor and had coordinated their attacks on major league baseball, Murphy claimed he had no intention of unionizing Mexican League players. Some may have interpreted this as a snub to the league, which was, in fact, tailor-made for Pasquel's autocratic style. He enjoyed the fruits of critiquing major league baseball for being despotic and capitalist, but would brook no outside interference or working-class labor movement, or criticisms of his operations on the same grounds.

## Mid-Season Legal Donnybrooks

Much of the 1946 baseball season was taken up with legal wrangling, each side issuing accusations and injunctions, and appearing in court. Following Chandler's banishment decree, the Brooklyn Dodgers and the New York Yankees filed injunctions against the Mexican League, seeking to restrain the latter from trying to recruit its players. What prompted this legal move, in part, was the presence of Pasquel's representatives in New York for the expressed purpose of signing a Yankee player. The *Laredo Times* headlined the story, "Pasquel Out Hunting in New York," reporting, "The

Mexican league baseball representative in New York was in the open today, identified as Bernardo Pasquel, a vice-President of the league, who said he wouldn't go home until he signs a New York Yankee star . . . and had talked to several Yankees, chief among them shortstop Phil Rizzuto who was offered $100,000 for three years, and infielder George Stirnweiss. Both refused, but Pasquel was undiscouraged."[85]

Oddly enough, Yankee owner Larry MacPhail held a relatively progressive view on the rights of dissatisfied players seeking the right to move on to the Mexican League. Commenting on the reserve clause, MacPhail said, "If, at the close of the 1946 season we fail to come to an agreement with any player on salary, he will have a right to go to Mexico or any place else if he can better himself. I don't think it's right to keep a man out of baseball because you cannot meet his terms."[86] Nevertheless Bernardo Pasquel was unsuccessful in signing one of MacPhail's players.

Though the ethics and legality of the attempted signings by Pasquel were being painted in the most unflattering and un-American terms, the ideology that the Pasquels used was the same antimonopolist argument that was used by the American Baseball Guild.[87] In fact, on the same day that New York Supreme Court Justice Julius Miller reserved decision on the New York Yankees' move to make permanent the injunction against the Mexicans, Pasquel was considering a court date on the Mexican League's contention, in the same court, that baseball in the United States was a monopoly and in violation of antitrust legislation. In this sense he foreshadowed the removal of trade barriers that has recently been ushered in by the North American Free Trade Agreement.

The attacks from the Mexican League, irksome enough to major league baseball, rattled them even further when the American Baseball Guild, in a flanking move, took on the national pastime in court. A small story in the May 17 *Laredo Times* indicated that the ABG had "all but two or three members of the Pittsburgh Pirates as members and served notice on President William Benswanger that it intended to begin collective bargaining negotiations very shortly."[88] Three weeks later the *New York Times* ran a longer story on the actual guild petition, which argued that the Pirates had formed a company union in order to undermine the ABG. Reading from the petition delivered in court, the attorney for the ABG declared, "On or about June 5, 1946, the company [Pittsburgh Athletic Company, owners of the team], by its officers and agents refused to bargain collectively with the American Baseball Guild, a labor organization duly designated by a majority of employees, in an appropriate unit as their representative and at all times since such dates it has refused and does now refuse to bargain collectively with said organization."

At various times subsequent to June 5, 1946, the company, by its officers and agents, has urged employees to deal with the management of the company through a players' committee instead of through the American Baseball Guild.[89]

These charges and countercharges between major league baseball and the Mexican League and the ABG went on continuously from May to July, at which point the major league club owners finally made a concession: in a "precedent-shattering move, . . . a joint committee of the National and American leagues. . . voted to consult the players in drafting a new uniform player contract," reported the *Laredo Times*. Significant in this story was the combined effect that both the Mexican League and the ABG had on shifting the owners thinking; the action "clearly was . . . designed to combat the American Baseball Guild and the players raids made by the Mexican League."[90] While the concession was minuscule by comparison to the post-reserve conditions of today's players, it marked the first time that these major league owners had had to make any concessions at all.

Which of the two was more effective in forcing change is debatable, but at least one *New York Times* writer argued for Murphy: "The Pasquel brothers, with their many millions and Mexican League, take one or two players at a time. Murphy, with nothing more than an idea, takes an entire club at a crack."[91] Pasquel had his rooters as well; one writer declared that "it remained for the Pasquel brothers of Mexico to strike the greatest blow for ball players freedom."[92] Another New York writer pointed to Jorge Pasquel's ability to critique major league baseball as regressive, as well as offer American players an alternative in moving players' interests ahead.[93] Whichever of the two were more effective may be difficult to assess, but it was clear that the Mexican League gained more from these attacks. Murphy's attempt at unionization ultimately bore some fruit, but undermined the existence of the union in favor of a series of concessions by owners. Writing of the impact of Murphy's efforts, economist Andrew Zimbalist writes:

> A joint committee was formed to discuss player contracts, and in 1947 a variety of reforms emerged: Baseball's first pension fund with owner and player contributions was set up; a minimum salary was established at $5,500 along with a maximum salary cut of 25 percent in the option year; spring training expense money for the players was introduced at $25 a week; the ten-day severance clause in the player's contract was increased to thirty days; the owners allowed two player representatives to attend meetings of their executive council although the players had no vote and could only attend when matters of player welfare were being discussed explicitly.[94]

## Major League Baseball Becomes Politically Isolated

The remainder of the season continued as a war of words in the press. What emerges is a picture of major league baseball as an entitled entity, struggling to maintain its position as a monopoly. While it may have liked to have had the press view the encroachments of the Mexican League as a purely nationalist issue, there was little sentiment for this position from sectors of the American sport establishment or from the State Department. If one reads the material it eventually seems as if major league baseball was somewhat isolated. It is also abundantly clear that Pasquel used a series of ploys to intimidate Commissioner Chandler and to fan the nationalistic flames among his countrymen. The reports coming out of Mexico City often used the language of combat to describe what Pasquel might do or to color the position of major league baseball: "We are ready to fight with them in any way that may be necessary. If they want to come and scrap it out they'll have to put out $30,000,000";[95] or "If the U.S. baseball officials want a baseball war, they will have it."[96] Referring to the contract breach by Vern Stephens and his protection by Chandler's office, Pasquel combined elements of nationalism and economic harassment: "I am going to show those baseball club owners in the United States who I am. I am going to fight them with everything I have. Of course I cannot lick them because they are big and belong to the biggest country in the world. But I am going to make them pay two and three times the salary that they now pay to their players, you'll see."[97]

The threat of the Mexican League could not be confined to a nationalist encroachment. Labor issues, we have seen, also loomed large. A number of members of the press pointed to the constraining influences of the reserve system in baseball [98]:

> But even without the legal technicalities that are more awesome than Bobby Feller's fast one, it is fairly evident that the boys from below the border have something when they holler "wolf" on the major league magnates.
>
> The players as a whole do not get a fair shake. They can't enter organized ball without signing of these contracts—and yet once they do, they are dead ducks.[99]

Other criticisms of major league baseball came from odd quarters. The athletic director of Louisiana State University, Red Heard, pointed to the poetic justice of the Mexicans' "raiding" of major league baseball: "They [major league scouts] have been raiding the campuses for twenty-five years, their scouts following college games as scouts of the Mexican League follow theirs."[100]

The State Department and the Mexican Embassy also felt that the position taken by major league baseball against the Mexican League worked at cross-purposes with international goodwill. The Mexican Embassy was quick to chastise Chandler's office for "missing the international pitch of a lifetime."[101] Commenting in the *New York Times* of April 6, one official, speaking for the Mexican ambassador, asked,

> Why all this fuss over some American players going to Mexico? It looks like a rare opportunity for baseball to go to bat in furthering the exchange of interna-

tional ideals. Here we are with the United Nations meeting in New York and baseball finds in its lap this rare opportunity for a practical demonstration of spreading ideas from one country to another.

Sportsmanship is a wonderful medium for learning about democracy. Both of our countries feel that athletics are vitally important in this respect. They could be used to tighten relationships between peoples. We exchange students, professors, artists and workers and so on, so why not ball players? After all, we learned baseball from Americans.

We even borrowed American coaches to teach our youngsters to play your game. Now that we're coming of age in the sport, are we to be cut off from this relationship? In the past Mexican players have played in American leagues, so why not the other way around?[102]

Here the Mexican Embassy is asking a series of questions that pose United States–Mexican relations as an equal partnership, as an "exchange of international ideals" when in reality major league baseball viewed it as one of hegemony. "Why not the other way around?" Because baseball's function was already being put forward as cultural imperialism, "to follow the flag."[103] The spread of the game was not one of international exchange to U.S. owners, but rather one of demonstrating U.S. political, economic, and cultural domination. Nevertheless, the benevolence of the Mexican embassy's message was echoed by the U.S. press in metropolises like New York, and burgs like Laredo.

Five days later, on April 11, the State Department echoed the Mexican sentiments when an official said that the major leagues were hurting efforts to build good relations between the countries; the official wished "'baseball would show some indication of a desire to clean up' its differences with the Mexican League." "Baseball is making it tough on us. We try to build up good will and this sort of thing tears it down. All of the responsibility isn't on one side, but we wish baseball would show some indication of a desire to clean this thing up. . . . The Mexican Government certainly will be angry over such statements as those attributed to [Vern] Stephens that big-shots down there go around with six-shooters on their hips."[104] Hence, the State Department was asking major league baseball and the commissioner to end the now-embarrassing problem: "We carry on other sports activities with Mexico in amateur, school and college fields with no difficulties, but this baseball squabble may make it embarrassing to continue those associations," said the State Department official.[105]

Put on the defensive by both governments, Chandler responded tartly, "The State Department has enough to do without meddling in baseball." The commissioner, formerly a U.S. senator from Kentucky, then attempted to show up the State Department by pointing to their own potential hypocrisy: "Suppose the Mexican Government did not recognize American oil concessions in that country. What do you think our State

Department would do about that? Don't you suppose they would put up a protest?"[106]

With these exchanges, the isolation of major league baseball was beginning to increase, prompting more editorials that called for settlements between the leagues rather than compliance from the Mexicans. Senior *New York Times* sportswriter Harry Grayson echoed the sentiments of both governments when he opined about the international implications of this situation:

> Here is a golden opportunity for Organized Baseball to further international ideals by helping instead of batting its brains out trying to disparage the newcomer south of the border. . . . For instance, wise baseball heads could advise señor don Jorge Pasquel to balance his teams before the opening of the season instead of shifting players from one outfit to another overnight. . . . Don Jorge Pasquel naturally is peeved at the dog-in-the-manger attitude major league owners are taking toward his efforts to make the game a popular and flourishing one in his native land. . . . With their fervor and the $100,000,000 behind them, one would think Organized Baseball would leap at the chance to play ball with the Pasquel brothers. There probably is nothing wrong with them that a little diplomacy wouldn't cure. Indeed, the major leagues could use all five of the Pasquels. What an improvement they'd be over some of the skinflints now running big league clubs.[107]

With the formal positions of each government put forward, the rhetoric turned decidedly nationalistic, but not antagonistic. Rather, the State Department was taking a conciliatory tone in its pronouncements, isolating major league baseball as the culprit and expressing the desire for "goodwill." Mexico was in accord, tactfully claiming that Pasquel was merely doing to the United States what the United States had done to Mexico without a thought to the local consequences. Pasquel more than anyone knew when to sound the nationalist theme, when to use it threateningly, and when to sound the call for binational harmony.

The American players in Mexico also contributed to the dialogue, as when Owen declared the Mexican League to be the "most democratic league in the world," but Danny Gardella, another "jumper," also chastised U.S. baseball along internationalist lines. Claiming that Commissioner Chandler and the owners were tarnishing the American image in the eyes of the Mexican sports public, he said:

> U.S. baseball has a chance to let its players come to Mexico and show the Mexicans what our country is like through a clean sport. But what do the money-bags up there do? A handful of birds like Branch Rickey, President of the Brooklyn Dodgers, are being unfair to America as a whole because they are kicking their neighbors in the face. They [the owners] got a chance to teach people [Mexicans] democracy through America's own game, but they fail to cooperate.[108]

Eventually, even the major league owners broke ranks. In late June, St. Louis Cardinals owner Sam Breadon traveled to Mexico City to confer with Jorge Pasquel, and in so doing demonstrated the growing dissatisfaction with Chandler felt among owners. When Breadon arrived in Mexico City, a "high powered limousine with Bernardo Pasquel, one of the five brothers,"[109] whisked him off to meet with Jorge. When the story broke on June 21, Breadon claimed his purpose was merely individual fact-finding, but he indirectly pointed to the absence of direct links of communication between U.S. owners and the Pasquels: "I'm here simply as an individual... I wanted to find out what was going on down here, so I came. I doubt that anyone at home knows where I am. Certainly I am not here representing anyone but Sam Breadon.... I haven't seen [Ford] Frick, [William] Harridge [presidents of the National and American Leagues, respectively], nor Chandler in weeks."[110]

The media speculated that Breadon might be in Mexico trying to sell the Cardinals to the Pasquels, a notion that would further fuel the ire of the owners. Also, some speculated that he was there to stem any further incursions by the Pasquels into his organization. Three players, Lou Klein, Fred Martin, and Max Lanier, had signed on with the Mexican League. Upon his return the following day, Breadon briefed the press that the issue of "raiding" U.S. baseball had not been brought up, and that he had "insisted there was nothing to rumors which sprung up during his trip that he might be negotiating for the sale of his club."[111]

The VIP treatment was extended to include a full dose of Pasquel forthrightness and charm. Explaining their intentions to Breadon, the Pasquels presented a human face to what had been a "foreign menace," and this impacted on Breadon's description of what the Pasquels were attempting to do: "They think they are doing the honorable thing in building up baseball for Mexico. They believe they merely are retaliating in a big way for what American baseball scouts in the past have done to Mexican baseball in a small way. Scouts from the United States didn't hesitate to sign players they found in Mexico and the Pasquels believe they have the right to sign any of our players in retaliation."[112]

Coming from the owner of a major league team, such objectivity was completely unexpected, but in such a pronouncement Breadon was in all likelihood indicting Commissioner Chandler for his handling of the issue. The *Laredo Times* ran an Associated Press story on June 29 that seemed to lay this out when it quoted Breadon as saying, "We are involved in a baseball war with Mexico and there is threat of a union among our players, but the Commissioner is up in Dakota sliding bases instead of doing something about it."[113] Filed from Cleveland, the story goes on to interpret the Breadon visit in two ways: as a snub of Chandler and as capitulation to "the enemy." The horn of nationalism had been sounded linking the "baseball

war" to political relations, and the presence of Breadon in Mexico frater-
nizing with the enemy was echoed in the following editorial:

> The man in the street . . . must feel that the big circuits lost face when the Presi-
> dent of the St. Louis Club sought out the chief of the baseball outlaws. It appears
> very much as if Breadon got down on his hands and knees and begged for mercy,
> "Jorge, old boy, don't swipe anymore of my players. The whole proceeding is
> absolutely un-Mexican," Breadon may have quoted, meanwhile tincturing his
> Tom Collins *con tequila* with that fine good neighbor policy which fairly frosted
> all over the injunction brought by the New York Yankees against the Pasquels.[114]

A subtheme, nationalist antagonism, never really came to dominate the
interpretation of the Mexican League's incursions. The press, players,
fans, and even some of the owners never quite took the bait.

Pasquel had no way of knowing that the press would distance itself from
major league baseball as much as it did. He had no idea that Americans
would see the baseball conflict with Mexico as partly a labor issue and
partly about weak leadership in major league baseball, with only a small
degree of nationalism involved.

The acrimony between the Mexican League and Major League baseball
was often seen as a personal conflict between Pasquel and Chandler, and
indeed it grew to be. Fortunately for Pasquel, the American press was
sufficiently distanced from Chandler to report Pasquel's side of the story
when and how he wanted it. In one typical exchange in the press, Pasquel
responded to the claim that Chandler's "office does not recognize Mexican
baseball because we've had nothing official on it."[115] Pasquel lashed back,
"Chandler says he has never officially heard about us. Well, I have never
officially heard of him either. I have merely heard of him through the
newspapers, and have heard that he is just a puppet in the hands of the club
owners."[116] This was delightfully carried throughout the press. Whenever
Chandler responded to the Mexican League with suspensions or when
major league owners filed injunctions against Pasquel, the latter responded
with nationalist-tinted threats.[117] This form of attack was fairly constant
through the season, as evidenced by the following stories reported from
opposite ends of the season. Back in early March when Chandler was in
Havana trying an end run around the Mexicans by enlisting other Latin
American baseball countries as allies against Pasquel, Bernardo Pasquel
was quoted as saying, "If the U.S. baseball officials want a baseball war,
they will have it."[118] When, in mid-August, Mickey Owen again leaped
back to the United States in hopes of reinstatement, the *Sporting News*
went on to report that former Dodger Luis Olmo would also seek reinstatement. Already angry with Owen's move, Pasquel became furious after
the report. The *Laredo Times* story reported:

Pasquel's latest fireworks were directed at J. Taylor Spink, publisher of the baseball weekly, the *Sporting News* of St. Louis. Pointing out that "we contracted 20
American big league players" in 1946, Pasquel told Spink in a telegram, "You
will be surprised to see what North American players will make up the Mexican
League for 1947."

Pasquel declared open warfare on the U.S. major leagues last week after
Mickey Owen, former Dodger catcher, jumped don Jorge's own Veracruz
team. . . . Pasquel said the "truce" was off and his agents were "working hard"
again to lure players to his Peso Circuit.[119]

## Babe Ruth Visits Mexico

Hostile threats and rhetoric are not the only ways to play the nationalist
card. Pasquel also used revered baseball figures to make his points. Baseball's greatest icon was Babe Ruth. Later in his life when Ruth was ignored
by the U.S. baseball establishment, Pasquel invited him Mexico. As he had
done in hiring Rogers Hornsby to manage in the 1944 season, bringing
Ruth to Mexico would, it was thought, stir up fan excitement. It would also
be carried in the American papers. The *Laredo Times* printed two stories on
April 27 and 30, announcing "Pasquel to Talk With Bambino" and "Ruth
May Become Commissioner of Baseball." As early as February 28 there
was a small story in the Laredo papers suggesting Ruth might be brought
on to manage a Mexican League team. The articles themselves revealed
few details but the headlines proposed the possibility of yet another swipe
at Chandler. Earlier in the month, Pasquel, in one of his nose-tweaking
moods, told the American press that his brother Bernardo had cabled
Chandler with a job offer in Mexico: to run his league at $50,000 a year for
five years with living expenses. The offer to Chandler to "jump" to his
league was pure media hype and illustrated Pasquel's willingness to wage
his "war" with major league baseball almost as guerrilla theater. So it was
too with his invitation to Ruth, who would make a better story in the press
than an actual commissioner. Prior to leaving for Mexico City, Ruth, recalling his trip to Japan for an exhibition series in 1931, espoused an internationalist position on the game, and in doing so struck a blow against the
baseball-as-American-hegemony position: "'Baseball belongs to the
world,' opined Ruth, 'not only to the United States. The Japanese, for
example, were insane about the game before the war. On my visits there I
knew of well-to-do business men getting up at 5 o'clock in the morning to
play it before going to business. Such enthusiasm should be encouraged, so
why knock the Mexican effort?'"[120]

On April 29 Ruth and his family were the guests of Pasquel, but instead of being put up at his home, where those he was seriously interested in were housed, they were put up at a hotel. As Ruth was shown around Cuernavaca and Acapulco, little of his future was discussed. Having essentially vacationed in Mexico at Pasquel's expense, yet keeping at a distance, Ruth was finally asked to give an exhibition of his hitting prowess, becoming little more than a circus sideshow. This somewhat pathetic occurrence happened at the end of May, when Ruth "appeared to give an exhibition of the famed swing that made him all-time home run king of the major leagues of America."[121]

In front of 22,000 spectators in Mexico City's Delta Park, the fifty-one-year-old Ruth stepped to the plate attired in "a red and white athletic shirt, gray slacks, a red baseball cap, and spiked shoes." Unbeknownst to Ruth, an argument between Cuban pitcher Ramon Bragaña and Mexico City manager Ernesto Carmona was brewing over how to pitch to him. Bragaña, of the 1935 La Junta team and one of the Mexican Leagues all-time best pitchers, was a fiercely proud man who would not agree to pitch Ruth easy-to-hit balls. "Bragaña tried to make it a pitching exhibition,"[122] declared the committee that leveled a suspension on him after he got into a fistfight with Carmona. The latter asked Bragaña to let another hurler, Romo Chávez, pitch to Ruth, thus further offending Bragaña, who insisted on pitching to the home run king.

Ruth remained oblivious to this backdrop as he put his out-of-shape and aging body in the batter's box. The following description provides a sad picture of the man:

> Then the Babe went to the plate and waggled a big bat. He cocked his right foot as he used to at Yankee Stadium, but the resemblance ended there.
>
> Ruth swung futilely at the pitches of Bragaña. He finally hit a foul tip, then sent a lofty fly into right center. The Bambino apparently hurt his right elbow and rubbed it vigorously. However, he kept swinging for another 10 minutes, mostly fanning or popping up weakly to the infield.
>
> Finally he rapped a hard liner deep against the right field stands 375 feet away and later connected for a 390 foot home run into the right center stands. . . . The fans greeted him with a great ovation when he first appeared, but got a little restless when he failed to deliver.[123]

Before this exhibition, Ruth had tried to show the pitching form that, earlier in his career, made him one of the premier pitchers of the American League, which turned out to be even more tragicomic than his batting: "Mexican League President Jorge Pasquel, wearing a white silk shirt, stood behind the bat as catcher and Veracruz third baseman Burbuja Vazquez was the hitter. Vazquez never got a cut at the ball. Ruth spent five minutes trying to throw two balls at one time. They generally squirted out of his hands, far wide of the plate, although Pasquel managed to get his hands on a couple of them."[124]

This woefully inept display and the fan reaction was not lost on Pasquel, although it appears he had never really entertained the notion of hiring Ruth to manage or serve as his commissioner. Ruth left Mexico as ignored as he had been in the United States. As a gringo icon who could be appropriated by Pasquel, however, Ruth was invaluable. And so for a month in 1946, Pasquel bought the bragging rights, such as they were, of yet another American baseball symbol for his collection.

Pasquel did many small things that were designed to annoy major league baseball rather than threaten it. His audacious job offer to Chandler aside, Pasquel would also plant grandiose stories of the future Mexican League. Painting the Mexican League as a visionary would, Pasquel often presented "future plans" that would tempt even the top major leaguers. His signing bonuses and contracts were widely known, but he also intended or at least publicly declared grandiose plans for building world-class stadiums in the cities housing Mexican League teams.[125] Along these lines, a winter league was planned so that Americans coming to Mexico would have more ample economic opportunity. The *Laredo Times* reported his ruminations on this plan: "'I think the winter idea is a good one for the players who want to stay in Mexico between regular seasons,' he said. If some of the players don't want to compete during the winter months, Pasquel said he would try to find other jobs for those who desire to set up permanent homes south of the Rio Grande."[126]

Taken together, Pasquel's handling of the press, his ability to take advantage of splits within the American baseball community, and his media presence all made his nationalistic message a more palatable one to people in the United States.

## The Two Laredos in the Pasquel Conflict

As noted in Chapter 1, the view of the border held by those far removed from it in both the United States and Mexico was anything but flattering. This was the case when it came to baseball as well. The citizens of the two Laredos were proud of their entry into the league, its history, and its accomplishments, but further away, *New York Times* sportswriter Arthur Daley disparaged the Mexican League as a whole, and Nuevo Laredo in particular. Commenting on how the Mexican League could not possibly provide the environment for real top-flight baseball, Daley concluded, "The harried moguls are asking each other how a town like Nuevo Laredo (population 10,000) can support ex-major leaguers in better style than that to which they are accustomed."[127]

After finishing second in 1945, La Junta was hoping to contend for the title the next season. Playing in the smallest stadium in the league (7,500 seats), and the furthest from the country's capital, Nuevo Laredo nevertheless had fielded a very scrappy team that reflected the border well. The owners, Colonel Rafael Pedrajo, Federico Longoria, and Pedro DeLeón sent Arturo García, the Tecolotes manager, out to scout talent with the equivalent of $60,000 at his disposal.[128] Many of the team's starters would return, led by their league-leading pitcher, twenty-three-game winner Agapito Mayor. It was hoped that the addition of major league talent would be the ingredient needed to win a championship.

Laredo's role in these events was supportive, to be sure, but included supplying talent. When in early preseason, with the La Junta team was still in the formation process there was talk of finding some players from the Laredo side. The February 4 *Laredo Times* reported, "One of the club advisors stated that arrangements were being made to have Laredo represented on the La Junta team. Nothing is definite but there is a strong likelihood that Freddie Levendecker, local schoolboy star . . . might join their ranks."[129]

Levendecker played at the outset of the season, but faded from view once the team solidified its roster with a combination of more established foreign players and Mexican returnees. Laredo's reduced role in the baseball scene was not taken all that lightly. Having its own tradition of and identity with the game, the city attempted to start a team that would retain some semblance of the game north of the border: "To give baseball-hungry fans what they want Laredo sportsmen are seriously considering starting a local baseball team with Pat McLaughlin, former pitcher with the Detroit Tigers, as their playing manager. . . . Since Laredoans have always been strong for the national pastime, local promoters feel that a good baseball club here would not only provide the city with some much needed athletic entertainment but would also be a paying proposition."[130]

As the conflict between Mexican and U.S. leagues escalated into an international media event, the Laredo experiment faded. This process was furthered by the amateur nature of Laredo's team, the Laredo Cardinals. The history of barnstorming semi-professional teams that characterized the region had begun to look a bit thread bare in the face of the organized, well-financed Mexican League. After a severe beating at the hands of the San Antonio Missions of the Texas League, the *Laredo Times* reluctantly admitted that the city's baseball experiment was in trouble: "Manager George Peters is having a lot of trouble booking games for his Laredo Cardinals since the locals played the San Antonio Missions of the Texas League here last Sunday. 'Since we played the Missions other teams around here seem to have gotten cold feet,' Peters said. 'We didn't beat the

Missions, in fact we lost 11–3. But we did give them a good game. We're ready to play any team, anywhere, anytime and for almost any amount,' Peters said today."[131] And, while local favorites such as pitcher Fernando Dovalina was still capable of generating excitement, it was clear that his era and that of semi-pro teams had passed.

For La Junta the season began on the road with the team losing four of its first six games. As the team limped home to Nuevo Laredo, they hoped to turn things around. The *Laredo Times* boldly reported, "La Junta To Get Giants' Players." Sal Maglie, a well-known pitcher whose name excited people on both sides, was mentioned as a possible addition to the twin border towns: "With dismissal of three players by the New York Giants yesterday, including a pitcher, La Junta is expecting to get one of these to bolster the club's pitching staff, it was intimated by Manager García. The pitcher is Sal Maglie, 28-year old Giant right-hander. The others are first baseman Roy Zimmerman and second baseman George Hausmann."[132]

The next day the Laredo press retracted their story on Maglie, announcing instead that he might be assigned to the Tampico franchise. He eventually wound up with Pasquel's Veracruz team which, in contrast to the oft-promoted ideology of equal distribution of foreigners, wound up with the best players. Nuevo Laredo did receive several players, including Roy Zimmerman and Tom Gorman (who went on to become a highly respected umpire), and a Pacific Coast League pitcher named Earl Porter. The latter was a bright spot in an otherwise dreary season. The ill-wind continued to blow, with La Junta unable to reach higher than seventh place, a situation that led to a flurry of trades and signings.[133] Through mid-May La Junta's record was 11–15.

Going into mid-July the Nuevo Laredo team began to show signs of turning things around, however. In a crucial three-game series against the star-studded Veracruz team, La Junta managed to show its character. In anticipation of a big game, the fans began lining up early the night of July 19. With the opportunity to watch former major leaguers such as Klein, Olmos, and Maglie, as well as local heroes such as Chile Gomez and La Junta's ace pitcher, Agapito Mayor, people in the two Laredos easily filled the tiny ball park. With the score tied 3–3, La Junta put together a typical leftover soup rally, starting with Roy Zimmerman doubling and two walks. Zimmerman scored the winning run when the next batter, Carlos Blanco, hit a ground ball to Veracruz infielder Lou Klein, who threw wildly to home plate. With the win La Junta's record stood at 28–28, bringing them up to fourth place.

Earlier in the evening the crowd became delirious when La Junta third baseman Carlos Blanco hit a home run just seconds after a local politician announced on the public address system that he would give Blanco twenty *pesos* if he would hit a home run. Locally, this was seen in the same light as Babe Ruth's famous "calling the shot" home run in the 1933 World Series, in which he pointed to the center field wall indicating he intended to hit a home run there, and then did.

While Laredoans were essentially reduced to cheering for their sister across the river, the town played a significant role in the dramatic wheeling and dealing surrounding the signing of foreign players. As both the northernmost extension of the Mexican League and one of the southernmost points in the United States, the two Laredos became the physical center for negotiating deals and moving players from the United States to Mexico. As a result, the Pasquels established a presence in Laredo. They built a warehouse in Laredo for the goods they regularly imported into Mexico, a structure that still stands. A Laredo mansion was also owned by the Pasquels.

Beginning with the Mickey Owen flap, Laredo became the Pasquels' "headquarters for the hiring of United States baseball stars," according to the *New York Times*,[134] and the meeting grounds for negotiations between the reluctant players and the Pasquel brothers. Treated lavishly while in Laredo, players would be presented to the press of both countries as media personalities. Vern Stephens was handled along these lines while in Laredo: "Alfonso Pasquel, who went after the home run king of the American league last year[,] came in a blood-red car, brought him from San Antonio on Friday night and lodged him at his palatial business-office-house. He stated that the Mexican League was prepared to give him anything he asked to play in Mexico. Owen arrived in Laredo where he was met by Alfonso Pasquel."[135]

To better handle these deliberations Bernardo Pasquel would stop in Laredo en route to the United States to contract players or oversee some of the lawsuits the Mexican League was handling.[136] Discussions with lawyers, meetings with American baseball officials and/or players, as well as transfers from the United States to Mexico all moved through Laredo. It is for this reason, as well as the presence of the La Junta club in the Mexican League, that the print media in Laredo was so attentive during that season.[137]

## The Conclusion of the 1946 Season

In the 1970s, with the warming of United States relations with China, international goodwill through sport became known as "ping-pong diplomacy." Nationalism, politics, and sport would come to be associated with each other. The events of the 1946 Mexican League season in some way presaged "ping-pong diplomacy" by a quarter of a century. Embassies in both countries took up the baseball issue; Miguel Alemán was able to exploit the issue in his successful bid for the presidency; and the perception that aggression against the United States could take place through our "national pastime" was not lost on politicians, baseball policy makers, or the press.

In the context of a Mexican-U.S. baseball "war," it is interesting to note that the battle lines were only erratically autonationalist. When the conflict turned autonationalist it was due to Pasquel's outrage over some move or public statement by major league baseball, and when he played this nationalist card he usually did so skillfully and with an objective in mind. Major league baseball, to be sure, would have had the press treat the conflict as a one-dimensional nationalist issue, but wound up being viewed as increasingly isolated and culpable. In part, this may have been due to the fact that baseball as a sport and cultural enterprise was not directly related to national interests and threatened no one other than owners. In part, the antagonism expressed toward U.S. interests from writers, players, and even some owners reflected the dissatisfaction with Commissioner Chandler's tenure in office. Pasquel's style served to deflect the nature of the conflict as well. Rakish and dapper, Pasquel had a presence that earned him a wide following north of the Rio Grande as well as at home. It was not even a hero's image so much as a celebrity's. Reporting on Pasquel's popularity with his compatriots, an outgrowth purely built on his posture against the United States rather than subjective feelings about the man, *New York Times* correspondent Milton Bracker wrote that interest in him and the baseball war:

> far transcends the realm of the diamond. People here who don't know third base from the bullpen are talking of the Pasquels. . . . In fact, it has even been said that not since the historic oil expropriation of March 1938 has any circumstance so delighted the Mexican national ego as that of "St. George" tilting the "dragon" of American baseball. . . . As one Mexican put it aptly, "Nobody really likes Jorge, but he's a national hero."[138]

At a time when Americans were tired of autocratic, top-down ruling, Pasquel's iconoclasm was refreshing. His *personalismo*[139] played well with the press and writers in the United States because he fused it with populism (e.g., his working in tandem with the American Baseball Guild), all the while playing the irrepressible cowboy who operated outside of the law and who embodied the hallowed American value of rugged individualism.

As for the claim that Pasquel really used the "raid" on major league baseball to get his friend Miguel Alemán elected president of Mexico,[140] I would conclude that it was a secondary motive, quite secondary to his efforts to get Mexican baseball recognized. The latter was most definitely fueled by his passion for the game, boosted periodically by his Mexican nationalism, a nationalism that was made more incendiary by American attitudes. Pasquel was no Third World lackey who subordinated himself to

his Yankee peers. When baseball's owners and commissioner acted arrogantly toward him, he responded in kind. He showed that he could give as
well as get. Faced with American dismissal of his league, Pasquel became
more entrenched in his position and became increasingly drawn into the
signings and war of words with Chandler, but his goal was always official
recognition by "organized baseball."

Before the season even started Pasquel was already making it clear that
he wanted an affiliation with major league baseball. As early as February
17, 1946, Bernardo Pasquel was vowing that "he not only will keep it
going [the new eight-team league], but develop it to the point where
American organized baseball would have to accept it as a member."[141]

Press reports scattered throughout the season reiterate this demand.
When on March 12 Chandler was busy in Havana trying to put pressure
on Latin American countries to comply with U.S. baseball's position on
renegade American players, Bernardo Pasquel was again reiterating Mexico's position. "If they [major league baseball] want to make an agreement
giving us treatment like the really big league we are, we're ready to enter
into it," Pasquel declared.[142] No less a personage than sportswriter Harry
Grayson, an outspoken critic of major league baseball, took up the call
when he wrote, "The Mexican League should be offered a classification
and given full cooperation."[143] Again at the end of June the issue of U.S.
recognition of Mexican baseball was voiced: "According to a report from
Mexico, the Pasquels want sub-major league rating and rights."[144]

That Mexicans, with their history of conflict with the United States,
and their decidedly Third World socioeconomic system, should seek to
usurp the U.S. national pastime represents an interesting twist on invented traditions. It seems that Pasquel was intent upon reinventing the
invented, by co-opting U.S. baseball to serve Mexican nationalist interests. Modeled on American major league baseball, the Mexican League
was every bit as gushing with ritual and tradition as its northern counterpart. From the opening day of the season, when President Manuel Avila
Camacho threw out the first ball in Mexico City, the game was linked
with nationhood. The structure and competition of the league itself had
the effect of regional integration, as did the playing of anthems and the
saluting of the flag before the games. In this respect, invented traditions
have a traditionalist caste. What differed in Pasquel's case was his use of
it as a weapon with which to attack the United States. Central to all this
is the multifaceted way in which nationalism is fashioned, utilized, and
modified by the forces at work: it is not a simple ideological reflex controlled by the state or other powerful agency (such as industrialists). In
this instance, Pasquel was able to secure his goal by playing out, as do
many Third World *politicos*, a strategy of nationalism and anti-imperialism. What was unexpected was his ability to garner a certain amount of

support from the very national press that he was attacking. Pasquel eventually got the Mexican League official AA standing as a minor league affiliate. Later, during the Peralta era in 1967, their affiliation was boosted to AAA standing.

Gaining such status came at a cost, however. When the 1947 season began, the numbers of players who had professional experience in the United States dropped dramatically from the 20 percent of the previous year. George Hausmann, former New York Giants second baseman, remembers contacting Pasquel for his second season in the league and being told his salary would be cut from $13,000 to $9,000 despite having had a very productive 1946 season. Financial losses mounted so that by 1948 foreign players were expected to accept a salary cap.[145] Altogether, for the three seasons 1946–1948 Gerald Vaughn has tallied the losses suffered by the Mexican League to be in the vicinity of $362,000, which was taken care of by the Pasquels. Economic catastrophe was followed by a mass exodus of former major leaguers when and where they could. Hausmann, for instance, stayed, citing that he had little choice. So in 1949 he began playing in Nuevo Laredo with his salary whittled down even more, to $5,000. Finally Commissioner Chandler lifted the ban on reinstating these renegade players, and men like Hausmann returned. The Mexican League had, by 1948, been reduced to a four-team league with all of the franchises playing their games in Mexico City, the only place the league could generate a sufficient fan base.[146] Pasquel stepped down from the post of baseball commissioner in 1949, though he continued to own the Veracruz team and remained a major presence until his untimely death in 1955, in an airplane crash. By then the league had begun to be ruled by a new strongman, Alejo Peralta.

Interestingly, Peralta was the antithesis of Pasquel in many ways, but they both claimed strong nationalist sentiments. Here too, they differed in how they expressed them. Whereas Pasquel employed the autonational antagonism associated with attacking major league baseball, Peralta boldly set out to field an all-Mexican team with his Mexico City Tigres. Many Mexican players were resentful of the number of foreigners Pasquel brought in, not to mention his special treatment of the them. Peralta's biographer claimed that August 4, 1960, was an important day in Mexican baseball history because the game was symbolically recaptured.[147] The challenge in the post-Pasquel era was one in which the league sought to recast "the Mexican League for Mexicans."[148] To this end Peralta established the concept of baseball academies, first for his own team, later for the league as a whole.[149] Changes reverberating through the league affected Nuevo Laredo's baseball fortunes as well. The team comprised a spotty presence in the league through the decade of the 1940s, although better times awaited them as 1950 dawned.

## The Tecos after the Pasquel Era: 1950–1994

Following a two-year absence after the rocky 1946 season, the Tecolotes reappeared in the Mexican League in 1949. But, whereas the Nuevo Laredo team had been the premier border baseball show since the early 1930s, for the first time in the history of border baseball there was professional baseball being played in both cities. The 1949 Laredo Apaches were charter members of the Rio Grande League which began that same year.

In its inaugural year the Rio Grande League was classified as Class D and boasted teams from all along the border, including Brownsville, Corpus Christi, Del Rio, and Harlingen. Trying out for a spot on the Laredo Apaches was yet another member of the Dovalina family, Lázaro, who was described as a "24-year-old Laredo rookie, trying out for the 'wide open" third base position. Dovalina is also a pitcher." This made it a trifecta for the Dovalina family, with three brothers playing ball for border teams. Also listed as playing on that team was thirty-five-year old Ismael Montalvo, still referred to as "Speedy" in the press. The paper acknowledged his age, but pronounced him "still a power at the plate [who] can also pitch."[150] He did not disappoint, hitting .322 with 112 RBIs that year and .334 with 18 home runs and 110 RBIs the next. In 1950, the league was upgraded to Class C baseball. For the Laredo Apaches the preseason was, one could argue, more challenging than the season itself. In 1950 their exhibitions included games against the Negro League Kansas City Monarchs and the powerful San Antonio Missions of the Texas League. To celebrate the upgrade, owner Nick Canavati went so far as to recruit Cuban ballplayers (as La Junta had done in the 1930s) to ensure a competitive season. Laredo made it to the playoffs that year, but lost to Corpus Christi in the first round. The league folded after the 1951 season. Apparently there just weren't enough solvent owners to make the league viable.[151]

In Nuevo Laredo, on the other hand, the 1950s proved to be a godsend.[152] Until 1953, no Tecolote team had climbed closer than four games to first place. In 1953, Teco owner Dr. Héctor Gonzáles decided to spend what it took to produce a contender, hiring Mexican League legend Adolfo Luque as manager as well as a new core of players.[153] Several veterans of previous lackluster Teco teams, such as Jesús Moreno and Barney Serrell, were brought back, but otherwise in 1953 the Tecos were determined not to embarrass themselves. While freely spending to buy talent does not always produce positive results, the Tecos' case paid off handsomely. In an eighty-game season, four Tecos batted over .300, and six players had over 40 RBI apiece. The pitching staff solidified around Moreno, who dominated the league that year with an 18–3 record and a 1.75 ERA. Ramiro Cuevas (father of Ricardo Cuevas, later Teco batting coach) and Martiniano Garay also had excellent years, each winning 12 games. For Cuevas, lightning was caught in a bottle on the night of August 14 in Mexico City's Delta Park. There, against the Diablos del Mexico, Cuevas caught fire, pitching the first perfect game in Mexican League history, allowing no baserunners for the entire contest. He was mobbed by the Mexican baseball world immediately afterward and went from being a serviceably good pitcher to an icon. A procession followed him to the hotel and later to the bus station when the Tecos were slated to return home. When they finally returned to Nuevo Laredo the city had given itself over to celebrating the triumph all over again, replete with convertible parade down Nuevo Laredo's main street, Guerrero Avenue, in front of thousands of cheering fans. Cuevas was also feted by the political elite and given a gold medal for sport merit during a special event in his honor. The golden season ended with the very first league championship for the frontier team.

The following year the Tecos won the championship again. Their .700 won-lost record (56–24) was by far the best in Teco history. With six .300-plus hitters and seven with 40 or more RBIs, the Teco batting order was even more potent than the previous year. Among the pitchers, Tomás Arroyo went 15–1, Ramiro Cuevas 10–7, and Jesús Moreno 13–5. The Tecos almost made it a three-peat in 1955. They tied Mexico City's Tigres on the last day of the season on the arms of Cuevas, Procopio Herrera, and Moreno. In the best-of-three-game playoff, however, they were thrashed twice.

In 1956, for reasons no one seems to be able to explain convincingly, the Tecos languished in last place, forty-one games out of first place. They did little better in 1957. With a new group of players, the 1958 Tecos won the championship for the third time in the decade. Behind batting leader Pablo Bernard and the power of Herminio Cortez, José García, and Ronaldo Camacho, the Tecos battered opposing pitchers. The Teco tradition of power hitting seems to have emerged during this period.

Even though the Tecos had a respectable year in 1959, finishing second, attendance was down significantly, prompting the owner to move his team away from the border.It would be sixteen years before the team returned to Nuevo Laredo, and in the interim the Tecos had unsuccessful stays in Puebla, Mérida, Isla Mujeres, and Villahermosa. In 1976 Tomás Herrera, a Teco player in the 1950s, sought to return the franchise to the border and, in conjunction with Cuauhtémoc Rodríguez and then-owner Ariel Magaña Carrillo, succeeded in ending the diaspora. The team played fairly poorly its first year back, finishing last in the standings, but no one seems to have minded. There was a general sense of well-being in having the Tecos again.

As 1977 dawned the team began where it had left off the previous year, playing perfectly pedestrian baseball for most of the early season. They failed to collect a single hit in a loss early in April, and suffered a 21–0 shellacking in Tampico in June; but in the final five weeks of the season they made a seemingly miraculous turnaround. Riding the born-again arm of Import pitcher Byron McLaughlin, who streaked through the months of July and August striking out batters at a record pace, the Tecos responded. McLaughlin would wind up with a record of 18–13, a 1.84 ERA, and 221 strikeouts. Jessie Trinidad, another Import, also came around, as did their top pitchers from previous years. The Tecos, ten games behind the Sultanes in late June, won twenty-four of their last twenty-eight games (including fourteen straight) to take their division title. They went on to beat Mexico City in the championship. It was a much-needed antidote to the baseball lethargy on the border. "Teco Mania" was born during that late summer run.

From 1977 to 1980 the Tecos continued to be the property of Carrillo, and enjoyed a small measure of success. This was a transition period leading to the Lozano era in 1981, but buried in obscurity was one of the best Teco pitchers of all time, Víctor García. For six years (1976–1981) of his nineteen-year baseball career, he proved dominating. Those six years were with the Tecos, coming a decade after he had entered the league. During that stretch of time García compiled a record of 86–51; and on a warm April night in the last year of his six-year "zone," García pitched a perfect game at La Junta Park in Nuevo Laredo.

In 1981 the team was bought by Nuevo Laredo trucking magnate Víctor Lozano and entered the modern era. Taking over the Tecos, Lozano and his vice president, Cuauhtémoc "Chito" Rodríguez, built the Teco machine that has been in contention virtually every season since. In the first years of the Lozano era the team once again forged an identity around power hitting. The Tecos continued to have the presence of pitchers Byron McLaughlin and Víctor García in 1981 and 1982, but what kept the team in contention was the home run combination of Alejandro Ortiz, Andrés Mora, and Carlos Soto. Through the first half of the 1980s *Los Tres Mosqueteros* (the Three Musketeers)[154] powered the team to playoff appearances in all but one season. Ortiz and Mora were charter members of what would become the 1993 Tecos. By 1984, there were five players who would still be with the team in 1993, and by 1988, there were ten Tecos who were on the 1993 roster. So much was power the signature of the team that these hitters could carry the team in seasons in which several starting pitchers had only .500 won-lost records. Fans felt that at any given moment this team could erupt for a truckload of runs, as they did on April 26, 1982, when four Tecos hit home runs in the same inning, in a span of thirteen minutes. Through the mid-1980s Teco players won home run crowns four out of five years.

By the mid-1980s the pitching once again became more consistent, focused on the efforts of Jesús Moreno Rivera and Imports such as Dave Walsh. The combinaton of power and pitching ultimately resulted in the Tecos' last Mexican League championship in 1989.

## Becoming Binational and a Community of Veterans

Two critically important features emerged during this decade: the declaration of the Tecolotes as a binational team in 1985 and the development of a large core of players who would, by 1994, become a community of veterans.

The team from Nuevo Laredo became the "Tecolotes de los dos Laredos" at the onset of the 1985 season. This was the first time on record a sports franchise had become binational, and for the most part the event went unnoticed. The formation of a binational team on this stretch of the border was only the most recent affirmation of what had been going on for a century. Still the Tecos were the first official binational sports franchise in the world.

The formulators of this team didn't see it in quite so novel terms either. For team vice president "Chito" Rodríguez and the Lozanos, Carlos Villarreal, and Larry Dovalina, it was strictly local and very much a marketing idea: "Before we played in Laredo I had started noticing that the media coverage from TV and the newspapers was as big on the U.S. side as it was on the Mexican side, and that meant that we had a lot of fans in Laredo who came to our games at La Junta Park."[155] Rodríguez initiated discussions with Laredo's politically well-placed Teco fans: assistant city manager of Laredo, Carlos Villarreal:

> Carlos Villarreal's father was a big Teco fan from the 1940s and 1950s. When baseball came back to Nuevo Laredo in 1976, Carlos's father was there, and Carlos himself followed in his father's footsteps as a fan. For example, in 1977 when we went deep into the playoffs Carlos followed the team wherever we traveled, and that's when we began to talk about bringing the team to Laredo.
>
> I first talked to Víctor [Lozano], but the one who closed the deal was [general manager] Samuel [Lozano]. Samuel was the one who pressed us to move forward and do something about it. He talked to Carlos and Larry [Dovalina], and they all talked to the mayor of Laredo, Aldo Tatangelo.[156]

As the 1985 season neared the Laredo media began to slowly warm to the idea that they too had a team. Initially Salo Otero, the sports editor for the *Laredo Morning Times*, was spare in his reporting of the formation of the two Laredos baseball venture, but within a four-week period (March 2–28), the level of discourse went from mild fascination to one heralding a new era. On March 2, in an article forecasting the new year for the Tecos, Otero brought up the new arrangement midway in a story that featured the local players on the Teco roster. Six days later he referred to the team as "Los Tecolotes de los dos Laredos, alias Nuevo Laredo's Tecolotes." Otero's editorial dug up some of the historic precedents of transnational baseball: the short-lived Pan American Association, a league that, between 1959 and 1961, fused the Texas League and the Mexican League in a seasonal thirty-six-game interlocking schedule. The hope then was that the part-time "hook up would be both profitable and pleasant."[157]

The binational effort was not simply a function of Carlos Villarreal and Larry Dovalina's exhorting the city to endorse the efforts. It involved a rather substantial amount of money to renovate West Martin Field—$700,000 to be exact, most of which Villarreal was instrumental in securing through a community development block grant. Otero's March 13 column was exclusively devoted to the impending debut of the new Two Laredos team, commenting on everything from the grant-getting coup that helped renovate the baseball park to the economic boon it would likely be for the community. Most significantly, Otero's column declared the historic importance of it all. Opening night of March 16, 1985, had all of the predictable marching bands and local pols out. Laredo Mayor Aldo Tatangelo gloated about this being "the only baseball that represents two nations."[158] Clearly the city of Laredo was sky-high for the opening of West Martin Field.

While baseball had been de facto binational or transnational for some time before 1985, it would be a mistake to think that the fans in Nuevo Laredo were beside themselves with joy. There was, and continues to be, a core of people who view the Tecos as national property. The media of Nuevo Laredo has, from time-to-time, played the antagonistic autonational card when talking about baseball in the two Laredos (see Chapter 7). The fans writing and talking to Chito Rodríguez reflected this as well, although they might have been more discreet: "At the beginning some of the fans in Nuevo Laredo didn't like it. We got a lot of calls at the office and letters in the newspapers complaining that it was the wrong thing to do, that it was for Mexican fans, that there was gonna be less home games, and they didn't like that. At that time we had a drop in attendance, maybe it was because of this or the peso devaluation of the 1980s."[159]

A March 15, 1985, editorial in the *Laredo Morning Times* echoed this as well, pointing out that while the economic crisis at the time might curb the likelihood of Nuevo Laredoans crossing the river to see their team, other factors might make it easier to see the Tecos. The editorial noted, "Thanks to modern technology . . . all 22 games played in Laredo would be aired on KLDO-TV on a delayed basis. That means that [Nuevo Laredoans] can watch the game without paying the price of admission, have a much better seat, and not have to buy their Coronas from some vender at La Junta."[160] The economic crisis eventually eased, and Nuevo Laredoans eventually warmed to the idea of the binational Tecos coming to constitute, by some estimates about 25 percent of the attendance at any West Martin Field game. Oddly enough, the reverse—the reciprocal flow of Laredoans to Parque La Junta—never was forthcoming. "It was a problem for people from Laredo to go to the park in Nuevo Laredo," commented Rodríguez.

"It was a problem because of the time change [during the summers, it is an hour earlier in Nuevo Laredo than in Laredo because of daylight savings time], because they are insecure in leaving their cars parked there, and the ballpark is not the best."[161] Others complain that the Nuevo Laredo fans are more rowdy, drunk, and unruly: "Yes, you can notice the difference in the fans right away. The fans in Nuevo Laredo are more into the game. Not that the Laredo fans are not, but the Nuevo Laredo fans express themselves more. Even when the fans come across from Mexico their behavior is a little different than when they are in their Parque La Junta. They calm down some. They know that Laredo fans and people expect different things."[162]

However one describes it, there are sociobehavioral differences between the fans of the two cities, a conflict discussed more fully in the final chapter.

A second feature that has come to characterize the Lozano era is the large core of veteran players. At times the team has come in for criticism in trading away popular players, but the fact is that as of 1993 at least ten players have been with the team for seven years, five who have been together for ten years, and three for twelve years. Ortiz began this nucleus fourteen years ago in 1982, joined by Andrés Mora a year later. Gerardo Sánchez, the Mexican League record holder for consecutive games played, joined them in 1983. Luís Fernando Díaz came aboard in 1985, and Enrique Ramírez in 1986. In 1988 five more players who would remain with the Tecos for a number of seasons joined the team.

The Teco players have grown to become a community of sorts. Even though they spend the winter months playing on different teams in the Mexican Pacific League, they, like pitcher Enrique Couoh, identify themselves as Tecos first: "Maybe because this team has been the one I played with first, but when I see others playing in the Pacific League, I feel as if we are family that is working temporarily in different places. We have been together such a long time, especially those of us who came in as a big group in 1988. We play together as a team and we never let the management or other players get in the way."[163]

# Part Two

BECOMING TECOS

# *Four*

## The Players and the Team

To PUT some flesh on the historical-structural skeleton, I have selected key personnel for which I offer biographical sketches. Clearly, the lives and careers of athletes and baseball administrators change quickly. Rookies become veterans or are dropped; injuries cut short careers; veterans finally decide or have it decided for them that their time has come; owners buy and sell players and clubs; franchises move. The world of professional sport is anything but stable, and the team that you first or last became enamored with is only a flash in time. The Tecos have gone through and will continue to go through all manner of changes. The local semi-pro La Junta club that vaulted into the Mexican League in the inaugural season of 1939 just as quickly dropped out in 1941 and 1942. Returning as the Tecolotes, the team played on the border until 1959, then deserted the area, playing in four different cities in Mexico for the next sixteen years. In 1976 the franchise was warmly welcomed back to Nuevo Laredo, where a decade later it emerged as a team straddling the international border, The Owls of the Two Laredos. The team changes as we speak.

### Team Structure

The sense of Teco community is based on a relative sense of permanence. In the world of sport, athletes all move through the life cycles at an accelerated pace. Birth to death may, in a long athletic life, be twenty years; hence a team that stays intact for five or so years begins to develop a sense of community. In real terms players play, stay, and go on at a disquieting rate. Yet despite the inevitable flux attached to the sport, the Tecos were, for a period of eight years ending after the 1994 season, one of the most stable sports franchises to be found anywhere. This section attempts to present a view of the Tecos as a collection of men, each with a story to tell, yet also a sports community. As such, there are structural relations to be described in addition to the select biographical sketches. The "ethnographic present," or moment in time in which these people are presented, is a span of two seasons, 1993 and 1994. Sources of both cohesion and tension are to be found within these stories. Issues of trust and mistrust, struggle over money and control, and personal demons are all handled differently but come to play a role within the group dynamics that have made the Tecos.

Although it is a "foreign" league, *La Liga Mexicana* is the only such league recognized by the National Association of Professional Baseball Leagues (NAPBA). Moreover, *La Liga Mexicana* enjoys the National Association of Professional Baseball Leagues (NAPBL) highest ranking, AAA status. Mexico's other league, the Mexican Pacific League, is distinguished from the Mexican League most notably by the time of year it operates—winter—and by the greater number of foreign imported players per team. The Mexican League plays at the same time as do the American major leagues, during the traditional spring and summer months (mid-March to August), a decision that is quite significant (see below).

The Tecolotes de los dos Laredos are part of the sixteen-team Mexican League, divided evenly into northern and southern zones. Being located on the northern border of the country, the Tecos are part of the northern division. Each team in the division plays a 132-game schedule, although the won-lost records may not reflect this (tie games are called after midnight and are not calculated into the standings). Beginning in 1993 the league divided the season into two parts, with points being awarded for each part according to whatever place a team finishes. The vaunted All-Star Game officially separates the two halves. The total number of points for the two parts is tabulated and the top four teams in each division go on to the championship playoffs.

Rosters are made up of twenty-five players, up to five of which may be "importados," foreign Imports, invariably from the United States, but they may also be Puerto Ricans, Dominicans, or Venezuelans. Clubs may sign Imports as free agents or, if they have "working agreements" with major league organizations, they receive an annual allotment. The remaining twenty-one players are Mexicans and are either signed as free agents for the season or, what is more likely, called up from the minor leagues. All Mexican League clubs have a minor league club from which they draw their talent.

From 1983 the league had a central academy called Pastejé, located north of Mexico City, from which all Mexican players were distributed, via a draft. Alejo Peralta, who even in retirement remains the most powerful influence in Mexican baseball, bankrolled the academy and had it built on land he owned. Following a 1993 fire that destroyed a major part of the academy, Pastejé was abandoned, but not before it had produced five generations of players (each class lasting two years). In 1995 a new facility opened, *Centro de Desarrollo del Beísbol Mexicano* (Center for the Development of Mexican Baseball), just outside of Monterrey and loosely modeled after Pastejé.

Player-management relations in Mexico still linger in an era of the reserve system. The central academy works to underscore the centralized power structure. Once signed, a player is the property of the club in perpetuity or until the club decides to sell or trade. Club owners have historically tried to exact comparatively high prices for their players when U.S. baseball scouts come to inquire. This has had the effect of dampening major league interest in Mexican players. Even if the player goes on to play in the United States, his Mexican club continues to have exclusive rights to him upon his return.

The stature of the relationship between the Mexican League club and their American affiliate is reflected in the caliber of players sent to the former. Accordingly, the Tecos probably enjoy one of the stronger relationships with an American major league team of any Mexican League organization. Chuck LaMar, Atlanta Braves Director of Player Development, saw the mutual advantages that could be had with relations in the Mexican League, but it was the future thinking of Teco Vice President Cuauhtémoc "Chito" Rodríguez that pushed for the relationship. Other Mexican League administrators sought to price their talent out of the clutches of U.S. interests. Rodríguez knew that the vast majority of his players would never make it to the major leagues, and would most likely return to play in Mexico after a few years. By making his players available to Atlanta, the player gets the advantage of receiving an opportunity to further his career, but also become trained in a way that Mexican League players rarely get. When these players return, they must return to the Mexican League club they started with and they come back schooled in baseball discipline.

## The Two Home Fields

True to their binational status, the Tecos have two home fields: Parque La Junta in Nuevo Laredo, and West Martin Field in Laredo. They play two-thirds of their home dates in the former and one-third at West Martin Field.

Parque La Junta, built in 1954, is a poured concrete, single-decked stadium that has a capacity of about 8,000. Approaching the stadium from the street one encounters a typical stadium design, a walled affair designed to keep the park and all that goes on inside separate from the warm street and people, a barrier marked by a single entryway turnstile. Upon entering, there is an antechamber, an outdoor area between the stadium proper and the walls around the park. In here can be found a bit of shared, hard-packed dirt grounds worn by the thousands of feet that hang around here each night. Here also can be found the concession stands offering beer, soda, tacos, hotdogs, and my favorite, "Frito-pies" (an opened bag of Frito chips with spicy melted cheese and jalapeño peppers poured over the contents, served up with plenty of napkins and a plastic spoon). The large commanding sign over the portal to the stadium proper declares the turf to belong to the Tecos. It blares: "Tecolotes de los dos Laredos," and a friendlier, ". . . *Un Asunto Familiar*" (a family affair).

Inside the park itself, the seating consists of eleven cement-tiered rows painted Dominican blue, and separated by a five-inch red band. There are no individual seats here, just white-painted vertical demarcations, each approximately two feet wide and numbered (e.g., E-79, E-80). The area ringing first and third base, known conventionally as box seats, are delineated as such by offering rows of individualized seats, cheap plastic seats such as those found in laundromats or small-town bus terminals. A canopy covers the seating area between first and third base, perched on top of which can be found the press boxes and owner's box, both simple affairs. Extending another 200 feet down both lines are the reserved seat and bleacher areas, demarcated as such by not being covered.

Advertisements abound. While ample evidence of the binational team character exists in signs (El Diario; Transportes Monte Mayor; Cemento Monterrey, as well as Dr. Ike's and Marlboro), the national stamp is always greater. Most important, perhaps, is the sign (in Spanish) in left-center-field declaring: "Thank you Mr. Governor! In Tamaulipas' dawn we will have a new stadium. Hand in hand, fans and government." Gratitude to the governor is more for what they hope he will do than for what he has already done. There is no denying the dilapidated condition of the park. While a fresh coat of paint perks up old parks like Fenway Park in Boston, it does little to change the run-down look of Parque La Junta. This sad old woman is light years apart from the grand dame that is Fenway. Plans are underway for a new stadium in Nuevo Laredo, and state support has been formally given; but the land for the edifice has not been forthcoming. So, while both the fans and owners of the Tecos are eager to see it, they will have to be patient for their dawn.

West Martin Field sits just about where Laredo's old Washington Park was. Built for the high school and other amateur teams, West Martin Field is a Walmart version of a minor league park. Like cheap, summer patio furniture, West Martin Field is made of contemporary materials (e.g., new concrete, aluminum, chainlink fencing), utilitarian with only a hint of aesthetics, and you can feel comfortable about leaving it out in the rain.

It seats about 6,000. The concession stands are new but have a makeshift quality to them, as if they are dismantled and carried away after the game. The stands are clean and appear swept, and the seats have not seen that many rounds of flesh. Brightly colored billboards for local businesses line the outfield wall. Like those in its Mexican counterpart, these advertisements reflect the national home turf: American Gym and Fitness Center and Laredo Paint and Decorating outnumber Mexican companies like Banco Atlántico. The most celebrated billboard is that of the Laredo restaurant, Taco Palenque, which challenges all Teco hitters to hit a home run over it and win $2,000. The lighting at West Martin Field is new (circa 1994) and certainly adequate for minor league baseball. On aesthetic grounds, the incandescent light works to highlight the rich copper-red earth and the elysian-green grass. Four hundred feet to dead center and 330 down each foul line makes this a respectable baseball park for a AAA franchise on either side of the border.

Comparisons between the two parks scream out to be made because, in many ways, they reflect comparisons between the two cities. Parque La Junta is a homely cousin that has seen harder times and shows it. People tend to fill a stadium and imbue it with their presence, but when a park is empty is the time to meet it. La Junta has been "rode hard and put up wet," as they say. The infield looks ragged, and the outfield is distressed with a ring of torn up ground outlining the fence. Workmen are trying to level this stretch of ground, but there are so many problems here. It is in the corners that the level of deterioration is most revealed: crumbling, cracked walls, rusted machines, overgrown with desert weeds.

West Martin Field is well cared for by comparison, but just as off-putting. While the Nuevo Laredo park is tired-looking, Laredo's park is a tad too fastidious, and players complain about the infield's hardness. It could do with some funk, for although it is new, West Martin Field is soulless. Experiencing rapid development and simultaneously suffering from distinct loss of aesthetics, both Laredo and West Martin Field seem to be hellbent on achieving a generic look that shuns identity and local character in favor of corporate chain culture. You might just as easily be in Elgin, Illinois, or Yakima, Washington, watching a game. Having been considered a third-rate town for so long, the attention Laredo is now getting leaves it responding with centuries of collective insecurity. It wants to be an instant Dallas and believes that expunging the past will only hasten the process. Rather than doing things with an aesthetic flourish and sense of its past, they do things fast and with money. The outcome is West Martin Field, a good place to play, but hard on the eyes.

## Biographical Sketches

### *Víctor Lozano, Owner of the Tecolotes*

In addition to owning a good-sized trucking company (Gazela), Nuevo Laredo's newly constructed bullfight ring, and the Tecos, Víctor Lozano is a record holder. Few people know that this sixty-three-year-old man holds the local record for *descuerando un chivo*, butchering a goat. He once completed the task in fifty-three seconds. There is more than just a hint of pride when he lists this feat, for don Víctor is the son of a butcher who never really left this family trade far behind. The headquarters for his trucking company and the Teco team offices on Obregón Street are, in reality, the small family home and his father's butcher shop enclosed and enlarged upon. Don Víctor was born in the small building that was home to all eight children and grew up being groomed to take over the family business.

Like most kids, young Víctor wanted to play ball and other sports, but he had to help out at home. As the oldest child he was expected to shoulder the burden of taking care of the others. He worked long, hard hours to put his brothers through school, and continues to look after them to this day. His brother's medical office is housed in the Obregón Street building.

Whenever time allowed, Lozano would try to quench his thirst for sports. He would play ball or attend bullfights. In fact, he was an amateur *toreador* of sorts, continuing to engage in his passion for the ring until his forties. Some of the Tecos even remember him trying to teach them an appreciation of some of the finer moves of a *toreador*. It was a day when a handful of players were at his ring and there was a young bull, still more calf than bull, in the ring. Lozano was feeling his oats that day and in his street clothes went about the moves. No longer as spare of frame as in his youth, Lozano did not emerge unscathed: the young calf-bull managed to graze his belly and tear his shirt. Pitcher Ernesto Barraza laughs remembering some of these episodes: "You can always tell when don Víctor has had a bit too much to drink and is enjoying himself because then a curl of his hair [usually brushed straight back] falls forward."

Lozano's dream of being a sportsman was deferred and transmuted into his commitment to developing sports in the city of Nuevo Laredo. He bought the Tecos in 1981. By then the team had been back on the border for five years and had been to the playoffs twice, including an emotional rollercoaster of a season in 1977 when they beat Mexico City in the championship series. Lozano was present for that season, waiting for the opportunity to buy the team, which came in the fall of 1980. Having two seasoned baseball people—"Chito" Rodríguez and Mexican superscout Jorge Calvo—prompted his decision and, together with his nephew Samuel Lozano Molina, Lozano hoped he would have the right amount of insiders and outsiders to assure a well-run and successful operation. The Tecos proved him right. From 1981 until 1994 the border team made the playoffs every year but two and won the league championship in 1989, coming close on three other occasions.

### Cuauhtémoc "Chito" Rodríguez, Teco Vice President

Within the space of five minutes Cuauhtémoc "Chito" Rodríguez is responding to a directive from Mexico City about the handling of thousands of machine parts destined for the United States, conferring with the Atlanta

Braves about the players he is to receive in a few weeks, advising the Teco owner in Nuevo Laredo on a Mexican holdout, and working with people in Laredo on how best to present a contract to the city council. He moves from one track to another almost imperceptibly, seamlessly handling business and sports, and sports as business in Spanish and English.

Having been with the team as either general manager or vice president since it first moved back to the border in 1976, Rodríguez is—more than the owner or the players—the essence of the Tecos. He has seen the Tecos through hard times and championships for the past eighteen years, and played a major role in turning the team into a binational enterprise.

Born in the state of Sonora, a Nuevo Laredoan since the age of two, and educated at Laredo's St. Augustine High School, fifty-eight-year-old Cuauhtémoc Rodríguez personifies the "Mexican binational" Oscar Martínez writes of.[1] Although he served in the U.S. Air Force and works and lives in Laredo, Rodríguez never gave up his Mexican citizenship and maintains he would never consider doing so. Since 1982 Rodríguez has headed Tanjore Corporation LTD, an import-export company owned by Mexican magnate Alejo Peralta, one of the world's richest men, according to *Forbes*.[2] This is the same Peralta who in the past directly—or in recent years indirectly, through his son—controls the Mexican League. Tanjore has done quite well in the wake of NAFTA, and Rodríguez has his whole family working at the company. That he is beholden to "the old engineer" (as some refer to Peralta) in Mexico City is clear, and Rodríguez does not deny it: "I'm 100 percent grateful to baseball. I met the Peraltas through baseball. I owe [to] them my economic situation."[3]

While Rodríguez was an administrative success in baseball by 1982, he was pretty much stuck as an accountant for a local hotel when Peralta decided to appoint him to head the new import-export firm he was opening up in Laredo. Since then Rodríguez's economic and baseball lives have paralleled each other in an embarrassment of riches. The parallel careers can, however, come into conflict. Because Peralta has been the owner of the Mexico City Tigres since 1955, his loyalty and identification are clear. He expects the same from those around him. So when, for instance, the father of Teco pitcher Ernesto Barraza, an engineer-owner of a Mexico City construction company who is linked to Peralta, was queried as to whom he supported in the upcoming championship between his son's team and the Tigres of Mexico City, he paused but declared his allegiance to the latter. Rodríguez, too, was a tad uncomfortable during the 1992 championship series. Traveling down to Mexico City, the Teco front office was eagerly looking forward to this championship series after destroying their opposition in the playoffs. At the park they all sat together, but Rodríguez split his time between Peralta's box and that of the Tecos. When the Tecos split the two games in the capital, Rodríguez was a bit on edge because of a joking comment made by Peralta: if the Tecos won the series, Peralta might have to renegotiate his contract with Rodríguez. His Teco compatriots shared a round of jokes at his expense.

There is no joking about Rodríguez's role in the binational success of the Tecos, however. His familiarity with both cultures and both languages has resulted in Rodríguez's being able to land a contract with the Atlanta Braves, arguably the best farm system in baseball. It is also his familiarity with Anglo ways that enables Rodríguez to accommodate the American players and other representatives of major league baseball that deal with the Tecos. No one else can do this, for despite having lived their lives on the border, neither of the Lozanos are bicultural. They speak little English and show no interest in doing so, nor do they spend much time on the U.S. side of the border.

The tendency to think of Rodríguez as more American than Mexican is quickly choked off in talking with him. Whether he is talking about how he prefers to be referred to (he likes Cuauhtémoc, though everyone calls him Chito), or what nationalism is, Rodríguez is most definitely Mexican first. On the border, however, it is the ability to function well on both sides that marks the successful man or woman. Rodríguez has been able to do that better than anyone else connected with this franchise. On any given day he is checking in with Mexico City; ironing out import players' contractual problems with Chuck LaMar of the Atlanta Braves (named in 1995 as general manager of the expansion Tampa Bay team), translating his dealings with Atlanta into workable equations on the border in both Nuevo Laredo and Laredo; and often ending his long days by crossing over into Nuevo Laredo for a game. At the game he shmoozes with players. Both Mexican and U.S. players look forward to his presence because both groups feel that he, more than anyone, is the man who can both understand their issues and do something about them. This is particularly crucial in dealings with Americans. Often these players come to the border and act out their initial culture shock. It is Rodríguez upon whom they rely when they encounter obstacles or have to face the border crossing for the first time. Rodríguez wears so many hats on any day that one has to wonder whether, at the end of an eighteen-hour day, even he knows who he is when he has to present papers coming back over the bridge.

### Larry Dovalina, Director of the Laredo Civic Center

The Dovalinas are one of the oldest families in the Laredo area. There were Dovalinas who were elected as Laredo deputies or alderman dating back to 1836. Following the demarcation of the Rio Grande as an international boundary in 1846, one branch of the Dovalina family became part of the founders of Nuevo Laredo, removing itself from newly minted U.S. soil to the other side of the river. They eventually returned, but the ambivalence over which side they most identified with remained. While there remain strong cultural pulls to Mexican as well as to U.S. soil in all of the Dovalinas, the family has always been solidly "American" in their political identity, however that is defined. Dovalinas have served in every war since before the Alamo. Dovalinas served in more than one civil war: they were in the Confederate army, as well as in the mini-civil war that was fought among rival political groups in the Battle of Laredo in 1886.

Dovalinas are also an old and reputable baseball family. In Chapter 2 we saw Fernando and his brother Lefty, two of Larry's uncles, stars for regional teams in the 1930s. Lázaro Dovalina, Larry's father, played for the Apaches in 1949. As the most current manifestation of the baseball Dovalinas, Larry has opted to develop baseball rather than play it. He and associate Carlos Villarreal carried out the binational baseball relationship between the cities, and Dovalina tends to it like one does a garden in the desert. From the post of director of the Laredo Civic Center, which he took over in 1978, he and Assistant City Manager Carlos Villarreal brought the Tecos to Laredo against great odds.

Structurally, Dovalina is not part of the Tecos leadership. Despite making daily arrangements with the Lozanos on the other side of the river, he is not part of the front office. Yet without his efforts there would be no binational team, or at least not as we know it. Everything on the Laredo side of the river, from securing a budget, to grooming the stadium, to recruiting the people at the concessions stands, to paying the Tecos, is handled by Larry Dovalina. It's safe to say that his Teco memorabilia–strewn office is the nuts and bolts of the team's operation on the U.S. side. But thinking of Dovalina as purely a team technician misses the point.

If Chito Rodríguez is the structural center of the team, then Dovalina is its essential margin, the critical outlier. For as devoted and tireless a functionary and fan as he is, he is also the only person in the Teco inner circle who is analytical. As in all things he does, whether it be in the running of the Civic Center, the city's cable television operations, or the Tecos, Dovalina is into delineating problems and fixing them. That takes a degree of candidness that escapes most of the Teco front office.

For all of his importance, Rodríguez is somewhat powerless, hemmed in on all sides by the powerful backers at whose discretion he serves (Peralta and Lozano). Dovalina's distance from the center gives him the critical perspective to be better able to see things. The inability of the Tecos to efficiently run their concessions and sell season tickets irked him, so Dovalina applied his expertise in running such things to solving the problems. This he can do on the U.S. side, and it has led to a noticeable difference in the way the same operations are handled in the two home parks of the

Tecos. It's also frustrating. Dovalina's face gets slightly more crimson when talking about the way that operations on the other side of the river have gone. "They just don't seem to understand the concept that we're in the business of providing entertainment and services. You gotta have promotions and contests and entertainments and good concessions or people will go elsewhere. We have twice as many season ticket holders on the Laredo side and twice the attendance because we worked at these things."[4] His voice is calm, but his blood is boiling as he vents his frustration at seeing how things could be better but aren't: "Samuel is my friend, but he's no promoter. That's just the simple truth."[5]

Few have worked as relentlessly as has Larry Dovalina on nurturing the "one team—two countries" concept. There has been a regular group of city functionaries that would prefer Laredo put its money to different use. The taxpayers' league has repeatedly attacked the idea of spending over $100,000 a year on a baseball team that has never generated money for the perennially hardpressed city. Each year Carlos Villarreal and Dovalina gird their loins for another round of meetings to fend off the attacks against the binational Tecos. Bottomliners have only one way of seeing the cosmos: if it doesn't pay for itself, axe it. It is visionaries like Dovalina and Villarreal who look at Laredo as more than a collection of businesses. They see a cultural past and future connected by the unique features of the two Laredos. Dovalina sees the Tecos as representing more than a team, an entertainment possibility; he sees a tradition that holds the key to the future, "There's more in common among ourselves than we have with people further to the north or south. You have Anglos here, but they become more Mexican with time. They speak Spanish. The two cities have always been one in their hearts, and you spend any time down here and that becomes obvious. That's our strength."[6]

### Dan Firova, Teco Manager

Dan Firova has a recurrent dream in which he is playing a major league game and gets the hit that he never got during his all-too-brief stays with the Seattle Mariners and Cleveland Indians. He was never able to tell me whether in his dream it was a day or night game, which team he was playing for, or even if the hit was a single or home run. It was simply the hit . . . the one that got away in September 1981, July 1982, and September 1988 when he had his three "cups of coffee" in the majors. The absence of that hit haunts him the way an amputee is haunted by his missing leg: the "presence of an absence" is the way Sartre referred to such things.

Firova was, in 1993, a thirty-six-year-old rookie manager, although he was no newcomer to the team. He was a catcher for the Tecos (in 1981–83 and 1991), and his career in Nuevo Laredo sandwiched other stints in Mexico with Saltillo (1984, 1988) and in the U.S. minor leagues with Chattanooga (AA), Calgary (AAA), Salinas (A), and Reno (AA). Firova is the proverbially well-traveled ballplayer, the kind that defines baseball. He only tasted the "show," living out his career as a catcher trying to get back. When he talks about it, he can taste it, and even his tight-lipped south Texas style is betrayed by this desire to be fulfilled.

Dan Firova is a quiet man, cut of the cloth of the south Texas male. He rarely initiates a conversation, although he will accommodate questions. At first I thought he might be shy, but gave up the notion after watching him get ejected from a game. The fact is, Firova is just one of those guys from Refugio, Texas, who was an excellent athlete as well as good-looking, and who lets his exploits do his talking for him.

His wife, Esther, concurs with my view of her husband. She summed up their first date: "I sat there with him across the table and thought, 'Is this guy for real? He just sits there!' It was boring!"[7] Dan, however, unbeknownst to Esther, described the date as a great time. They and their three children have endured his rollercoaster career in baseball, which has taken him to play in Canada, Mexico, and the United States. Esther, a vivacious woman who has been the bedrock of the Firova family, has over the years seen enough of baseball to write a book about the game and the men-boys who play it. It wouldn't be pretty.

As much as his playing career coughed and sputtered, its end came suddenly and ignominiously. He was catching regularly for the Tecos in 1991, and in fact was beginning to get hot, hitting safely in fourteen games. In his last game, in his last at-bat, he hit a home run. What malice lay in the hearts of the Teco front office? What had he done in this or in another life to prompt such a move? After the game, an unsuspecting Firova celebrated with a beer or two.

In the front office there were the weekly, sometimes daily, maneuverings that require people to think far ahead. It was the last day of the season for the team to sign someone, and they were desperate for a pitcher to take them through the playoffs. With each team limited to four import players, and Firova counting as one, he was expendable. The pitcher they found was an Import; and so despite showing signs of a revived bat, Firova was dropped. "That's baseball for you, nothing personal," recalls Firova. The decision was based on the team's best interests, but Firova's interests had been completely ignored. If this was to be his last day, it would have been thoughtful of the Tecos to let him go as early as possible so that he could catch on with a team in need of his skills. The Tecos did not do this, however. Seething, Firova only managed to tell the front office that he thought it was a "shabby" move. Perhaps because they felt guilty or not guilty enough, the Teco management told him that they would put him on the "disabled list" for ten days to see if the pitcher would pan out. He would coach during that time and at the end of it they would let him know if he was coaching or playing. For a player facing extinction, such an offer does not seem so cold: "I thought I might still be *alive*," he said. The days flew by quickly and as day ten came, he must have been tied into emotional knots, though nothing creased his face. As the evening lights were turned on for the game, there was yet no word. Then, as casually as someone mentioning that you left the garage door open, a coach sauntered up to him and said, "Are you gonna warm up these pitchers or am I?" End of tale. Firova's playing career had just been squashed with about as much thought as someone snuffing a cockroach. That's when he started having "The Dream." It turns out he could endure the rebuffs and the bad bus rides and callousness as long as he was playing, for by playing he could hope to get back to the majors for one more day.

What hard-hearted, brutal man so coldly erased baseball player Dan Firova from the earth? It was the same man I had come to know and re-spect as a player's front office man, the very person who later went on to hire Firova first as a coach in 1992, then as manager the following year. The push came from Teco Vice President Chito Rodríguez, who had sized up Firova during his tenure with the team, liked his youth and experience, and appreciated his more professional (i.e., American) style of managing. Firova's personality, his hold-it-in demeanor, also impressed Rodríguez, and so, against the inclination of Víctor Lozano, Rodríguez pushed for this *pocho* (Mexican American) to manage the team. Once again, Firova was rescued from total baseball extinction.

But there were problems. Firova was replacing José "Zacatillo" Guer-rero, a Mexican Hall of Fame legend who managed the team to a champi-onship in 1989 and was revered by the fans in Nuevo Laredo. Difficulty gaining popular acceptance would face anyone who followed in Guerrero's wake, but for Firova, a pocho from across the river, it was even harder. The abuse he had to endure during his first season occurred with the regularity of the lunar tides. His Job-like stoicism stood him in good stead, for no anger, disappointment, or hurt seemed to sully his composure. He hurts, of course, but it is seen by only the few who know him. Part of this abuse was the rookie rite of passage, which passed as he entered his second sea-son, but part is directed at Dan Firova, the foreigner, and that he has never overcome.[8]

### Ernesto Barraza, Pitcher

Ernesto Barraza unabashedly admits to having discipline problems. It's not his complete lack of it so much as his contradictory relationship to it. At times he values discipline highly, and then, inexplicably, he quickly seems incapable of focusing. This has resulted in problems with control while pitching and a checkered baseball career; but because he is the most erudite of the Tecos, Barraza seems to enjoy his contradiction. He mulls it over like a valuable artifact in a private collection.

At twenty-six years of age he is already a seven-year veteran of the league. Barraza's entry into baseball is somewhat atypical, however, and here too we see the theme of discipline at work. In 1984, seventeen-year-old Barraza was already somewhat of a problem for his parents. As far as his father was concerned, young Ernesto needed the discipline that boarding school or military service provide. When Ernesto, oblivious to the problem, hinted to his dad that it "would be nice to travel to Europe with some friends for the summer," his father, a civil engineer in Mexico City, gave him a counterproposal: "Because I was not studying, my father's boss, Don Simon, told him to send me to an Israeli kibbutz. . . . My father works with a lot of Jews, constructing buildings for them. I wanted to go to Europe with some friends for a couple of months. [My father] said, 'If you wanna go out there, then go three or four months to this place and study and work there. My boss will pay for your schooling in Tel Aviv.' "[9]

That summer his family had already planned their vacation at Mazatlán on Mexico's Pacific coast, and Barraza would decide about the Israeli offer while there. "I was 16 or 17 then. I was going on vacation to Mazatlán and for this my mother bought a new car, and bought a car for me too. While we were down there, they stole my car."[10]

Israel was off indefinitely. The auto insurance they were getting had not yet kicked in, so they were out the cost of a new car, and Barraza didn't feel that he should be an additional financial burden to the family. "I was ashamed to ask for money to go to Israel. The car had no insurance; we lost all of our money in that car. So I went to work in Mazatlán."[11]

While in Mazatlán in April 1985, he was invited to go to Pastejé, the national baseball academy that trained all Mexican baseball prospects. Barraza remembers it more like a setting for a Dickens novel: "It was very remote, about a 100 miles from Mexico City and in a very poor part of Mexico. Very cold! All of us [ballplayers] came from warm parts of the country and this was very cold. It's a place that was sealed off, where they demanded a lot of sacrifice, but they gave you nothing. It was hard. And we would never really get to the U.S. because they wouldn't let you go easily."[12]

Still, Pastejé could easily be considered an appropriate substitute for the kibbutz. In addition to honing his fine baseball skills, Barraza learned the virtues of structure and physical discipline: conditioning, running, weight training. Upon graduating from the academy as a pitcher in 1986, he was drafted by Campeche. Two years of minimal pitching made him bait for a trade to the Tecos, who were looking for young arms. From 1988 to 1992 Barraza began to slowly mature, building a repertoire of pitches with varying degrees of success. For instance, in 1992, when his won-lost record was

13–7, he was actually throwing more or less a like .500 pitcher with an ERA around 4.00—nothing that would get noticed. But his strikeout-to-walk ratio and number of innings pitched steadily progressed until he was a clearly serviceable pitcher who could keep his team in a ball game long enough to spare your bullpen, all of which takes discipline. His trajectory peaked in 1993 when he went 13–8 and finally brought his ERA under 4.00.

A trickster, Barraza could either dominate the opposition or sputter, and both are a function of his ability or his failure to focus. On any given night you might get Barraza "the Beam" or Ernesto "the Distracted," such is the nature of the mythological trickster in Native American mythology. This was the case on—appropriately enough—April Fools' Day in 1992 when Barraza pitched a no-hitter against Cordoba. The trickster showed up that night and Barraza came out throwing laser strikes that pinched only the corners of the plate. All night long he made hitters swing at his first offering and all night long they grounded out. Only two balls were hit to the outfield the whole night. Barraza barely worked up a sweat, throwing only seventy-three pitches (47 strikes, 26 balls) and completing his feat in slightly less than two hours. It was only the fifth no-hit, no-run game in Teco history.

But the trickster could also show up and present us with Ernesto the Distracted, which he did one clear May night at Parque La Junta in 1993. Fieldnotes discussed his lack of concentration from the first pitch on: "He seems tense out there, talking to himself, nodding at something known only to himself. By the third inning he is still struggling. After having the first batter in the hole with no balls and two strikes, he walks him . . . again."[13]

Between innings in the dugout he seemed distracted, but uncharacteristically he still seemed congenial and ready to talk. It is assumed that pitchers get into a frame of mind that they must maintain even while in the dugout and to do so they often focus on the mound or action on the field and tune out other distractions, sort of like having an actor stay in character between takes on a movie set. Barraza did neither. Surprisingly, at a time when one must maintain a "game face," he began venturing into a poorly timed self-criticism: "I like pitching better when I'm behind. I know this isn't good but I have problems concentrating when we are ahead. . . . This year they're [batters] hitting, me. I don't know, last year hitters were only .220 against me. This year it's like .280. I don't know what to do. I have movement, I'm aggressive out there, but they're still hitting me. I'll have to talk to my pitching coach in Veracruz."[14]

While never really quite getting into the game, and barely escaping without a loss, five days later Barraza the Beam is facing the Saraperos of Saltillo and pitching a rare complete game shutout, striking out eight and walking only one batter.

Barraza is the Bill (the Spaceman) Lee of the Tecos, perhaps of the whole Mexican League. Like his major league counterpart, Barraza is educated, yet a chronic underachiever. He is the youngest son of a relatively well-off family in Mexico City. His sisters are, as they should be, talented at a variety of things and at least one attended college in the United States. He is impressively bright and quick (he was offered a college scholarship to Brigham Young University, but stayed in Mexico), but like Spaceman Lee, he makes a point of approaching life at an oblique angle when the world is locked on 90 degrees. He actually translated one of my books to his teammates, reading passages aloud during a game and essentially lecturing them (as if they cared). Were he on the straight and narrow, Barraza might have been on a fast track to a career in law or politics, but instead he is the last Teco to throw a no-hitter, an enigma that intrigues his teammates, and they accept Barraza as the team bohemian: "He will drive to San Antonio in the afternoon," says a teammate, "just to see a movie, or he'll come to the park missing some part of his uniform."[15]

The day before the opening of the 1994 season, Ernesto Barraza was sold to the Mexico City Tigres (along with veteran slugger Alejandro Ortiz). The shock waves of this news spread quickly through the Nuevo Laredo sports community and the outrage was so widespread that owner Víctor Lozano had to call a press conference to quell the anger. Barraza was quite surprised as well: "They offered me the same contract as they did in '93, and I had such a good year! They said that the team needed to cut expenses because they lost so much [money]. I told him that if that's the case they should trade me. I didn't think they would."[16] Since Mexico City is his family's home, he's not unhappy there, but the sense of family that marks the Tecos is not to be found among his Tigre colleagues. No other team has such a core of players who have been together so long.[17]

### Alejandro "Pato" Ortiz, Third Base
### Andrés Mora, First Base

With their thirteen seasons on the Tecos, these two veterans have so defined the era of the Tecos de los dos Laredos that one might think they each live in one of the cities and meet at the bridge each day to foray to the park. They each live in one of the Laredos, but they are not so joined at the hip.

It's only April, and the 1994 season already seems old to Andrés Mora. Characteristically quiet on the bench, Mora suddenly turns to me and says, "You know, I think I may retire after this year. I set a goal for myself of twenty home runs, but I feel like my bat has slowed down, and my legs hurt like hell."[18] He's been thinking about this for a long time, because the words just flow with none of the restraints so typical of him. But it has to be sad because the twenty-year veteran Mora, who has 411 career home runs at this point, needs only 43 more to break the all-time Mexican League record set by Hector Espino. It might as well be 430 more home runs the way he's been swinging the bat lately.

"Pato" Ortiz, thirty-three-year-old third baseman, has been with the Tecos for his entire thirteen-year career. He is among the top ten lifetime home run hitters in the league, having hit his three hundredth in early May. He often speaks as if he had been born a Teco and will die one. He ponders the future and past from the Owl's perspective only, ignoring completely his roots in Veracruz.

Mora would have passed Espino's home run totals several years ago were it not for a three-year stint in the major leagues (two with the Orioles and one with the Indians). He is one of only about seventy Mexicans to ever play in the U.S. major leagues. In only 682 at bats Mora powered twenty-seven home runs, good enough in his estimation to have qualified him for more playing time from Oriole manager Earl Weaver. The latter felt differently, however, and traded Mora to Cleveland, where he started the 1978 season. After about a month he was sent down to AAA to get more seasoning, a move that angered him. He opted to return to Mexico. "I think if I stayed in AAA I might have had another chance at Cleveland, but I was mad. I hit good but they still put me in AAA. I don't really feel too bad [about it], because I did a lot more down here, and it's my home."[19] Here we see one of the unique features of the Mexican League. Other Latin American players rarely choose to return to their countries of origin, but Mexican players often do so because in their leagues one can earn a reasonable salary, play under more stable conditions, and not have to endure the cultural and linguistic dislocation.[20]

Ortiz also chose playing in the Mexican League over life with a AAA franchise in the United States. "It's easier," he explained. "No language or food problems. You can stay in a place longer. Over there, you get moved around a lot from one team to another."[21] He never grew up thinking he was going to play baseball as a profession or as a vehicle for bettering his life. On the contrary, he never even played the game until he was seventeen, and someone looking for players in a sandlot team coaxed him into trying it. His love was soccer and Ortiz argues that he had potential in that sport, though to me it seems he possesses the prototypical power hitter's upper body, not that of a soccer player. He likes to joke about his missed career.

When he's not joking around raucously, Ortiz's strong Indian features give him a contemplative look, which at times reveals a layer of resentment that his easy smile covers. Not long ago he let loose on one Laredo reporter who had spent most of his time interviewing the import players. In a show of nationalist pique Ortiz sneered at the reporter, finally questioning him, "What's wrong? You don't want to interview any more of those damn gringos?"[22]

If Ortiz is mercurial, Mora is, by contrast, patient. Not that long ago, however, there were problems between Mora and the Teco front office. He walked out over a contract dispute, fought with manager Zacatillo Guerrero, and was even traded away in 1989, sadly and ironically missing the Tecos' only championship during his playing years. At this juncture of his career, though, Mora wants to get into coaching and managing and is trying hard to be the responsible team player. He won't room with the beer guzzlers anymore, and he was among the hardest-working players in spring training. There is every reason to believe that in doing this he is only tapping into a part of himself that was always there, rather than fabricating something that wasn't. An incident that occurred in spring training should serve as an illustration.[23] Two American instructors from the Atlanta Braves' organization, down to teach and otherwise work with the Tecos, were going about their business watching players perform, assessing and instructing them. In the Americans' presence at Parque La Junta was an implicit understanding that they were real ex–big leaguers in the land of students, wannabees, and generally inferior players. When the American hitting instructor, a knowledgeable veteran of eleven big league seasons, watched Mora take his swings in the batting cage, he directed the Teco coach to "send the big guy over," as if Mora was just another rookie. I cringed at the thought of someone so highly regarded in Mexico being treated invisibly and assumed that some kind of tension would result. Mora was told that the American instructor wanted to talk to him and so he sauntered over, sweat beads on his slightly chubby face. Smiling and shaking his head, the American said slowly and loudly, "Very . . . good . . . swing"—pausing between each word so that this Mexican might understand. Then, turning to the coach, the American continued, "Tell him, on his body, I'd like to see his balance shift a little, like so"—and he demonstrated how he would like it done. Mora listened in rapt attention, and answered in English, "If I do that I'll have to keep my hands down like this"—and he demonstrated to the gringo, who was shocked that this player could speak.

I interjected on Mora's behalf: "He knows English from playing for three seasons in the majors." The American instructor's eyebrows jumped in surprise and instant respect was conveyed on his face. I added, "And he hit twenty-six dingers over in Baltimore under Weaver." Mora casually but pointedly corrected me: "twenty-seven home runs." I forgot that for most players their time in the big leagues is built on hundreds and hundreds of games in the minors, so that the difference of one home run is significant. Mora and the American became solid associates over the next weeks. Mora has seen many things in his baseball life, experienced many slights and kindnesses, and understands that gringos make such mistakes all the time.

The history between Mora and Ortiz is deep. They seem emotionally joined at the hip and often don't even need to talk to be able to communicate. Rather they use the slightest facial gestures and hand movements. Sometimes it looks as if they are trained sign language experts, but it is only the two enjoying their special shorthand. Sometimes it's just shared quiet, as it was on the night Mora hit his four hundredth home run. The fans went crazy, giving him a standing ovation as he crossed home plate. Mobbed by his fellow Tecos, Mora made his way back to the dugout. Someone quickly tried to retrieve the ball, and an interview was done as the stadium rocked with gratitude and adulation. Mora gets applause whether he succeeds or fails, but somehow in the middle of all this hoopla there is a sweet sadness about him, almost a loneliness. Moments later Ortiz and Mora sat quietly next to each other in the dugout sharing a moment and a cigarette as if completely separate from all the action on the field.

Mora began 1993 with a goal of twenty home runs and for the first half seemed on course, but as the season wore on, he slowed at the plate, at times hobbling to reach base. It was becoming clear that the end was at hand. Still, an off-season would, it was hoped, provide the old warrior with enough rest to move on. In 1994 Mora had few at-bats and eventually was used only as a pinch hitter. At season's end I sat on the bench with him and jokingly told him that I needed a good ending to this book. Having been on the bench most of the season Mora seemed less and less animated, but the conversation seemed to stir him. I said, "Maybe we could end it with you coming up to bat?" His face lit up. "Yeah. Mora comes up with the bases loaded and POW—home run over the center field wall. I put one over the crown there in center field scoreboard. It was 1979 or 1980."[24]

### Juan Jesús Alvarez, Pitcher

Each time he finished pitching his half of an inning Juan Alvarez would come back to the dugout in pain. No trace of it in his face, but as he tried to stretch it out quietly, in the corner of the dugout you could see that his back was giving "El Indio" trouble. That was 1993. By 1994, his seventh year in the league, this twenty-five-year-old required back surgery. "That [surgery] was the most difficult moment of my career. To win or lose games is inevitable, but to recover from serious back surgery and come back to win a game was difficult."[25] Alvarez would come back at the end of the season to pitch and win. In his first game game back he battled for seven innings, leaving with a 3–2 lead. In baseball parlance, Alvarez is a "gamer," a "horse" in his toughness and durability.

Until he went down with the back injury Alvarez had, like others in his cohort who had frozen at Pastejé, annually posted up ever more impressive numbers. For four straight years he had hovered around eight wins per season, but with him what was impressive was not in the stats. Alvarez is the kind of pitcher that keeps you in the game long enough to spare your bullpen. In 1993, however, he posted thirteen wins, with a respectable 3.07 ERA. More importantly he pitched a hefty 194 innings, unusual in the Mexican League, and his 163 strikeouts were good enough for second place at the end of the year. He was coming into his own at the very time that his health was failing him.

Some of the Tecos call him "Chief," some "Indio" (Indian), in reference to Alvarez coming from the Yaqui Indian community of Potam, Sonora. Everyone in that part of Mexico follows Guaymas in the Mexican Pacific League. Like a generation of young American kids growing up in the 1930s and 1940s, Alvarez and his siblings secretly listened to night games on the radio that they hid in their room. Their parents heartily disapproved of sports, thinking it took young people's minds off of more important things like farming. But young Alvarez excelled at sports, not farming: "I began to play sports when I was twelve years old, at first basketball, then baseball. I played for some championship amateur teams at home, but never really thought that I would become professional. I stopped playing sports for a while when I was fourteen, fifteen, until I was about eighteen years old. I am the only native to play professionally. There were other baseball players, good ones, but they were unable to join a professional league."[26]

While Alvarez thought he was playing in obscurity the scouts attached to the Mexican academy at Pastejé who roam in search of talent noted his potential and, in 1986, invited Alvarez to attend. He was so happy he could have burst, but Yaqui culture and his parent's low view of sports muted his outward display. He walked around with that written invitation in his pocket for weeks. During that time reality set in. As heady as it was to get invited to Pastejé, realistically there was no way Alvarez could attend. The family lacked the money for a bus ticket or clothes for him. As with all things in these small communities, word of Alvarez's invitation leaked out and people started quietly gathering donations for the bus trip. His personal fortune had turned into the celebration of Yaqui pride for the community who might be producing the first Yaqui to pitch professionally.

That winter at Pastejé, Alvarez says he almost froze because he had no warm clothes to wear. Like Barraza who preceded him to the academy by a year, Alvarez adapted physically, honed his skills, and was eventually drafted by Guaymas, which he is convinced was providential. "After that [being drafted] I knew I would make it, because Guaymas was the team of my childhood."[27]

He joined the Tecos in 1988. While adjusting to a new team is an issue for every ballplayer, Alvarez's adjustment was compounded by his sense of being an Indian: "It was a challenge to me to become as good as my teammates. It was critical that I feel an equal among them, but as you can see,

I made it."[28] He not only made it, he did it on his terms. At the risk of invoking the romantic image of an Indian, I found Alvarez to have the most dignified bearing of anyone on the team. His presence is not built on macho bluster or conspicuous movements or looks. This 6'2" righthanded pitcher has a quiet power about him, at once removed from the world around him, yet accessible to anyone. It would be difficult to imagine him getting ruffled or losing his temper the way some of the others do. Even the presence of the Imports don't phase him. Willie Waite, who managed to systematically alienate everyone in the Teco organization in less than one month, had no effect whatsoever on Alvarez. "Last year there was a lot of discontent coming from the import players. Many [Tecos] became angry with them over the season. I, on the other hand, never had a conflict with them. I was even able to maintain cordial relations with the most troublesome one among them."[29]

If anyone could function on an even keel with some of the mercurial moments of the 1993 season it would have been Alvarez. For him, playing professionally in the two Mexican Leagues is a Yaqui odyssey in which he is forever discovering that the world around him is loaded with strange people. Somehow he holds on to a quiet core that enables him to keep a healthy perspective. He is a Teco, respected by his teammates, socializing with other players and their families. He can never forget, however, that he is from Potam. "I can't wait to get back to there. We, my wife and daughter and I, return after the playoffs. When I play in the Pacific League [during the winter months] my family stays with me at Nayarit and we leave for games from there whenever possible."[30] What he failed to mention, but others told me, is that he goes back to his people each year loaded with gifts for everyone in the community. For Alvarez giving back is part of the Yaqui Indian sense of keeping a balance in the community and universe.[31]

### Enrique Couoh, Pitcher

If form follows function, then Enrique Couoh is the perfect embodiment of a fork. He is thin, delicately-boned, slightly sloping, and every part of him seems to end in a point, particularly his long tapering fingers. He was made to throw the forkball, and does so with devastating results. Twice now, Atlanta Braves' instructors have sent for Couoh to attend their spring training in West Palm Beach because they too are intrigued by his forkball.

Couoh came to the Tecos as part of the class of 1988. In the ensuing years this twenty-five-year-old native of Mérida, Yucatan, has put together a respectable record, but one that has to be deconstructed in order to be appreciated. It seems as if the Tecos' management can't make up their minds whether to use him as a starter or a reliever. He has done both well.

In 1990, as a starter, Couoh was 14–8 with a 3.83 ERA. In 1993, out of the bullpen, he went 7–2 with an impressive 2.24 ERA. His strikeout-to-walk ratio has always been high and with each year, as he has gained control of his pitches, he has become impossible to beat when he's on. One is hard pressed to characterize Couoh as overpowering. That is reserved for beefier pitchers. This *flaco* (skinny guy) is more like quicksand: you swing and come up empty, and the ball just oozes into the ground. Couoh is one of only a handful of professional ballplayers from Yucatan and, like Alvarez, Couoh carries his regional identity with him, at once a source of pride and responsibility. These traits can mix to make for memorable moments, as when in 1990 Couoh got to pitch in front of family and friends for the first time:

> We were playing the Yucatan Lions in my hometown of Mérida. Coincidentally, the game took place the day after my mother's birthday. I was named starting pitcher and had a great game. I pitched twelve innings and left the game tied at two runs. You know, being in a stadium in my hometown, having my parents there, having my mother's birthday just the day before, made all of this a special moment. The fans really responded to me as well. I am Yucatecan. It didn't matter that I pitched for the Tecos.[32]

Enrique Couoh is the only Teco I met that seems as if he could be my neighbor, friend, or colleague. By this I mean that he comes across less as a ballplayer than a young lawyer or accountant. He is married with a two-year-old child, and he doesn't seem to have the ego problems of some of the other players.

While he may seem bookish, there's nothing abstract about Couoh's split-finger fastball that's at least AAA caliber in any league, anywhere. Nor is his slightness to be thought of as somehow weak. His strength is slippery speed and fluidity, not blistering fastball of some 210-pound power pitcher with twenty-two-inch thighs or the hairy bashing of home runs. Just as he runs unphased with long, easy strides for miles in 100 degree temperatures, Couoh angers straightforwardly. In response to my question as to what the story of the 1994 season might be, other Tecos raged against the dismantling of the team; Couoh simply said without emotion, "You want to know the story this season? The owners fucked up the '94 season for the Tecos."[33]

Typically in discussing the difficulties that the Tecos have had with imports, players are given to glower and growl angrily, dotting their speech with "pinches" and "chingados." Couoh momentarily held his breath and then softly said,

> Many of them feel humiliated by having to come and play in the Mexican League. They feel like trash because they inculcated preconceptions held by

their organizations [the major league clubs that signed them and assigned them to Mexico]. I think the opposite. For instance, the case of Foreman who did a great job for us. He got called back. American players must put both feet on the ground. In other words this may be their last chance to do well, but if they dig in, they will get back.[34]

For me the essence of Couoh was summed up on a night in 1994 when he threw against Mexico City Tigres. Each inning he went out there to pitch, he looked hittable in his warm up tosses. When the batter came up he would throw with the same fluid, almost casual motion and the ball slid like quicksilver into the earth, leaving behind another cursing batter. Between innings Couoh seemed neither distracted nor intensely focused; he seemed like an ordinary man, until it was time to go back out again. After nine of these cycles, Couoh had thrown a two-hit shutout and fanned sixteen.[35]

## Pedro Meré, Second Base

It's been said half seriously that when you are twenty-one years old in the Mexican League, you're already an old man. If so, twenty-four-year-old Pedro Meré is the most geriatric youth in professional baseball. He's been playing professionally since he was sixteen, almost eclipsing Joe Nuxhall, the Cincinnati Reds' pitcher who threw his first major league game at the age of fifteen.

Meré is a fluid second baseman with soft hands and fine instincts. Despite being 5'7' he has real power, averaging almost fourteen home runs a year, and his numbers continue to get better. Twice Meré was looked at by major league teams that brought him up to their spring training camps, and both times he was asked to go to their instructional leagues. He went to Atlanta's instructional league but became disillusioned when he didn't get the kind of playing time he was used to. "It was not until about two weeks before the end of the season that I was asked to play. I had a conflict with them because of this. I returned home because I felt I had wasted my time there."[36] I had known Pedro Meré for two years before I knew this about him. He is not one to dwell on such matters.

This quiet, gold-toothed young man comes from the baseball rich state of Veracruz, the city of Medellin de Bravo, and from a baseball rich family. "My father used to play ball but only locally. I do have an uncle, Luís Meré, who pitched in the Mexican League from the 1970s until about 1980."[37]

Meré smiles when he talks about his hometown and the prospect of returning briefly at season's end. Like most of the Teco starters, going home is but a stop before resuming play in the Pacific League, but he nevertheless makes the most of it: "Returning home is always nice after being away for so long. You get to see your family and friends. We catch up on things that happened during the season. Some of them ask me to clear up some rumors that surface during the season. We just have a lot of small talks about what's been going on with me, with them."[38]

The great passion for baseball among the people from Veracruz comes from the long tradition of the sport there. Local people were drawn to the sport by the arrival of many Cuban players via the coast and the inclusion of native Veracruzanos in their games.

Meré is deceptive-looking. One can immediately see his gentle face, a visage that seems free of malice, perhaps even a bit gullible. When he smiles, however, there is a sense that he's savvy. Should one miss that, his gold front tooth gleams incongruously to offset his apparent docility. While never initiating complaints or pushing player issues, Meré's sense of the team and the life of a Teco is laserlike, cutting to the bone without the smile ever leaving his face. Meré's rendition of the unusual sense of Teco collectivity is the best I encountered:

> The Tecos, as you see them, were founded by young players who, along with me, arrived around 1988. The foundation of the team included pitchers [Alvarez, Barraza, Couoh] and Ramírez. A year later came Díaz, and Romero. The most important characteristic of this team is that we have worked harmoniously; we have built a unified spirit because of coming to this team within such a short time. And because of that spirit we have been able to handle gringos like Baller who are difficult.[39]

Because he was so young when he came in, Meré essentially grew up as a Teco, but in spite of lacking the distance from which to examine his life, he calls on any issue with both passion and maturity. In speaking about travel, for instance, Meré reveals a bit of the team's social psychology:

> Unfortunately we are aware that travel arrangements are contractual agreements by which we must abide. I have always felt that Mexican players suffer from these arrangements. Our travel schedule makes us the most exhausted players in a league filled with exhausted players. The numerous trips and poor accommodations become a serious disadvantage to us. When Imports travel better than us we are also unhappy, but we are also aware of contract agreements by which these foreign players must abide. We can't make changes on this issue. In the meantime, we just arrived on a bus trip from Mérida to Laredo, forty hours, and we hardly stopped along the way. I think we stopped twice for food. It was an injustice considering we had been struggling to qualify for the playoffs. I was really upset with the managers [front office of the Tecos]. It makes you think that they don't care a thing about players. However, we try to overlook such unfair

treatment. When I'm on the playing field, I tend to forget whether the management has paid me or whether I have just arrived at the park exhausted from a
forty-hour bus trip. We show them all by winning for us, not the managers.[40]

Meré's quiet nature seems to stand in contrast to some of his other more
outgoing and aggressive teammates, giving one the sense that he acqui-
esces to the issues that faced the team during the two seasons I was with
them. Clearly, nothing could be further from the truth. The controversies
that came to engulf the Tecolotes were deeply felt by each and every
player, whatever their temperament.[41]

### *Jay Baller, Pitcher*

Fieldnotes: May 1. Just returned after a six-week leave. The gringos have joined
the team in the interim. Standing by the batting cage at West Martin Field
watching some of the Teco sluggers stroke balls over the left field wall, I hear
two very different conversations behind me. Ortiz, the pranksterish third baseman, is chatting with two Monterrey Industriales players about an umpire who
ejected some Tecos a week earlier. They are roasting him over a very hot fire.
Out of my other ear I hear some of the *importados* from both teams laughing and
making social connections through friends they have in common. The first conversation is Mexican in character, replete with expressions, close physical proximity, and hand gestures; the second is American. They are the same insofar as
either group could be having the same conversation, but their social makeup, for
the moment at least, is nationalist.
   The big guy in the midst of the American group is the loudest. Pitchers running the outfield fence can hear him bellowing the details of a story about some
ballplayer that the four at home plate all know. A thick-necked white guy, who,
in the interest of telling the story is faking—badly—an African-American accent.
After delivering the punch line—"Shit, I ain't done that since seventh grade!"—
he is also laughing the loudest.[42]

In this case, the "big guy," Jay Baller, seemed to me at that first meeting
to be all this and more. His in-your-face quality, which was reminiscent of
the burly first baseman, Marco Antonio Romero, when I first met him, put
me off. At 6'6" and weighing about 240 pounds he didn't need to wear a
shirt with the sleeves cut off and up.

A week passed before I decided to introduce myself to him; when I told
him what I was working on, he replied, "Hey man, what you're doing
sounds interesting. Let me know how I can help." The honest, sky-blue
eyes and rapid patter of his speech somehow negated the "beefy redneck"
I thought I saw a week earlier. Two very different impressions of the same

man emerged: a blustery and abrasive character on the field, and an eager and open (almost vulnerable) man off it. These two were complexly inter-twined into a thirty-three-year-old relief pitcher.

Even though he never thought of himself as a reliever when he started his career with the Philadelphia Phillies in 1982, he now defines himself as one. Were one to judge by numbers, he is also quite a good one. Between 1988 and 1992 he saved 103 ball games in a potpourri of AAA cities such as Calgary, Indianapolis, Omaha, and Scranton. In 1989 he set a minor league record of thirty-four saves with Indianapolis. Baller is no stranger to Latin American baseball either, having spent two seasons in Venezuela before joining the Tecos in 1993. Like the other *importados*, Baller arrived three weeks after the March 23 start of the season, yet by the middle of June, with less than one half of a season behind him, he had already com-piled a 6–2 record with thirteen saves. These are all good credentials, a fact recognized by the Kansas City Royals in 1990, the Phillies in 1982, 1992, and the Chicago Cubs in parts of 1985, 1986, and 1987; in each case Baller was brought up to the majors. At some point in his career he began to relish the danger of being a closer (someone who preserves wins for his team by coming into close games in the late innings and shutting down the opponents). "When I go in there's no room for error. One pitch can ruin it. I like knowing that I can be that perfect."[43]

When the Imports came to Laredo, Baller became their de facto leader. "I wasn't tryin' to be boss or anything. I just thought I'd help us all out," he said. The other Imports had no problem with Baller's informal and egalitarian style. When someone needed something fixed, or a car to drive, it was Baller who often handled negotiations with the Tecos' front office. When the family and girlfriend of fellow Imports Orlando Lind and Bobby Moore came in, Baller made himself available to help out, and all three players lived and worked well together.

There was, however, the unfortunate problem with the fourth Import, Willie Waite. He would not brook Baller's leadership. At first, all the im-ports thought it was a matter of initial adjustment and backed off when Waite said or did something inappropriate. But after a series of smaller incidents, Waite woke up Baller's baby daughter by playing rock music loudly until 5 A.M. in the apartment complex where they all lived, and all tolerance vanished. The following day, en route to the local Walmart the Imports had it out. Baller bellowed at Waite to get out of the car. "I was gonna punch his lights out," he recounted matter of factly.

The most impressive thing about Baller is not his fastball or the way he sets a hitter up, but rather his sense of just where in the sport he is and what he makes of that. While Waite was cursing the heavens for putting him in Mexico, Baller was figuring out how to make the best of it. This was admirable. The Mexican League is not a place that ex–major leaguers or wannabe major leaguers choose to go. In fact, until recently, it was just the place you avoided going to. Rather than succumb to the stigmas, Baller chose to maximize his opportunity:

> I figure that if I continue to put up good numbers they gotta look at me, and if not the Braves, well maybe the Rockies or Expos, somebody out there will notice. I can't worry about that shit 'cause I can't do nothin' about it. All's I gotta do is continue to save 17 to 20 games a year.[44]

His pragmatism was nicely blended with an optimistic view of the world. Even more impressive was Baller's mature sense of why he is in the game. There is a point that some people reach who are in pursuit of their dreams where one sheds the grandiosity of the dream, while being able to fully enjoy the pursuit. This is not scaling down, or giving into reality; rather it is living the dream. Being cognizant of all the little things like going to the ball park each day, suiting up, having your loved ones come to see you, traveling as a team is what this dream is about. You may have earlier taken your career and playing time for granted, but no longer do so. This usually comes from having developed a sense of mortality, some newfound sense of vulnerability that cocky youth cannot fathom. Jay Baller has come to this sense of appreciation of late. Before 1987, he was as raucous and careless with his career as any one of the thousands of young ballplayers who squander their moment in baseball without a shred of consciousness.

By late 1987 he had separated from his wife, which in his eyes made his downward spiral complete. But it wasn't. He decided to ponder his future while vacationing in Clearwater, Florida. He fished and hung around for weeks before returning home. But once he got back, he began to experience odd sensations. He became dizzy but attributed it to the stresses he had been under. He started losing balance. Again, he thought it was due to stress. But when he started having difficulty filling out a check one day he finally realized something was dramatically wrong. "Luckily the hospital was five minutes away, 'cause if it was any further I'da been wiped."[45]

By the time he checked himself into the emergency room, his heart rate was over 200. They quickly gave him something to slow it down. Whatever the dose was that he took didn't do the trick, so he was given a second one. "That's when I redlined for the first time"—meaning that your heart stops functioning so that on a screen it is a flat red line. The emergency team jump started him with their electrodes, but he redlined again. His temperature had now spiked to 107 degrees.

The treatment he received was risky, because it resulted in Baller slipping into a coma. Five days later he opened his eyes: "The first thing I saw when my eyes focused was my mom's face. You know how special that bond between a mother and her son is. I've thought about how she must have felt in Oregon, thousands of miles away when the hospital called to tell her her son wouldn't make it through the night and that she should get on the next plane."[46]

Spring training was just a few months away when Baller decided to resume his career. He walked into camp thirty pounds lighter and everyone thought it was over for him. "But I still managed to put up some numbers. Got my velocity up to where it was respectable." And he posted the lowest ERA on the team. Before camp broke, manager Don Zimmer called him in and gave it to Baller straight: "Look, I'm not gonna fuck with you. We're going up north with twenty-eight guys and you're not one of them." Baller wanted to know the reason. Zimmer said it was his loss of velocity.

His next stops were with the minor league affiliates of Seattle, Minnesota, Kansas City, and Philadelphia. Everywhere he went he "put up numbers" and never let the situations deflate him. Meeting his present wife, Terry, was, without question, the most positive step in this most recent phase of his life. Terry, along with new daughter Sierra, prevented Baller from sinking into an emotional abyss as he went from city to city trying unsuccessfully to get back to the majors. This late-model Baller is a man who has been forced to come to grips with life's big questions. The Teco stopper Jay Baller can appreciate the chase itself, and that has helped him focus down on smaller things—such as buying a good coffee pot so that his fellow Tecos can share some java at the game.

Jay Baller was, in the first half of his season with the Tecos, one of the *importados* who was appreciated. One veteran Teco pitcher characterized him, "Well, he [Baller] and Orlando [Lind] are those who have been better able to adapt. They are the ones with whom you can relate most. They don't wait for you to come to them to be friendly. They go and let it be known that they are willing to make new friends." His stature was further secured both by his willingness to confront Waite and by his success as the team's closer. The Mexican players saw Baller openly challenging Waite and appreciated it.

With so much going for him, it was quite surprising to encounter the situation reversed when I returned in the second half of the season. In the wake of Waite getting the call back to Atlanta's AAA ball club in Richmond, Baller seemed to have taken on the mantle of the Ugly American. It's hard to say exactly what precipitated the shift, but a Baller-inspired collective Import desertion of the team several weeks earlier in Mexico City (see Chapter 6) was most certainly the turning point. After that incident, relations on both sides soured. For his part, Baller's behavior was more aggressive, less conciliatory than earlier. He openly declared that he "did the work of three Mexicans," a remark that infuriated many. He left the park at odd times, returning just before the game. He readily con-

fronted people he might not have earlier, prompting one teammate to conclude, "In some ways, he is worse than Waite."

For their part, the players were only slightly more hurt than angry by the
Mexico City incident. They had trusted Baller, and because he was so successful on the mound, they could more easily think of this gringo as a team
member. Some Imports are just seen as *refuerzos* (reinforcements), but
Baller seemed to be the other type. Was he angry at not being in
Richmond? Was there some other reason? Certainly from his point of
view the ineptitude of the Teco front office knew no bounds and acted as
a constant irritant. Conditions of his contract were repeatedly not met.
The simplest thing might turn into a week-long string of phone calls and
badgering. He may simply have grown tired of it all, but it was not confined to the front office. Rather, his relations with the players grew
strained, and the season ended in psychological shreds with Baller itching
to leave and the Tecos breathing a collective sigh of relief once he did. "I'm
in the Land of the Lost down here, and I'm looking for the key to get out,"
concluded Baller, who nevertheless led the league in saves that year. Had
he played the entire season he very well might have set the league record.
On a very small scale the Baller reversal was an unfortunate and unneces-
sary blow to relations between gringos and *mexicanos*. With a bit more
introspection on Baller's part it could have been otherwise.

## Social Organization

Management, foreign and Mexican players, veterans and rookies, the cities
of Nuevo Laredo and Laredo all comprise the structural properties of this
team. All but the bimetropolitan element are germane to the Mexican
League. A description of the structural relations would benefit from the
use of a metaphor; in this instance, the Tecos can be likened to a city. As
a social microcosm of a metropolis Teco City has its "old town" section in
the presence of veterans like Mora, Ortiz, and Sánchez. It has a newer
suburban section made up of those who came in the 1988 wave (e.g., Barraza, Couoh), as well as an exclusive neighborhood generally reserved for
foreigners. Relations between groups of Tecos reflect relations between
parts of cities too. The historic center of town, long accustomed to controlling the direction and pace of life, resents the newly emerging power
stemming from the suburbs and their more youthful leadership. This is
certainly the case in Laredo, and among the Tecos as well. The older players assume their position as team leaders and are, for the most part, so
treated, but there is a certain amount of resentment on the part of the
younger ones. It was very interesting to hear that the older players thought
of themselves as willing to act as mentors to the younger players. "There

are many rookies who think approaching us is impossible. I don't understand why they don't speak with us. Maybe they're afraid, but we try to help them understand us," declared one old-timer. The younger group, however, experienced their early days differently:

> Well, I was in the rookie group of 1988. We didn't talk to Ortiz or Mora. They were a separate group. We saw them in the bus and only talked in passing. Sometimes we shared a laugh. They woke us up at whatever time they pleased. They insulted us.
>
> Now we are more equal. They are now leaving and we are on the level that they were when we first arrived six years ago. They now respect us. We are a respected group.[47]

To some extent the early treatment received by the class of 1988 was a form of "rookie" hazing. But these differences are more attuned to structure and temporal phenomena than simple rites of initiation. The newer players, who are now in the prime of their careers, are a group that is becoming politicized in a way that the older never were. Newer players are more easily angered by the way in which the owners have handled them. Older players have had to endure the baseball players strike of 1980 and the renegade league, ANABE, that was formed in its wake.[48] During the several years of the strike, the owners were particularly ruthless and intimidated many players of the time, with the result that players were less likely to express their resentment. These newer players, on the other hand, show a bit more willingness to confront issues. For instance, they are less likely to forgive the Imports for their racial and cultural intolerance. On the Tecos, because these post-ANABE players came up together and have played so long in each other's company, they have a sense of being born of the same mother:

> This team has a single foundation. This helps the players become closer. I think we are closer friends than players of any other teams. The rest of the teams base their recruitment on buying players from other teams. In other words, in many of these teams, the majority of players have not begun with them. On our team there are almost no players who started with another team. Most of us started in our organization or came over when we were very new so we have known each other since we began playing. We have known each other all of our life in baseball.[49]

If there is an old core and a newer suburban ring to this Teco City, there is also the presence of an exclusive neighborhood of non-Mexicans who live physically separated from the rest of the city. I refer, of course, to Imports who reside in Laredo. The quota of foreign players has fluctuated over time. During the Pasquel era it was as many as ten. For the decade from 1983 to 1993, the quota was four, but has, since the 1994 winter meetings of the league, increased to five. The presence of Imports is, both from the perspective of the Import as well as his Mexican teammates, ambivalent. On the one hand, they are welcomed as valuable additions in the team's quest for a championship. On the other hand, either by showing intolerance and disrespect for Mexican customs or by behaving as entitled ballplayers, Imports often create difficulty for teammates, the front office, and fans. Thus the Imports' presence highlights the perceived inferior status of Mexican baseball—that it must retain these reprehensible individuals in order to succeed. To many this smacks of cultural imperialism.

By virtue of the preferential treatment of foreign players, the Import-Mexican team relationship is structured to reinforce the foreigner's sense of superiority. Constituting a separate, somewhat privileged caste, the imports get paid more and separately (by the major league team they are representing, if the Mexican team has a working relationship with one), travel better, and sometimes occupy better quarters on the road. At least one Teco prophesied, "This situation may very well be the cause for the future rupture of our team and hurt our ability to act as one." Imports rarely speak Spanish or seriously try to learn, nor do they easily adjust to food and other cultural differences. Worse still, for many foreigners, playing in the Mexican Leagues has come to symbolize the end of their careers, and they commonly take their frustrations out on their Mexican hosts. In Baller's case, his disappointment at getting his career on track was palpable, and a good deal of his acting out was probably venting frustration. To his Mexican teammates, however, Baller was spoiled in ways they could only fantasize about, and they had little sympathy for him.

Some *importados*, such as Lee Upshaw, who played with the Tecos in 1992 and briefly in 1994, adapt fairly well, seeing their experience in Mexico as a cultural opportunity. Early accounts also reveal Imports who enjoyed playing and living in Mexico. For a number of the Negro Leaguers who played on Mexican teams in the 1940s, this was certainly the case, as we saw in Chapter 3. On occasion, *importados* really take to their Mexican experience and wind up staying for a long time, or as in the case of Jack Pierce, permanently.[50] Pierce, now a scout in Mexico, played twelve years for seven different teams before he retired in 1987. He powered his way into the Mexican League record books with a Ruthian effort in 1986, when his fifty-four home runs set the single season mark. Rounding out his numbers that year was a .381 batting average and 148 RBIs. Pierce is one of those rare Imports who liked it enough to stay, marrying a *mexicana* and raising a family. Pierce, alas, is quite an exception. Imports have tended to be synonymous with problems. In Teco City the problems are somewhat isolated by having Imports live apart (across the river) from the rest of the team.

On the field, relations between Teco Imports and Mexican players are cordial. These men are professional enough to know that success between the lines is a collective effort, but outside the game, they rarely mix. There is a marked tendency for exclusive grouping based on nationality, and this is, of course, underwritten by the inability to communicate. Even when the chasm is bridged and players attempt to interact, there is a withered quality to it that is particularly telling in the context of baseball life. Asked if they ever socialize with Imports outside of the game, one veteran replied, "Oh yes, sometimes if they invite us we all go: rookies, Americans, and veterans. Yes, sometimes I take a walk with the American players." To understand this more fully, one has to recall just how much downtime there is in baseball. Players have so much opportunity to hang around between, before, during, and after the game that it can lead to problems. Players will party together, at times violating team rules and/or getting into problems with women and/or the police. Players hang around together so often that they can find all manner of mischief to get into, so "taking a walk" with Americans constitutes a particularly paltry moment shared among players, and underscores the nature of these relations.

Teco City is also a company town. Everyone who lives in it works for the Owls, and while they don't live in company housing, by virtue of having to move to Teco City from their hometowns, they are occupying Teco space. The relations between players and management is problematic anywhere in baseball. The traditional reserve system that American major leaguers worked so hard to rid themselves of is still operative in the Mexican League.

The ways in which these relations are manifest are in the control exerted by Mexican League owners over their players, and most particularly in the opportunities for Mexican players to play in America. Latin American baseball researcher Milton Jamail has already discussed the prohibitive nature of Mexican league contracts with their players:

> Owners of Mexican Summer League teams have not been anxious to see their top prospects leave. All Mexican player contracts must be purchased from the Mexican League teams and this fact has served to severely limit the number of Mexicans playing in the USA . . . and up until very recently the asking price was very high. So while a U.S. team might sign 20 Dominican prospects for $100,000, they've had to pay that much for one Mexican prospect."[51]

The Tecos all pointed to this issue as well: "I believe the main reason hampering the opportunity of Mexican players to play in the U.S. is the Mexican League's control," argued one Teco. "The cost of contracting Mexican players is excessively high. . . . For this reason, if U.S. owners consider a Mexican player, they must be certain the player has the potential."[52] A second Teco points out, "Some teams, like Saltillo, sell their players at very low fees. I remember Armando Reynoso [contract] was sold to the U.S. at a very low fee, maybe $10,000. That year Reynoso won 21 games. In Nuevo Laredo, if a player has won 21 games, the owners would ask at least $70,000."[53] Another echoed this: "The main reason hampering the participation of Mexican players in U.S. leagues is Mexican League owners unwillingness to provide opportunities for this exchange. They set the cost too high. The cost of ten or twelve Dominican players is the same as one Mexican player. The owners are the ones who have the control."[54]

For their part the Teco owners argue that they encourage their players to spend time playing in the United States: "We prefer for them to play there. That way, when and if they return they will be better trained. It helps our team."[55]

The control of the owners extends also to the press, which is seen as a public relations arm of the team. One Teco commented, "Mexican newspaper and others are paid for by the owners. Yes, this is how it is. For instance, if a radio commentator speaks negatively about any of us in the league, our owner orders the commentator not to do this again."[56] Milton Jamail modifies this view somewhat, commenting that although many journalists are unprofessional, there is a growing number of first-rate journalists.[57]

Relations between players and the front office clearly contain a strong element of tension. In such a climate anything is liable to be interpreted as an act of malevolence; certainly this is the case with the players. No doubt some of their charges can be shown to be fact, such as the failure of the front office to pay into the players retirement fund for a couple of years. Some issues that generate anger have occurred but may have had alternate explanations. For example, in July 1994 the Teco players were not paid on time. They were going on the road and the front office said they would be paid by the time the team returned. That the players were not paid was a fact. How it all was interpreted is filled with innuendo and charged with mutual distrust. Regardless of the actual facts, the instance furthered the resentment of the players toward the front office. One story has it that Samuel Lozano, the general manager, told the players that the city of Laredo had not come through. In fact, the city pays the Tecos immediately following the game, but it seems that Samuel was trying to get the city to pay before the game. Word on the street was that don Víctor—through Samuel—was busily trying to get money for his bullfight arena. According to fans and the press, the Lozanos had, by 1994, abandoned the Tecos by selling off some of its stars and seeking a buyer for the team. A survey of fans in Nuevo Laredo in 1994 (see Appendix C) clearly indicated that they felt the Tecos owners had mismanaged the team: eighty percent of the respondents faulted the owners in one way or another. Even as rumor, however, the sentiment and lines of tension can be assessed, and in 1994 engulfed the entire organization.

Some issues with the front office reflect charge and countercharge between players and the owners, and short of a court case cannot be proven to anyone's satisfaction. There was the players' claim that the front office had cheated the players out of playoff money in 1993. Playoff money in the first four games of each series is to be split 50–50 between owners and players. The players asserted that the owners deliberately undercounted the attendance and shortchanged them out of thousands of dollars. The front office scoffs at this charge, but it matters little because each incident adds a layer of resentment on the part of the players, and indirectly furthers their sense of cohesiveness. "Whenever someone has a dealing with Samuel, he comes back and we all talk about it," commented one player. Sensing their powerlessness in the Mexican League they do what they can in response. While no one likes to discuss it, there is a level of play called *la tortuguismo* (the tortoise) involving a deliberate slowdown of play (see Chapter 7). Following the lead of James Scott,[58] who has argued for "everyday forms of resistance" when structural barriers prevent more open confrontation, *la tortuguismo* is a systematic slowdown of play, a behavioral response fashioned by players. In any event, the management-player relations are strained (as in the case of Pedro Meré, above), and there is little goodwill sensed on either side. While much of the players' resentment centers on Lozano because he is the most direct contact they have with the front office, the anger is really directed at the management-owner relationship. "We can't do anything because we have no Free Agency like you do in the U.S. *Chinga*, they could pay us a thousand [dollars] a month and we couldn't do anything but complain. I can't go to another club. If Samuel is still here next year I'm gonna ask for a trade."[59] The next year this player was traded. Were someone else in Lozano's position, communication might or might not improve, but the structural relations would be equally tension producing. These are worker-management issues, and individuals only shift the balance a few degrees one way or another.

While looking at the team as a single social microcosm helps us to understand Teco relations, we must also look at the team as binational, made up of two entities. The relations between the two Laredos is the unique feature of the franchise. There have been other teams along the border since the founding of the league (e.g., Reynosa in 1963–1976, 1980–1982, and since 1995; Ciudad Juárez in 1973–1984), but the Tecolotes were the first border team and binational venture. Both Reynosa and Ciudad Juárez have American cities as counterparts, but it is only the two Laredos that have the historic and current social makeup that can allow such a venture. Only the two Laredos were born of one. It took more than having Tecos fans on both sides of the border to enable the project to move forward; it took a historic and social bonding that comes of constant denial of international boundaries, the bonding that comes of having a *mexicano* population in Laredo that has some power and is merged (at social points) with Anglos. And it takes an ideological sense of common origins.

The region's transnational baseball past enabled people to envision a team for both cities. Teams from Nuevo Laredo had long since become accustomed to playing across the river as the hometown team (see Chapter 2). The press fostered the idea of transnational baseball as well, with its feature stories on La Junta and the early Tecolotes. When the Lozanos and Rodríguez pushed the binational project, they merely tapped into a tradition that had been going on for eighty years. Playing in the relatively more professional Mexican League following World War II, however, did have the effect of taking the game out of the local arena and thereby harming the transnational character of the game. Players were less and less likely to be locals, and more and more likely to be Anglos or Latinos with no connection to the two Laredos. The game, the team, and its players increasingly reflected autonational issues in their feelings and behavior toward each other, mediated by their binational need for each other.

# Five

## Culture and Masculinity on the Tecos

AUTONATIONALISM and machismo seem well suited to each other.[1] Jorge Pasquel blended them effectively in his confrontations with U.S. baseball, as did Commissioner Chandler in his response to Pasquel. The puffery, bluster, and saber-rattling that accompanies testicular politics blends readily with the drive to dominate one's fellows and, even more, women. The machismo-nationalist connection was provocatively made by Paredes, who examined nineteenth- and twentieth-century Mexican *corridos*, or ballads.[2] Among other things, he pointed out that Mexican machismo was a product of the steady hostility that existed between Mexicans and the Americans whom they had fought and who seized Mexican land in the war of 1846. "Don't back down on me, you *bravos*, and carry your blades at the ready" was the admonition of the *Man from Guanajuato*.[3] These earlier songs talk of "dying like men," remaining "valiant" to the end—a straightforward patriotism and hostility toward the enemy. A half century later, during the Mexican Revolution, Paredes points out, there developed a brand of *corrido* that expressed the same resentment but with a hypermasculine twist that is more reminiscent of macho chest thumping found in many societies:

> What did these big-footed gringos think,
> that they scare us with cannon.
> They may have piles of airplanes,
> but we have the thing that really counts.[4]

Or:

> It will be a pretty sight, to see all those gringo corpses;
> they will flinch from the tortilla, and they will sweat up to here.
> In truth, I hope they will bring their gringo women along,
> because we are getting tired of loving our Indian girls.[5]

This brand of autonationalism clearly lends itself to macho boasting that denigrates the enemy and glorifies *la patria* through sexual threats and linguistic form. We find ethnographic parallels of this in the descriptions of relations between Tecos and Imports (see Chapters 1, 6, and 7). This chapter pursues a slightly different yet related track by looking at machismo as a cultural marker of Mexican masculinity. In brief, the Latin macho stereotype is examined, less for its nationalist implications (dealt with elsewhere) than for contrasting masculine styles between Mexicans and Americans. These contrasts work to reinforce the autonational resentment presented throughout. For the Mexican players, the contrasts that highlight the cultural differences between the two groups not only separates them, but also fosters tighter cohesion within each.

As a blueprint for Latin American masculinity—or at least one form of it—machismo is comprised of a set of beliefs, behaviors, and relations. The cornerstone of this code of masculinity is power, and its main manifestation is aggression: against men and women, sexual, psychological, and linguistic. Most people have come to loosely think of it in the vein of Mexican poet and essayist Octavio Paz: "One word sums up the aggressiveness, insensitivity, invulnerability and other attributes of the macho: power. It is force without the discipline of any notion of order: arbitrary power, the will without reins and without a set course."[6]

As a pervasive set of institutions we expect to find machismo in baseball as well. The study of the Tecos shows machismo to be choreographed in the game, as well as in the lives of the players, both of which are caught up with displays of masculine power and aggression. Whether it is the rugged look of, say, Andrés Mora or Alejandro Ortiz, or the emphasis on jock-talk centered on baseball prowess, male aggression, or dealings with women, the Tecos are very much adherents of the machismo school of masculinity. This broader view is inculcated by their wives as well, one of whom characterized her husband (and all males) as follows: "He [a *macho*] has to be tough. He has to be the head. What he says, goes with his girlfriend or his family. He has to be in control. My husband had to be tough. His no's were no's. His yes was yes. If he wanted to go out, he'd go out. It wasn't a matter of asking. They'd call each other *mandilón* [henpecked] if the wife said 'no' and you listened."[7]

This broader view of Latin American masculinity has, however, come under increased scrutiny and critique over the past twenty years,[8] with the result that the concept has become nuanced and elaborated, and that as its primary manifestation Latin American men have been shown to incorporate a broader range of behaviors than previously thought. Machismo, then, has been reconfigured, according to some: "Macho has nothing to do with how much salsa you can eat, how much beer you can drink, or how many women you fuck. You can be macho as a farmworker or judge. It's a real mixture of pride and humility. . . . if I live up to my code of ethics, I will gain respect from my family, my job, and my community."[9]

This broader view of men is also evident among the Tecos, in men like right fielder Luís Fernando Díaz. When a call went out to the Tecos to take part in a fashion show, Díaz was the only Teco who appeared. The woman who staged the show, herself a Teco wife, said of Díaz, "I invited him [and others] to take part in a fashion show, and thought 'They're never gonna buy this.' But he showed up with his family. He wanted to come and he took his wife to pick out his clothes. And I'm like, 'What?' This is one of the last guys I expected to show. His wife picks out his clothes and he comes out of the dressing room and asks, 'Is this okay?' She's dressing him!"[10]

Clearly, we are dealing with a range of behavior and style that includes very different, at times diametrically opposing, codes for behavior—which requires some analysis. Teco ethnography can help us understand the disparate elements of Mexican and Latino machismo, and through it help refine our sense of how autonationalism gets played out.

Ironically, in its more pompous and bullying form, machismo, Paredes claims, first entered Mexico as part of the gringo invasion of the nineteenth century in the personage of the Anglo Texan cowboy and Texas Ranger busy carving out a piece of Mexico. Propelling this imperialism was rank economic opportunism, sanctified by a sense of manifest destiny, social Darwinism, and masculinity. Doubly ironic, the American Texas cowboy is an outgrowth of the Mexican vaquero—diffused to Anglos as part of the ranching economy that sprang up along the Rio Grande River from the eighteenth century on.[11] The cowboy differs from the *vaquero* most significantly in his racist views, and in his social use of the pistol, which, along with icons such as the Stetson, all meld into a form of nationalist machismo. If the "national character" school of anthropology, in which cultures were distilled into a set of social-psychological portraits, were still in vogue, Mexicans would be characterized by a sense of machismo. Through the cultural construction of gender, behavior and emotion become means of distinguishing the gringo from the *mexicano* and thereby fueling nationalist resentment, but a sense of just what is meant by the term "machismo" must be developed.

## Machismo and Masculinity

After centuries of tacit acceptance by men and women in a wide range of societies, the institution and cultural concept of machismo has finally come to be challenged. Machismo is one of those concepts around which there is little consensus and extreme reactions. Differences in machismo exist along class, ethnic, age, and regional lines,[12] as well as individually. To the degree that machismo is bound up with notions of hypermasculinity and virile demonstrations of masculinity, it joins the fray of current combatants trying either to save or resurrect traditional masculinity, to find a new one;[13] or to critique the essence of masculinity.[14]

Even when it is shown that the characteristics of machismo are found in a wide range of societies, there nevertheless remain cultural variations of it that are heavily associated with Latin American and particularly Mexican masculinity.[15] The task, then, is to explain machismo, both socially and culturally, so that it is neither ethnocentric or a post-hoc rationalization for any and every masculine excess.

Most definitions of machismo center on male determination to dominate and control all social relations. In its most conventional usage machismo is synonymous with an aggressive display of masculinity built around intimidating, posturing, fighting, carousing, and competitive behavior. Most often thought of as male domination of women, machismo runs the gamut from simple monopolization of all marital and familial decision making, to aggressively conquering as many women as one can, even to abuse of women.[16] Likewise there seems to be a strong current of proving oneself vis á vis other men. Acceptable forms include, but are not limited to, competition of a social, political, and linguistic nature.[17] This view of machismo brooks no softness, compromise, or subordination.

In the classic *The Labyrinth of Solitude*, Octavio Paz dramatically outlines his view of Mexican machismo through his social analysis of the Spanish verb "chingar." We have become familiar with this verb as the invective and hostile declaration of intramasculine war, *chinga tu madre!* (fuck your mother). Wherever in the Spanish-speaking world *chingar* is found, the verb implies an act of aggression, of violation in word or deed, whether in business, politics or, against a female in someone's family:

> There are two possibilities in life for the Mexican male. He either inflicts actions implied by *chingar* or he suffers them himself. . . . The person who suffers this action is passive, inert and open, in contrast to the active, aggressive and closed person who inflicts it. The *chingon* is the macho, the male; he rips open the *chingada*, the female, who is pure passivity, defenseless against the exterior world. The idea of violence rules darkly over all the meanings of the word, and the dialectic of the "closed" and the "open" thus fulfills itself with an almost ferocious precision.[18]

If Paz is given to portraying machismo in somewhat dramatic terms, he is nevertheless describing a set of male attitudes and behaviors that actually exist in some form or other. Social scientists have examined this institution as well, and without exception agree that such a construction of masculinity exists. Studying Nicaraguan masculinity in a barrio in Managua during the Sandinista Revolution, Roger Lancaster extends and concretizes machismo in defining and chronicling it as a *system* of male aggression capable of withstanding attempts to undermine it: "Like racism, homophobia, and other forms of arbitrary power, arbitrary stigma, machismo is resilient because it constitutes not simply a form of 'consciousness,' nor 'ideology' in the classical understanding of the concept, but a field of productive relations."[19] Lancaster's view of machismo adheres to the 'bully' definition, critical from a quasi-feminist point of view.

Others, beginning with Mendoza,[20] and continuing on with Paredes[21] and Mirandé,[22] have argued for a view of machismo that is bipolar. The excessive bully is counterbalanced by a man who is measured, generous, dignified, responsible. Mendoza referred to the bully as the "false macho" and the more positive construct as the "true macho."[23] I would like to argue for the macho as containing elements of both within himself. In fact, the expression of a more gentle side coexists with, rather than stands opposed to, traditional machismo within the individual. Comparing Mexican and American players in this way reveals not only cultural differences of masculinity; it also revealed, by separating these teammates along national lines, subtle dimensions of autonationalism.

## Making Sense of Teco Machismo

With ten straight playoff appearances and two league championships since 1977, the Tecos are considered a force to be reckoned with. Their signature, appropriately enough, is power. Their hitters "talk that talk, and walk that walk," with two-day growths of beard, cutoff sleeves, and a fondness for pounding their jocks with bat handles because, as they sometimes declare, *tenemos muchos huevos* (we have a lot of balls [literally, eggs]). The Teco's power hitting and machismo is further demonstrated in the way the Tecos tend to perform as a team—seemingly doing everything to hamstring themselves, then putting on a last minute power surge that catapults them into their division's lead. While speed is valued, there is little effort to acquire it. As the sine qua non of machismo, power is expressed in powering the ball for a 430-foot home run, or at least a 400-foot single. At least half the Teco hitters swing with the idea of gulfing one out of the park; and when they succeed and round the bases to meet their fellows at home plate, they, like their American counterparts, choreograph a group macho fist-slamming-fist exchange, except that the Mexicans cap theirs off with a mutual Mexican salute (hand sideways chopped out from chest).

On the day-to-day baseball level there are other expressions of macho posturing as well. Language is often double-edged with literal on one side and sexual one-upsmanship on the other. Hence, *ese vato no se raja* (that guy doesn't back out, he's not a pussy) not only means he's tough, but conveys an image of a male who is sexually-anally aggressive as well. So too with the oft heard, though less sexual baseball expression, *se fajó* (he bore down, or tightened his belt, often applied to a pitcher). Machismo, however, is not designed to be subtle. Paz notes that the macho's aggressiveness "provokes a great sinister laugh," even turning humor into "an act of revenge." The macho's "jokes are huge and individual, and they always end in absurdity."[24]

In the very first Tecos series I watched in the summer of 1992, I witnessed an illustration of the fusion of aggression, joking, and machismo in a game against the Leones from Mérida.[25] The plate umpire was calling the kind of game that brought on murderous cries from the Tecos faithfuls. He had been consistently "squeezing" both pitchers, reducing the strike zone significantly; but since this was a home game, the Teco fans were convinced he was doing it only to their pitcher. This umpire, a huge rotund man, completely obscured the catcher when viewed from behind. In about the third inning the Teco battery had had enough with his calls and decided to retaliate: the catcher called for a fast ball and then shifted ever so slightly to the side, allowing the pitch to hit the umpire. This worked much better than expected—the umpire took a ninety-mile-per-hour pitch in the groin. He instantly dropped down on all fours, to which the fans roared their approval, screaming "Burro!" and "Check the ball!" and whistling their derision. The downed umpire fought to catch his breath. The fans continued their stomping and cheering until he finally stumbled to his feet, face red and sweaty. A huge, malevolent sneer spread slowly across his lips, and he turned to face the crowd. Holding up both arms as if signifying a halt to the game, his voice shouted for all to hear, *"Chingen sus madres, pendejos!"* (fuck your mothers, jerks!). The stadium fell stunningly silent by this completely unexpected behavior; then, understanding the impact he had had, the bear-of-an-umpire laughed aloud. Within seconds, the fans rebounded and continued heaping abuse upon him, which lasted right through the game. It mattered little, however, for in the contest between umpire and fans the latter had been bested by this sudden outburst of machismo.

That laugh is also the signature of the story or joke that puts people down. Often the veterans, who nightly hold court before the game, recall someone's *faux pas*, or recount someone's colossal failure; but the humorous story has an edge to it, one that comes out not so much in the narrative as in the inflection and laughter that punctuates the tale. This is illustrated in a story about Teco slugger Marco Antonio Romero.

Romero is one of the most macho of the Tecos. He cultivates the look. His thick jet-black hair combed neatly back from his forehead and bushy Vandyke beard, setting off a two-day growth of beard, fit predictably upon a powerful beer-swilling body that swaggers. But what one remembers most is his laugh: gravelly, loud, explosive, and potentially a bludgeon. In the early part of my fieldwork, when I was very much an outsider and not trusted, I sought to chronicle some of this behavior, but it spilled over to engulf me:

Reynosa: This afternoon the veterans were giving a workshop on Teco-lore in the dugout. Seeking respite from the mid-day heat, they straggled in one by one until a small group had gathered. Then each of the veterans (Mora, Romero, Ortiz) would hold center stage talking to the rest about some encounter with other players (usually involving besting someone). Always sentences are punctuated with "*Chinga!*" or "*Pinche*" or any of the standard off-color terms that pass for an exclamation mark. Romero recounts a time when he took off after an opposing pitcher, mimicking the feeble, cowardly way the latter ran around the diamond trying to avoid Romero and his bat. Ballistically, Romero flew into the face of one of the players imitating his fury with a scowl and raised gloved fist on an overly hairy ham-of-a-hand. Then, that menacing laugh of his boomed from his goateed faced, and was joined by a chorus of laughter. . . . Turning his attention to me (he noticed me listening), Romero's smile slid smoothly to a sneer, and he used what limited English he knew to refer to my book, making it clear that he does not welcome my presence. He used the English word "book" in his otherwise Spanish diatribe: "Look at this one, the barbón [bearded one], writing a "*book*.". . . "*fuckin' book, fuckin' book.*" Each time he spit it out more loudly and more threatening, and always with the sneer-smile. The others were keenly interested in seeing what I would do. They smiled at me in thinly veiled friendliness that belied my foreignness.[26]

In a related set of events occurring about the same time, some of the veterans were challenging the stewardship of the Tecos' new manager, Dan Firova. Issues at the heart of their resistance had to do with nationalism, but the style of the challenge was pure machismo. Firova the *pocho*, who betrays his Mexican roots by acting more like the classic tight-lipped Texan that he is than a Mexican, no doubt generates some low-level resentment. Romero, more than the others, seemed to be in Firova's face. On the surface there was no real reason for the reaction to Firova. He was relatively young, an ex-Teco himself, having been a teammate of many of the players he was now managing, and so theoretically better able to relate to them. The anti-Firova sentiment was also felt by the fans and press of Nuevo Laredo and was directed at his gringo style of managing (e.g., he refused to coach third base) and his American identity. To make matters worse, Firova followed an extremely popular manager who had become something of a baseball institution in the two Laredos.

Romero was the one whose actions seemed most designed to offend. His (and many others') weapon was the transparent comment or joke. Something is said, the meaning of which exists at two very different levels: the benign and malevolent. For instance, the term *cachucha* means baseball cap, but if one is talking about or to women, one can also mean expendable women, "because like a hat you can put it on or take it off whenever you want." Or consider the oft-heard refrain *sácala!*, meaning "take it out (of the ball park)," as in a home run. It also means "take it (penis) out of your pants."

Romero, however, only occasionally used these linguistic devices in dealing with the Teco manager. He preferred to be a bit more direct, stopping just short of a direct confrontation. Romero's intentions were clear, however, as in one pregame episode in which the players were out taking fielding drills and doing light running. Firova entered the dugout, where Romero had come to drink some water:

> Firova [joking]: "Hey Romero, what's this? Let's get out there." Grabbing a bat, Firova turns and goes onto the field to hit grounders, standing about forty feet from Romero. Romero commences to growl to others in the dugout, but loud enough for Firova to hear: "*Chinga!* Go out and do what? I need water, not more work, *Pinche!* [an adjective whose approximate translation is 'damn']." Firova turns ever so slightly, deliberating for a second whether or not to go after Romero, and then goes on hitting grounders. Others in the dugout make eye contact with each other and Romero, saying nothing yet saying everything.[27]

This is the kind of quasi-challenge that is often uttered and, in the macho Mexican world of men, demands some sort of response. The manager, however, is very much a Texan and is ready to respond to a direct challenge (which this stopped just short of being) but not to something as ambivalent as this seemed to be. For the American there are options for handling a borderline insolent player like Romero, but not so for the Mexican. In head-to-head encounters as above, Firova's handling of it was not the most manly, and it cost him some measure of respect.

## Male-Female Relations

My dealings with Teco wives was primarily limited to the ballpark or team functions, yet I felt I could still draw from them some conclusions, most of which reflected a traditional machismo. Only one Teco wife worked, and she was Mexican American. Only one wife/girlfriend was attending college. There was a marked gender hierarchy, with men subsuming women in matters of decision making, familial authority, and economic control. That the wife may in some instances control the household—the public/ private division of authority—does not preclude the fact that men are able interpersonally to preempt women in most matters. One baseball wife summed up her husband's machismo and that of Mexican ballplayers in general: "The machismo is boosted by the uniform. That uniform makes them feel big. It's like a policeman in Mexico. The guy thinks he's macho 'cause he's got a police uniform, badge, and power to tell you what to do. These baseball players feel the same way. That uniform adds to their machismo. Without the uniform you oughta see them."[28]

Controlling one's woman is a requisite for machos. One wife presented this process as she had repeatedly seen it develop between players and wives:

> Every year I see the players and I see them walking the same path. I see them all starting the same and winding up the same. They start off being playboys and then get married to a pretty, popular girl. Then, as machos, they got to control the girl, so they make it so she doesn't work. However, she's probably more educated [than him]. She dresses up nice, but he'll control her. He'll give her everything to keep her happy. That's being macho, "You don't work. Anything you need, I get for you."[29]

The combination of professional baseball and Mexican machismo leads unavoidably to infidelity. One wife claims that 95 percent of the players philander to one degree or another; but in this regard Mexican players differ little, if at all, from their American counterparts. Said one player, "We go back to our hotel. We get showered and get our adrenalin going 'cause there's gonna be some women from the game at a bar. We're baseball players, so of course we're gonna score."[30]

The wives and girlfriends understand this as well, and attempt as best they can to prevent this:

> I do see them [wives] at the park, going through a few insecurities. They're always there after the games taking care of their husbands to make sure they come home after the game. I did that. . . . I know some Mexican [players] wives confront their husbands. Some of the girlfriends [of players] call the wives when the husbands are gone. Fireworks! What's unbelievable is that they [husbands] would deny everything. You'd think there was a script and you hand it out from one generation to the next. You call a guy 2 o'clock in the morning and he's not in his room [when they are on the road], and he says, "I went out to eat." "At two in the morning?" "Well, hon, the game went fourteen innings." The other excuse, "I was in Solano's room playing cards." And you feel like a fool. They all use those lines, and nobody plays cards.[31]

Needless to say getting caught up in this kind of never-ending cross-cultural baseball bachelor behavior leads to a high degree of insecurity among the wives, and much of this spills over into somewhat dysfunctional relations between wives, as well as between wives and husbands:

> When they can't take it any longer, they fight with their husbands. They challenge them. When they [wives] get together they cat fight with each other about each other's husbands fooling around. They gossip about another player making a move on someone. "And did you see this girl at the game? She was looking at him with those binoculars," or "I heard that your husband was dancing at a disco-

theque in Acapulco." When the husbands are gone they get together and say, "Well, we're gonna call them tonight. And if they're not there we're gonna do this or that. Remember they're [husbands] macho though, and won't take a challenge. A guy like [so-and-so] says, "Enough, I been here and here, and that's final!"[32]

Infidelity is endemic to sports figures in many parts of the world, but what may mark off the Mexican player from his American counterpart is refusing to take into account his wife or girlfriend's anger or disappointments as anything less than a challenge to his manhood. If the above interview material is at all reflective of their actual behavior to each other, there seems to be some sort of resignation on the part of these women to their husbands' philandering and general behavior. Taken in conjunction with other elements of behavior and style, the macho emerges as a cultural complex rather than as a single trait or two.

## Tender Machos

There exists a parallel range of behavior somewhat at odds with conventionally perceived machismo, which I call "Tender Macho." This style bears a closer relationship to the "true macho" (honorable man) discussed by Mendoza,[33] Paredes,[34] and Mirandé,[35] although I believe my sense of Tender Macho offers an even softer dimension of emotion than these scholars have discussed. My observations were limited to three areas: players' interactions with children and fans; players' expressions of feelings and vulnerability; and demonstrations of physical affection between players. All of these forms of behavior occurred frequently enough to be considered normative.

Through the development of a large nucleus of returning players, over the years the Tecos have encouraged feelings of family and community among teammates that mirrors Mexican kin-based values around *familia*, and *compadrazgo*. All but one of the Mexican players live in Nuevo Laredo and tend to reside in clusters, which increases the amount of interdependence between men and their families. Unlike most professional athletes, the Tecos have come to take for granted their seasonal gathering. As with many of the more accomplished Mexican players, the summer season in the Mexican League is supplemented by their playing in Mexico's "other league," the Pacific Coast League, which plays in the winter. One of the Tecos who plays in both leagues underscored both his introspection and the unique camaraderie of the Tecos:

The money is better over there [in the Pacific Coast League]. The quality of players is higher, but I don't like it as much in Mexicali [the PCL team he plays for]. You see, I'm not an easy talker. I'm shy. Over there [in Mexicali] they have a lot of big-name players and when they talk they don't make it easy for others. It's like they're the main people and we're less. Here [among the Tecos] there is a solidarity that allows everyone to feel like they belong. I can talk with others about anything. There, all I talk about is baseball.[36]

A sense of community spills naturally over into male-female relations. Where relations between men and between men and women intersect, there may exist a discrepancy between macho ideals and behavior. Nelson makes this point in her study of a central Mexican village when she quotes one of the local men:

Yes, at times we men want to be very strong and macho, but at the bottom we are not. When it is a question of morality or a family thing that touches the very fibers of the heart, it hurts and a man cries when he is alone. . . . Many drown themselves in drink and others grab a pistol and shoot themselves because they cannot bear what is inside . . . and at times those who believe themselves to be machos are really not so when they are alone with their conscience. They are only braggarts of the moment.[37]

Whether we want to consider this a "value stretch,"[38] as would some sociologists, or more akin to Goffman's "front stage vs. back stage" distinction,[39] what strikes me as impressive is the fact that men, most often those who are poorly educated, can verbalize these issues to outsiders, strangers, or to their own friends in the form of conversations, ballads, and songs.[40] More particularly, through the study of the Tecos we can add a wrinkle to the study of Latino and Latin American masculinity by seeing it as conflict between divergent cultural ideals, and that conflict exists in tension with actual behavior. The ethnographic observations of the players' behavior illustrates the nonmacho behavior, acting as a kind of brake against a runaway view of Latin American men as macho. Díaz, Romero, Cuevas, and others are machos who claim to live by the code of machismo, but as one wife remind me, "They also bend the rules. They wash dishes. They carry the baby. They change diapers. So, that's not a real macho."[41]

## Relations with Fans and Children

The relationships between the Tecos and their fans, particularly children, were filled with instances of two-way social intimacy and concern. It can be seen, for instance, in second baseman Pedro Meré engaging a fan as he walked off the field between innings one night. Meré stopped to listen patiently as the fan (a regular), who had a neurological disorder, struggled to tell him that he should hang back a bit on the curve balls being pitched to him. Despite being in a slump and in the middle of a game, Meré acted as if he had all the time in the world, exchanging his views on the pitcher with the young fan. This was no publicity stunt, nor was it an attempt to lure fans to the park. These fans and players have been together for a long time and have developed a genuine affection for each other; some fans often bring homemade gifts or baked goods for various players. In players' relations with children at the games one also sees this affection, whether it is the seemingly constant requests for signing balls or scraps of paper (as many as fifty such requests on some evenings) or as in the following incident that occurred at West Martin Field:

> Romero, with his three-day growth, looks like central casting's choice for a Mexican bandido. He laughs like a three-pack-a-day convict, but when he holds his little baby girl and zooms her around like a little pink dirigible [she wore a pink headband], he's the warmest, most comforting man imaginable. Each time he stops, she cries to be picked up and zoomed, and so the others all take turns suspending her as effortlessly as the moon hangs overhead.[42]

Another time, Ortiz, having struck out, returned to the dugout in Parque La Junta, ready to explode:

> Ortiz storms over to the time-out corner of the dugout, curses loudly, and slams his bat against the bat rack. Without losing a step, he moves to the other side of the dugout, still glowering, his cleats clicking angrily up the stairs to the chain-link fence that separates the players from the fans, and spots the baby of one of the fans he knows sitting on her mother's lap. Not missing a beat, he sweeps from fury to smile, losing twenty years in the bargain, and voice piping, pleads, "Give me a kiss, Elisa."[43]

Ortiz's actions are noteworthy, underscoring the time-out zone as not merely a place, but a period of time in which the player is inconsolable and completely isolated from his fellows. So furious is the individual in this state of mind that others will avoid even eye contact with him. In this instance, the close proximity of machismo and tenderness in Ortiz is demonstrated by his ability to move readily from anger to affection. There is a cultural comparison to hint at as well. Anglo players, while friendly, are not nearly as emotive and spontaneous as the *mexicanos*. The Imports would sign autographs, or indulge the children's request (within reason), but because of cultural and linguistic dislocation the Anglos could not possess the feel for the fans in the same way as their Mexican counterparts. Were this the only index of Tender Macho, there wouldn't be enough of a case to make. After all, similar instances of player concern (at least among individual players) with fans and children in the U.S. minor leagues can be found. But this was merely one of what I think constitutes a complex of behaviors.

## Expressions of Vulnerability

In direct contrast to the macho image of either Mexican or American players is the ability of Mexican players to express vulnerability. Just as easily as
some of these men seek to intimidate and dominate, they also beseech one
another (and on one occasion, even me) for help. One example comes from
the 1993 championship series between the Tecos and Olmecas, after a
Teco loss. Third baseman Ortiz had made an error that had cost the Tecos
the game. The following morning he appeared at the office of the manager's wife, who is an administrator at a local hotel (the two families are
very close, enabling Ortiz to converse relatively freely with his friend's
wife). What makes this particularly telling is that he goes beyond the emotional rules for Mexican machos by asking for help, from a woman no
less.[44] She described the meeting:

> He comes to my office, practically gets on his knees and wants me to tell him that
> he's doing okay, that he didn't make a mistake, that he's gonna snap out of his
> slump. He went to *my* office. He hadn't gone to sleep. He'd been drinking all
> night, and like, "God, where have you been?" And he sits down, puts his head
> down, grabs his forehead, and says, "I let the team down. I let my friends down."
> He was really emotional. He said, "I tried! I lost the ball and I couldn't make up
> for it with a hit. I let Dan [Firova] down and you don't know how much that
> hurts me. I'm really trying. What am I doing wrong?" He kept asking me, prac-
> tically crying. He was in my office for two hours, and I'm thinking, "Man, this
> macho guy? And him coming to a woman?"[45]

Even some of the stoic players, not usually given to expressing their
feelings, on occasion surprised me with the depths of their feelings. Andrés
Mora, facing declining skills and health, had begun seriously contemplat-
ing retirement. What made this doubly difficult for him was that he was
only thirty home runs short of the all-time Mexican League record. In
Chapter 4 Mora was characterized as being so in control of his emotions
that his lows and highs are virtually indistinguishable behaviorally. This
stoicism and heightened sense of privacy combined with the esteem in
which he is held by teammates make for an emotional distance between
him and almost everyone else (except Ortiz). All of this made it more surprising when he suddenly turned to me one night early in the 1994 season
and said, "You know, I'm thinking of quitting after this year." I asked why.
"My bat slowed down and I have aches and pains everywhere. I can't move
my leg back any further than this [he shows me]. It's just that I don't know
what to do. Baseball has been my life. I'm lost without it. It's very sad."[46]

An especially important area of emotional management is the way in
which the Tecos deal with their gringo Imports. Several typical illustra-

tions of this troubled history and of the slights felt by the Mexicans at the hands of the foreigners have been presented in the Introduction and will be presented in subsequent chapters; yet here, as in other areas, the Mexican player expresses his feelings as hurts (not simply as anger) with a mixture of sadness, incredulity, and pity for *norteamericanos*. This was the case with one of the younger players when he discussed his feelings about the way he was treated when he went to Atlanta's spring training facility:

> I had a good spring training here, then a got an invitation to West Palm Beach with the Braves. They paid for my ticket, food, everything. And they wanted me to stay there. They told me they wanted to send me to the Rookie League. They wanted to pay me $40 a week. Then I got that problem that my Dad died last year and now I have to send money to my mom; 'cause we owe money to the bank and I'm helping her. I told them, "I'll stay here if you send $200 a month to my mom. Don't give me nothing, just send it to her." And they said they couldn't do that. They said all you can do is call Laredo [the Tecos' front office] and have them send the money. Then I called here to Laredo and they never talked to me. And I said, "Okay, I'm gonna sacrifice this and go back to Mexico." And J. [a pitching coach for the Braves] said to me, "We want you here. If you go back to Mexico you're not coming here no more." I said, "I'm sorry. I appreciate that you invited me." I told him that I have the certificate of my Dad's death and I'd show it to him. He didn't care. What kind of a man is this that doesn't care about family?[47]

It is difficult to think of these expressions as exemplifying macho stoicism, impenetrability, or concern with seeming tough. Of course American players are capable of verbalizing their feelings, disappointments, fears, hopes. The difference between the two groups was the relative ease with which so many Mexican players could and would so express themselves. Considering that I shared with the American players the status as gringo outsiders, as well as our common culture and, to a lesser degree, a linguistic limitation, I would have expected that the American players would have expressed their alienation and other emotional issues more easily with me. In general, it was the Mexicans who, despite my foreign status, actually opened up more easily. Gringo players talking about sensitive areas of their lives or careers more often cloaked it in defensive joking, anger, or sarcasm. Feeling the pressure of time against him, one Import stated it rather typically: "Hey, shit man, I'm gonna be thirty, and I'm fuckin' wasting my time here. I don't have much more time, and I'm sittin around here!"[48] Another of the Imports talked about his days in the Texas Ranger organization and in particular a manager who "told all of us to hit movin' our front leg up like this [shows me]. No way can I do that, man. He said if you do it you'll move up the ladder [get promoted to a higher league]. Man, you can't fuck with a man's swing like that."[49] In both cases the tone is angry, and defensive, and the frustration comes out as invective. The hurt and pain, however, cannot be shown, either in word or facial expression. The Mexican players I dealt with would also get angry, but they showed the ability to express their hurt, and this I found impressive in the wake of their reputations as "machos."

## Physical Expression

Despite the pretense of male bonding, the expression of physical affection between American players (and by extension, all males) is carefully legislated. The fear of being labeled homosexual is a key part of the socialization of young men in America, and the category of behavior that is considered suspect extends to showing signs of physical affection.[50] Basketball greats Magic Johnson and Isaiah Thomas were close friends who would hug and kiss each other before their teams' contests with each other. This display of affection led to the persistent rumor that they were gay, which seemed the only logical way of explaining such behavior.[51] In a column in the nationally syndicated Sunday magazine, *Parade*, the question was posed: "Why Can't Guys Hug Each Other?" The two young men whose responses were chosen as representative illustrate the internalized homophobia in our society. One wrote: "A lot of times, when you're confused and stuff, and you feel lonely, just to hug somebody—the human touch—would be nice. But if I'm with guy friends, I can't say, 'I'm feeling down right now. Would you hug me?' They'd be like, 'what?' And if I went over an hugged a friend, like to give him support, I would immediately be called gay."[52]

Public display of affection is limited to moments following success or victory. A no-hitter or a touchdown run warrants hugs, a slap on the behind, even a macho kiss on the top of the head in front of twenty-five million viewers. That same hug in the parking lot could get someone punched. As pointed out by Curry[53] and White and Vagi,[54] American athletes tolerate touching in the locker room only if accompanied by a good deal of homophobic joking. The Tecos offered stark contrasts here as well.

Eric Yelding and Puerto Rican–American Boi Rodríguez (two Imports) routinely hang out with each other between games. They also interact frequently in game settings, such as in the dugout or during batting practice. When one says something positive or flattering to the other, it is typically couched in macho obscenity—"That was a nasty fuckin' catch back there, Homey"—as is much of the interactions among Mexican players. Yet among the Imports I saw little of the softer side to break this uniformly testicular facade of machismo. Their camaraderie was bolstered by their import status, their living on the Laredo side in the same hotel, and their traveling together; but while they were close, I never witnessed any physical affection between them except when one would hit a home run and the other (along with the rest of the team) would mob him with high fives and slaps on the back.

Early on I noticed that the Mexican players expressed physical affection more easily and without the need for the cover of a joke. It was not at all uncommon for men to be watching events on the field with one using another as a leaning post; players could also be seen standing on the steps of the dugout watching the game with arms around another player's waist. There was no self-consciousness about these acts, nor odd looks of any sort from the other players. Sometimes the affection was fused with more conventional macho forms. On one occasion at Parque La Junta I saw two of the Tecos play-boxing in the dugout:

> It started out typically enough with each man circling around, throwing phantom punches at the other and moved into a flurry of body slamming. As they dodged and ducked and flicked jabs that barely missed, the thought ran through my head that this could escalate into something serious. A headline flashed through my brain, "Play Fighting Turns Deadly for Two Tecos." Instead, these two moved from their Mexican version of capoeira [a Brazilian martial arts dance] to gliding around the dugout in a waltzlike embrace, settling finally into watching the game with arms around each other's waists. One punctuated this choreographed event by pinching the others behind. Headline in my brain altered to read, "Play Fighting Turns Dearly."[55]

Somewhat later I observed a more significant incident that sealed my revised view of machismo. One night in May 1994, the Teco players were sitting, as usual, in a row of plastic seats that was placed in front of the dugout so that they could take advantage of any cool breezes. The row was filled and everyone seemed preoccupied with the man on the mound pitching against them. He was vexing the batters with his array of forkballs and curves, and as of the sixth inning no one had yet gotten a hit off of him. The Tecos were busily trying to unlock the riddle of his pitching and everyone was caught up in the discussion. Two or three additional Tecos were standing behind the row, also in the conversation, when I noticed that one of the players standing behind the row was talking animatedly about a short slider while repeatedly stroking the hair of the player seated in front of him in a front-to-back fashion, as if grooming him. Again, this was as public as one could get, yet no one seemed even the slightest bit struck by this action . . . except the anthropologist.

It was at this point that I thought I would try to determine just how many on the team engaged in various forms of physical affection and how often it occurred. For two periods of one-week each (separated by two months) I tried to count the number of times I saw players showing physical affection for each other. I wrote down their names, the context, and the form the affection took. Not all the Tecos were so given to demonstrating physical affection. These are, after all, men from widely different cultural and regional backgrounds within Mexico. The two men who are Indian, while warm and genuine, were not openly physically affectionate, for instance. And Mora, the macho with a socio-emotional moat around him, while friendly, would only interact within a strictly baseball context. Of the twenty-four *mexicanos* on the team, I counted nine whom I regularly saw display some form of physical affection (such as holding or leaning on each other), and another seven who occasionally touched or were touched by others. Those exhibiting affection could be married or single, rookies or veterans; the only pattern I found was that seven of the nine players who exhibited regular affection were pitchers and catchers. Perhaps these two positions involve a degree of mutual dependency that encourages such familiarity. Of the twenty-five total affectionate acts I counted in those two week-long periods, twenty-one were in and around the dugout area or bullpen, and the other four were in the clubhouse. I detected no homophobic joking to legitimate these acts. In fact, given the ease and frequency with which the Mexican Tecos expressed physical affection, I feel fairly certain that these men were barely if at all conscious of their behavior. American players, on the other hand, never showed this degree of physical closeness with each other (with one exception) in the two seasons I observed these players.[56] Finally, I told one of the Mexican players that I was impressed with how easily Mexican men showed affection, that in the United States men are worried about doing this for fear of being considered homosexual. He looked somewhat surprised and puzzled; then, after a moment, he seemed to come to a realization: "When I went to spring training in the States," he recalled, "I remember once putting my arm around one of the gringos who was a good guy. He looked at me like—[face recoiling in horror]. I thought he just didn't like me and I was surprised because we got along good, but now maybe I understand this thing better."[57]

The Anglo players expressed a degree of discomfort when queried about this kind of behavior. When I shared this observation with one of them, he replied, "Yeah. Now that you mention it, I sorta noticed that too. But I can't get behind that kinda thing. I mean I can bear hug a guy or 'five' him or 'mosh' [mutual chest bump] a guy, but these [Mexican] guys. I don't know it's different. They put their arms around each other and leave 'em there, man."[58]

By and large the view of both the American male and the male athlete as homophobic are critical, showing him in one way or another shooting himself in the proverbial foot. His limited range of accepted masculine behavior and attitudes hamper his ability to promote gender security, as well as his attempts to live a more rewarding life. That men, for instance, sicken and die more readily than women has been linked to, among other things, male views of their bodies and to their inability to respond to crises such as illness or stress.[59] This is mute testimony to how men in pursuit of masculinity often wind up harming or killing themselves. Kidd summarizes some of these shortcomings as the inability of males to express feelings of vulnerability or concern for others.[60] Sabo points out male inability to admit to physical injury (a kind of vulnerability).[61] Others have discussed the homophobically fueled inability—except through highly visible macho sports rituals—of men to show physical affection toward each other.[62]

While the gringos I observed in the same two-year period exhibited social and psychological differences amongst themselves, they functioned similarly on key indices. Gringo players were less likely to talk about their vulnerabilities, and when they did so they would more likely discuss issues angrily or with humor, keeping their masculinity intact. Americans would be affectionate with their children and those of other players, but they were never seen emotionally gushing over children, especially if they had their "game face" on. This was not lost on the Mexican players and their families and prompted one of the Teco wives to comment: "In our culture a gringo, we know, is cold. They may be good guys—not mean—not machos, but they're also not gonna be emotional."[63] On the key issue of showing physical affection, I never witnessed Americans behaving as emotionally open as I saw the Mexicans behave. The only exception during my stay was an incident in which one of the Mexicans felt comfortable enough around Lee Upshaw to lean on him.[64]

Tender machismo is presented both as a corrective to the traditionally held view that Latin American masculinity is one-dimensional, and as a way of furthering autonational perceptions. To the most extreme macho who mindlessly equates male posturing, aggression, and "bullying" with masculinity, tenderness could be associated with weakness. In keeping with the "masculine protest" perspective, such a view cannot tolerate even a hint of something that looks like weakness, precisely because its proponents are the least assured of their strength.[65] The tender elements, it is argued, reflect men who are secure enough to permit gentleness in the construction of gender. Such men can also claim ideals of familial responsibility, care, and nurturing.

Paz's view of Mexican masculinity as a cultural response to the history of colonial domination has inadvertently fueled pejorative views of Mexican men long held by segments of Anglo America and by social scientists as well. The Mexican machos, and by extension other Latino men, have been depicted as aggressively posturing, irresponsible to family, philandering, abusive of women, hard-drinking, and criminal. These attributes lend themselves quite readily to racist views of Mexicans and Latin Americans, while dialectically functioning to morally self-aggrandize Americans when comparing themselves to Latinos.

Beginning in the 1970s Chicano(a) scholars launched a series of critiques and studies against what they asserted was an ethnocentric depiction of Latino/Latin American men as machos. The Chicano community studied by Baca-Zinn, for instance, was shown to distinguish between cultural ideals of machismo and structural relations between men and women in the family.[66] The latter evinced a greater degree of egalitarianism than one might presume based on widely disseminated cultural assertions about Latino machismo.

Another recent effort to further the revisionist view has come from Matthew Gutmann, an anthropologist studying a working class barrio in Mexico City. Among his findings, he noted that Mexican institutions are undergoing change, some of which have fostered a decline in importance of traditional machismo.[67] A goodly number of Mexican men Gutmann studied seemed to eschew traditional machismo and its converse (the *mandilón*, or female-dominated man) in declaring themselves "*ni macho, ni mandilón*" (neither macho, nor *mandilón*). The Tecos seem to approximate Gutmann's view of Mexican men as well.

On the three indices used here, the gringo Imports seem less diverse. Contrasting with the Mexican players along the dimensions discussed does not make one group less sexist or more progressive toward women than the other. It signifies, first, that Mexican players deviate more from traditional perceptions of men (and perceptions held of Latin American men) by exhibiting a greater range of behavior.

These contrasts are also cultural ones. As such they function to exacerbate a range of social divisions. Certainly any difference that gets generalized to the nationalist level (i.e., "gringo" versus "Mexican") works to fuel autonationalist antagonism, and here we have looked at several dimensions of masculinity in its service. That a Teco wife could so easily characterize Anglo men as "cold," or that Dan Firova's handling of a truculent Mexican player would be interpreted as more or less manly, or that Anglos could viscerally respond to Mexican male physical familiarity (leaving one's arm around another player too long) as discomforting, illustrates a variety of responses that are not simply masculine contrasts but national ones as well. If we view these manifestations of machismo as criteria for inclusion and exclusion within the true Tecos, then we see that the gringos can be on the team but not of it (i.e., within the Tecos community). Machismo can aid the nationalist cause through shared or contrasting styles of behavior. The cultural differences in being men can promote a greater sense of cohesion among the Mexican Tecos just as the slights they receive from gringos works to alienate them from their American teammates. Through a combination of structural factors (such as travel and living arrangements) and emotional-behavioral factors (such as physical affection) the Tecos are joined and split along national lines. The next chapters will reveal this in greater detail.

1. The 1935 La Junta team barnstormed through the northern Plains states: Fernando Dovalina is in the second row, third from left, and Ismael Montalvo is in the second row, third from right. (Photo courtesy Fernando Dovalina.)

2. Teco pitchers Obed Vega, far left, René Rodríguez, and Aron Quiroz loosening up before a game.

3. Children in Nuevo Laredo grow up attending many Teco games each year.

4. Young fans are a regular feature in and around the dugout. This youngster delights in the rough-housing.

5. The Tecos begin each game at West Martin Field with two flags and two national anthems. Here we see the color guard marching off.

6. The temperature at game time routinely tops 100 degrees Fahrenheit. Teco catcher Marco Antonio Cruz must endure this and more while swathed in protective gear.

7. As a rookie pitcher in 1993, Obed Vega anxiously waited for a chance to break into the starting rotation.

8. The years of playing in Mexico's summer and winter leagues have taken their toll on slugger Andrés Mora.

9. Pitchers Enrique Couoh, left, and Ricardo Moreno waiting for the second half of a double-header.

10. Ernesto Barraza, right, with teammate Evarista Mena. Barraza was the last Teco to throw a no-hitter while the team was still *de los dos Laredos*.

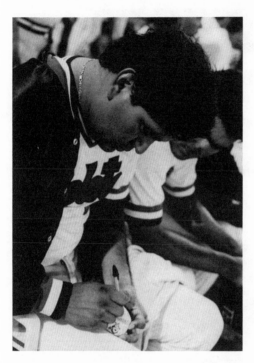

11. Mexico's first (and thus far, only) Yaqui Indian baseball professional, Juan Jesús Alvarez, autographs a ball for a fan.

12. Pedro Meré, veteran Teco infielder, enjoying the quiet of an empty clubhouse.

13. Alejandro Ortiz, for over a decade one of the Mexican League's most feared hitters.

14. Marco Antonio Romero, Teco first baseman, represented the newer era of Teco slugger.

15. Romero was one of the most influential Tecos. Here he laughs after skewering a rival with a tale designed to showcase Romero's machismo.

16. Twins Obed and Edgar Vega flank Evarista Mena.

17. Orlando Lind, Import pitcher from Puerto Rico, was one of those rare players who could bridge the world of Imports and *mexicanos*.

18. Import relief pitcher Jay Baller.

19. Arriving three weeks after the season started in 1993, Baller nevertheless wound up with thirty saves, to lead the league.

# Part Three _____

THE RIVER JOINS AND THE RIVER DIVIDES

# *Six*

## 1993: The Best of Times

THE BASEBALL SEASON lends itself very nicely to being discussed as cyclical; in anthropological circles it is called an "annual round." A round connotes a series of unending sameness; certain things always occur in spring, followed by summer, and then fall and winter activities, in an unending circle of events. The sameness works to bear structure, allowing us to situate and analyze activities and ceremonies, and associate events within a sequence of related times and settings. Unexpected events serve to test the norms and markers and ultimately work to further institutionalize them. In the case of the Tecos I sorted out the markers within the season that proved to be both routine and exceptional. There was a unique and wonderful drama that unfolded around each portion of the annual round. More importantly, the whole thing made for a good story, one in which disaster and victory paralleled each other at almost every turn. Some of the story derives from the predictable structure of the season, and other parts of it were never to be repeated; and while it may be fashionable to eschew linear descriptions, there was in 1993 a strong narrative that should be presented.

### Spring Training

The parallel between nature's cycle and the onset of the baseball season is widely worked in countless poems, essays, stories, and plays, such as the following by poet Donald Hall:

> The game wakes gradually, gathering vigor to itself as the days lengthen late in February and grow warmer; old muscles grow limber, young arms throw strong and wild, legs pivot and leap, bodies hurtle into bright bases safe. . . . Clogged vein systems, in veteran oaks and left-fielders both, unstop themselves, putting forth leaves and line drives in Florida's March. Migrating north with the swallows baseball and grass's first green enter Cleveland, Kansas City, Boston.[1]

Depending on who you are speaking with—fans, players, club officials— the dates may vary, but all baseball efforts head toward Opening Day. The beginning of anything is made more vibrant when it coincides with the beginnings of nature's growth cycle, a theme sounded in the title of Thomas Boswell's book, *Why Time Begins on Opening Day*.[2] Although Latin American baseball is seasonally focused on what is for us winter, the

Mexican League has always insisted on paralleling the American annual round (see Chapter 7) and has wound up paying a price. Because both leagues play at the same time, the quality of Americans sent to the Mexican League is not as good as those sent to play in the Pacific Coast League, also in the winter. To play summer baseball was very much a conscious political decision. It actually makes climatic sense in the two Laredos to begin the season at the same time as in American baseball. Even in April, it can get pretty raw in these cities if there is a north wind, making it feel more like south Buffalo than south Texas.

It's spring time and everywhere in the baseball universe local ballparks are repaired and painted. Predictions of success are cast about like grass seed. New players are nurtured like saplings delicately placed in balanced earth. There are also the businessmen running ball clubs who buy and sell horseflesh in the hopes of fielding a winning team and turning a profit. For the front office there really is no end to the season. They are busy scouting year round, and beginning with American baseball's winter meetings, the Tecos' staff is embroiled in trades and sales of players. By January they are focusing their efforts on bringing players who need to be signed back into the fold. For most players the season begins some time in February when they report to spring training, but even here there is a range. Many Tecos, like Ernesto Barraza or Luís Fernando Díaz, have been playing winter ball in the Mexican Pacific League, coming to camp in late February or early March. Others might come early. The veteran slugger Andrés Mora came early, looking to bounce back after an injury-plagued year; he wants to make sure he's ready and healthy. Rookies are eager to make the club and have been practicing on their own for weeks before the February 17 startup date. Holdouts, who are exasperated with their contracts, threaten not to come at all. *Importados* don't show up until April. Despite this variation, baseball remains a cultural rite of spring, and in the Mexican League that means being ready to roll by March 17.

In spring training the outsider is able to see the dormancy in which nothing much appears to be happening, but in reality the team is forming. Going through spring training affords one a rare view in which a team-as-aggregate becomes a team-as-collective. While there are a few ways in which Mexican League spring training is different from that of AAA leagues in the United States—such as players coming in ready to play from winter ball—in most respects they are similar. At this early stage there is an easy quality to the training, with the first few weeks devoted to calisthenics and a few baseball basics.

On February 17, the first day of the Tecos' spring training, manager Dan Firova casually and quickly dispenses with the introductory remarks. Everything about Firova is casual and somewhat abrupt, but on this first day, with a cold north wind blowing and an overcast sky, the brevity is

appreciated by everyone. Since he is a rookie manager, he introduces himself and his staff, as well as me, to this gathering of about twenty novice
players. They blow on their hands to warm them up as Firova lists what he
expects from his charges that day. Housed at a hotel in another part of
Nuevo Laredo, these rookies and tryouts arrive at Parque La Junta at 9
A.M. each day on the red, white, and blue Tecobus. They appear somewhat
excited and seem to enjoy wearing their new Teco uniforms. These are the
blue road uniforms with LAREDOS emblazoned across the front in striking
red letters. The only veteran here this day is the oldest Teco, Andrés Mora.
Rehabilitating himself from injuries, Mora is determined to wipe out his
disappointing numbers of 1992. That a man en route to becoming a legend
is here this early raises some eyebrows. Mexican veterans still believe the
preseason is for the untested.

More in keeping with this youthful gathering is Julio Trapaga, a young
infielder who shows real promise. He realizes that breaking into the Tecos'
starting lineup, which in the previous season featured players who had an
average of nine years of experience, will be, barring an injury to one of the
veterans, impossible; and this only makes him look that much more serious. I don't think he cracked a smile during all of spring training. Rubén
"Cartucho" Estrada, a twenty-four-year-old utility infielder, knows the
difficulty of cracking this lineup all too well. After riding the bench for a
few years, he was finally able to contribute in 1992, regularly filling in
throughout the lineup and delivering clutch hits and fielding performances
in the championship series against Mexico City. As a result Estrada smiles
easily, a bit more secure in the knowledge that his spring will be a prelude
to a full season with the club. The multitudes of rookies and tryouts are
more skittish, fearing that they will be demoted to one of the team's minor
league clubs or will simply be told to go home. They move through the
routines of spring training furtively.

Most days during this stretch of the year are typically unpredictable. If
the wind is blowing from the north it is bound to be cold and damp, making the entire morning unpleasant. Hitting is difficult, as is throwing, and
the temperature, in the mid-fifty-degree range, feels much colder. Should
the wind be blowing in from the south, however, it feels more like baseball
playing weather. The sun will loosen limbs and nicely dry out the field
revealing the red earth. Spirits are boosted, and even the seasonally normal
rainfall is not as unfriendly when the wind blows from the south.

After his announcements and the obligatory roll call, Dan Firova gets his
coaching staff to start the day. Pitching coach Mario Valenzuela, a rookie
coach from Nuevo Laredo, begins the day with a series of physical routines, the first of which is a light stretch and a casual jog around the perimeter of the ball field two times. His graceful movements and good conditioning are somewhat unusual for a pitching coach. This jog around the

park functions as sort of a wake-up call to a groggy gathering. Upon completing the second lap, Valenzuela begins a more serious fifteen to twenty minute routine of stretching. Except that he's using Spanish, Valenzuela's counting and cadence could just as easily be a Jane Fonda workout tape or an aerobics instructor anywhere north of the border: "Uno, dos, tres . . . nueve, diez. Cambio!" or "Suave! La derecho alto, otra debajo!" Some of his charges move through this routine easily, others with great effort.

Stretching is followed by sprint drills in which the players, in groups of two, sprint toward coaches stationed fifty yards out, then jog back. This is done for fifteen or twenty minutes and is followed by the heart of the spring training day: batting practice. Pitchers continue to run and take throwing practice. The standard procedure for many professional teams is a combination of the following routine. The players form groups of four for batting practice. In the first batting sequence each player bunts twice, executes one hit-and-run, hits one "get-em-over" (hitting the ball to advance the runner), hits one sacrifice fly, hits one suicide squeeze, and eight to ten "swing aways," with some effort to hit to the opposite field. In the second round they swing away eight times, in the third round six, then four in the following round, and two in the last.

In the past this routine would have been followed daily for the month between the onset of spring training and Opening Day, with the days increasingly punctuated by exhibition games as the first day of the season neared. In 1993, however, the Tecos had a very different spring training. Illustrative of the new, stronger working agreement between the Tecos and the Atlanta Braves, the latter sent down a pair of their top instructors for two weeks to assist the Tecos. No other Mexican League team received this sort of aid, and since the Mexican League has had the reputation as being the last gasp of one's baseball career, it is unlikely that many others ever will. In a radical departure from such thinking, however, Chuck LaMar, then Atlanta's director of minor league operations, felt that Mexico had been given short shrift. LaMar contended that, with the proper resources, Mexico can produce talent on par with other Latin American countries. For this reason two former major leaguers were spending two weeks in Laredo and Nuevo Laredo, and two very unlikely fellow travelers they are.

At first glance, Leon Roberts and Jerry Neiman look like baseball's version of "The Odd Couple." At six feet four inches tall and 230 pounds, Roberts, in his mid-forties, is a bear of a man. Neiman, on the other hand, is short (5'8") and wiry (perhaps 155 pounds). Neiman's hawklike visage is counterpoint to the bruinlike, comfortable face of Roberts. They differ in temperament as well. Roberts, who fills the ballpark with hitting instructions and can easily work a crowd, is clearly heard all over the field, even when he is greeting someone. Neiman's chiseled face, on the other hand, suggests someone who is accustomed to silence (indeed, he is an avid out-doorsman, hunter, and guide), someone who deliberates before speaking. Beyond these rather superficial differences, however, the two men share their lifelong commitment to the game, which reduces their differences to naught. Their playing careers behind them, they have given themselves over to teaching talented young men how to better their skills. Roberts and Neiman care little for advancing up the ranks of coaching, ultimately land-ing a job in the major leagues. They are rare in that they are happy doing just what they are doing. Managing the Durham Bulls in the A-level minor leagues (the team made famous in the movie *Bull Durham*), as well as peri-odically instructing young players in other locales, is just the occupation that Roberts wants: "Hell, I got one of the best jobs in baseball."

Neiman feels similarly. In response to my questions about moving up the ladder in the Atlanta organization, he eschewed the discussion of poli-tics that usually accompanies the subject of upward mobility. He actually prefers lower level minor league pitchers "because they're still passionate about the game; they're not jaded."

These two also share a very serious orientation to work. When they came to the two Laredos they hit the deck running, eager to look at Mexi-can talent. It was the first time in Mexico for either. Neiman studies and watches hard as first one pitcher, and then another, goes through his reper-toire of pitches. He stops one of them very suddenly and directly and makes a biomechanical assessment to the bilingual Valenzuela: "You see him casting the ball. He's not getting behind it. If he gets more behind it instead of letting it slide out, then the problem with his hip will be taken care of. His hip will be cocked to allow him to drive the ball."[3]

That they have just two weeks to work with a strange team and do not even possess a rudimentary knowledge of Spanish only serves to intensify their sense of purpose. Neiman is slightly critical of the more laidback Teco style of practice. "Too much standing around. Look at those pitchers standing stock still in the outfield. They should have been doing 'rundown' drills by now." The pitchers have never done such drills, but sure enough, within days of Neiman's and Roberts' departure, the Tecos' pitching coach implemented the drill in which pitchers simulate pitching situations with runners at first and third. They throw home quickly, then move into posi-tion for a rundown of the base runner. As the runners at first and third try to get the pitchers to err, the rest of the Tecos have stopped to tease them and delight in any miscues made. Neiman, in short order, introduced an element of discipline and routine into the team, no small feat in itself, but his modesty is the understated confidence so characteristic of westerners: "If you can help just two pitchers a year and not screw up any, you're a good pitching coach." While humble, Neiman knows the value of a pitch-ing coach: "Pitching coaches and third base coaches are essential. They are keys to a successful team, and I do my job as well as anybody. Bullpen coaches [and] first base coaches are the managers' drinking buddies." Impressed by a pair of pitchers he has seen for these two weeks, he has decided to send them to the Atlanta Braves' spring training site in West Palm Beach for further examination. This is not a symbolic gesture and certainly should be replicated by major league clubs who, while hungry for Latin American talent, shun Mexico. Neiman entered the Mexican League with no preconceived notions of what Mexican players can and cannot do, which may be in part why he was chosen. Certainly, Neiman is in the minority among coaches and scouts in this regard.[4]

Leon Roberts has also been busy. His style is more informal than Neiman's but just as effective. He combines questioning, critique, motivation, and visualization in his admonishments to young hitters:[5]

Roberts: "How many home runs did you hit last year?"
Teco: "Seven."
Roberts: "That's good. If you work on off-speed pitches, you could improve on that. You ever hear of Kirk Gibson?"
Teco: "Kirk Gibson? Yes."
Roberts: "Five years ago he hit twenty-eight dingers. How many do you think were off-speed pitches?"
Teco: "Maybe half?"
Roberts: "26 of 28. Now you think you wanna look at swinging at more off-speed stuff?"

Roberts then tosses him some off-speed pitches, varying the speed and location, while the Teco youngster waits on them—holding back on an off-speed pitch is the key to this exercise—then hits several hard. "Good!" shouts Roberts. "Perfect! Fifteen home runs and a .325 batting average!" he proclaims, implanting the idea in the player's head. "Even if he hits .300 with ten or eleven dingers," he tells me later, "it's a good season and he'll get more money too. Raise expectations."

Considering their brief stay and lack of familiarity with language or culture, the overall impact of these two instructors is palpable. When they are on the field the players hustle more, play harder, shout more. When they leave, however, their absence is also evident, although by that time the Tecos are ready to launch their exhibition series.

## Exhibition Series

During the last two weeks of spring training the Tecos typically play exhibition games against nearby Mexican League rivals, such as Monterrey's Sultanes and Industriales, and Saltillo's Saraperos.

The team travels on the Tecobus, and why it has Texas plates on it is a mystery to me. It doesn't travel in the United States beyond West Martin Field in Laredo. Additionally, Texas plates are more costly. The upkeep and insurance would be less expensive in Tamaulipas. Moreover, the Tecobus is a decidedly unattractive vehicle. Some would argue that it is one of the oldest and ill-equipped buses in the league. I prefer to think of it as Nuevo Laredo's version of Ken Kesey's Merry Pranksters bus: one is socially identified as a Teco by either being "on the bus or off the bus." The 1983 Chrysler bus has the red, white, and blue Tecos colors on all sides declaring *"Los Tecolotes de los dos Laredos."* The interior shows signs of long road trips: worn rubber mats in the aisles, seats clean but discolored with age and sagging from years of bodies sleeping in uncomfortable positions. Customizing consists of twin-berth bunks that take up the back of the bus and luggage racks converted to encase a sound and television system, all of which lack finishing touches. Despite its funkiness, the Tecobus is the single most identifying feature of the team, and traveling with the team is, perhaps, the most important way of identifying oneself as part of the subculture.

The first trip of the 1993 season had the Tecos traveling to the sleepy town of Anahuac, Nuevo León, for a game against the Sultanes of Monterrey. We left from a motel on the outskirts of Nuevo Laredo that housed the unmarried, nonlocal players during spring training. It was a hot afternoon in early March when we piled onto the Tecobus for our one-hour trip to Anahuac, a small city of 20,000 some fifty miles south of Nuevo Laredo. On this trip we carried many rookies and tryouts in addition to a smattering of veterans. That day, March 4, wasthe deadline for signing with the club, and several players embroiled in contract disputes were still holding out.

At Dan Firova's instructions, the bus was full, the engine running, and the door about to close at precisely 4 P.M. Firova looked at his coaches, who quickly did a mental roll call. One man was missing. Alejandro Ortiz, the slugging third baseman, was not on board, posing for Firova the question: to wait or not to wait? On his very first trip as manager, Firova paused only a minute past 4 P.M. before he nodded to the bus driver. The Tecobus's engine gurgled and coughed as we eased into the 1993 season; and everyone on board knew that Firova, a close friend of Ortiz's, was taking charge. Unfortunately, not everyone who played regularly for the team was on board and the lesson would have to be repeated in the days to come.

We could see the city give way to mesquite and cactus in the desert countryside. The expanse of this arid country suddenly became more impressive as tiny roadside rest shacks that sell produce and other items began to highlight the enormity of the landscape. Curving south, we turned one bend after another, losing ourselves in the Mexican desert. No sooner had we settled into its undulating and immaculate hills than the landscape convulsed, as we found ourselves ensnared in plastic refuse on all sides: a sea of Styrofoam containers and bags of every size and shape coated the land like an industrial snowfall. This shocking reminder of Nuevo Laredo didn't look as if it had been dumped, since then it would have been in piles, so much as blown there by the winds. As the bus passed through, we all registered one sort of facial incredulity or another. Then, just as suddenly as we entered this surreal world, we left it. In the distance we made out the perimeter of Anahuac. As the bus slowed to enter the main street, the one-and-a-half-foot-long crucifix that loosely hung from the rearview mirror swung more wildly, making me wonder if the crack in the windshield had been made by this god-sized cross. Rolling slowly into town gave everyone there a chance to fully take us in. It was a scene that must have resembled those involving barnstorming baseball teams in the 1930s. As we cruised past houses, people sitting or working would stop what they were doing, stand up, check out the team logo, and then, at the same slow cruising speed as the bus, begin walking toward the park at the far end of town.

Most excited of all were the small packs of children who would run wildly, waving their twiglike arms at us. We waved back. As we got to the ballpark there were already some fans milling about waiting for the "big city" teams. The children continued to come in gaggles of five to ten, running, their dust-covered limbs churning away in anticipation of the holiday we were ushering in, one of the year's special days. We were the circus come to town, and everywhere there were wide eyes, grins, and waves—but none more than from a little boy who hobbled toward us as fast as he could on a broken old crutch, waving his dusty baseball cap with his free hand.

The park is an all-dirt affair: no infield grass, just dirt with white lines and a big white "T" and "S," chalked out for Tecos and Sultanes, freshly laid on the on-deck circles by each dugout. Being roughly halfway between Nuevo Laredo and Monterrey, the 2,000 fans were split over who to root for. The Sultanes finally arrived and all of the players began exchanging jokes and high fives. While the Tecos must play until the third week of the season without their Imports, the Sultanes already had theirs, giving them a decided edge.

As the sun set, bringing the distant mountains into relief for the first time, the game was about to begin . . . four fights and one hour late. Fans had been drinking since mid-day, enjoying the mariachi music being played much too loudly over the PA system, as the players shaved their bats and put on their "sanies" (sanitary white socks).

The game started, and the teams quickly exchanged zeroes. By the second inning, however, the skies darkened for lanky Teco pitcher Enrique Couoh, unable to douse the Sultanes' hot bats, which struck for a five-run inning. Disputed calls by amateurish umpires followed and the Tecos began showing signs of exasperation. Luís Fernando Díaz was called out on strikes despite having clearly signaled from the box for a time out. Teco pitchers were being squeezed. By the sixth inning the score was 10–0. Ever-testy first baseman Marco Antonio Romero was already out of his uniform and smoking cigarettes on the bench. The game had broken down as players in twos and threes were telling jokes with their backs turned to the game.

When the game mercifully ended around 11:30 P.M., the combination of road travel, the late hour, and the final score quieted even the most rowdy of the Tecos—all except Andrés Mora, who despite his age and a lifetime of abusing his body was buoyantly taking questions from press and fans and signing autographs. Again I saw the tiny one-legged lad with his crutch and dusty old hat. Mora turned to him among all the children hovering about and gave him a signed baseball, which the little one held in complete disbelief. That Babe Ruth–like moment would remain with me—a bloated old slugger and a handicapped waif in a gesture emblematic of concern and gratitude in its purest sense.

Although I was hoping to return to Nuevo Laredo, Anahuac officials had planned a feast for their guests; so at midnight both teams piled into their buses and followed the mayor's car to another part of town where a peeling yellow stucco building housed the town's social club. Two policemen sharing a single uniform (one wore the pants and holster, the other the shirt and hat) stood outside and directed us in.

Tables had been hastily placed end to end, forming two long rows. The room itself was large enough to accommodate the sixty or so players who were coming, and waiting for them at one end was a bar with barrels full of ice and cans of Tecate. Behind the bar was a huge pot of stew made up of frijoles, potatos with chunks of bacon floating in it. Most of the players were grateful that something was being provided and quickly lined up and consumed all the food and beverages. It was a more sedate gathering than I would have thought possible for so many ballplayers, but the hour was late, and I could see yawns sprinkled around the room.

The festivities had just begun, however. A three-piece band started playing typical Mexican mariachi-like form, and the singer could be heard yip-yipping along with his guitar and accordion accompaniment. All three musicians were stocky and short and wore blue or brown Dacron jeans with long-sleeved plaid shirts. The lead singer impressed me more with his long, pointed, anachronistic sideburns and short, thin moustache than with his crooning, which bore only a passing resemblance to the more contemporary northern Mexican musical forms known as *conjunto* and *norteño*. The presentation of the celebration, despite its frayed and make-shift qualities, had a lavish air about it. The singers performed as if royalty were listening. The cooks dished up ladles full of greasy concoctions as if the food were the creation of gourmet chef Wolfgang Puck. And the policemen outside were at attention as if there were hordes of paparazzi waiting to get into the gathering inside. As we filed back into the Tecobus in the early morning hours, the streets were empty. Ernesto Barraza and some of the others who had the presence of mind to get to the Tecobus quickly commandeered the bunks at the back of the bus, while the rest of us settled into the seats. As the driver started up the engine I settled in for what I hoped would be a short snooze in the darkened bus, but this was not to be. Someone slipped a porno videotape into the VCR unit installed behind the driver's seat. Barreling through the Mexican desert in the middle of the night hearing the sound of a woman's orgasm was not conducive to sleep. Mile after mile of moans, as well as huge semis passing us at high speeds on a two-lane road, made sleep virtually impossible. The porno tape, I would soon discover, was played after all games until it had lost the ability to titillate altogether, at which time the players began substituting their favorite music for the film's soundtrack. The extreme closeups of oral sex began to be mediated by mariachi or Salsa or Rap until everyone looked out bleary-eyed as the lights of Nuevo Laredo came into view.

## The First Half of the Season

The 1993 season began poorly for the Tecos. They lost five of their first seven games—none by close scores—and found themselves alone in the cellar. Two weeks later (April 8) they were still there, having lost games at a two-to-one clip. Not to worry, assured one long-time Teco follower: "The Tecos are always slow starters. You'll see, they'll be in the championship playoffs in the end." Their problem was quite simple; they were the only Mexican League team playing without their import players. The agreement with Atlanta that sent four (and, in 1994, five) Imports to the Tecos would not occur until the first week in April. This left the pitching corps dangerously thin, as was evidenced in their April 6 game against the Petroleros of Minatitlan. There, the Tecos set a Mexican League record for most walks allowed (sixteen) in a nine-inning game, en route to a 20–7 shellacking by the Petroleros. The Teco pitching staff was clubbed for eighteen hits during that spree and wound up using every last player who could throw a ball. That included pitching coach Valenzuela, pressed into service because no one could stop the bleeding. Three weeks into the season, the relievers' ERA was over 7.00. And not only were the Tecos minus their gringos, but they had passed along two of their own players to Atlanta for the duration of the Braves' spring training. Normally the perennial favorites and the scourge of the northern division, the Tecos were 7–14.

From the moment the Imports, as well as the two returning Tecos, came on board, the team rebounded. In the April 10 contest against Jalisco, import Willie Waite was pitching. He won, going seven innings and giving up two unearned runs. More important still was the ability of the bullpen to hold the win—Enrique Couoh came in to nail it down. Bobby Moore, one of the Imports, came through with a run-scoring double and a single. The next night another Import, Orlando Lind of Puerto Rico, pitched eight strong innings but left the game with the score tied 2–2. The Tecos forced a run across in the ninth, and then the fourth Import, Jay Baller, came on in relief. Baller got the win, but more importantly the Imports were yielding immediate results. And their success was contagious. The anemic Teco bats began to come to life. In the month following the imports' arrival, the Tecos turned their record around, going from 7–14 after the first three weeks of the season to 16–8 over the next month. On May 8 they were in fourth place in the eight-team division.

The Tecobus rolled into Monterrey, carrying a team of contenders who were coming in for a crucial three-game series with the Industriales. Everyone was on board . . . but me. Captain Firova, true to his policy of punctuality, pulled the bus away from the Teco offices on Obregon Avenue on time. I had trouble getting across the bridge and missed the bus. Luckily, my colleague Milton Jamail was going to Monterrey and we headed out together, intending to meet the team at the hotel. At the twenty-five kilometer government checkpoint (north of Nuevo Laredo), where the Mexican Government checks documents, we saw the familiar red, white, and blue logo of the Tecos ahead of us. Excitedly, I jumped out of the car and pounded on the Tecobus door. It opened, and I bounded up to hear catcalls: "*Barbón, tienes que pagar una multa!*" (Beard! You'll have to pay a fine!). They were surprised that I had intercepted them, and I heard no end of the ribbing all the way to Monterrey. Once there, however, everyone grew more serious. The Industriales had to be beaten.

The Estadio Monterrey, in which both of Monterrey's teams (the Sultanes and the Industriales) play, is state-of-the-art. It is easy to see why many claim that if major league baseball ever expands into Latin America, Monterrey would be a likely city to land a franchise. Its fan base in a city of over three million is more than ample. Its affluence as a center for manufacturing could provide all the capital interests and owners needed. And it already has an impressive facility that could be expanded further. The city is surrounded by some of the most spectacularly shaped mountain ranges I have ever seen, clearly visible from within the park.

While we pulled up to our hotel and piled out, intent on getting a few hours rest before the game, Baller, Moore, and Lind drove in by car. Waite, too arrogant to go with the team and too hated by the other Imports to accompany them, had to be chauffeured down by the Teco general manager.

During batting practice reporters flocked around Mora, who was nearing his four hundredth career home run, and Ortiz, who was one shy of his three hundredth. Pregame ebullitions abounded: taping, scraping, stretching, nursing. Ortiz made sure I noticed the huge bruise on his ribcage from getting hit by a pitch two days earlier. "Check this out!" he yelled at me as the team trainer readied a syringe to inject into his posterior. "Steroids!' I joked. "I knew it, Ortiz. I knew you were using them." He laughed but made sure that I knew it was a vitamin B shot. Mora also declared his injuries, two very raw-looking abrasions suffered two days earlier in two very rare—for him—slide attempts. Cartucho Estrada busied himself with shaving a bat handle with a glass shard. He felt that his declining batting average would improve with this kind of small adjustment. Long ago George Gmelch,[6] himself a former professional ballplayer, documented and examined the ritualistic lengths to which players go to ensure success. It is no different down here.

Like most baseball teams, the Tecos banter when and wherever they can. That night my friend Milton Jamail was in the dugout chatting with general manager Samuel Lozano. He commented about the translation of the word fungo, which the Mexicans use as well. There is no translation for it—it simply applies to hitting fly balls to the outfield. Lozano was trying to make sense of it by transforming it into a Spanish verb, "fungar," and conjugating it. Ortiz and others were standing around listening, and thinking it to be simple-minded trash, they chimed in with other examples. "*Cagar!*" (meaning "to shit"), announced Ortiz. Laughs all around. "*Miar!*" (to piss), offers Romero. "*Mamar!*" (to suck), hollers Lind on his way down the dugout steps. The dugout was filled with vulgar infinitives and laughter before Lozano and Jamail suddenly pulled up short and enjoyed the chuckle.

As in most male settings, these men use their banter to test one's social eligibility, as well as to signify inclusion or exclusion.[7] During spring training the Tecos treated me cordially but distantly. I knew I had to endure this until I could find a way to cross over, but being an older, non-border gringo with only serviceable Spanish seemed an awfully heavy cloak to discard.

My chance came much earlier than I would have anticipated, while traveling with the team to games. Being on the bus conferred a degree of authenticity that separated me from journalists, the group I was most often confused with. Traveling with the Mexican regulars also distinguished me from Americans. Some of the players were already a bit predisposed to me, while others, including most of the veterans, were not. The difference proved to be my willingness to share their accommodations and road lifestyle. The breakthrough came in the form of joking, both with me and at my expense, but always openly and easily.

It was in an exhibition game in Reynosa in March that a wicked line drive, hit foul by one of the Tecos' batters, whacked me on the leg. I was standing far enough down field that the velocity had slowed some so as to escape without damage. To these guys such occurrences are hilarious, Chaplinesque fiascos. They roared. I made nothing out of it. The very next inning another batter lined a shot into the dugout that slammed against the back wall just a few feet from my head. Mora, walking by, said, "Hey man, you must be a magnet." "Sure," I responded. "I'll chop my leg off and let you bat with it so you can get your [batting] average up." Two of the other veterans liked that comeback. An inning later as I was walking to the other end of the dugout when Romero passed me and suddenly yelled, "Esquive!" (duck). I did, and everyone roared. I high-fived him, enjoying this more than any of them could have known. Having the opportunity to be the butt of their jokes was the opening I was looking for. For the next game or two they tried the "duck" number on me at least a half-dozen times (with decreasing success). No matter, because now they joked about an array of things and I responded in kind.

Unlike in American ballparks such as West Martin Field, there was no national anthem played in Estadio Monterrey, just a "play ball" call that served to initiate the event. That night it would be Orlando Lind on the mound for the Tecos. Lind, despite a disastrous early outing that saw his ERA swell to 6.00, had pitched masterfully since; and coming into the game he had a league-leading 1.59 ERA. The Tecos quickly jumped out to a 1–0 lead on a home run by Bobby Moore, and Lind eased into a groove and stay unruffled for the rest of the game. Only once was he threatened, when in the third inning James Steels, an American playing for the Industriales, came to bat. Steels had been tearing up the league's pitching. In the previous series between the two clubs in the Laredos, Steels hit a rare home run into the teeth of a northerly wind, blowing in from right field. The ball jetted out of the park so fast that it looked as if it had been assisted by the wind rather than hampered. Now Steels was up again, with a tough at bat against Lind. Everything the righthander threw he fouled off, but the fourth or fifth foul ball was a monstrous blow knocked clean out of the stadium. Everyone just watched in silence, and when it was clearly foul the Tecos breathed a collective sigh of relief. Steels wound up weakly grounding out. A pumped-up Lind resumed mowing down the opposition.

With his last pitch, he had gone eight innings, given up two hits and one walk, and struck out six. In the eighth inning Lind was squeezed by the umpire and visibly showed his disgust with a bad call that should have resulted in a strikeout. Upon returning to the dugout he screamed to the umpire, "What was wrong with that pitch?" The umpire turned to Lind and put his fingers to his mouth, which Lind interpreted as the umpire calling a ball because he (Lind) went to his mouth (possibly throwing a spitball). Lind swore at the umpire, who seemed to reciprocate by giving Lind the finger. At this point Firova stepped in, informing Lind that the umpire was actually making a rare admission of error by indicating that he "ate the pitch" (meaning he made a mistake). Lind bowed deeply and apologized loudly and comically. The umpire responded with a toothy smile and bowed as well.

Jay Baller came in and pitched a perfect ninth to preserve a tight 2–1 win. The Tecos were getting used to this. Winning is addictive.

We climbed onto the Tecobus and wound our way back to the hotel. In a buoyant, yet not infantile mood most opted to be let off a few blocks from the hotel at the Taco stands that stayed open past 11 P.M. It was a subdued dinner and we sat around talking quietly, squeezing lemon juice and a pinch of salt into our Tecates. There was little inclination to party since the park and hotel were some distance from the center of town. Or maybe some, like Couoh, were trying to save as much money as possible: "I've got a family to care for, and some time later I'd like to have enough to go into business for myself."

No one straggled into the lobby of the hotel before mid-morning. By then we had already spent an interesting morning at the Mexican League Hall of Fame, located in the heart of Monterrey. Some of the players had friends and family in the area and spent the day with them, but most simply slept till mid-day, later stumbling into the restaurant looking for that first cup of coffee. With a 5 P.M. call for batting practice, the lobby was taken over by rookies and bachelors sitting around making small talk and generally enjoying each other's silent company.

The second game of the series pitted Waite against an ex-Teco, Luís Huerta. Again, the Tecos came out early and scored in their first at bat. The feeling of confidence in the dugout had even spread to taciturn Dan Firova, who found himself cursing the umpires with more venom than usual. "Burro, goddamn umpires can't get a call straight!" he scowled, following with a mortar lob of chewing tobacco to the dugout steps. Before the first inning ended the floor was glistening from Skoal and sunflower seeds.

The Tecos coasted through the first four innings in under fifty minutes. Each time they returned to the dugout they sat in their accustomed places that no one has to publicly declare. Barraza likes to sit on the steps in the closest corner to home plate. Mora positions himself near the water cooler near the ramp leading to the dressing rooms. He likes it there so he can enjoy an unobtrusive cigarette. The far corner, which is the side of the dugout furthest from the plate, is empty. That's tonight's time-out zone, where Díaz, furious with himself for striking out, has just gone to scream invectives and kick the bench. Waite lives in or near the time-out zone, wherever it happens to be. Even though he was pitching well, he gravitates to the most marginal spot in the dugout because he has, in part, come to understand that he is being shunned. Baller, of course, swears the loudest in the zone. Others are more circumspect. Mora never seems to lose it. Even in his present mini-slump he walks back at the same pace each time.

Taking his batting glove off finger by finger, he holds the offending bat under his arm. When he gets to the bat rack he places the bat down, then sits. This time he drops the bat—not hard, just drops it. Walking to the time-out zone, he seemingly does nothing; then in a muted expression of outrage he steps on a plastic cup, slowly and most definitely crushing it. Nothing more. He then goes to the water cooler for a drink. However one thinks of these behaviors they are licensed venting, similar to the ritualized running amok in certain New Guinea tribes.[8]

In the dugout, the Tecos clamor for a hit: "*Vamos chingados!*" (Let's go, fuckers), and "*Carreras!*" (runs), as they try for some insurance runs to pad their 1–0 lead. Nothing doing. They wind up relying upon Baller to nail down the win in the final two innings, which he efficiently does.

The Tecos ride back home on the new and very accommodating toll road between Monterrey and Nuevo Laredo, buoyant over their recent charge. They would take on the Saraperos of Saltillo the next day. Juan Jesús Alvarez, *el indio*, would be on the mound for the Tecos. He had been a quiet mainstay of the pitching staff, dignified whether eating in a roadside dive or in a crisis situation on the mound. Even in his previous start, in which he experienced back pain, he made no mention of it. No grimace, no word. Between innings he would stretch inconspicuously in the corner, the discomfort registering only in the line of his mouth tightening. Yet when I looked quizzically at him as if to ask if he were okay, he smiled ever so slightly. He was ready.

Alvarez, like other pitchers, prepared for this game by running back and forth along the outfield wall at Parque La Junta in a blistering ninety-two degree heat. "It's dry now, much better for running," he said, gliding along side of me. As a Boston runner, I think of how relative all this is. In Boston heat, most run either early in the morning or late at night. These Teco pitchers impress me by comparison. After the initial warm-ups and batting practice, the players adjourned to the dressing room to switch from their practice jerseys into game whites. Barraza and Vega, with energy to spare, pumped a little iron with a rusty weight set, while the old man, Mora, sweat still dripping from batting practice, blandly looked on. Luís Díaz, how-ever, was very animated, and having missed the first game of the Monter-rey series because of the birth of his little daughter, was busily handing out tiny peppermint patties to everyone. "Now we're both pápis (dads)," he said, referring to the recent birth of my son.

Firova wanted the players to be loose, but because Saltillo is in last place he feared a Teco letdown, so he was making everyone aware that the *mul-tas*, the system of fines he had instituted early in the season, was doubly in effect now. As with its counterpart in the United States, this system fines players for not hustling, missing signs, missing the cutoff man on relays, and so forth. Firova also rewards players for getting game-winning hits and pitching shutouts. In cases of disputes there is a kangaroo court made up of various Teco players to issue decisions.

The Tecos were indeed loose this night. Romero elbowed me, motioning to the stands where the Teco cheerleaders were trying to lead a cheer. Six young girls dressed more or less identically (white sleeveless jerseys and shorts made of jeans) were waving blue and white pompoms. They weren't quite in sync, but it hardly mattered. This was a high point of the season. The team was beginning to jell, running their record to 20–10 since the *importados* arrived. It was still early enough for everyone to expect the best, no matter how they had done until now. Even the dispiriting presence of Waite, the quintessential "Ugly American," had worked to allow Americans and Mexicans to pull together around a commonly disliked presence. In fact, though Waite tested everyone's patience, no one really believed him when he said he was going to leave, which is why everyone was shocked when, ten days after returning from the Industriales road trip, the announcement was made that Waite and Baller were being called up to Richmond (the Braves AAA franchise). Waite left in a flash, not triumphantly (although he did try to rub everyone's face in it), but more like someone slinking out in the dead of night. Surprisingly, Baller elected to stay. One would think that a player would not hesitate to move up the ladder when the opportunity presented itself. But Baller's reasoning was to play regularly in the Mexican League was better than to play less frequently in Richmond. If he could put up big numbers, then the Braves would be more likely to take him on in September than if he wiled away his time in the American Association.

This collective sense of "willing" wins, together with a drive to be professional, whether on Mexican or American terms, is what enabled the Tecos to wake up on May 26, the end of the first half of the season, and find themselves in second place. The points they earned from this second-place finish would stand them in good stead for the next half of the season and the playoffs that followed.

## The Second Half of the Season

Three conditions defined the second half of the Teco season: the play of the team and players, relations within the team, and the weather. The first two vary; the third is constant.

Laredo's television meteorologist, "Heatwave" Berliner, is a quirky-looking character. Each morning and evening he appears on Channel 8 looking for all the world like a bookish science nerd. His face and demeanor is bespectacled and studious, clearly out of place on the border. His forecasts are delivered deadpan, with a tin voice that never wavers. His nickname, connoting blistering, intense heat, and his presence are oxymorons. It's brilliant. Part of Heatwave's appeal is his unchanging, bland quality, as if he had no age, no peaks and valleys. Just like the weather! The temperature routinely climbs to 110 degrees Fahrenheit at this time of year, cooling off to between 85 and 90 at night. There's no chance of rain and nary a cloud in the sky until sometime in late October. Things bake if left in the afternoon sun: cassette tapes buckle if left on the dash, keys left exposed to the heat would sear the flesh if touched. The Tecos not only play in this weather, they train in it. Games start at 7:30 or 8:30 P.M., but batting practice might start at 5:30 when it is still intensely hot. And always the pitchers could be seen loping along in front of the outfield wall unphased.

Appearing in the playoffs and gaining the all-important home field advantage is based on total points derived from where a team finishes in the standings in each half of the season. The top four teams in points advance to the playoffs. Having climbed in the first half of the season to the second spot in the eight-team division was very satisfying, but for the Tecos to seal their appearance in the playoffs they would have to finish strong again in the second half. The second half has traditionally been good to the Tecos, but the border team began quietly this year by splitting a four-game series against the Sultanes of Monterrey, winners of the first half. The second series against Aguascalientes went more poorly still, with the Tecos salvaging only the third game. Seven games into the second half, the Tecos were 3–4 and tied for last. Seven straight wins later, however, they jumped into first, where they would remain the rest of the year. In the end, their second half record was 40–24, which, combined with a 36–29 slate in the first half was good enough to win their ninth North Zone championship since 1977.

While the goal of the team may be to win a championship, and the additional goal of the players to earn fame and fortune, the season has its own story to tell. Clearly, for the team, the first half of the season was dramatized by the gringo cavalry rescue and the coming together of the team in response to the noxious presence of one "ugly American" (see Chapter 7). By comparison, the second half seemed flat. The Tecos were clearly the team to beat in this phase. The players were loose, even giddy. If anything, overconfidence and maintaining the drive might have been problematic for Dan Firova's team.

When I returned during the second half it was a happy group of players that greeted me in the clubhouse. "Alan Klein!"—this from the other end of the dressing room—"Damn! Alan Klein, here in Nuevo Laredo," facetiously bellowed a freshly showered Dan Firova, with a smile and a towel wrapped around him. How un-Firova! If this was how buoyant their most reserved member was, things were going well indeed.

Orlando Lind was busily handing out batting gloves to his teammates, gloves he had received from his brother, José "Chico" Lind, then an infielder with the Kansas City Royals. Gerardo Sánchez took two pairs of red gloves and was trying them on for size when Orlando quipped, "You better get me a couple of runs or I'll take them back." "Tonight, I'll give you two," responded Sánchez, who in 1996 would set the Mexican League record for most consecutive games played.

Because of the heat, everyone was taking advantage of a yellow ice chest full of soda (when the Tecos win, the chest is full of beer following the game). Ernesto Barraza was searching the chest for a couple of chunks of ice to put on his pitching elbow. He was listening to a cassette of Pink Floyd's *Wish You Were Here* and wearing a Floyd T-shirt. He is the first, and so far the only, Floyd fan on the team. He and a few of the others liked to spend the time between batting practice and the game pumping some light weights. Some of the Tecos were just outside the clubhouse where it opens to the stadium, busily trying to hit on some local women.

The light-heartedness remained even as the first Saraperos players jumped on Orlando Lind for two runs. While he and catcher Edgar Vega stormed back to the dugout cursing, the others sauntered back casually. Lind was doing time out as the Teco's leadoff man, Bobby Moore, stepped to the plate. "C'mon Bobby, Bobby!" "Andale Bobby!" shouted the players. There was no pressing note in their voices, and Moore obliged by singling to center, setting the Tecos on a roll. They tallied six runs in the bottom of the first, sparked by a two-run homer by Jerardo Sánchez, who smiled at Lind on returning to the dugout; and after high-fiving everyone, he shouted to Lind, "I'm taking the tags off of the gloves now, okay?" The Tecos won 19–2.

I arrived at Parque La Junta early the next day. It's 105 degrees, "but it's dry." Still , it's too hot for me to go out for my usual 6 A.M. run. Too hot for a workout at the air conditioned gym. Too hot to stand in line in my air conditioned car on the bridge going over to Nuevo Laredo. Too hot. But the Tecos were out there running, taking batting practice. I had an excuse; I had just arrived from New England and had not physically adjusted yet, but Jay Baller, who has been here since April and was acclimated, had no excuse. He was quite agitated, however, at having to practice in the heat of the day: "It's all about pigment," he bristles in the clubhouse. "I just don't have it. I can't go out there. I don't know why the fuck he [Firova] has gotta call BP this early." Overlooked was the fact that Ricardo Moreno and Ernesto Barraza were as white as he was but had just put in four and five miles, respectively. Fact was, Jay Baller did not resemble the same man who came here in early spring. In April Baller would have gone along with the program. In less than four months he had gone from a "hail fellow well met" kind of guy to someone frustrated and surly and ready to take it out on anyone around him. Earlier in the season Baller had seen how Willie Waite whined, and he quickly worked in the collective effort to marginalize his Anglo compatriot. Being more hopeful about his career and not wanting to be perceived as a pushy gringo, in the first half season Baller was definitely more upbeat about life in the Mexican League and his chances for going on to a later stint in the majors. As July wound down he had grown resentful that the right opportunity had not come (the deadline for being picked up from the Mexican League had passed); he had become frustrated with the ineptitude of certain people in the Teco front office, and tired of what he saw as the shabby conditions attendant with playing in Mexico. In response to it all, he had begun taking it out on the Tecos. Other situations preceded it, but the defining moment of the second half of the season came on a road trip to Mexico City.

## The Mexico City Incident

On July 11 the Tecos were in Mexico City for the second game of a two-game series against the Diablos. The game was slated to begin at 1 P.M., so when at about 10:45 A.M. Firova saw Baller, he thought nothing of it until an hour later when he noticed that both Baller and Moore were now in their street clothes.[9]

"What's goin' on?," the manager asked Moore. "You playin' or what?"

"Nawh," answered Moore, "we've gotta fly back."

"You know, if you go, you're goin' without permission, and, you're gonna have to deal with Lozano."

Baller and Moore laughed dismissively: "Yeah, we'll take our chances."

As it turned out, all four Teco Imports did not play that day, flying back to Laredo instead and beginning what would become known in Teco baseball circles as "The Mexico City Incident": the Imports temporarily abandoning their teammates for purely selfish reasons. The Tecos went on to lose both the game (19–1) and their grasp on first place.

It was one of the team's most humiliating defeats in years, prompting some to ask how they could lose so badly with one of their aces (Barraza) on the mound and a lineup that had been battering pitchers all over the league. Rookie pitcher Ricardo Moreno recalled that once the players were aware of being "abandoned" by the Imports, some grew angry and determined: "We wanted to know from Dan why he let them go. They [*importados*] do whatever they want. The team was angry. We are a team and we had to stay together. When they left us before the game we wanted badly to win. Some said, 'Hey, we did it (win) before, we can do it again.' But we played badly, made six errors."[10]

Another Tecolotes insider, however, felt that the one-sided loss was a function of collective foot-dragging, and likened the team's play to a tortoise, *como la tortuga*, he said. According to this thinking, by not putting out their best effort, the Tecos were sending a message both to Imports and the front office. This was strikingly at odds with the psyched-up mindset that Moreno claims for the team. These two interpretations—playing poorly but trying to win versus purposely playing poorly—cannot be easily reconciled. In the light of the deep wound caused by the importado abandonment, there was enough demoralization to at least open the floodgates of this rout, though once it had started, it quickly took on a life of its own. However one explains this humiliation on the diamond, the real repercussions were felt off of it.

The Imports returned to Laredo completely confident that no action would be taken against them. In their minds they had disrupted nothing and had not insulted anyone. Jay Baller spoke candidly about the incident: "Three of us [pitchers] had already pitched and weren't gonna go out again that day. We had an off day comin'."[11] They invoked the need to be with their families on that day as additional moral leverage. The way that travel arrangements were handled, according to Baller, left a lot to be desired. Imports, as well as Teco starters, were scheduled to fly back on Monday, the day after the game. Baller considered this ridiculous since it was their off day and they desperately needed that day of rest. He checked into flights on Sunday and found two, one at 3:30 and another at 6:00 P.M. He claimed to have spoken with Lozano about the available Sunday flights and asked him to take care of booking. The fact that the team was not booked on the latter flight was, according to Baller, proof positive that Lozano was "penny-pinching again."

The antagonism between Imports and the Teco front office, unfortunate though it was, had begun long before. Whether or not they realized it, the Imports had been given the pampered treatment from the beginning. Waite, Baller, and, to a lesser extent, Lind and Moore were chauffeured around by the front office almost at will. Teco Vice President Rodríguez had treated Baller and Waite to his exclusive country club for several rounds of golf, a courtesy extended to Baller for the entire summer. Every time they needed something all they had to do was make a phone call and the team's general manager and vice president would do it for them. It is easy to see how the Imports had come to feel entitled.

Many contradictory things can be attributed to Baller, but on two issues he is unwaveringly straight: he works hard at his craft, and he feels he should be treated well. He brings these expectations with him wherever he plays, but in addition, he and Waite, as former major leaguers, both felt that coming to the Mexican League was tantamount to being given final notice, which in some ways it was: Atlanta would release them if they couldn't prove themselves with the Tecos. The difference between the two gringos was that Waite whined his way around Laredo, and Baller demanded to be treated in accordance with his status as an ex–major leaguer and a record-holding minor league veteran.

The treatment Baller expected was nothing less than what his agent had negotiated for him, which included use of a car and monthly living allowance while in Laredo. All the Imports were paid by Atlanta and given a living allowance for accommodations, but Baller received a larger allowance and the car was an additional perk. Unfortunately, Chito Rodríguez and Chuck LaMar never quite managed to get together on the contractual obligations that each of their organizations had toward the Imports, and the void that existed was filled by the opportunistic Baller, who routinely maintained that his demands had been approved by the Braves. Rodríguez had difficulty in confirming these demands with LaMar, but because he wanted both to fulfill the expectations that Atlanta might have of the Tecos and to provide a constructive atmosphere for the Imports, he agreed to each demand, no matter how absurd or uncongenial.

As Teco general manager, it was left to Lozano to deal with many of the details involving the Imports. It was he who had to arrange the elaborate travel to and from games outside of the Laredos. It was he who was supposed to deal with management around the living arrangements and the payments to the players. In fairness to both sides, there were times when Baller (as self-appointed spokesman for the Imports) was overly demanding, just as there were occasions when Lozano didn't hold up his end of the bargain, with the result that the Imports grew restive and the front office frustrated. At such moments the Americans threatened to play their trump card: they would bolt and leave the team.

The car that Baller received was the right size for the strapping 6'6" reliever and his wife and child, but the wrong year: it was nine years old with at least 90,000 miles on it. Repairs were frequent on the old beater, and each time it broke down, Baller would get more and more hot under the collar since it meant a major inconvenience to his family. Laredo is not a walk-about city. People, especially nonlocals, need a car to drive from one air-conditioned place to another. Worse yet, his wife was stopped by the Laredo police for driving an unregistered and uninsured vehicle; when Baller found out about it, he went through the roof. He called Rodríguez repeatedly, who had Larry Dovalina handle the matter. It required some paperwork and a small fine to be paid, but eventually it fell to Lozano to move the papers. For whatever reason he didn't; and several weeks later a letter arrived at the Ballers' apartment from the police, warning them that if the fine, now having accumulated, were not paid immediately there would be a warrant out for Terri Baller's arrest. Baller threatened anyone and everyone with the only thing he could, "packing up and leaving." And no one could really blame him. The Teco front office had blown it, and whether it had been accidental or intentional, from Baller's point of view it was only the latest in a long line of difficulties he had faced since coming to the border.

He knew two things: the Imports were largely responsible for the success of the Tecos, and that by threatening to withhold their services he was able to get what he felt was rightfully his. What he and the others didn't know, or fully comprehend, was that they were contributing to a cultural and national drama that would have consequences for subsequent groups of Imports.

While they are foreign professionals, these *importados* are not simply mercenaries hired to get a job done. They are also team members, individuals engaged in a collective pursuit of a goal and dependent upon others from start to finish. If Imports do well they aid their team's pursuit of a title, and (they hope) get noticed by the parent club. Additionally, however, the Imports are also cultural representations: symbols of the United States. The power differential that exists between the two countries, and the attitudes attendant to their citizens, is mirrored on the team as well. This was imperfectly understood and/or disregarded by Baller and the other Imports.

The aftermath of the abandonment was revealing because all of the Tecos responded the same way. The dressing room in Mexico City was like a tomb following the loss. Players quickly picked up their gear and headed for the Tecobus to return to the hotel and shower. According to Firova, "Nobody said nothin' after the game, but those guys [Imports] were abandoning the team and the players were hurt by that";[12] he was characteristically understating the gravity of the incident. The humiliation was made worse by the trip home to Laredo. The starters all flew back on Monday, while the manager, coaches, and the rest of the players rode for fourteen hours on the Tecobus.

This two-tier travel system is one of the most pernicious and structurally divisive institutions in the Mexican League. For road games within a team's division, all Imports fly to cities that are more than a six-hour drive away while their Mexican teammates travel by bus or car. On the big cross-country tours both Imports and Mexican starters fly, and the rest endure bus trips as debilitatingly long as seventeen hours. On the night following the Imports' desertion, players were quietly seething. Alejandro Ortiz, for one, was so disgusted with the way things were that he came to Firova and said simply and elegantly, "I don't like this anymore. Everyone goes or no one," referring to both the desertion in question as well as the two-class travel plan. He gave up his airplane ticket so that sixty-year-old coach and trainer Pini Jiménez, far and away the oldest man in the organization, could be spared the discomfort. Another suggested that the team "let the *culeros* [referring to the Imports derisively as people violated anally] go. We don't need them!"

By the time the team reassembled in Nuevo Laredo Lozano had informed the press on both sides of the river that the Imports had been given permission to leave a day early:

> They called from Yucatan [after the previous week's series against the Leones] and told us that depending on the wins and losses during the trip, they would take the 3:30 P.M. flight from Mexico and wouldn't be able to be in the game. Furthermore, had they played on Sunday, the whole team would return by bus the same day, but the players from Atlanta would have to wait for the next flight until Monday and would lose a day of rest. I would also like to point out that the players haven't rested in the last twenty-four days and that decision [to allow the Imports to leave] was just.[13]

Strictly speaking this was a fabrication. The front office was backing the Imports because they feared that if the Mexican League commissioner's office got wind of this they would suspend the players for the remainder of the season, and the fans would be outraged. Chito Rodríguez had a somewhat different slant on his dealings with the Imports: "I can put up with Jay because he is an ex–major leaguer and he's used to being treated as one. You have to understand, he's adjusting psychologically to being here for the year. Also, he's done very well here. Mostly, he's frustrated. But Preston Watson [Waite's replacement after he was called up] has bad numbers, yet he also thinks he can act like Baller. We can't put up with that."[14]

The Mexico City incident further soured relations between the American and Mexican players. There was little socializing between the two groups outside the ballpark before the incident, and even less afterward. Nevertheless, considering the presence of two major irritants in their midst, I was impressed by how tolerant the Mexican players were of gringos in general. Ernesto Barraza had been in the Mexican League for six years and seen his share of "*pinches* [damn] *gringos*," but he continued to fight against the tendency to generalize about them. This may be in part a tribute to his cosmopolitan Mexico City background, and in part a tribute to the fact that not all the Americans who come down are intolerant, spoiled, or racist. When Rodríguez claims, "I can tell you that our groups [of Imports] have been better since we have our relationship with Atlanta," he means that the players coming over remain hopeful of returning to play for the Braves. Theoretically, then, they are more disposed to fit in or at least to regulate their behavior during the season than someone who has no parent club to answer to or has little hope of playing in the majors. Apparently 1993 was atypical.

**Playoff Series**

Most of the Tecos had come to think of the playoffs as part of their athletic birthright. The entire starting lineup, and pitchers Barraza, Alvarez, and Couoh, had been there virtually every year of their careers. For Mora and Ortiz it had been ten of the past twelve years, but even newer players had been there four or five times. The players think of the playoffs as a short, intense third season following the two halves. To win the championship a team has to take three best-of-seven series. The Tecos last accomplished this in 1989 and came close in two subsequent seasons.

The Tecos once again found themselves in the post-season, thanks to the combination of their dependable performers (Ortiz's 30 home runs and 102 RBIs, Mora's 20 home runs, and Romero's .300 batting average and 17 home runs); their Imports (Moore's .340 average); and the career year of Meré (.328 average and 18 home runs). In addition, the pitching staff more than carried its weight. They dominated in a range of categories. Alvarez led the league in strikeouts and was among the leaders in earned run average and innings pitched, despite a record of only 6–7 in the torrid second half of the season. Barraza overcame a tough July to lead the team in victories, finishing fourth in the league in that department with a 15–8 record. Lind pitched very effectively, compiling a 13–7 mark with a 2.95 ERA, good for fifth in the league. Baller's 30 saves led the league and came within five of the Teco record (even though he missed the first three weeks of the season). Enrique Couoh compiled a deceptive 7–2 record to go along with a sterling 2.24 ERA. All cylinders were firing as the Tecos prepared for their first post-season rival.

They opened against the Aguascalientes. For the fans, this was the time to jack themselves up. Not only were more fans in attendance during the playoffs, but also more *sonájas*—rectangular wooden boxes with handles that make grating metallic sounds as they are turned. The catcalls that punctuate the games are also intensified, so that in addition to the whistles and cries of "burro" one could hear all manner of epithets, both vulgar and creative. The insults that most anger are the personal ones, such as "Hey _____, instead of playing baseball you should be home taking care of your good-looking wife." The Tecos sliced through the Aguascalientes in their initial series like a hot knife through butter. In the first two games in the Laredos, Lind and Alvarez pitched masterfully into the seventh and eighth innings. Again the long ball played a role. In the first game "El Hombre," Andrés Mora, having tailed off somewhat in the season's second half, rebounded by sending a long arching shot over the left field wall to give the Tecos a lead it would not relinquish. He seemed fifteen years younger as he rounded the bases and headed for the dugout, the puffiness around his eyes and weariness gone for the moment. He even forgot about his customary cigarette following each at bat. On the other side of the bench, Baller, much to his dismay, was passed over as the closer in favor of Couoh. The skinny Mexican pitcher closed both games virtually flawlessly (four and a third innings, no hits, no runs, six strikeouts). As the series moved to Aguascalientes, Barraza won handily, 4–3, behind home runs by Romero and Sánchez. This time Baller relieved, crisply. The series would have been a sweep but for the 9–2 loss the Tecos suffered behind the ineffective pitching of American Preston Watson. Nevertheless, it was a very strong Tecolotes team that headed for the Northern Zone finals against the Monterrey Sultanes.

The Tecos had not fared well against the Sultanes during the year, losing six of seven against them in Monterrey and barely playing them even at home. Fortunately for the Tecos, the postseason favors a team with momentum, and after splitting the first two games on the border, the Tecos went on to win three more in Monterrey behind an excellent combination of pitching and hitting.

The Sultanes series was interesting from yet another vantage point. Zacatillo Guerrero, who, until 1993, had been the most successful Teco manager of the era, was now managing the Sultanes. To both fans and players Guerrero had become somewhat larger than life. Unlike Dan Firova, who liked the professional low-key approach to managing, Guerrero was a mercurial taskmaster, known to belittle his players in public if he felt it necessary. One couldn't find more different management styles anywhere than between the rookie *pocho* from Refugio, Texas, and the Mexican League Hall-of-Famer.

In the second game of the series something occurred that turned long-held feelings toward Guerrero in the Laredos from glowing to glowering. Guerrero suddenly decided to alter the chemistry of the game by psyching out his opposition. At West Martin Field, in front of the Teco faithful, Guerrero yelled to the third-base umpire to check the cap of Teco pitcher Barraza for a controlled substance. The umpire did, and found nothing. That, however, did not satisfy Guerrero, who, in violation of Mexican League regulations, stormed out to the mound and checked Barraza's cap for himself. His brazenness shocked the fans of Laredo into silence, until an irate Firova charged out to confront him. In Firova's anger the Teco fans found their voice and began booing Guerrero, an act strange to them after so many years of adulation. Leaving the field, Guerrero pointed to his head with his index finger, indicating to the fans that he was smart enough to psyche out the opposition. The incident immediately chilled what had been a warm, six-year relationship, and the fans hurled enough abuse at their former hero to shake the stadium.

The overall effect of this incident seemed to work. It was an unnerved Teco team that wound up committing five errors (three by Ortiz), en route to losing the game 6–2. That night a despondent Ortiz went out and drank himself into numbness. The next morning, when questioned about his horrible condition, he shook his head and said, "The things he said bothered me a lot. He insulted the whole team."

Guerrero's action was vaguely reminiscent of the dysfunctional influence an abusive father has on his children who, even after they break away from him, are easily threatened into undermining themselves. In the Sultanes-Tecos series, however, Guerrero had spent his emotional currency. The Tecos did not crumble beyond that game; rather they went on to beat the Sultanes three straight times in Monterrey. During the last game, amid the waving brooms brought by Teco fans in Estadio Monterrey, a frustrated Guerrero stormed out to the mound to remove his pitcher (an American Import). The imperious and berating manner of the old master did not play well with his gringo pitcher. One thing led to another, and before anyone knew it the pitcher and manager were ready to go at it until the team rushed out to separate them. The Tecos had exacted their revenge. Guerrero was no longer the unruffled and venerable maestro in Nuevo Laredo, while the *pocho*, Firova, had come full circle, reconstituted into a latter-day David victorious over Goliath. As the Tecos rushed about high-fiving and hugging each other, Firova went and got one of the brooms with which Teco fans had been taunting their opposition and waved it about as if it were a banner. The win was doubly sweet for him, advancing the team to the finals and silencing his critics.

The eight bottles of champagne he purchased were brought down, and after a short dousing ritual someone shouted, "Don't waste it, drink it." A very dusty and tired Teco team made short work of the beverages.

## Championship

In the end there were but two: the Tecos (as predicted) and the scrappy (and unlikely) Tabasco Olmecs. Third seeded in the playoffs in the southern division, the Olmecs had clawed their way to the finals, beating a heavily favored team from Mexico City. This was the Olmecs' first final round appearance. During the regular season the two teams had split four games between them, each winning in their home parks.

For ten straight years the Tecos have gone into the playoffs, and five times they have gone to the finals. After a disquieting loss to Mexico City the previous year, the 1993 Tecos found themselves in the finals again and were determined to avenge the loss. The borderlands around the Laredos were high with anticipation, as was Villahermosa, home of the Olmecs, in the south. Each side was busy heaping derision on the other, as in all good rivalries. In this respect, sport is timeless.

The Mexican League championship series hearkens back to the baseball-crazy days of Jorge Pasquel in the mid-1940s. Wild enthusiasm and throngs of aficionados in the stadiums are commonplace. So too is the vilification of opponents and the mass preoccupation that consumes the fans for the entire two-week period of the series. Heroes and revelers are caught up in a dance that plays just as well with a mariachi beat in Nuevo Laredo as it does with piped-in rock music over the sound system in Oakland or Toronto.

The fans had already packed Parque La Junta by the time the Tecos began taking batting practice for the first game, two and a half hours before the opening pitch. This was the first time all year that there was standing room only. Many of the Teco starters, smelling a championship, were ready for the game to begin early. "We banged their heads pretty good when they were here in April; I can't wait to get to them again," exclaimed second baseman Pedro Meré. Firova once again cautioned against overconfidence: "They're in the finals and there for a reason. They're a type of team that tries to make things happen. Not too much power, but hit and run and steal bases."[15]

The initial contest seemed like a repeat of much of the second half of the season: steady pitching and power displays by the Tecos. Orlando Lind pitched solidly. As was typical of much of the season, the Teco pitchers had a shaky first inning. This time they spotted the Olmecs a run, but in their customary fashion got it back, and more, in their half of the first inning. The diminutive Meré started things off with a home run. The next three Tecos got on base before another of the smaller Tecos, Bobby Moore, showed uncharacteristic power by hitting a grand slam to give the Tecos a commanding 5–1 lead.

The script moved along predictably. Lind settled down, allowing no more runs. In the fourth inning the big guns of the Tecos came to life: Romero pounded a three-run home run over the left field wall, giving the "Border Birds" an 8–1 lead. He struck again in the seventh with another home run, and the game ended mercifully with the Tecos winning 12–1. The fans, press, and even the players themselves were getting used to this sort of dominance, and all left the stadium feeling good—not euphoric, but satisfied.

The second game was played across the border at West Martin Field. Again, it was a bit odd to see the stands filled to overflow with 5,000 fans (many from across the river) whistling, stamping, and using their *sonájas*. "Better late than never," quipped Firova on the sudden surge in attendance after a disappointing turnout through the season. Enthusiasm was turned up several notches and an air of expectation hovered over the white-yellow light of the field. For the Tecos the game may have seemed ripe for the picking, which, of course, is often precisely the time when things begin to unravel.

It's hard to say just where the karma shifted and went south. I tend to think that the world turned upside down for the Tecos beginning with slugger Marco Antonio Romero's impulsiveness. The second game seemed to begin on the same charmed note as the first. The Tecos jumped out to a 2–1 lead on a two-run blast by Romero. For a two-week stretch Romero was so good that it was as if he were playing by himself. No pitch was too fast or too well placed and his timing could not be upset. It was his third home run in two games, his league-leading seventh of the postseason, and he was feeling very aggressive, the way all good power hitters should. In his next at-bat, however, he popped up weakly after being crowded by an inside pitch. Ever the macho, Romero swore at the night sky and choked the life out of his bat as he approached the dugout. He had the perfect face for fury: dark and fiery eyes, a growl for a voice, a thick lawn of stubble on his face, and a mustache that seemed to frame his mouth in a permanent scowl. Romero descended the steps in total disgust with himself, walked to a neutral corner, and smashed the dugout wall with a loud, open-handed swat so characteristic of time outs. Unfortunately, this time there was a nail sticking out of the wall that he had not detected, and it drove a good inch through his hand. He was immediately taken to a local hospital to be treated. Though Romero returned for the next game, he played hurt from that point on, unable to grip the bat with authority. If, as baseball people claim, "hitting is contagious," so is the lack of it. With this unexpected injury to their hottest hitter, the bats of the Tecos began growing silent. Alvarez pitched a tight ball game, but so did the Olmecs' Ricardo Osuna, and for eight innings the two were locked in a duel in which one wrong move could spell doom. The Olmecs pushed across a ninth-inning run off Jay Baller, and the Tecos lost 3–2. The series then shifted to Villahermosa in southern Mexico.

Villahermosa is the provincial capital of Tabasco. It is known around the league for having some of the wildest fans, but also, ominously, as having a ball park unkind to hitters. "In Villahermosa the air is heavier and the ball will not carry as much," warned Olmec manager Juan Navarrete. This was a prophetic statement, not so much about atmospheric attributes as about baseball strategy. As Baller later commented, "They knew we lived and died by the home run and had their pitchers just pitch us away all the time. That makes it real hard on your power."[16] Many a hit ball died in the outfield, the victims of effective pitching to a home run–happy band of Tecos as well as the heavy air.

While the Tecos were mostly seasoned veterans used to playing under all sorts of conditions, there was no question in my mind that the homefield crowds in Villahermosa were an effective weapon. Firova disagreed: "Look, when a guy's out there, he's so focused that he forgets everything. During games I'd forget I was playing in front of fans altogether until I was in the dugout."[17] But with the players sitting at field level and with only a chain-link fence between them and the fans, it was hard to tune out the Marat/Sade mob scene in Villahermosa.

Many factors made the fans' presence significant. Foremost was the din: "Those incessant drums," Larry Dovalina recalled, shaking his head. "They started before the game and didn't stop even when it was over." Both he and Rodríguez agreed that the Villahermosans are among the most ferocious fans that they have encountered, and their experience goes back almost two decades. "You know how at the games sometimes guys will holler, '*Chingen sus madres!*' Well, here even the women were scream-ing, 'Chingan sus madres, Tecos.' I couldn't believe it." recounted an in-credulous Rodríguez.[18]

There were other factors at work as well. The decision to open the gates at 7 A.M. for a 1 P.M. game and start serving beer hours before the game clearly was incendiary, as was the open seating arrangement of the ball-park. The latter allowed seating on a first come, first serve basis, which meant that the most avid (and often the most out of control and inebriated) fan was likely to get to the park early and sit closest to the field. Outfielder Gerardo Sánchez had to deal with drunken fans periodically rushing him during the game and screaming incoherently. As many years as he'd been around he was able to fend them off, defiantly crossing his arms in front of his chest and staring the intruders down until the police arrived. "When the cops finally got him," recalled Sánchez, referring to one fan, "they pulled him away. He looked like a pig, slipping in the mud on the field and covered all over with beer and foam."[19]

Given their first opportunity to let it all out in a championship series, the Olmec fans were thinking only of excess. Villahermosa made sure that *brujos* (witches) attended as well. They would bring *piñatas* of yellow and purple owls, which they would burn. One *brujo* burned incense and had the crowd chant slowly with him, "*Mata Tecos*" (Kill Tecos), while he waved the incense around the Teco dugout. Smoke seemed to be everywhere, and delirious, sweating fans danced around the roasting owl, lending the whole scene a warlike, tribal cast. Yet another fan, face painted to resemble Olmec warriors of old, cleverly crafted a sign reading, "*Tecolotes asada al carbon, gratis*" (free barbecued owls—a takeoff on the grilled meat dish Carne Asada al Carbon). But it was the cherry bombs, "as big as hand grenades," that unnerved outsiders most, including Mexican League Com-missioner Treito Cisneros. Action was stopped while the smoke from these bombs cleared near the pitcher's mound or first base. After admonish-ments over the public address system by league officials, threatening for-

feiture of the game unless the disruptive behavior ceased, the fans sim-
mered down and limited their cherry bombs tosses to between innings.
Remarkably, amid this bedlam, what followed was a string of hard-fought
pitchers' duels with precious few hits and no more home runs.

The fourth game between the teams epitomized the series. For eight
and a third innings the teams were locked in a scoreless duel. Orlando
Lind, who pitched the series of his life, had shut down the Olmecs with
only six hits. He left in the seventh in favor of Enrique Couoh, who continued the scoreless string. Three times the Olmecs threatened with runners
on third, and three times the Tecos escaped unscathed. On each occasion
the Tecos lined up in front of the dugout to high-five either Lind or
Couoh for their clutch pitching. Each time they shouted, "*Andele Tecos!*"
(move it, Tecos) and "*Carreras!*" (runs)—and each time they failed to drive
in a run in their half of the inning. Eduardo Salgado, the tricksterish young
reserve outfielder, thought he stole a run when he tried to score on Rubén
Estrada's single in the sixth. The plate umpire called him out on a ques-
tionable play. But in the Olmec ninth, the runner reached first when third
baseman Ortiz dove for a hard-hit grounder. He gloved it and from a
kneeling position tried to throw out the lead runner going to second. As
many times as he had relied on his arm in such situations, it failed him this
time, sending the ball into right field while the runner dashed home with
the winning run. Pandemonium gushed everywhere. The Tecos melted
away into the night. Formally, the series was over the following evening,
but the Tecos' emotion and momentum ended with that errant throw.

Anyone present at the park has to remember the bedlam that punctuated
the Olmecs' series victory in five games. The sight of a dejected Samuel
Lozano leaving the field as a fan held aloft a huge replica of an Olmec head
stands out in my mind as one of the most memorable statements of the
one-sided series. It was a slap at the heavily favored Nuevo Laredo team.
Even more unexpected than the loss was the post-mortem treatment the
Tecos received back home after the series. No congratulations, no city-
wide or bicitywide appreciation. Nothing but a few isolated, almost embar-
rassed, acknowledgments of the team's spectacular climb. It was a sad way
to end a day, a month, or a season.

There were a smattering of fans present when the Owls of the Two Laredos touched down at Laredo International Airport after their defeat in the
championship series. Instead, the players should have been feted for their
success and for the high drama they provided to the fans all season. The
front office did not take the initiative, however, to create such an event, and
the players merely proceeded to scatter about to their second seasons in the
Pacific League—dejected perhaps, but confident that they would probably
rap at the championship door in 1994. Teco families packed up in semi-
nomadic fashion emblematic of the seasonal flow. Imports left, not certain

where they were going; Baller was glad to be on his way. Lind, on the other hand, actually cried, hating to end the season partly because he had had such a fine year, but also because he knew that the ambience and community on the Teco team is something rarely encountered in professional baseball.

Lind is an Import who ameliorates all the negative perceptions of foreign players conjured up in Mexican baseball circles. He is a throwback to the kind of *refuerzos* seen in Mexico in the 1930s and the era of the legendary Martín Dihigo, Santos Amaro, and Ramon Bragaña, all of whom were from the Spanish Caribbean and were of African descent. Mexico has historically accommodated such players, as well as the early Negro Leaguers (see Chapter 2); it is, as we shall see, the Anglos who pose specific problems.

The attitudes of Imports and their contributions weigh heavily on the Mexican teams they play for. The structural inequalities in their contracts account for much of the Mexican resentment, and reinforce the Imports' sense of entitlement and superiority. This leads into a discussion of nationalism in the next chapter. The Tecos, because of their unique arrangement, underwrite binationalism far beyond the mixture of foreign and locals on the team. Off of the field, however, relations between players are more antagonistically autonational. These two faces of nationalism play off each other as a kind of dysfunctional dance, in which symbiotic need is systematically balanced and undermined by the resentment of each party.

# Seven

## 1994: The Worst of Times

THE SOCIAL FUSING and splitting of the two Laredos expressed in the river metaphor is more comprehensible as a set of fluid and unceasing existences. Hence, depending on the specific situation, people on the border engage one another using some combination of transnational, binational, and autonational identities. This chapter will discuss the way the three nationalisms are found in the most recent period, culminating in the destruction of the Tecos' binational agreement in 1994. Teco binationalism is the outcome of cycles of "good times" that bring a spirit of cooperation to the two Laredos, while hard times and crisis sets in motion mutual recrimination.

### Baseball Binationalism

"Even in an era when regional franchises like the Minnesota Twins, the Tampa Bay Buccaneers and the Golden State Warriors are an established part of professional sports," wrote Larry Rhoter of the *New York Times* in 1988, "Los Tecolotes de los Dos Laredos are an oddity. For the past four seasons this Mexican League team has been a truly international franchise."[1]

This binational label is built upon the notion that the team has a dual structure and identity based on shared proprietorship. Their split home schedule, divided between parks in both cities, and binational division of labor in the running of the club, reinforces the view of partnership between cities and countries. Binationalism also conveys a sense of sovereignty, and along with it equality. Articles in the *New York Times*, *Wall Street Journal*, *Dallas Morning News* have featured the Tecos as a newsworthy and futuristic form of binationalism. "The fact that Los Tecos have been doing baseball business back and forth across the border for almost ten straight years shows how the seemingly endlessly incubated NAFTA might work," begins a feature article in the *Dallas Sunday Magazine*.[2] The article goes on to discuss the cultural accommodations and cooperative nature of the team as if such ventures between countries rarely occur. Indeed, most distant views of the border presume a hard and hostile boundary between the countries, when in fact the local coupling of towns and cities along the border has been shown to generate all manner of linkages.

While many cultural linkages between the two Laredos have been discussed throughout this book, one could argue that none has the depth or range of the Tecolotes. Certainly none of these ventures has garnered the international attention that the Tecos have.

It is the unexpectedness of binationalism that proves so captivating to people from a distance. The two countries are most often depicted as being so different that venturing jointly into anything seems unlikely, risky, and even slightly unreal. An element of *National Geographic* cultural voyeurism pervades much of the American view of Mexico and, even more, along the border.[3] This extends to depictions of Mexican League baseball as well. Anyone can find the exotic in Mexico, New Mexico, or even New Jersey, for that matter, if that's what they are looking for. Indiana Jones exoticism is certainly what writer Gary Cartwright had in mind when he described baseball in Veracruz:

> On a sweltering Thursday morning in mid-April, Jack Pierce was picking his way among the stalls and pushcarts of the old market in Veracruz, Mexico, side-stepping baby pigs and turkeys and half-dead iguanas, when an old man in a tattered sarape appeared out of nowhere. . . . Ball games in Veracruz—or any-where else in Mexico—have a wacky, gaudy, Fellini-esque quality that teeters somewhere between illusion and madness. For one thing, batboys are often old men. The Aguila's batboy is a gnomelike fellow named Carlos who looks as though he would be comfortable in the bell tower at Notre Dame.[4]

This one-dimensional view of Mexican baseball, and Mexico in general, shades quickly into more racist stereotypes, as seen in Cartwright's sudden expertise as a physical anthropologist: "Unlike the Imports, who are usually in pretty good shape, the stereotypical Mexican ballplayer is short, fat, slow of foot, and chronically lazy."[5] Fortunately there are some well-placed and progressive experts to counter such depictions. Milton Jamail has thoughtfully responded directly to the racism and cultural ignorance of such reports, countering the faulty thinking with cultural and historical fact point by point.[6] Even when the journalist is not demeaning his subject, there still exists the tendency to exoticize, to separate rather than find the connections. Exoticizing is fine when done to intentionally distance the reader for the sake of some larger cultural point or when it has interpretive depth, but so often it is resorted to because there is neither intention nor ability to move beneath the surface. Exoticism is often inversely proportional to familiarity with the subject. Even the normally incisive and progressive baseball writer Peter Gammons slips, on occasion, into a booze-broads-and-mariachi characterization, as he did in his coverage of the 1989 Caribbean Series in Mazatlan, Mexico: "Even the next night, after Mexicali had collapsed like the peso against Las Aguilas de Zulia from Venezuela, the good people of Mazatlan chugged their Pacifico beer, sang their songs ('aye, yi, yi, yi') and danced the night away."[7] Thankfully, Gammons's sensitive depictions swamp these occasional lapses.

In the case of the Tecos, the exoticism is magnified by having a baseball franchise where Mexican and American cultures meet. Invented tradition plays a particularly interesting role in this context: whereas the concept has been used to discuss the fomenting of national identity, the Tecos as invented tradition foster binational invented tradition (e.g., playing both anthems at West Martin Field, the ritualized crossing through customs).

The Mexican League understands the full import of all this as well. While initially tentative about the experiment, the commissioner's office now fully endorses the binational arrangement. In fact, there are efforts currently underway to broaden this facet of the invented tradition. In 1994, the Mexican League and Texas League played a pair of All-Star games against each other, one game in each country. In part, building on the Tecos' success, the Monterrey Industriales relocated to Reynosa on the Mexican border and across from McAllen, Texas, with an eye toward possibly starting a binational relationship at some future point.[8]

Assessing the nature of these international relations involves looking at the Tecos not simply as a momentary relationship between nations. The long view is needed because any single windfall or crisis is capable of highlighting either the harmonious or acrimonious—but in either case the constant—polarism of the relationship. Whether discussing environmental border crises or the border baseball season, the attraction and repulsion felt must be kept in mind.

## Autonationalism and the 1993 Season

In terms of their talents and attitudes, Imports are often a mixed bag of treats and toxins for their Mexican League teams. For the Tecos in 1993, the presence of Orlando Lind and Bobby Moore, who adjusted fairly easily to the Mexican League, only partially offset the ill effects of Willie Waite and the back-sliding of Jay Baller. Beginning the season late meant that the Imports missed the chance to bond with their teammates during spring training, which contributed to setting them off socially throughout the year. Fortunately for the Tecos, in this case the Imports truly were *refuerzos* (reinforcements) and provided an instant boost to the club.

How this social tension plays itself out on and off the field is critical for understanding nationalism(s) and baseball. For the most part these men are all professional enough to meld their skills on the diamond. It is the "other game," the one off the field, one in which the culture of the team is involved, that brings to the fore the autonationalist antagonism. In some ways the presence of Imports is like a foreign army called in to protect a citizenry. The foreigners may be working to save a people from something that seriously threatens them, but they remain a noxious presence to be tolerated only, in this instance, at play. What the Mexican players hope is that some of the Imports will get over their initial contempt the league or the country (as in comments such as, "Baseball-wise, this is the land of the lost," or "I can't believe I'm in this horseshit country,") and develop a limited sense of camaraderie.

The two-class system of Imports and Mexicans that characterizes all Mexican League teams is based on the preferential pay and treatment accorded Imports. Most Mexican players can deal with these structural inequalities even though they find them unjust and irksome.[9] The Imports generally play a good caliber of baseball; and since getting into the playoffs and winning the playoff money is what the players are all after, the gringos' abrasiveness is easier to handle.

Not all Imports are problems, however. Some are like Lee Upshaw, who played two seasons for the Tecos: an easy-going, Baby Huey kind of young man who actually enjoys playing in Mexico. During Upshaw's second, albeit brief, stay with the Tecos in 1994 he showed an eagerness to assimilate to border culture and was remarkably free of cultural pretensions. When his wife moved down he made a point of introducing her to the wife of catcher Marco Antonio Cruz, since she speaks some English. Together the wives planned a barbecue. This was the only time I saw such an attempt at friendship made between Imports and Mexicans and their families. In 1995, Import oddity Jeff Perry, an Anglo from Colorado married to a *mexicana* from Torreón, set himself off socially from the other gringos by deciding to live in Nuevo Laredo rather than across the river with the other Imports. This was a rarity; most often there is an invisible wall that not only keeps the social worlds of the players entirely distinct off the field, but entails having members of the same team live in different countries. By living in Nuevo Laredo, Perry was accepted better than any Import in recent memory. Most Imports do not share Perry's views, however.

The Mexican players seem prepared to admit that Jeff Perrys exist, but experience has taught them that most Imports (gringos in particular) are difficult. While they are required to play alongside them and they try to tolerate both intentional and unintentional slights, they fabricate a range of responses designed to promote their own solidarity and, indirectly, their nationalism, at the expense of the Imports. This borrows a page from James Scott's work on cultural resistance and deserves some elaboration.[10]

Being lower in the social hierarchy, Scott argues, precludes direct confrontations ("public transcript"), calling instead for a disguised confrontation ("hidden transcript"). In this way, some of the Tecos sought various ways to confront the Imports indirectly. After the Imports complained about one of the hotels, a Mexican player took an Import off to the side and cautioned: "Listen, you gotta be careful about these beds. They got lice. And not only lice, but bedbugs too."[11] That was all these gringos had to hear. They ran back to their rooms and rearranged their bedding in the face of this new threat. Beds were off limits. Something new had to be devised, so they arranged their suitcases and duffle bags to serve as beds, throwing sheets and towels over them and tightly cinching the sheet bottoms under their travel bags. No one knows whether or not they took turns on guard that night, but that is the story as it was told to the other players. While the laughs that were shared among the regulars that night were small potatoes by comparison to the abuse most of the Mexican players put up with during the season, they enjoyed getting back at these gringos.

As pointed out earlier, Firova didn't confront the four Imports when they deserted, rather informing them that they were leaving without permission. Later, Firova reflected on this: "I've gone to the wall for these guys. Let's face it, in the Mexican League some hotels are good, some bad. What they did is just not caring for the team. Nobody said nothin' at the game when the Imports were gone, but those guys were abandoning the team, and the players were hurt by that."[12]

Various insiders saw the lopsided loss as a collective and willful sabotage, a surreptitious response by those unable to directly confront.[13] "It's not the first time we've seen this, nor the last time. It's the players' way of saying, 'Fuck you' to somebody they're pissed off at," confided one player.

Even the stigmatized "Mexican only" bus rides can facilitate the building and expression of resistance. By providing a social and psychological place to vent their feelings safe from the eyes and ears of the Imports and management, the bus can offer a setting for the creation of "hidden transcripts." In one instance of this, Barraza was lounging on the bus ride with his feet propped up, looking absently out the window at the desert stealthily passing in the twilight. In his Pink Floyd T-shirt and Anglo looks, Barraza could have passed for any young American man. It was he who had lost the game that was the season's most embarrassing defeat. Foolishly, I tried to apologize for the Imports' abandonment. Barraza, impatient, cut me short. He smiled grimly, speaking facetiously and loud enough for all to hear: "Hey, that's the American way, no? You are taught that you are the best, so when you come down here, you come to be served. You're on vacation and expect others to serve you."

The hidden transcript was being written. Barraza's angry comments quickly brought out pitcher Ricardo Moreno's ire:

> They [the Imports] do whatever they want. We're angry! We're a team. We have to stay together no matter what. When they left us before the game, we wanted to win. Some said, "Hey, we did it before they came, we can do it again." But, we played pretty badly, with no enthusiasm, and made six errors. If this happened

last year, the manager would have suspended them. But not this year, not this manager. Last night Preston Watson [another Import] just left the game with his wife. Just like that! You believe it? He went back to Laredo, I guess, but how can a teammate do this?[14]

Baller later argued that G.M. Samuel Lozano was to blame for poor planning of the travel arrangements. Baller's excuse was that he didn't want to travel on an off day, he had a rest coming, and he found a flight that Lozano couldn't book. The others all found reasons to go as well, although Moore was a position player who had no day off coming. Lozano had a long record of being unable to handle details, certainly with the Imports, so there was something to Baller's claim that Lozano could have handled the travel plans more adroitly.

Men like Jay Baller have tasted life in the major leagues. They are used to teams who see to it that travel arrangements and contractual obligations are efficiently handled. In his defense, he had already spent a summer bickering with the Teco front office about details of his contract that were signed for but not delivered, so his reservoir of good will had run dry. The conditions of his contract included living arrangements and travel (a car) for his family while in Laredo, as well as road arrangements. Chito Rodríguez oversaw these issues, sometimes having to go back and forth with the Atlanta Braves who were paying his salary while with the Tecos. As Teco Vice President and President of Tanjore Corporation in Laredo, he was hardly responsible for personally seeing to it that Baller was taken care of on a daily basis. This was responsibility delegated to Samuel Lozano, and Samuel was often unable to respond to some of these details of life for players in Laredo. It is within this context that Baller had soured over the season, and it is within this context that Jay used his only remaining weapon to get his contract acted upon: withholding his playing. Hence, between Baller, Rodríguez, and Lozano (and at times Laredo's Larry Dovalina) there was a dance going on that involved leaping partners that were often not caught. Baller was demanding, but not unjustly entitled. Everything he wanted had been agreed to by Atlanta and the Tecos. And he was worth it, as far as he was concerned. He had put up some large numbers during his stay.[15] Unfortunately, in making his case, Baller couched things in a most unfortunate way, arguing at one point that he ". . . did the work of any three Mexicans." He may not have meant it to be racist, but that is precisely how it was taken when the regulars on the team heard about it. The Teco players and coaches were rarely privy to broken deals; rather they saw Imports who seemed forever to be demanding something. The Mexican players were also aware of Samuel's lapses, but by comparison to what they saw gringo Imports getting, these *Indios* had little sympathy for their foreign teammates and their issues.

Some of the younger Tecos, like Moreno, were still incredulous that these Imports could have abandoned the team, but old timers like Ortiz had seen this kind of thing before. He spent a good part of the trip back railing against the two-class travel policy. As a starter he had a plane ticket home from Mexico City, but gave it to Pini, the old batting coach employed by the Tecos. The idea of taking that kind of beating on this southern swing was too much. The team had driven for almost 40 hours to get to Mérida and now were winding their way back. The effect of this on a young man's back was clear enough, but for the old guy who never let on that his back was hurting, this was too much for Ortiz, who at one point cursed both the Imports and the Teco front office.

The Mexico City incident of 1993 underscored the strain between nationalisms. On this occasion as on several others I witnessed, Alejandro Ortiz found the Imports to be the most convenient object of anger. When the source of a problem could be interpreted as either management or the foreigners, there was a better than even chance that outrage would be focused on the latter. In short, whether it is legitimate to call the foreigners scapegoats or not is secondary to the preference for singling them out. This kind of autonationalism is used by the front office as well, as it was when Lozano missed a payroll, explaining to the outraged players that it was the rapacious gringos that used up his payroll money—even though it was the Atlanta Braves who pay the salaries of the Imports. The foreigners were always considered safe to blame in such circumstance because they so readily fueled the acrimonious relationship with Mexicans.

In classic autonationalist fashion, the cases of both Waite and Baller had the effect of enhancing Mexican solidarity while fueling anti-American sentiment. In all fairness, Baller initially didn't hold pronounced anti-Mexican views. Later, after developing an adversarial relationship with the front office and growing frustrated with not being called up to the major leagues, Baller began to scapegoat his Mexican experience. When he sensed that others were angry with him, he no longer cared, which made his presence all the more tragic. Nevertheless he was a charitable person, willing to help out some needy person at the ballpark with clothes or money, but these acts of kindness were lost on his teammates, who had already suffered his cutting remarks and attitude.

In the course of making negative comments about Mexico, Baller also made an incisive observation about transnationalism. On one occasion, Baller tried to enter the park from the a side entrance rather than the front gate and was confronted by a burly security guard who refused him admittance. Baller went to complain to Larry Dovalina about "the fat prick out back." Dovalina, who like everyone else had had enough of Baller by this point, motioned for the security guard to come over. The latter looked every bit like someone forged in a prison weight room and moved toward

Dovalina like a tank, while Baller went on a tirade against everyone and everything, including Dovalina and Laredoans. "You know, it's starting to spread from over there," he said, eyeing both Dovalina and the guard. The guard moved closer and in a low, menacing voice growled, "Fuck you!" Baller flinched and backed off, saying, "This fuckin' border should be 100 miles north so you could all be together." Without ever having read a book on Texas-Mexican history or ever having heard of the Republic of the Rio Grande, Baller had unwittingly made an important and accurate observation. He had come to see the border as irrelevant. He understood, on some level, that culturally and psychologically Laredo and south Texas still shared much with Mexico.[16]

While the Imports tended to have the effect of forging stronger bonds among the other Tecos, there were occasions when the gringos undermined Teco solidarity. One example should suffice. At the end of the season, rookie pitcher Obed Vega was taken out by manager Dan Firova after a rough outing. Vega, like most pitchers, was convinced he could still get out of the inning. When Firova insisted he head for the showers, Vega, uncharacteristically, threw the ball on the mound in disgust, which, according to Firova, was "showing me up in front of the fans and players." Firova then decided to bench Vega indefinitely.

As a Mexican American, Firova has had his share of national and cultural problems in Mexico, but he is not one to leap to conclusions about Mexico. He sees things as a function of individuals. I asked him how he would handle issues such as this differently next year:

> I'm not gonna put up with showin' me up, [that's] one thing. Alvarez did it. He threw the ball down when I went to take him out. He apologized a few days later through one of the other guys and it got back to me. Watson [a gringo] did it after he gave up a whole bunch of runs. The last one was a home run. When I went out he walked right off the mound to the bullpen. Two innings later he said, "Hey Dan, I'm sorry about that. I'm not that kind of guy but I got hit hard." The last time Vega did it. He gave up five or six runs and about nine hits. I started walking out to yank him and he throws the ball down and walks off the mound. I stepped back down the dugout steps and motioned for relief. When he walked past me I let him have it. "Who the hell do you think you are? You're a damn rookie and I'm not taking any shit from a rookie. You're not pitchin' on my team again."[17]

Firova tends to speak in English when angry, so most of what he said about not pitching again was lost on Vega. Vega was confused and distraught when he was passed over in the next rotation of starters and sought out a conference with Firova. The pitcher began by formally apologizing: "I'm sorry about what I did. I shouldn't have. I'm a rookie." Firova was satisfied with the apology: "Look, that's all I ask for. It's over, okay?" Vega, however, had not finished his train of thought: "But it's just that the others did it too, Baller, Watson." Firova shrieked, "I don't give a shit what anyone else did! They were wrong, but you were doubly wrong 'cause you're nothin' but a rookie!"[18]

While Firova saw this as individual issue, the Mexican players connected his exchange with Vega with his handling of Imports—in other words, that Firova, a *pocho*, was weak on disciplining Imports and tough on Mexicans. Vega's justification couched his behavior in a nationalist cast. This was echoed by other Mexican players, who faulted Firova for caving in to the gringos during the Mexico City incident as well.

The hiring of Firova as manager itself had autonationalistic implications. In the winter of 1993 Rodríguez announced Firova as his choice for manager. Considering the legendary status of Zacatillo Guerrero, the previous Teco manager, in Nuevo Laredo, Rodríguez's full backing was needed to hire Firova. Principal resistance to Firova came from his being a Mexican from *Mexico de afuera* (Mexico abroad), a colloquial expression for Mexican Americans. The Nuevo Laredo press spearheaded the anti-Firova sentiment. On February 16 an article appeared in *El Mañana* with Dan's passport picture, erroneously claiming that he wouldn't be able to manage the Tecos because he had no work visa. To some degree the disappointment of Nuevo Laredo fans with the successor to Guerrero is understandable. The opening salvo of resentment of a "pretender" taking over the team was clearly cast in autonational terms, however. Firova was a former Teco, a pitching coach, and a life-long border resident who should have garnered some support, but there was nothing but a steady stream of abuse from the Nuevo Laredo side.

Predictions appeared in the press that Firova would not last beyond the first half of the season. During the early part of the season, for instance, the Nuevo Laredo press took a decidedly anti-Firova stance in its reporting. In the ninth inning of a May 6 game against Unión Laguna, with men on second and third, one out, and the Tecos trailing by one, Firova elected to pinch hit for crowd favorite Mora, going strictly with percentages and choosing utility infielder Rúben Estrada, who was batting over .280 while Mora was batting .220. The move failed, and *El Mañana* lambasted the decision, pinning the loss on Firova: *Firova Regala Juego* (Firova's hands over the game), it blared.[19] Two nights later against the same team, Mora hit two home runs and the Tecos won 8–3. *El Diario* opened its story as follows: "Yes, the bat of Andrés Mora that pegged two home runs against rival pitchers and a slap at manager Dan Firova was the difference in the Teco 8–3 win."[20] Photos of Firova were rare but when they occurred they were usually unflattering, such as one that appeared of him dejectedly sitting in the dark concrete corner of the clubhouse with his head in his hands, with the caption, "Goodbye to the title: Dan Firova, manager of the Owls of the Two Laredos, laments the loss." Salo Otero of the *Laredo*

*Morning Times* felt that the treatment Firova received from the Nuevo Laredo press was definitely related to his being a *pocho*: "They feel that Mexican Americans get many more opportunities than do Mexicans. So, they get resentful. Getting Firova was an outgrowth of that kind of feeling."[21] The Teco front office made a concerted effort to get the press to print more flattering articles, with only limited success.

Following the final victory over Guerrero's Sultanes in the playoff series, the Tecos came triumphantly back into the dressing room to a crush of reporters. It was ironic that it was that particular series that led to the demonization of Guerrero and the legitimization of Firova, but for the rookie manager, who had to put up with the press's insults, it was payback time. He stood in front of the reporters and began pointing: "You, you, and you, out! I'm not talkin' with you guys. The rest of you can stay on." Later, when Firova encountered one of the reporters he had earlier dismissed hanging around outside the clubhouse, he called him a "goddamn liar" and menacingly poked his finger into his face; the reporter, bathed in sweat, swore he had not written the things that he in fact had printed. Was this only typical antipathy between press and sports figures? Perhaps, but there was definitely an autonational tone here as well.

The Nuevo Laredo fans also heaped abuse on Firova. No matter what he did, they would blame him for something. Each time he left the dugout they would scream, "Take him out!" or "I could do it better!" Part of the problem was that Firova's managing style was not sufficiently Mexican. Whereas most managers in the league manage from the third base box, Dan does so from the dugout, and this merely serves as a reminder that he is a foreigner doing the job that a Mexican had previously done. As one reporter put it, "Firova gets blamed for a loss, and called lucky if he wins." Firova's relationship with fans and press improved slightly in 1994, but there were still problems. In one incident in Parque La Junta, a fan who had been calling Firova all manner of names finally caused the manager to crack. The taciturn Texan started screaming back at the fan, even giving him the finger. According to Firova's wife, Esther, he continues to be an object of blame there even though he is no longer with the Tecos. She continues to write angry letters in response to attacks on her husband by radio talk-show hosts and callers in Nuevo Laredo. "He was a *pocho*, and that's all they cared about over there," she said recently. "Dan never got a break."

## The Crisis of 1994: Dueling Nationalisms

All three manifestations of nationalism were brought to bear on the 1994 Teco season. Within the short space of nine months, the binational agreement went from being vibrant to almost dead. In all of this, cycles of trust and mistrust, cooperation and antagonism, played their familiar border ballad. It was not the first time nor would it be the last that binational arrangements became frayed and partners grew to distrust one another.


## Opening the Season

Despite—or perhaps because of—the fact that the Tecos were soundly trounced in the championship series for the second straight year, fans in both communities eagerly awaited the start of the 1994 season. Joking analogies between the Tecos and the National Football League's Buffalo Bills were regularly being drawn, urging the Tecos to break the Bills' losing streak. No one seemed to doubt that the Tecos would once again go far in the playoffs. The core of veterans were still young enough to pound and hurl opponents into submission, and the Imports sent down from the Braves were usually of high quality.

Yet on the very eve of the 1994 season Teco owner Víctor Lozano hurriedly called a press conference in Nuevo Laredo to announce that pitcher Ernesto Barraza and third baseman Alejandro Ortiz had been sold to the Mexico City Tigres. Something was vaguely mentioned about players "to be named later" coming to the Tecos in return, but all anyone in the room heard was that two of the finest players ever to don a Teco uniform had been sold like prime cuts of beef. To say that people were shocked is an understatement. After slugger Andrés Mora, Ortiz was the team's most senior player and his 32 home runs and 102 runs batted in from the previous year proved that he was still very much at the top of his game. He was a particular fan favorite not only because of his sense of humor and his leadership, but also because Ortiz had married a woman from Laredo and personified the transnational marriage ties and social bonds that existed between fans and players. Barraza had been with the team for seven years and had become a consistent winner, leading the club in victories (fifteen) the year before. As an intelligent, zany, and good looking pitching hero, he had also become a darling with many of the young women who attended games.

Chito Rodríguez tried hard to justify the sale to the fans and press by arguing that the core had done very well over the years but that there were many qualified rookies who needed a chance to play on a daily basis. He called it a "strategic" move, but none of the baseball-savvy press or fans bought that for a minute. *Laredo Morning Times* sports editor Salo Otero bluntly stated in his editorial that money was at the root of the deal. "Yes, the Tecos are saying they will get three players from the Tigres, but it was money that was the biggest motivating factor. Lozano also put it bluntly, 'We need the money, and there was money involved.'"[22] Indeed, Lozano had been claiming financial losses from the Tecos for several years, and 1993 had been particularly disappointing for him. The front office claimed that it needed 140,000 in paid attendance to break even. The year in question, they claimed, yielded only a combined attendance from the two parks of 120,000.[23] These figures, however, most likely do not take into account the Tecos' three postseason playoff series, which should have lifted them well beyond the break-even point.

Whether or not the Tecos made money in 1993, Lozano was casting about for ways to generate interest. The front office's concern, however, was too little and too late. The relationship with the fans had been souring for some years, but following the bargain sale of Barraza and Ortiz in the first month of the 1994 season, the fans were deserting in record numbers. Responding to a crisis largely of their own making, Lozano began making vague threats to sell the club to ease his fiscal burden. Critics argued that Lozano was preoccupied with his newly constructed bullfight ring, Plaza de Toros, and they speculated that he was probably siphoning money away from the Tecos. However rational such a move might be in any other business, baseball fans saw Lozano as a turncoat.

Thus the sale of two popular players precipitated in part Lozano's eventual sale of the Tecos. The media drilled the move and the fans stayed away in droves. Opening day, typically one of the larger crowds in Nuevo Laredo, ranging from 3,000 to 5,000, saw not many more than 500 in the stands. When I returned a week after opening day, there were no more than 400 fans at Parque La Junta for a game against the Mexico City Tigres. One longtime Teco fan put it simply, "The attendance has been shitty. When 'he' sold Barraza and Ortiz he really upset the community. There's a boycott across the river [in Nuevo Laredo] from what I understand. It's an undercurrent and if you talk to any of the guys in the media who handle the Tecos they'll tell you off the record that everyone they've talked to says that they ain't going back to the park until Víctor and Samuel get out."[24]

The players talked among themselves about it all. The Lozanos had long been viewed by players as adversaries, particularly general manager Samuel Lozano. While some, such as Mora, tried to minimize the loss of Ortiz and Barraza with a "that's baseball" rationale, there was still a palpable sense of loss among the players. One Teco veteran said, "Last year we were a team. This year everyone is thinking only about his job. We have no leaders, no feeling of camaraderie."[25] Another said, "I don't know, it makes me sad. But they've done this two or three times in the past, but we always had a good group of rookies ready to take over. This time I don't know. It's more than just losing good players."[26] A third opined, "Ortiz was a leader here, and now there is no one to take his place. Not Romero, not Meré, no one. Not Mora who is trying just to hold on. Ortiz would hang around with everyone, rookies, veterans, even gringos. I don't know [about the sale]; it's not right."[27]

Morale was slipping, fans were angry and distant, and by June 16 the press was discussing the sale of the team. While local owners was being sought, there was concern that the team might wind up leaving the border as it had in the 1950s. It is difficult to determine how real this threat was since such things are often said to intimidate fans and cities into complying with the desires of owners. Lozano had grown tired of the foot-dragging of Nuevo Laredo's mayor on his promise to build a new stadium, and the threat of selling the team to anyone might have been directed toward opening up this gridlock. Throughout this public posturing the fans continued to boycott, and Lozano's losses—and his need to sell—increased. League Commissioner Pedro Treto Cisneros became increasingly aware of trouble on the border. In an interview with the *Laredo Morning Times*, Cisneros discussed the Tecos' problems with finances and attendance (fewer than a thousand fans a game in Nuevo Laredo): "Víctor has had some heavy losses [but] Laredo should stay in the league. I will do my best to help them stay there."[28]

Why were the fans staying away? According to a survey I conducted in both Laredos at the end of the 1994 season, the sale of Barraza and Ortiz and the failure of owners to manage personnel and/or handle the team in a fiscally responsible fashion were the most frequently mentioned reasons for fan apathy (see Appendix B). In Nuevo Laredo, 88 percent blamed the team's misfortunes on the owners. In Laredo, where attendance had not fallen as much, only 45 percent felt that the owners were responsible for loss of fan interest. A sampling of typical comments:

[Laredo]

Samuel Lozano is too cheap to buy or pay players. He just plain sucks.

Lozano is too much of a money-grubbing scum.

I think that Lozano, by trading away Ortiz and Barraza, showed what an ill-mannered G.M. he is.

[Nuevo Laredo]

That Víctor is an enemy of the team.

Now with the bulls [referring to Lozano's new bull-fighting ring], he does not attend to the team. Be careful, Víctor; it's a good team.

My advice is that they should treat the Tecolotes as they do the bull fighters.

A minority of Nuevo Laredo fans (13 percent) felt that the real problem was that the Tecos played in the decrepit Parque La Junta. More Laredo fans (43 percent) declared lack of facilities and promotions as the reason fans deserted the team. No matter which side you look at, or even if you split the difference between the two figures, the owners were perceived as being out of touch with their constituency.

Of course, having a losing team did little to win back the disillusioned. The loss of Ortiz's thirty home runs was amplified by the withering away of Mora as a power hitter. His twenty home runs of the previous season dwindled to three in 1994. Marco Romero partially offset the power drain with thirty home runs almost doubling his previous year's output, but overall the rest of the lineup could not fully compensate. Puerto Rican Import Boi Rodríguez initially replaced Ortiz at third base, showing some power but proving so horrendous in the field that he was quickly converted into the team's designated hitter. Moreover, he only hit seventeen home runs. The other Import players fared worse. The five Import pitchers who shuffled on and off the Teco staff during the year won only a total of fifteen games and saved only six. By comparison the Imports of 1993 amassed thirty-two wins and thirty saves. To make matters worse, Teco stalwart Juan Jesús Alvarez finally succumbed to his back injuries, having surgery early on and missing most of the season. The loss of the steady Alvarez and the absence of a closer in the bullpen meant that Enrique Couoh shuttled between starting and closing, which wore on him as well. At the end of the first half, the Tecos were solidly buried in seventh place.

### Closing the Season

For the first time in twelve years and only the third time since returning to the border in 1976, the Tecos failed to make the playoffs in 1994. After the heady success of the previous season, the collapse was sobering. It was also perplexing. No one thought that the Tecos could degenerate so quickly. There were periodic efforts by the players to make light of their early exit—"Come on! We got a three-month vacation coming!" shouted one player, comically trying to spur on his teammates in the waning days of the season. But such quips fell flat in 1994.

Coming back at the very end of the season to witness this turn of events I found things more or less the same, at least on the surface. The pranksters were still at work. Díaz was still clowning during the playing of the national anthem, trying to insert whatever odd bits of English he was learning into the singing of the American national anthem ("You must find the time. He found the time"). His English had improved. Pitcher René Rodríguez was also still making grunting noises into the ears of his neighbor, while Ricardo Moreno whacked himself repeatedly on his cup in time with the music. But, beyond these typical routines one discerned changes. Where the uniforms were so white last year and even a few months ago, they now seemed dingy. The stitching on the uniform numbers was beginning to unravel, metaphorically marking the end of a long and bitter retreat. Despite having a career year, Romero was emotionally removed in ways I had never before seen. Pitching coach Mario Valenzuela said he'd been that way more often this year, not joking as much. I surprised myself by wishing for the old, arrogantly infuriating Romero rather than this subdued version.

[Parque La Junta:] The Imports are the only ones happy to see this season end. One comments, "This is the time of year in baseball when you think, 'I can't wait to get home and make my own friends.' Too many bus rides, road games, hanging around hotels." He is obviously not a Teco, just a hired gun. The Tecos know about the hardships of minor league baseball and playing in Mexico, and they endure it stoically. They are the border team and must travel the greatest distances and unfortunately under the worst conditions. The Teco bus is their jet. This trusty but antiquated bus looks like the survivor of another era when compared with the beautifully appointed bus of the Industriales or Sultanes. The owner's cry of poverty has resulted in travel costs being cut to a minimum, so the Teco beast must travel ungodly hours to get to games.

One recent southern swing began with a fifteen-hour drive to Mexico City for a three-game set, followed by a three-hour drive to Puebla for a two-game series. An eighteen-hour ride to Campeche came early the morning after, and instead of freshening up at their hotels, the Tecos were trucked right to the ballpark. They played three more games before taking the relatively light ride (three more hours) to Mérida. Finally these *maratonistas* endured a forty-hour bus ride back to Nuevo Laredo, arriving a mere four hours before a big series against Laguna. Disheartened? Resentful? Perhaps, but they came out to play. The gringos? They all flew back. These bus rides, where they might stop only twice to eat, only make them more aware of being Tecos. They know who is and who isn't "on the bus" (gringos and owners), to borrow the phrase from Ken Kesey. Winning teams can make even such trials worthwhile, but a losing season tests them all, and the 1994 Tecos more closely resembled Napoleon's legions retreating from a Russian winter than a sports team. Resentment abounded, but not, as in the past, primarily directed at the gringo, who faded into the background. Rather, 1994 was a season scarred by an accumulated disgust with the front office to the point where it could no longer be ignored. "The [front] office fucked up the '94 season for the Tecos," said one of the survivors of the long march.[29]

While leaving the park after the last day of the season, Chito Rodríguez and I spoke briefly and he dropped a twin bombshell. "Alan, this is off the record, but Mr. Peralta wants me to work for the Tigres in Mexico City. I'll stay here until Víctor [Lozano] can sell the team."[30] Now it was definite: the Tecos were definitely going to be sold and Chito would be leaving. The latter seemed more inconceivable than the former. The only man left from when the Tecos returned to the border, Chito was the heart and soul of the team.

*An Act of Cannibalization*

Rodríguez waited, as he said he would, until the team's sale was imminent before announcing his departure. On September 3 the *Laredo Morning Times* carried the story. Seeking to mute any adverse reaction fans might have, the paper trumpeted the fact that the border would continue to have a franchise. If the fans thought they could now rest easy, they were soon jolted by yet another news story. It was reported that Rodríguez would not be leaving for the Mexico City Tigres alone. Rather, he intended to take just about everybody with him. Virtually every worthwhile starter was going along with him. Veterans Romero, Meré, and Díaz, and pitchers Couoh and Alvarez were going, as were newer players: the Vega brothers, pitcher Ricardo Moreno. Rodríguez was also taking super-scout Jorge Calvo, the man responsible for signing most of the Teco talent for the past decade, and pitching coach Mario Valenzuela. Even the working agreement with Atlanta was being relocated. Finally, late in January 1995, it was formally announced that Teco manager Firova was also moving over to Mexico City in that capacity. Together with Barraza and Ortiz, virtually the entire franchise had been relocated, prompting sports editor Salo Otero to refer to the former Tecos now signed to play in Mexico City as *Tigres del norte* (a humorous reference to a popular northern Mexican musical group). Rodríguez's reaction to the predictable outpouring of rage was also predictably defensive: "Why are they angry? The most important thing was to make sure that there was a team in the Laredos." But, no matter how he sought to rationalize it, his moves had eviscerated the team. Some discussion of players in exchange for those leaving was being tossed about to make it look as if this were a large-scale trade, but the wholesale liquidation of a franchise that had become legendary, partly for its stability, swamped the sense that a trade was taking place.

Rodríguez depicted himself as a defenseless pawn in the game, which, structurally speaking, was true. Nevertheless, his rationalization (that all they needed to do was give the fans a reason to go to the ballpark) is more culturally revealing than a personal justification. There is, among Mexican men of power, an element of disregard—at times arrogant—for the needs of subordinates (fans) that reflects a social relationship between owners as men of power and the vast majority of those without. This arrogance is also characteristic of Mexican male power relations, and is more revealing when we compare attitudes between those in charge of the Tecos on the Laredo side with Samuel Lozano.[31] Larry Dovalina and Carlos Villarreal viewed the relationship of the Tecos to the people of Laredo as more egalitarian, both a contract and relationship of sorts to be developed between these men who feel as if they have a worthwhile product and consumers who can find other ways of spending their discretionary dollars. By contrast, those running the show in Mexico by and large tended to be haughty, caring less for their fans and seeing them as ingrates when they either complain or don't attend. Where Dovalina was forever looking for promotions to boost attendance at West Martin Field, Samuel Lozano couldn't be bothered until attendance had dropped precipitously, and by then it was too late.[32] Where Dovalina got the city to install new lights in the park, Lozano was ineffective in pressuring the government of Tamaulipas to improve or replace the facilities in Nuevo Laredo. Whereas other owners would try to make up for poor facilities with promotions, Lozano was mute, actually laying off his director of promotions for a time. Dovalina's efforts paid off and attendance in West Martin was almost twice that in Parque La Junta during the hapless 1994 season. In true binational fashion, Rodríguez was instrumental in linking the two sides on several issues, such as handling his players in a sensitive fashion; but he likewise found it expedient to stay clear of issues that threatened to expose the vast differences that also characterize this relationship.

The Mexican management model, which mirrors social hierarchy and distance in the society at large, also includes a relationship with the press that borders on disdain. Mexican owners feel little need to explain their actions to the media. They, more than their gringo counterparts, see the media's role in sports as little more than cheerleaders, and think that sport journalists are often paid to be promotional copywriters for their local teams. It is not surprising that one rarely finds sports journalists involved with serious exposés or critical examinations of institutions, although this does not mean that these journalists are content with their relationship. The fans of Nuevo Laredo were also taken for granted.

In the Tecos' case, front office insensitivity is best illustrated by the sale of Ortiz and Barraza. For all his sensitivity and knowledge of the game, Rodríguez not only failed to take into consideration the fans; he failed to consider the chemistry of the team. His formal rationalization—giving "opportunities" to rookies—may have historical precedence, but if the need to recoup losses prompted the sale, there remains a lucrative postseason that would guarantee enough revenue to break even, and the Tecos had been playoff regulars for a decade. If this is even close to the truth, than the desire to sell all or part of the Tecos was even more clearly expedited without regard for the community. Tampering with the highly successful chemistry of the team shows a lack of concern for team and community. Admittedly, team chemistry is not quantifiable, and most team officials would not place too much weight on it, but in the case of the Tecos there was such a large nucleus that had been together for so long that chemistry should have been taken into account. These players had deep roots in the communities, often—as in the case of Ortiz or Díaz—marrying local women and setting up permanent homes there. Larry Dovalina contends that such marriages have the effect of generating substantial fan loyalty to the team, a point well worth any cultural anthropological consideration. Carrying this one step further, the fan's "relationship" to the Tecos had become part of the team's structure. It was the fans who legitimated the "invented tradition" of the Tecos, and in the relationship between players, fans, and the media, one can find an outstanding example of binational institution concocted in the modern era but legitimated through the past. For the front office to have diminished this is less oversight than callous disregard by those in power toward others. In bitter irony, the case could be made that, in carving out such a large chunk of the organization to take with him to Mexico City, Chito Rodríguez understood the notion of Teco chemistry better than anyone.

## The Death of the Owls of the Two Laredos

Finally, after months of speculation, a new ownership was emerging. In Campeche, at a Mexican League meeting in late September 1995, Manuel Canales of Nuevo Laredo was introduced as the new president and majority owner of the Tecos. Along with sixty-three others, Canales bought out most of Víctor Lozano's interest in the team; Lozano still remained as a minority owner. The new list of owners included representatives of most of Nuevo Laredo's business and political community, including the mayor, Horacio Garza, and a former mayor, Manuel Canales. Tellingly, no Americans, even from Laredo, were to be found among the investors. There is no Mexican League regulation that prohibits American investment in the franchises, but as trendy as it is to own minor league franchises in the United States, it is curious that Lozano could not seem to find an interested party north of the border. A year before, however, in one of his periodic efforts to find a partner, Lozano rejected at least one American who was interested in majority ownership.[33]

While such a thorough change in leadership to completely wash away the old with the new, the good with the not-so-good, ironically one person remained in place. Samuel Lozano, general manager of the team in the old regime, was actually elevated to vice president in place of Rodríguez. With that promotion, the baseball relations between the two cities were sent into a free fall. It seemed to some that everything that was good about the Tecos had been stripped away, while the key problem remained. On the Laredo side, the key backers, Villarreal and Dovalina, were visibly disturbed at the prospect of wholesale trades or sales of players and the new/old Teco management. They began asserting to the press that Laredo would have to "reexamine" its relationship with the Tecos.

By October and November, baseball is replaced in people's minds by the Texas football frenzy, but in 1994, the border baseball drama continued to claim its share of media attention. Entering the uneasy situation was the Texas-Louisiana Baseball League, formed by Dallas businessman Byron Pierce in 1994. In its initial efforts, this successful league had failed to land a Laredo franchise. Now the ground seemed fertile and Pierce's group was met with interest by city officials. Within a month a formal proposal was drawn up by the Texas-Louisiana League, which would pay the city of Laredo a set amount of money and move a franchise into the city. Rather than pay the Tecos in Nuevo Laredo ($160,000) for having the team play in Laredo, the city would be in a position to receive money and jobs would be generated. The message was well received, and pressure to leave the binational agreement mounted. When an editorial appeared in the *Laredo Morning Times* advising local citizens to take on the new league's offer, Dovalina urged caution, citing the binationalism at stake: "This is about the relationship, dynamics and cohesiveness of two cities. It's probably the only place where this could work."[34] For a city as financially strapped as Laredo, guaranteed revenues rather than payouts carry weight. The kicker, of course, was the demise of *Los Tecolotes de los dos Laredos*, but within days Villarreal and Dovalina shifted their allegiance away from binationalism and toward their own city. On November 19, the city council met and agreed to sever its contract with the Tecos and establish one instead with the Texas-Louisiana League.

Suddenly, the "invented tradition" forged between the cities that had been broadcast throughout the baseball world lay shredded on the ground, and representatives of each city and country stood eyeing each other angrily. The "river" had, indeed, come to divide these people. The 1995 season would feature the Nuevo Laredo Tecolotes and the Laredo Apaches: two franchises, two leagues, two cities, two countries.

### Conclusion of Crisis

The reality was that the binational agreement was structurally flawed. The Tecos are a Mexican team first and foremost. They are owned and primarily run by Mexicans and play in the Mexican League. Laredoans have virtually no say in team policy. Considering that Laredo's contribution over the past several years has meant the difference between profit and loss, the inability of the Laredo contingent to have any real input into team policy proved vexing to Dovalina and Villarreal, who had been responsible for maintaining the binational agreement in an often hostile Laredo city governmental environment.

Binationalism shows itself to be particularly vulnerable. When ruptured, it is startling to see how quickly autonationalism rebounds. We saw this in the ways that Rodríguez and Dovalina shifted their identities between the two nationalisms within a single conversation. Even in the wake of this serious baseball rupture, the binational identity is not easily shrugged off. Commenting on a position that the Tecos would consider taking in the upcoming 1995 year, Rodríguez said: "When we went to Victoria, Samuel, Suárez, and I were talking about it [the relations between cities], and the way *we're* going to approach it. *We* want to continue being the team of the two Laredos including keeping the name. We know that the fans had nothing to do with it, that it was a city decision [to separate]. We thought that ten years of a relationship is hard to let go."[35]

The fluctuation between various forms of nationalism is also noted in the following story of the reaction of the Mexican League's commissioner, Pedro Treito Cisneros, to the news that Laredo was severing its tie. "The league president was against it," said Rodríguez. "When it was mentioned to him that the Laredo side was not signing a new contract he was very mad. He said, 'We're gonna inform the press that we took the team out of Laredo because of Proposition 187.'[36] He was mad at the time, but we argued that the best approach was to let the fans know that we are still the team of both Laredos."[37] Here the shift in a single conversation moves from binational (Cisneros wanting the relation to continue) to autonational (his threat) to binational (subsequent advice received).

## Dovalina's Binational Response to the Crisis of 1994

Few were as committed to baseball binationalism as Larry Dovalina, but there were moments triggered by the crisis of 1994 that pushed him toward an autonationalist position. In responding to the *Laredo Morning Times* editorial calling for the city to drop its binational tie with the Tecos, Dovalina responded binationally: "This is about the relationship, dynamics, and cohesiveness of two cities." Yet in finally agreeing to sever that tie, Dovalina also played on his identity as a Laredoan, and by extension, a nationalist. In speaking for the community of Teco fans in Laredo, Dovalina plays off of a we–they dichotomy that always threatens to separate these border dwellers [italics mine]:

"*We're* going [to the Texas-Louisiana League] based on the fact that *they* [Teco owners] are going to make a wholesale trade of about nine players. *They're* gonna decimate the team. *They* haven't said anything officially, but *we're* privy to information, so *we* feel it would be next to impossible to get anyone to attend. . . . The Laredo community [*we*] wants the Texas-Louisiana League. People in the community feel that Samuel and Víctor have screwed us over the ten years. They feel that they [Laredo fans] have never counted for anything as far as the other side is concerned, and that they [Nuevo Laredo] do basically whatever they want. *We* have no say so or control. For some people it would be easier to identify more closely with a Laredo team because they felt that the Tecos were from Nuevo Laredo all along.[38]

Here we see the events of 1994 discussed, not in the spirit of binational cooperation, but antagonistically. For their part, the Mexican ownership did little to reduce the isolation and alienation that the Laredo side felt. When a press conference was suddenly called in Laredo on November 10 to announce ex-Teco Andrés Mora as the manager for 1995, Laredoans were snubbed: "We weren't told about it," said a glum Dovalina. There was precedence for this insult as well. Throughout 1994 Dovalina located American investors for the increasingly desperate Lozano, but none were ever brought on board. When the dust settled the Tecolotes remained a wholly Mexican-owned club even though Laredo contributed about half of the team's operating budget. The inequity of the relationship and the Laredo-perceived incompetence of those across the river was, in the wake of the events of 1994, too much to bear. Always, however, the binational relationship tended to mute the anger and outrage felt, so that even as each side was talking about separating, one would hear about "well wishing" in the new endeavors.

## Continually Invented Tradition

The rock-solid binationalist spirit of the 1993 Tecos was in the following year rent asunder. The tradition was shown to be easily undone and actually imagined. Anderson's "imagined community" lends a cultural layer to the discussion of nationalism as culturally fashioned: "In an anthropological spirit, then, I propose the following definition of the nation: it is an imagined political community—and imagined as both inherently limited and sovereign."[39] The nation perceives of itself as *limited*, that is, having boundaries which set it off from other nations. Likewise, the nation imagines itself as *sovereign*, which is "the gauge and emblem of freedom."[40] And finally, the nation perceives of itself as a *community*. The first two features promote a sense of boundedness and boundaries, potentially or actually set against other nations. The third operates within the realm of culture enabling the nation to design and use ideas and practices that reconstitute the sense of community which is not, in fact, operative. The Texas-Tamaulipas border lends itself nicely to this fusion of geopolitics and culture.

Invented traditions open the possibility of linking the discussion of nationalism to a temporal dimension that shuffles easily between past and present. As mentioned in the introduction, actual studies of sport as invented tradition are hard to find, and the cultural creativity involved in this process has never been adequately studied. Built upon Benedict's sense of imagined community, the invented tradition can provide us an opportunity to look at the actual building of cultural formations, in this instance through sport. Both through its sense of structure and through its ability to invoke a sense of being connected to the past, sport is reminiscent of what anthropologist Robert Redfield called "the greater and little traditions";[41] that is, sport is distinguished locally from the way it operates at national and international levels.

By positing the idea of a nation imagining their communities, identity can be furthered beyond actually having to share such things as religion or community, both of which refer to demonstrated collective past. Rather, one can invent traditions, hence direct identity formation to the present and future: "The term 'invented tradition' is used in a broad, but not imprecise sense. It includes both 'traditions' actually invented, constructed and formally instituted and those emerging in a less easily traceable manner within a brief and dateable period . . . and establishing themselves with great rapidity. The royal Christmas broadcast in Britain (instituted in 1932) is an example of the first; the appearance and development of the practices associated with the Cup Final in British Association Football, of the second."[42]

Sport, like other forms of popular culture, may reflect society, but always from a particular socially configured position (e.g., different, even competing, groups, classes, or regions) Hence, while baseball may reflect classic autonationalist distinctions, we must determine what other social relationships one can see in the way the game is handled. Hobsbawm's sense of invented tradition serves us nicely by fusing newly minted cultural practices with traditional ones giving, us a way of linking past, present, and future in observable social behavior. In this regard a sport may not simply reflect society as already established, but serve as a blueprint for social experiments that are also underway.

Baseball, an example of invented tradition in the first sense, provides a stable structure through its codified rules, rituals, regalia, measures of excellence, and repetitive behaviors, all of which fosters a view of the sport as "timeless." This is best demonstrated in the playing of the game itself, with its rejection of time keeping and its atavistic uniforms (relative to other sports), as well as the mythology of the game originating in a nineteenth-century rural setting (when it was actually an urban phenomenon). Even the length of the baseball calender year (eight and a half months) reinforces the sense of timelessness in that it lasts longer than almost any other team sport. The most spectacular international sports events, the Olympics and the World Cup, by comparison occupy little time.

Baseball, as well as other sport competitions, also fosters links with nationalism through its naturally dramatic structure. As in most sports, there are historic links between combat and political maneuvering between rival entities, be they classes, ethnic groups, or nations. Here sport works to foster both internal cohesion and hatred of others much more immediately and readily than other noncompetitive forms of mass culture (e.g., music or art). Hence, winning and losing contests both result from commonly understood and appreciated prowess, strategy, and error, in combination with the socially constructed attributes of heroism and vilification: good and evil, risk and struggle, and morality all work to lend meaning to sport. These moral imperatives are linked to local and regional identities through sports teams. The Boston Red Sox–New York Yankee rivalry, for instance, most certainly incorporates these elements. Going back to the second decade of the twentieth century, the rivalry contains—in a baseball timeline—a very respectable depth, but relative to the cities themselves, that rivalry is a product of the modern era. A sense of age-old rivalry permeates anticipated contests, often treated as morality plays in which each opponent serves as the embodiment of everything vile. In the Boston area, this "invented tradition" even spawned its own bumper sticker: "I love New York, It's the Yankees I Hate." Routine fisticuffs between rival fans at the ballpark also attests to the attribution of hateful characteristics to the opposition. Such intense emotion over a sporting event is nothing new. I only wish to draw attention to the way it manifests itself, and to the fact that in many cases such rivalry may overlay older forms of competition. New York and Boston baseball rivalry is an outgrowth of an older rivalry for the preeminence on the north Atlantic seaboard. In this instance baseball actually intensifies or "reinvents" tradition.

Sport at more local, metropolitan, and even regional levels actually comes closer to constituting the kind of identity that the nation-state envisions for itself. When *Boston Globe* sports columnist Dan Shaughnessy writes of the "Red Sox Nation," he is describing both a sports link, and an existent, though weaker, regional identity held by many New Englanders. It is not an actual face-to-face community that forms the Red Sox Nation. Red Sox Nationalists do not know each other and do not share any trait across their wide-ranging world other than their slavish following of the team. Rather, the Red Sox Nation is an invented tradition cast in sport and drama (e.g., the trade of Babe Ruth to the Yankees, the rivalry between the two cities, the repeated failure to win a World Series since 1918, as well as the fans' eternal hope each spring) that furthers this sense of imagined community. The task for nationalists, sport impresarios, and visionaries is the same, namely to enlarge the sense of community as effectively as these local sport traditions have.

These cultural inventions are, in Hobsbawm's words, "responses to novel situations which take the form of reference to old situations, or establish their own past by quasi-obligatory repetition."[43] Invented traditions are, in short, "facetious." Their interest to social scientists lie in at least three areas: (1) attempts to slow the fast-paced contemporary world by appealing to a sense of an immutable past; (2) to further establish a cultural domination of one group over another, and (3) to establish, through the use of invented traditions, the presence of historically disempowered peoples. All three impact on nationalism.

Locally, the most thoroughgoing example of Laredo baseball as invented tradition was the annual July 4 contest between Laredo and Corpus Christi that took place through the latter part of the nineteenth and early twentieth centuries (see Chapter 2). The importation of the holiday to the border was, in itself, an invented tradition, and the playing of the baseball contest was an *intensification of that tradition*, as well as a further layer of "Americanization" to border culture. There could be no better occasion than the birthday of the nation for inventing tradition because all of the spectacle is directly filtered through the lens of autonational identity. The emergence of an annual contest between two south Texas cities was, by the turn of the century, considered an institution, a tradition. The charter trains leaving Laredo in 1912 were expected to carry at least 800 local backers of the team for the July 4 tournament in Corpus Christi.[44] The descriptions of these events depict the institutional nature of the celebration, which is part of a larger cultural-metropolitan exchange involving Laredo's Washington's Birthday celebration: "Corpus Christi people always come here in force for the annual celebration of Washington's birthday anniversary, and Laredo reciprocates by sending a large crowd down there for the annual Fourth of July celebration," wrote the *Laredo Times* in 1924.[45] Hence, this spectacle-laden invention of tradition encompassed Washington's Birthday, the Fourth of July, and baseball as a local form of autonationalism.

Mexican versions of this were not as far-flung. While Mexican League baseball most definitely contains predictable elements of invented tradition, such as flags, one is hard-pressed to match the complex described above. As a postscript, however, Fiacro Díaz Corpuz's altering of dates to "prove" that baseball entered Mexico via the Nuevo Laredo area (Chapter 2) might constitute an unusual instance of invented tradition. This might be interpreted as an instance of mutant local pride getting the better of a professional journalist. What is intriguing is the willingness to consciously alter information in order to create a tradition of baseball for the local area. We must also remember that this invented (read: partially fabricated) tradition actually necessitated the use of baseball players from both sides of the river; thus Díaz was actually describing a kind of transnational invented tradition.

In 1995, the case of the Texas-Louisiana expansion franchise in Laredo offered another interesting possibility for looking at invented tradition. In place of a home-grown institution carrying forward a local tradition, we have an outside corporate effort (expansion of the league) attempting to enter a local area. From the perspective of invented traditions, the Laredo Apaches are somewhat intriguing in that everything that they were attempting to do to assure their success is couched in business, rather than baseball, terms. As expressed by the team's general manager, Derek Leistra, the Laredo franchise is "service oriented" (something that Nuevo Laredo ignored in its dealings with fans): "I want us to be the thing to do in Laredo this summer. Because of that, we owe it to our fans to give them the best service we can."[46] Points of articulation between corporate interests and local cultural interests center on the very feudal concept of service. To serve the community, even if for profit can, in this instance, aid the establishment of tradition where one no longer exists.

The taking of the name "Apaches" worked to foster a sense of the past in two ways. The actual Lipan Apache were a formidable and feared presence in eighteenth-century Laredo, just as the Laredo Apaches were the last professional team to play in the city. In one move the new Apaches linked themselves to a baseball and a historic past. In the opening day celebration, ten surviving members of the original Laredo Apaches baseball team were introduced, creating a further link between the community and the latter-day Apaches. There was an unsuccessful attempt on the part of the new team to find local talent worthy of playing, but they did go out and hire ex-Teco coach Ricardo Cuevas, and the team itself had a heavy Latino presence, all of which was an attempt to rapidly develop a fan base and a local presence on the team.

Adding to the hoped-for welcome on the part of the city was the very real lack of alternatives for sports-minded public in Laredo. This is less a comment on the city than it is a statement of the possibility, if carried out well, of replicating the atmosphere of a local fair. Invented traditions can have nationalist motives, to be sure, but as in this instance, they may be purely local in origin, with indirect larger social implications.

Alas, all the promotions and careful market studies as well as the tipping of their hats to the local history of border baseball could not get the Apaches through a complete season. Citing losses in excess of $200,000 for the first half of the season, the Laredo Apaches ceased their operations at the half-way mark of their inaugural year. At the time they were drawing fewer than 700 fans per game, needing 1,700 to break even.[47] At least some of those fans felt that the team had not given the town sufficient time to warm up to the club. One editorial in the *Laredo Morning Times* accused the Texas-Louisiana League of not having sufficiently grasped the entrenched Mexican cultural orientation of the city.[48] Combined, these two explanations for why the Apaches failed point to the insularity of the border city and also to a holdover of the suspicion with which outsiders are viewed.

Bereft of a baseball team, Laredoans will have to shift attention elsewhere, prompting some to already wonder whether the rapid failure of the
Apaches will reignite interest in the Tecolotes de los dos Laredos.[49] The
fluid nature of these arrangements, at times antagonistic, while at other
times cooperative, reflect the social and historic ways in which border
identity shifts. The forms of identity discussed here reflect actual structural
and historical arrangements. Baseball as one cultural product shared between the two cities reflects the fluctuating arrangements, which at times
are things each side claims for itself and at other times is mediated by the
presence of the other; these are forms of identity that Chapman, Mc-
Donald, and Tonkin refer to as essentialist-versus-relativist identities.[50]
Whatever it is called, a study of baseball, ballroom dancing, or bridge
building will reveal that the "river joins and the river divides."

## Conclusion

A major problem with using most definitions of nationalism is that they
take little if any account of internal sociopolitical differences: the nation-
state is assumed to be monolithic and homogeneous. One reason for the
weakly developed nationalism in Mexico has precisely to do with the state's
inability to fuse its regions and populations. Indigenous people in Chiapas,
for instance, are barely integrated and functioning members of the nation,
a fact made poignant by their recent uprising against the government. The
alienation of people in the south is mirrored to a lesser degree by norteños,
but with similar results. The northern Mexican states have always been
considered inferior and marginal, and even in their recent economic boom
the central Mexican elite still think of them in those terms. The internal
sociopolitical weaknesses of developing nations must be always be accounted for in defining and empirically demonstrating nationalist success.
While less of a problem for industrial nations, internal differentiation nevertheless still poses an issue. The United States is really no different in this
regard. Granted, there is no underdevelopment for the population as a
whole, nor any lack of industrial infrastructure to tie the country together,
but there are underdeveloped pockets in which people feel disenfranchised
and in which parallels to developing nations can be found.

The two Laredos reflect these conditions and more. Each side of the
Laredo border represents a region that is somewhat at odds with surrounding areas. Webb County, Texas, is an underdeveloped pocket by comparison with nonborder counties, while the Nuevo Laredo region is more economically developed than the more southerly reaches of the state of Tamaulipas. Yet when compared against each other the two cities do an
abrupt about face. Laredo seems more prosperous and more developed

than its counterpart. Economic differences between the two are apparent to anyone casually walking the streets of either city. The tendency for one side or the other to feel vastly superior or inferior to the other is then somewhat muted by their reversal of fortunes when compared with the regions adjacent to each.

The relations between the two Laredos is as much defined by external interactions as internal ones, and each city brings their history of relations with either Mexico or Texas to their daily interactions with each other. Hence, the river is more than a metaphor for relations between two border cities; it is in some sense a microcosm of international relations. The tale of the Tecos incorporates a range of these issues. So, for instance, the autonational antagonisms within the ranks of the players, part of each and every Mexican League team, are exaggerated by the binational character of the Tecos. That the Teco gringos live in the United States while the others all live in Nuevo Laredo serves to further separate and intensify structural differences between Imports and Mexican players. The same was evident in the events and interactions that took place between Teco administrators in Laredo and Nuevo Laredo in the crisis of 1994. In both cases the Tecos represented an excellent way of viewing tensions between nations and the cultural and ideological means used to overcome the potential for divisions.

## Tecos as Imagined Community

Considering the employment instability and frequent movement among baseball players both in the United States and Mexico, the Tecos were a remarkably stable community. In addition to living in clusters (e.g., adjacent apartments), the Tecos were often seen waiting for each other just to go to the supermarkets, or assisting each other's families. Group longevity may foster the establishment of mutual assistance and dependence, but for many their relative gratitude for good fortune is also at play, as one player summed it up: "Nine years ago I was in the fields sweating and walking behind an ox and plow. Now I'm playing well. I have an apartment and a car. We all came here together, and even though I come from Veracruz and the others come from other parts [of the country] we all take care of each other. We all had to work hard, and now we are fortunate.[51]

Benedict Anderson was careful to point out that while nations sought to artificially extend the sense of identification of people with the nation-state, it was not a fabrication, but rested upon concrete cultural elements common to a historical period. In the case of the Tecos we are not looking at the grand plays of an age, but at one small cultural form shared only by two cities. Yet the concept of imagined community applies as tellingly.

We have seen how the historic roots of the two Laredos presaged the tension of joining and dividing residents on either side of the river. The Laredo of the eighteenth and early nineteenth centuries was a genuine community, organically joined yet fractious. With the advent of the international border in 1846, Laredo suddenly had two identities, two political nationalisms foisted upon it. These competing autonational personae were also in contest with the traditional organic community now seen as transnationalism. Intermarriage between the two Laredos and the creation of festivals unique to them (such as the Washington's Birthday celebration) continue as modern-day survivals of this past. This continued sense of real community functions in direct contrast to the promotion of outside influences, most notably the attempts at national integration working on both sides of the new border.

The establishment of baseball in the area followed the same trajectory. Questions of origin aside, once rooted in the area, the sport was transnational. Players from one side played on the other, as did teams with no limitations. When, in the early twentieth century, national pride or bragging rights were at stake as they occasionally were, the players might momentarily realign to reflect citizenship, but the flow back and forth would quickly reestablish itself as the norm (see Chapter 2). This was particularly marked when outsiders came through to play in the greater Laredo area.

It was with the introduction of outsiders (first Cubans and Mexicans, then, during the 1940s, Anglos) that the transnational or local quality of baseball began to erode. The powerful La Junta teams of the mid-to-late 1930s first brought them in. Even then, the structure of the sport remained local, but the outsiders were a harbinger of the increasingly professional level of play along the border and elsewhere in Mexico. La Junta became a charter member of the Mexican League in 1939, eventually changing its name to Tecolotes, after which the numbers of locals rapidly diminished.

While continuing to draw interest from the Laredo side, the *Tecolotes* became the cultural property of Nuevo Laredo in the post-war period. After a sixteen-year diaspora, the Tecos returned to the border in 1976 and picked up where they had left off. By this time the only facsimile of transnational baseball to be found was in the amateur ranks, primarily in the Laredo Community College team.

### *Transnationalism in Laredo Community College Baseball*

The close proximity of Monterrey with its large baseball playing population ties in very nicely with Laredo Community College's interests. As the southern pole of Laredo's borderland sphere of influence, Monterrey was a logical place for LCC assistant coach Ricardo Cuevas to scout.

Troy Van Brent, the head coach of the LCC Palominos, has built this junior college team into an internationally recognized contender. During his eight-year tenure at the school, Van Brent has managed to get the Palominos ranked as high as first in the national junior college polls (in 1992). Without question, much of the success of the program lies in LCC's ability to draw talent from Mexico—on average three players a year—and for this blessing Van Brent is indebted to Cuevas. This is the same Cuevas who coached the Tecos. "The way it all first started was, we went down to Monterrey and we had a little tryout back in 1987," said Van Brent. "I took my gun down there and my stopwatch and everything, and we saw about fifteen to twenty kids first time we went down there. And then after that it started to be that a few kids came up here 'cause it was in their paper. And before long we started gettin' other kids callin' us from Monterrey and comin' up."[52]

What prompted Van Brent to look to Monterrey in the first place was his desperation for pitching. Cuevas took off to Monterrey, coming back with two players in what would in short order become a regular flow of talent from Mexico. As the Laredo program became better known in Mexico, players from all over the country would seek out Van Brent or Cuevas. One such recruit, Hector Castañeda (drafted and later playing in the Baltimore Orioles' organization), was from Mexico City. "Actually, his father brought him to the college when he saw it in the paper and paid his tuition for the year. He was from the Mexico National Team, and those players would hear about this or that kid playing in Laredo and after that it really picked up."[53]

The rest of the team also reflects Laredo's borderland, with the majority of players coming from San Antonio and Corpus Christi. Van Brent estimated that he has had fifteen players drafted during his tenure at Laredo. While many do not manage long stays in American pro baseball, they often parlay the skills learned with the Palominos into careers in the Mexican League.

The movement of Mexican ballplayers to *el norte* is not only characteristic of the Laredo area. The same has been reported in San Diego and Tucson. Major leaguers such as Texas Ranger infielder Benji Gil are products of the transnational baseball phenomenon.[54] Born in Tijuana, Gil moved to a San Diego suburb with his family for the educational opportunities. Gil's father, a landlord in Tijuana, stayed behind to tend the family's business. This transformed the Gils into binational commuters, and Benji Gil would often crisscross the border to play three games a day.[55] The opportunity for career advancement in American baseball may have lured the Gil family, but Mexico's greater commitment to the game exerted its own pull: "In America, the kids don't seem to want to play as much, like they're forced. . . . In Mexico most kids want to play baseball."[56] This popularity is apparent in the stands as well: crowds of 5,000 are not unusual in semi-pro games in Tijuana.

It is within this relatively greater devotion to the playing of baseball on the Mexican side that a related transnational baseball development has taken place. The 1991 discovery of forty pounds of marijuana in the duffel bags of two LCC players driving north of Laredo for a game in San Antonio prompted an investigation that revealed the entanglements of the Mexican drug traffickers with borderland baseball. The proliferation of semipro leagues in cities such as Nuevo Laredo has been used by drug lords to find recruits for their trafficking. "Some of the sponsors throw post-game *pachangas* [parties] near the fields complete with live music and tasty barbecue," wrote the *Laredo Morning Times* in a series documenting the connection between drugs and baseball. "This, and other fraternization, leaves time for people to get to know each other and for the monied to get to know the needy and unscrupulous. There are many poor neighborhoods, or *colonias*, situated just north of the border."[57]

Transnationalism by definition has no boundaries: not between countries, nor between institutions within a country. The way of life in the borderlands has fostered a range of institutions (baseball being one) that come under local control. Part of the inability of federal attempts to eradicate smuggling and trafficking stems from the fact that these are local institutions that automatically resist attempts by outsiders to alter them. Transnational baseball has continued to exist, albeit in truncated fashion.

## *Closing the Book on the Tecos*

Professional baseball in Nuevo Laredo had taken an autonational turn from the days of Jorge Pasquel. Having only had a professional team for two years, 1949–50, Laredo was merely an adjunct until the Lozanos acted on the idea of making the team binational.

The main criteria for binational status—sovereignty and roughly equal partnership—was more apparent than real in the Teco case. The team was wholly owned by the Mexican side, with Laredo simply paying for a string of appearances in their park. The Laredo office had no input on policy. This is important, because were the Tecos truly a joint property with decisions hammered out in cooperative fashion, it is likely the team would have looked very different. Structurally speaking, then, the binational label was one of appearance only. It is in this sense that the Tecos become a facetious imagined community, and the binational performance on the field becomes just that: performance.

The Tecos were a binational phenomenon more as ideology than as fact, and it was in the distinction between the two that the relationship failed. Here we encounter another Goffmanesque use of "front-stage vs. back-stage" event, in which the front-stage performance is one of binational cooperation in fielding a team and playing contests on both sides of the border, while the behind-the-curtain control remains on the Mexican side.[58] Binational arrangements cannot long function in this vein.

It was the frustration and resentment associated with this structural imbalance that allowed the autonational hostility to resurface so quickly. One could look at the relations between the principles in this mini-drama and conclude that the breakup of the binational agreement was the result of incompatible personalities or irreconcilable differences over team policy and, to some extent, be right. But that would miss a key ingredient. The national identity of either party is very much a conscious part of the arrangement. In this instance, when someone is speaking of "them" or "they" (as did Larry Dovalina or Samuel Lozano) it is clearly understood that they are referring to those living across the river. The Tecos were very much an example of a facetious imagined community, a failure of Anderson's principles of nationalism and imagined community to root regardless of a common past or hoped for future.

Because the Tecos were supposed to be a shared cultural (Laredo and Nuevo Laredo) and binational (Mexico and the United States) property, they invented certain traditions. The uniforms were changed to reflect the binational arrangement. "Laredos" was emblazoned on the road uniforms; the hats, instead of reading "Tecos," were changed to "Laredos" with a large "2" in the background. The publicity generated by this unique relationship was beginning to be noticed, as were the inquiries about possible duplication of this elsewhere on the border. Ironically, despite the dual parks and anthems, and the history of fans crossing from one side to another to watch the games, on some level the Tecos were more convincingly thought of as an invented tradition by outsiders writing about the team than they were at home. In short, the Tecos failed to completely capture the public fancy, and hence failed to become an invented tradition at the level of local culture. I see this as a failure of the cities, first to see the Tecos as a cultural property, and second, to promote them in the most effective way.

It is at this juncture of culture and sport, that promotion, media representation, and civic interest can have a profound effect. The inability of ownership and, to some extent, the supporting institutions (the media and city officials) to fully comprehend the cultural potential of the Tecos resulted in a loss for the two Laredos. Despite initially pushing hard for the binational arrangement, the Lozanos never had the vision of their team being a cultural phenomenon. They ran it in the most pedestrian and traditional fashion: put out a team that can win and all else will follow. They put out a winning team, but after a time the fans started finding other things to do, and the revenues started dropping. This prompted some unpopular fiscal moves and, in turn, continued the decline. While Hobsbawm discussed invented traditions in national terms, I have been arguing that in the case of the transcultural border traditions, invented traditions can play somewhat different and innovative national roles. These local traditions have always functioned to short-circuit autonational antagonism. The Tecos, like all of the cultural performances in the two Laredos, fostered an identification with the region, and to the degree that the tradition was amplified and built upon, local transnationalism would deepen. When the first games were played in Laredo, one young Teco fan, Ricky Velásquez, who had attended many Teco games across the river, was moved by the playing of both anthems at the games at West Martin. "I think it's great," said Velásquez, referring to the binational character of the team. "Like for any other game [in the United States], they play the national anthem, except this was the Mexican national anthem. I really liked that, because I had never heard it [here] before."[59] It took the game coming over to Texas for a young Mexican American to hear and appreciate his roots.

I also argued that, because of the length of the performance (five months), the Tecos had the potential of deepening the transborder tradition in ways no other cultural enterprise could. It afforded the ideological mythmakers (the media and arts) a unique opportunity to compose something distinct to the Laredos as the only binational sports franchise in existence, and thereby increase attention paid to the area. Media, marketing, and mythmaking fully converged on the Tecos.

The binational quality of the team could have been converted into a marketing success had the Lozanos understood the cultural and public relations gold mine they had in their hands. Larry Dovalina, in my estimation, worked tirelessly to promote this vision and was the only one who truly comprehended the Tecos as cultural capital. Outsiders had been intrigued by the Tecos for just those reasons, but because it was so close to home, the Laredo media never managed to see the Tecos as anything more than a local sports phenomenon. It was also a major source of frustration for *Laredo Morning Times* sports editor Salo Otero, who, restrained by insufficient staff, worked hard just to keep the Tecos as the lead sports story during the season. Laredo institutions never quite came through in this regard.

For the Tecos to have become an invented tradition they would have had to enlarge their fan base beyond the diehards and move into the cultural arena. This would have necessitated a promotions and public relations chief with vision and imagination, neither of which the Lozanos were willing to back. In part, I have concluded that they ignored these possibilities because it would have entailed a loss of control over the franchise to the other side. The Laredoans were more able and willing to promote the Tecos as an ideological and cultural property, and the Lozanos would rather have demonstrated their control than further the success of the franchise. This is as much a function of the Lozanos' idiosyncrasies as it is a Mexican-U.S. issue. And here is where we find personal and autonational issues lying one on top of the other.

The U.S.-Mexican border is a stretch of territory along which people of sometimes vastly different economic development, culture, and race are arrayed. They simultaneously share much and hold little in common, all of which requires a more varied sense of nationalism than most scholars offer. I have tried to use a three-dimensional view of nationalism, but there are other dimensions to be explored. Most certainly the subtleties and nuances of structure, behavior, and identity along the border would accommodate a range of nationalism(s) that involve culture, economics, and politics. The Tecos baseball team has provided a lively starting point, as full of international camaraderie and conflict as any NAFTA meeting, as spectacular and meaningful as July 4 and 16 de Septembre, yet as local as the backyard barbecue.

A big crowd of over 3,000 was on hand for the opening of the 1995 season.[60] The new ownership latched onto a variety of funds to improve aging La Junta Park, and they lowered the ticket prices to entice hard-pressed Mexican consumers to consider watching the Tecos. Andrés Mora was introduced to the fans as the new manager and received the biggest hand. New faces dominated, however. In the dugout one saw many of the same interactions as before—not surprisingly, as these are professional players, used to moving from team to team. To be truthful, I don't know if I was alone in missing the sense of family that I had grown to recognize in this club. The few players left from before, such as Enrique Rámirez, Marco Antonio Cruz, and "Cartucho" Estrada, seemed resigned to the new players in their midst, but the sheen of confidence that always characterized the Tecolotes was not to be seen; perhaps it would come during the course of the season. Baseball has a habit of recreating its myths.

On the other hand, for the *Tecos del Sur* (a.k.a. the Mexico City Tigres) the 1995 season opened dramatically. The Mexican League commissioner was in attendance, as were some of the more powerful people in the nation. The stadium was filled with 24,000 fans anticipating a new contingent of players from the border that now composed approximately half the team. Opposing them this day was the other Mexico City team, the Diablos. There was a shared sense of nervousness and excitement among many of the ex-Tecos to get on with the rest of their lives. The wives of the ex-Tecos filed in, some of them still wearing their Teco jackets, and they too were somewhat struck by how much larger the scale of everything was.

Taking advantage of the jitters of the new contingent and two Tigre pitchers, the Diablos quickly jumped out to a 5–0 lead in the first inning.

The Tigres came back in their half of the first with three runs, but the Diablos continued to get timely hits. The Tigres' pitching could do little to quell Diablo bats, so that by the fourth inning it was a 9–3 Diablo lead. Unfamiliar with the way that the Tecos would manufacture runs in late innings, the Mexico City faithful grew quiet. In the fifth inning, however, the Tigres began whittling away at the lead, while a string of pitchers (among them ex-Tecos Moreno and Barraza) kept the Diablos from scoring again. Ex-Teco first baseman Marco Romero's two-run single tied it in the seventh inning. In the ninth inning the Tigres had men in scoring position when the Diablos once again called upon their bullpen to stop the rally. In what can only be called poetic symmetry, the Diablo bullpen disgorged a figure quite familiar to the ex-Tecos on hand. It was none other than Import pitcher Jay Baller, who had spent the previous season in Japan, "the Land of the Rising Sun," only to return in 1995 for another season in "the Land of the Lost."

He marched to the mound and wasted no time, overmatching his Tigre opponent and retiring the side. The ex-Tecos in the dugout watched and clinched their teeth as Baller strutted off the mound: "Anyone else would have been bad enough, but with Baller it was worse. No question," recalled one.[61] In the tenth inning the Diablos could do nothing offensively, and the Tigres took their turn. New Tigres manager Dan Firova had watched Baller very closely for signs that he was drifting or losing concentration. As an ex-catcher Firova keys in on pitchers, but as Baller's former manager he felt particularly acute. Sensing a pattern that he had seen before, as well as a chance to weaken Baller's concentration, Firova waited until the big ex–major leaguer was about to pitch to his one-time teammate Romero, who was to lead off the tenth inning. Romero was awaiting Baller's delivery when he heard his manager call for time. Firova walked toward the batter's box, smirking just a bit at Baller. Romero was puzzled when Firova asked him if he was feeling okay: "You tired? You want me to put someone in for you if you get on base?" asked Firova. Romero looked at Firova and shook his head: "No, I'm okay." "Well, then," said Firova, "put it out of here and we'll all go home." Going back to the dugout he again seemed to smirk in Baller's direction. Was this a psych-out job? Or did he know something?

It was a beautiful moment as baseball moments go: power hitter and power pitcher completely transfixed with each other; a clever manager looking to tip the scales just the slightest bit in his direction. The ex-Tecos in the dugout knew this type of moment well, and they lined the top step of the dugout in anticipation as the first two pitches missed wide. Romero knew just where the next pitch would be, and he got to fully extend his hairy arms. He later admitted that he wanted this pitch as much as any in his career. From the time the smirking Firova headed back to the dugout to when the rocket left Romero's bat barely a minute had passed. As the ball arced into the left-field bleachers, it was as if these *Tecos de afuera* had never left the border. The bench erupted and emptied even faster than the 24,000 fans that came to be introduced to the Tecos del Sur could yell their joy. It was as if Romero's home run negated the lost championship of 1993, or the misery these ex-Tecos had endured in 1994. The crowning touch was that the winning stroke was off Jay Baller, former teammate and antagonist. The moment was as much the end of one era as it was the beginning of a new one, but it was a moment that only these refugees from the border baseball wars could fully savor.

POSTSCRIPT

As this book goes to press word comes to me that the quarreling cities have decided to patch up their baseball differences. The 1997 season will once again feature a Tecos team playing in both Laredos, keeping the image of the river as a social metaphor central to understanding the border.

# Acknowledgments

It is to the people of Laredo, Texas, whose aid and encouragement nurtured and enriched this project, to whom I am most grateful. Larry Dovalina served as my gateway to the culture of baseball and the borderlands. His views on both were incisive: filled with the depth of an insider, yet critical. It was also Larry who introduced me to Laredo's baseball past through his father and uncle—don Lázaro and don Fernando Dovalina—both players from Laredo's rich past. These three Dovalinas opened up a world of border relations that rests at the heart of this book.

Esther Firova was my guardian angel. From the moment I came to Laredo and my path crossed hers, good things happened. In her capacity as hotel administrator she found me the best accommodations. As wife of the Teco manager, Dan Firova, she quickly connected me with her husband, and through him, of course, the team. As a baseball wife, Esther also provided me with a uniquely female perspective on life in the Mexican Leagues that is at once understanding and penetratingly honest. She even introduced me to her uncle, don Ismael Montalvo, once one of the area's finest ballplayers with a career that spanned the 1930s to the 1950s. Don Montalvo regaled me with humorous accounts of the life of a ballplayer in the early days. Thanks to you both.

A particular debt of gratitude goes to Cuauhtémoc "Chito" Rodríguez, former vice president of the Tecos (now holding the same position for the Mexico City Tigres) for granting me access both to the owner of the club as well as to its players. More steeped in the Teco tradition than anyone, having been with the club since it arrived back on the border in 1976, Cuauhtémoc had the best command of the workings of the Mexican League of anyone in the area and always shared his insights with me. Cuauhtémoc is the very epitome of the concept of binationalism that is explored in this book. I'm sure that when the study periodically revealed warts in connection with the Tecos, Cuauhtémoc may have winced a bit; but he always understood that the overall project praised baseball on the border. Thanks also go to don Víctor Lozano and Samuel Lozano, who granted me access to the team, and special thanks to don Víctor for a fine feast with his fun-loving friends in Nuevo Laredo.

Salo Otero, sports editor of the *Laredo Morning Times*, was always ready with a pun or point on any Teco topic. Whether we ran into each other at the park or at the gym, he unselfishly shared his lengthy experience as a sports writer with me. Milton Jamail, close friend and colleague, initially encouraged me to take the subject on, then made himself available whenever I needed his expertise. His vast experience in Latin American baseball served to cast the structural framework for much of this study. When questions came up or issues needed addressing, Milton and his wife, Margo Gutiérrez, went out of their way to answer them, often in the warmth of their home, which became my refuge in Texas. Fran Lloyd and Heidi Dobrott willingly attended to the logistics of the study, in a warm and supportive way, providing me with timely connections to people and institutions such as the Laredo Public Library, Laredo Historical Commission, and Los Caminos del Rio.

Colleagues outside of Laredo also supported me with ideas and material. Gerald Vaughn, whose work on the Mexican League of the 1940s served as a basis for one of the chapters, offered his work and encouragement. So, too, did historian David LaFrance, who has studied Mexican baseball in the 1980s. Joseph Arbena continues to serve as the torchbearer for Latin American sport in the academy, and generously served as the bridge between his field of history and mine. My colleagues at Northeastern University, Arnold Arluke, Daniel Faber, and Michael Blim, provided me with the emotional and scholarly support one needs when far from the field.

My family came through in a variety of ways. I am thankful to my oldest son Jedediah, who accompanied me on one of my trips and photographed many of the players. His work nicely captured many of the players I have written about and serves as the photo essay in the book. He also served as a spot-researcher in Austin. My youngest son, Cody, was kind enough to nap often, allowing his aged father the time to write; and my wife Mary kept it all going at home while I was in Laredo and derelict of duty in Boston. Thanks, my love.

# Appendixes

# A

## Bibliographic Essay: Border and Nationalisms

For THOSE of us who grew up far away from the border, differences between Mexican, "American," and Mexican American are often easily made, almost as if the further one gets from the border, the more clear the definition of nationalism. For those living closer to the Rio Grande, however, the sense of identity is layered. This book has attempted to examine one structural dimension of this shaded identity—nationalism—leaving aside the more complexly fashioned issues of race, class, and regional identity among people in the borderlands. What follows is a review of some of the more pertinent definitions of nationalism and my attempt to tease out general and heuristic elements that I can use to look at contemporary border relations and regional border baseball. I also attempt to place the study within the context of studies of national identity in sport sociology.

### Definitions of Nationalism

In his introductory text on the subject, Alter states, "The plethora of phenomena which may be subsumed under the term 'nationalism' suggests that it is one of the most ambitious concepts in the present-day vocabulary of political and analytical thought."[1] Benedict Anderson similarly points to the operational chaos surrounding the term in quoting Tom Nairn: "Nationalism is the pathology of modern developmental theory, as inescapable as 'neurosis' in the individual, with much the same essential ambiguity attaching to it."[2] The ambiguity is also at the heart of Breuilly's treatise on nationalism.[3] Because nationalism may refer to either political programs, sentiments, or actions, an operational definition, for Breuilly, is too vague for an informed study.[4] Nationalism can span the political spectrum from right (e.g., National Socialists in Germany or the reform nationalism of Meiji Japan) to left (e.g., Latin American liberation movements). Chameleonlike, nationalism is used in a wide range of fields involving an equally broad variety of perspectives, whether it be psychological, Marxist, communicative, or functionalist.[5] Breuilly argues that in order to eliminate the chaos in the subject in general, nationalism should be examined purely as a political phenomenon. However, to further refine our understanding of the myriad ways nationalism emerges or works, one must continually assess specific cases, and in so doing nonpolitical factors (e.g., culture, ideology) reenter at every level. Some of the difficulty in comprehending nationalism derives from our insistence on treating it in a too positivist a manner. Terry Eagleton reminds us that nationalism, seen as a process, moves over time from a progressive force to a reactionary one.[6] Raymond Williams understood this too when he penned the following lines for one of the characters in his novel, *The Second Generation*: "Nationalism is in this sense like class. To have it and feel it is the only way to end it."[7]

Culling a wide variety of sources, studies, and definitions, it is safe to say that minimally nationalism is *a political program containing a specific integrated set of cultural practices and ideology existing among a group who seeks to promote their sense* of enlarged community. For Gellner this is expressed as the convergence of politics and culture around the modern nation-state,[8] but in accepting this sense of the term we will note several variations. Importantly, the formation of this modern community comes at the expense of others. Moreover, since nationalism covers the political spectrum, it may be more explanatory to think of it, as Weber[9] and later Anderson[10] suggest; that is, in relational terms. Weber conceives of nationalism as a "specific sense of solidarity *in the face of* other groups."[11] By this he means the specific forms of language and culture (e.g., shared history, religion, day-to-day social forms) that set off all or part of one nation from others, then reintegrate the separation as part of the group's self-definition. Structurally, Weber emphasizes the use of social specifics that exist both to provide identity within the group and to provide a baseline separating one group from another.[12] While Weber and Breuilly may have emphasized the group solidarity function of nationalism, its innate tendency to divide is just as important. A nation-state need not actively be operative to promote a sense of nationalism (e.g., Scots, Armenians, or Kurds who presently share little of the nationalism of the countries that they are part of maintain their sense of national identity based on an earlier political autonomy).

The relations between nations, and hence nationalisms, are by no means conducted on a level playing field. Colonial and postcolonial relations that characterized the rise of capitalism were built around economic exploitation, a relationship that would in time spawn a response, an anticolonialism often termed "risorgimento nationalism."[13] Lenin first discussed nationalism in developed and developing nations in terms of anticolonialism.[14] Later, Wallerstein,[15] Frank,[16] and others exhaustively studied the relations between core and peripheral areas as engaged in a mutually reinforcing set of behaviors. As when borders are shared between such disparate nations, the uneven qualities tend to be exaggerated and affect the expression of nationalism.

Amplifying certain of Ernest Mandel's ideas about late capitalism,[17]

Michael Kearney looks at transnationalism as an aspect of uneven political-economic and social-cultural ordering of late capitalism.[18] As surplus capital was exported away from developed nations to underdeveloped ones, altering the latter as the process deepened, we see the maturation of mid-twentieth-century capitalism. In the latest period we see peripheral economies of the Third World unable to utilize the available labor they generate, pushing it into the developed nations (e.g., Turks in Germany, Mexicans and others in the United States). Culturally, this plays havoc with the traditional notions of border and border identities by making the border (on both sides) a contested terrain. For Kearney, the notion of nationalism and rigid boundaries is synonymous with the increasingly dated sense of the "modern state," while transnational ("a blurring" of boundaries) reflects the present state of nations.

The U.S-Mexican border contains a particularly pronounced juxtaposition of industrialized and developing nations. Issues such as undocumented labor, contraband, and maquiladoras play out of this political-economic difference. James[19] and Fanon,[20] among others,[21] have discussed the colonial mindset with implications for nationalism. For Third World countries nationalism links national pride with anti-imperialism. Both here and elsewhere I have tried to show how essential Third World anticolonial nationalism is in building a sense of autonomy.[22] Since so much of the hegemonic relationship between core and periphery has to do with social self-loathing and a veneration of the foreign, building Third World nationalism must not only work to build national pride, but simultaneously demonize the industrial powers with which third world nations relate.[23] Anderson's notion of "imagined community" works nicely to illustrate the national identity that is fostered through construction of common culture, but does less to show the anti-imperialist nationalism. In relations between nations as politically and economically distinct as those between the United States and Mexico, and given the cataclysmic history that binds them, identity fueled by antagonism and resentment is as essential a component of nationalism as is that garnered directly through positive identity.

## Approaches Used to Study the Border

Since the border has steadily grown in importance, the scholarly attention to it has also grown. Looking at a range of studies shows us that each discipline, while contributing something of its own to the understanding of the border, nevertheless rediscovers some essential qualities of the border. Since I come to this region so lately, I benefited greatly from some of these works.

## Geographers and Economists

Border geographers such as Lawrence Herzog talk extensively of "transnational space" along the 2000-mile border between the United States and Mexico.[24] With the aid of dependency theory, and political economy, Herzog examines the ways in which this region's cities simultaneously reflect their national centers and forge a distinct regional identity. Speaking of the twentieth century, Herzog writes, "Demographic shifts in both the United States and Mexico have transformed the boundary corridor into a field of confrontation of social, political, and economic forces native to the two nations. The border zone has become a place unto itself. It has developed a measure of autonomy, economic dynamism, and its own rules."[25]

In their study of Mexican border cities, geographers Arreola and Curtis have thoroughly dissected the border city. Examining "zones of tolerance," the center, residential, gates and bridges, tourist zones, and "commercial spines," they have detailed those features that give the border its unique as well as derivative qualities: "the border cities remain hybrid cultural landscapes. They display a heritage that is Spanish and Mexican, but they also incorporate and testify to North American landscape tastes."[26] Having acknowledged the fusion of traditions, Arreola and Curtis do not, however, formally subscribe to the thesis that the border comes to have its own identity. Instead they treat the borderlands as binational. And indeed, their preference for examining the features of Mexican border cities that are distinctive are important and valid, but they implicitly leave the door open to making leaps to the transnational level. In the final pages of their study the authors comment on the two-way diffusion that both characterizes and portends changes along the border, quoting Richard Rodríguez: "The Tijuana that Americans grew up with was a city they thought they had created. The Tijuana that has grown up is a city that will re-create us."[27] Whether or not one subscribes to the notion that the border constitutes its own political, economic, or cultural entity, so long as one can point to attitudes, ideas, and behavior on the part of border dwellers that refers to their border, one has entered into a dialogue that is transnational. It matters not whether the citizens of Tijuana and San Diego believed that their cities were growing more interdependent, as one survey proposed to show,[28] because, as Arreola and Curtis demonstrate, the cities were in fact becoming so. Likewise, it matters little whether a steel wall is erected to separate the two countries, as it has been along a five-mile section near San Ysidro, California. The sentiment behind trying to separate the two countries only bears witness to the flow of people and culture across to the United States and to the federal policy committed to relocating these people back into Tijuana, only to repeat the exchange, and thereby establish a cultural pattern that characterizes the border as distinct from the normal occurrences elsewhere in either country.[29]

At bottom the population developments along the border are rooted in economic interplay between the two neighbors. The growth of *maquiladoras* that triggered this population expansion was itself a function of the border. Manufacturers, most of whom are U.S.-based, were looking for a place to set up low-cost operations as close to the United States as possible. The result was that as of 1990 there were almost 1,600 *maquiladoras* along the border in Mexican towns and cities. Nuevo Laredo was the site of 93 of them with a working population of 16,162.[30] Tijuana's 530 *maquiladoras* led all cities, and Juárez's 320 plants was second, while the 134,838 workers topped all Mexican cities.[31]

As northern Mexico, particularly along the border, attracted more industrial enterprises there was a predictable labor migration to that region from other areas of Mexico.[32] The *maquiladoras* that have popped up from Tijuana to Matamoros have shifted Mexico's demographics and economic growth to the previously underpopulated and unimportant north.[33] Arreola and Curtis, among others, have presented these figures in terms of population growth.[34] Nuevo Laredo went from a town of 6,548 at the turn of the century to 350,000 today. In all likelihood the latter figure is an undercount. Juárez, during the same period, mushroomed from 8,218 in 1900 to 797,679. Tijuana's growth is the most striking: from 242 to 742,686 in the same ninety-year period.[35]

The integration of northern Mexicans into the U.S. consumer economy is so marked on the border that many Laredoans consider Mexican retail trade more important than sales to fellow Laredoans or Texans. Estimates of how much of the Mexican border dweller's dollar gets spent on the U.S. side run as high as ninety-one cents.[36] That is certainly the case in Laredo, where the retail trade spearheaded the boom during the 1970s, with one of the highest retail-sales-per-resident figures in the country.[37] The devaluation of the peso in 1982 and 1994 devastated Laredo's merchants, who have always been heavily dependent on Mexican consumers; but even this did not destroy the mercantile trade. The wholesale trade with Laredo merchants continued, as Mexicans bought large quantities in Laredo's stores to resell in Mexico at a small profit, although this was more limited than in the pre-1982 days. "When I go into a store here in town I buy a couple of pairs of sneakers. When a Mexican comes to that store he buys 100 pair, so the store owner is geared to the Mexican rather than me," commented one Laredo resident.[38] Even now, in the wake of a crippling Mexican law that places a fifty-dollar limit on Mexican citizens' purchases in the United States, the retail trade of Laredo is the anchor of the economy. They are mobilizing their considerable strength by enlisting Texas's senators and governor to pressure the Mexican government to drop the spending limit.[39]

Population growth comparable to that experienced in Mexico over the past fifty years is found on the U.S. side of the border as well. The "Sun Belt" has experienced its gains on the back of what Herzog calls "population interest groups," primarily military personnel, retirees, and amenity seekers.[40] In conjunction with energy development, land speculation, tourism, and agriculture, the U.S. southwest has experienced unprecedented growth.

The growth of northern Mexico and the southwestern United States is not, however, equivalent. In fact it is the economic asymmetry that marks this borderland. There are curious ironies to this. While earnings on the U.S. side of the border are five times those on the Mexican side, the same U.S. wage earners are invariably worse off than those in other parts of Texas. Hence, Herzog mentions that wage levels in Laredo and elsewhere in the Texas border country are only half those of all Texans. Another irony is that northern Mexicans, poor by comparison to U.S. border dwellers, are better off than Mexicans in the interior.[41]

Border political-economists, such as Fernández, have done much to structurally demonstrate the transnational character of the border region.[42] Working on a twin base of economic differences between the two nations and the differences in political-economic development, Fernández builds a case for the gradual interpenetration of the economies as one approaches the border: "In terms of demographics, industry, commerce, trade, agriculture, and tourism, the border region is nowadays an area integrated into the economic and political spheres of the United States and Mexico."[43] The integration, however, is "based on uneven development of the two economies,"[44] a condition that distinguishes the U.S.-Mexican border from most others. While the northern Mexican border region has witnessed dramatic economic growth since World War II, it has not been able to outsprint the population growth that so many new jobs spawned, nor the jobs that were found north in the United States. Fernández points to a weak development in the capital goods industrial sector of Mexico as the main reason. The U.S. border region, on the other hand, while economically better healed than its Mexican counterpart, is impoverished relative to the rest of the states in which they are located.[45] The growth of U.S. border economy has been in retail sales. The combination of heavy consumerism from northern Mexico, American tourism, and military bases and their personnel has resulted in this burgeoning area. Also, the economies are merging as a result of the flood of legal and extralegal labor that must be regulated, as well as an informal economy that includes enormous amounts of contraband.[46] The result is a region that manifests political-economic differences but strong regional characteristics as well.

## Historical Studies

Historians also share this transnational perception of the border. The border's preeminent historian, Oscar Martínez, has documented the transnational/transcultural qualities of the region for three decades.[47] He grounds his view in the distinct regional culture that was established first in Spain, then in Mexico's northern provinces (which includes territory on both sides of the Rio Grande) from the eighteenth century on. The view that the region and its people were different than the rest of Mexico was shared by residents both in the interior as well as in the north: "Mexicans recognize a norteño culture distinct from that of other parts of Mexico. Norteños are said to be different in their manner of thinking, speaking, acting, and dressing. A strong spirit of struggle, determination, adaptability, and hard work are attributed to norteños."[48]

Following the demarcation of the United States and Mexico in 1848, there emerged quasi-distinctions between Mexican Americans and northern Mexican nationals. For Martínez, these differences are real but not substantive enough to eliminate the transnational/cultural unity of the area. Martínez points out that unity is forged in part out of deprecatory assessments that each nation has of its border dwellers. Norteños are seen by Mexicans in the interior as being coopted by *agringamiento* (Americanization), while Mexican Americans are seen as northerly extensions of Mexicans by their Anglo countrymen in the interior. This is furthered in the perceptions that exist of each other by border dwellers themselves. Mexican Americans are often referred to as *pochos* (characterizing their cultural and linguistic identities as chopped up) by their Mexican counterparts across the river. Mexican Americans respond by derisively terming Mexicans on the other side as *mojados* (wetbacks). Despite this sometimes mutual derogation, the inhabitants along both sides of the Rio Grande continue to develop their collective sense of identity through their common goals, interpenetrating economies, and determination to find solutions to problems unique to them, such as pollution or mutually benefiting infrastructure: "People on the U.S.-Mexico border view the boundary and the function it is supposed to serve, in terms fundamentally different from those of their compatriots in interior regions."[49]

In his widely acclaimed social history of Texas, David Montejano also chronicles the qualities that made the Rio Grande region transnational.[50] Montejano documents the border region's intrinsic cultural transnationalism. The history of settlement in the region speaks directly to a common origin, roots that preceded the 1848 Treaty of Guadalupe Hidalgo. Its earliest settlement involved families living on both sides of the river as early as 1757. Sánchez, the town's founder, was frustrated in his efforts to get settlers who preferred the south side, to relocate across the river where the town's center was.[51] Later, in describing the Catarino Garza affair of 1890, a Texas-led rebellion against Mexican president Porfirio Díaz, a journalist encountering the Rio Grande region for the first time commented that the area was "an overlapping of Mexico into the United States, and the people, though they have been American citizens for more than forty years, are almost as much an alien race as the Chinese, and have shown no disposition to amalgamate with the other Americans."[52] Montejano goes on to chronicle that "Mexicanization" was also the fate of Anglos living in the region:[53] "There was neither racial nor social distinctions between Americans and Mexicans; we were just one family. This was due to the fact that so many of us of that generation had a Mexican mother and an American or European father."[54]

### Folklorists and Anthropologists

Folklorists and anthropologists working the area attest to its unique identity as well, by seeing the border as a transcultural zone. Américo Paredes has helped pioneer this view. As with the others who preface their views of the border with the area's unique history, in particular the lower Rio Grande, Paredes conveys in everyday behavior the power of the area's collective roots to operate within and around larger political realities:

> When the Rio Grande became a border, friends and relatives who had been near neighbors—within shouting distance across a few hundred feet of water—were now legally in different countries. If they wanted to visit each other, the law required that they travel many miles up or down stream, to the nearest official crossing place, instead of swimming or boating directly across as they used to do before. It goes without saying that they paid little attention to the requirements of the law.[55]

Paredes's sense of transcultural is rooted in the bicultural experience of Mexican Americans. Moreover, his primary contribution to cultural analysis lies in demonstrating Mexican American forms of resistance to Anglo assaults on their culture. Paredes shows the border *corrido* (ballad), for instance, to be a patterned, conscious expression of Mexican and Mexican American resentment to gringos. This view of the transnational identity specifically targets one of the two major populations on the American side, but Paredes also details the Anglo presence and contribution to the border culture. In his examination of the border corrido of Gregorio Cortez, Paredes chronicles the cultural fusions between the Mexican ranchero culture and the Anglo cultural predilection for handguns and macho that resulted in the creation of the cowboy archetype that later spread throughout the west.[56]

José Limón's work on culture in South Texas has carried Paredes's work into a more contemporary interpretive milieu.[57] Looking at current cultural practices among Mexican Americans in south Texas, Limón has provided a vivid cultural-studies analysis of a wide range of everyday practices, such as barbecues among working-class men and dances. Embedded throughout has been the post–World War II cultural presence of Mexican immigrants in south Texas, known as *fuereños* (foreigners). Limón gives these people a central role in the creation of cultural fusions between them and already-established Mexican Americans. Combined, Limón and Paredes form a powerful body of cultural analysis for this region, and the transcultural nature of this region is duly highlighted.

In a more socioeconomic vein, anthropologist Michael Kearney has examined the northern emigration of Mixtec populations from Oaxaca, Mexico, as they reformulate their identities into something transnational.[58] He usefully distinguishes between borders and boundaries in the nation-state. Boundaries are legal and spatial formulations, while borders have to do with geographic areas that are cultural and that cross boundaries. He looks at the transnational characteristics that constitute the border as a function of the most recent period of capitalism and the nation-state, that is, the peripheralization of the core in which the traditional centers of power and economic control must cope with large populations of reserve labor from the periphery. This also exerts a powerful cultural force along the border in the form of Latinization of the Anglo-American side of the border. The result is a border area that is neither conventionally American nor Mexican, but rather its own dynamic entity.

*Literary Scholars and Artists*

In his book on Chicano satire Guillermo Hernández looks at the use of humor and invective in Chicano literature.[59] This is rooted in the transcultural position of the Chicano, or the Pocho. In a study of the works of various Chicano authors, Hernández chronicles the sometimes labyrinthine path of the Chicano's attempts to forge a path that can accommodate and resist both Mexican and American onslaughts to their unique position between the two societies and countries.

Guillermo Gómez-Peña, a performance artist, living on both sides of the Tijuana–San Diego border, most poignantly expresses the ambivalence with which both Mexicans and Americans view Mexican Americans:

> Despite the fact that I spend long periods of time in Mexico City, still write regularly for Mexican publications, and maintain a close dialogue with many artists and writers from "the center," in Mexico City I am referred to as a Chicano,

or *americano de orígen hispano*. The anthologies and festivals of Mexican border culture rarely include my work because "Guillermo, you live on the other side." To live "on this side" still implies a form of betrayal. When I go back to perform or give a talk, I have to do so as a Chicano. My Mexican brothers have managed to turn me into "the other," along with 15 to 20 million Mexicans spread throughout the United States.[60]

## Interrelations of Nationalisms

These nationalisms mutually influence one and other. We can generalize a bit by declaring that the interrelations between the three nationalisms begin with autonationalism. The border marks the establishment and site of national guardedness between nation-states. The adversarial relations (real or potential) that mark autonationalism serve to promote internal identity, and the border marks a point beyond which no one identifies. Emphasis is on "We *versus* They." In the case of Texas (and the United States in general) and Mexico, autonationalism is particularly virulent. The history of strife often marked in the course of the past century and a half has, at times, enabled each side to loath the other (e.g., for Texans the memory of Goliad or the Alamo; for Mexicans the Mexican American War). At times the antagonism is played out racially between Anglos and Mexicans, which places Chicanos in a difficult position of having their national loyalty regularly questioned.[61]

With any two entities aligned along a border there will be various forms of exchange, no matter how guarded and cold the relations may be. Even minimizing or sealing off the movement of people or goods entails an exchange. The Berlin Wall, for instance, necessitated not only its construction but also ongoing maintenance of checkpoints, thus presupposing attempts to cross it, in large measure promoted by the West Germans. Hence, there grew an ideology and set of behaviors devoted to the wall on both sides, and whether or not they realized it people created a cultural institution and exchange. In most cases, movement of goods and people were routinized, moving through both official and unofficial (illegal) channels. This binationalism was the product of cooperation and the needs of nations sharing a border. Here the emphasis is on the border as fixed but open to goal-directed exchange. Emphasis is on "We *and* They." Binationalism feeds off those periods of time when international relations are positive, as opposed to autonationalism's tendency to close the border to exchange. It is a naturally occurring cycle and particularly marked immediately along the border.

National policy and international relations between the centers of power often have little to do with the relations that grow up between the people and locals existing on the border. For instance, the *"Bracero* Program" of the 1940s grew out of the agreement between Washington, D.C., and Mexico City to send Mexicans to work at jobs in the United States in response to the U.S. war effort that had drawn thousands of American workers away. When they were no longer needed these *braceros* were shipped back. But thousands of Mexicans began moving north toward the border in the hopes of getting some work in the United States, and this shift ushered in the period of labor immigration that has spawned a slew of institutions on both sides devoted to the control of illegal aliens into the United States. The border has become a "staging area" from which Mexicans hope to cross legally or illegally into the United States to work. If they are successful, they make the move; if not, they are caught by the U.S. Immigration and Naturalization Service or Border Patrol and shipped back, or their work arrangement ends and they are sent back. From the point of view of binationalism, the border has generated agencies to handle both sides of the issue. The same applies to virtually anything that involves a movement of goods or people, or the problems shared by the two sides of the border, such as smuggling or pollution of the Rio Grande.

The relation between transnationalism and binationalism is less fraught with tension than either is with autonationalism. Binationalism can spawn transnational relations by building a level of common culture through building of continued interaction and crisis. Much of the more recent "browning" (or increased Mexican national presence in search of work) of the area just north of the border has had the effect of adding a further layer of Mexican culture to what is already there. Conversely, the binationalism can be a function of an earlier bicultural tradition. Much of the Mexico-Texas border includes coupled cities whose origins can be traced to the colonization efforts of Nuevo Santander in the mid-eighteenth century. Certainly this is the case for the two Laredos. While don Tomás Sánchez founded the villa of Laredo on the north side of the river, subsequent settlement took place on the south side,[62] and much of the early conflict among these settlers stemmed from Sánchez's efforts to get the "south siders" to relocate to the other bank. The formation of Nuevo Laredo, and the binational operations that marked the two towns from the 1846 inception of the border, was only a continuation of the relations and identity that preceded it.

In the case of the Laredos, common culture and social roots were forged from the outset. Later, the distance from Mexican and American political centers reinforced the transcultural and eventually transnational characteristics of the border. Nevertheless, national identity and its antagonistic properties continually eroded the border region's common identity. Aspersions can often be heard cast between Laredoans and Nuevo Laredoans that reflect their differing national identities. The unflattering *pocho*, used by Mexicans to refer to Mexican Americans north of the border, comes up often enough, while Laredoans can be heard to counter by referring to Nuevo Laredoans as *mojados*, wetbacks. But, when dealing with outsiders, the two sides merge, as when Spanish-speaking residents of either city refer to Federal district Mexicans as *chilangos*.[63]

Even in cultural spectacles designed to reflect a singular national identity, such as American or Mexican Independence (July 4 or 16 de Septembre), the transnational proclivities show themselves. In the wake of the railroad coming to the Laredos along with the Anglo merchant and late-nineteenth century invasion of professionals, there was a conscious attempt to move local traditions away from their Mexican roots. The Washington Birthday celebration was part of this "Americanization" effort.[64] The July 4 Independence Day celebrations were also part of the effort. These two holidays were, interestingly, linked to a larger, emerging south Texas regionalism. The cities of Laredo and Corpus Christi established a tradition of exchanging celebrants between these holidays. This tradition dates back to at least 1888, when the *Laredo Times* noted, "It is understood that Corpus Christi will give a grand tournament on the fourth of July and our boys will doubtless go down on that occasion."[65] Baseball contests between the two cities had taken place the previous year, but this was the first time it was linked to the national holiday. The tradition grew, so that by 1912 the announcement of the annual trip included six coaches on the Texas-Mexican Railway with over 800 citizens of Laredo.[66] By 1924 the celebration had grown to several thousand.[67] Importantly, accompanying the Laredo celebrants were "the Third Artillery Band of Mexico City and the Nuevo Laredo Municipal Band which furnished music in Corpus during the celebration,"[68] and which returned to play two concerts in the twin city in Texas. Nuevo Laredoans were an anticipated part of every Laredo affair, even affairs at a distance from the two Laredos that were designed to promote national identity somewhat at odds with Mexican identity. In the case of the two Laredos, the three forms of nationalism melt readily into one another.

### Blurring Licit and Illicit Institutions into the Transnational

The border has built a set of unique institutions dealing with the legal and illegal movement of goods and people across it. These institutions foster the creation of a border identity that can incorporate like and unlike people. Not only is there a powerful ethnic, linguistic, and cultural bond between Mexicans and Mexican Americans; but, because of the behaviors and attitudes that are now part of the border, people who do not share culture, subculture, class, or race have become part of a common set of institutions. The gringo, pocho, and Mexican are engaged in a range of exchanges and mutual roles that form border culture. In this dance, the Border Patrol, the coyote, and the illegal alien, while adversarial, wind up not only creating a novel institution, but a mutual dependency on each other. They have their own language and behavior, and come close to their own subculture. In this respect border culture is multifaceted, built as much out of commonality and mutual interest as out of competition, resentment, and criminality.

The economic growth of northern Mexico and the internal migration within Mexico to the border has also increased the likelihood of larger numbers of Mexicans seeking entry (legal and illegal) into the United States. The "alien" issue is a direct function of the border and more specifically the recent history of the border. It is within this context that Kearney has studied as transnationals those Oaxacans who have moved from their homes in southern Mexico to the border and beyond to the United States.[69] Bustamante[70] and Hansen,[71] among others, have shown how cheap Mexican labor built the infrastructure of the U.S. southwest and contributes to the profitability of a range of economic sectors in these border states (e.g., agriculture). Two million "aliens" legally crossed into Laredo during May 1994,[72] but one can only guess how many crossed the river into the neighborhoods (La Azteca or South Laredo) where they are shielded in safe houses until they can go further north.[73]

Smuggling is by definition transnational, and it is as intimately related to border economics as is labor migration or *maquiladoras*. The assistance between townspeople on both sides of the river had always been freely lent, and with the establishment of the international boundary become a function of nations and states.[74] Day-to-day life, however, continued to move across the river in defiance of these new governmental restrictions. Marriage, as well as many economic and cultural activities, continued from before.[75] Montejano mentions the powerful economic position that Mexican border families, with branches on both sides of the river, garnered through controlling trade in the 1850s.[76] Much of the movement of goods across the border, however, was contraband. In his 1853 report to Congress, the American consul discusses institutionalization of smuggling growing up alongside of the border: "Practically every American along the international line preferred the career of a merchant; and smuggling with the best part of the population had entered into the romance and legend of the frontier."[77]

The Merchants' War of the early 1850s helped provide the smuggling rationale for many merchants on the border, as when the Mexican government proved hostile to their interests and the U.S. government was slow and lax.[78] *Norteños* in conjunction with Laredo's Mexican American and Anglos demonstrated their regional colors in conducting their trade that included regularized smuggling. To aid the economically struggling border communities that existed across from more viable U.S. communities, the Mexican government in 1858 decreed that their northern border towns would pay no tariffs on imports. The impact of this caused American cities on the border to stagnate, and led directly to an increase in contraband.[79] Smuggling and the economics of border relations grew up together.

Even today smuggling takes place at all levels of the two Laredos. The movement of drugs across the river is the best known,[80] but smuggling of large volumes of manufactured wares by American merchants also takes place. In the summer of 1994, the head of Hachar Industries, one of Laredo's largest and oldest enterprises, pleaded guilty to two counts of falsifying statements and invoices in an attempt to defraud the government of importation duties.[81] The report also mentioned the widespread nature of these acts among reputable business people.

Smuggling of goods from the United States into Mexico is also ongoing.[82] Until the North American Free Trade Agreement removes the duties that apply to it, various goods will continue to be illegally moved across the border, as was the case with electronic goods up until the General Agreement on Tariffs and Trade (GATT) of 1988. One longtime ex-smuggler of electronic equipment whom I queried candidly stated that it was only the international GATT agreement that prompted him to leave such a lucrative field. While this individual left the life of a smuggler for a staid business career, others simply tap into new merchandise. The easy and fluid movement between licit and illicit commerce is important to keep in mind when discussing the transcultural and national character of the border, however.

Tourism is the fourth economic pillar of the Laredos' border economy. Two-thirds of Mexico's annual visitors confine their Mexican stay to the border, making tourism a major industry, but this industry is built upon a set of poorly visible cultural relations.[83] The presence of American tourists who visit Mexico, going no further than the border to buy curios and cheap border trade, also works to fuel the disdain of Mexicans toward gringos. Each party walks away from their economic exchange (whether it be buying wares or visiting "Boy's Town"—the brothel district) with a revitalized sense of self and another layer of distance between themselves and the foreigner. The fact that this relation is now in its fourth generation indicates its normalization. Again, like the relations between border patrols, illegal entrants, and coyotes, tourism is a function of the border; and it matters not whether any of these forms are positive and functional, or negative and dysfunctional. They are in every way as distinct as they are related. The following is a simplified chart of the three nationalisms.

## The Three Nationalisms

| Auto-nationalism | Bi-nationalism | Trans-nationalism |
| --- | --- | --- |
| · Focus on creation of sense of national identity through common ideology and imagined community. <br> · Emphasis on "We *versus* They," or adversarial internationalism. <br> · Use of border as fixed and impenetrable | · Focus on points of cooperation between bordering states, e.g., common needs, problem solving. <br> · Emphasis on "We *and* They," or cooperative internationalism. <br> · Use of border as fixed but open. | · Focus on merged identity into something new. <br> · Emphasis on "Us," or hybrid internationalism. <br> · Use of border as fluid and open. |

## Tecos in Sport Studies

The case of the Tecos represents a corrective of sorts to the overly generalized sense of nationalism and sport present in the field of sport studies. The latter feel that, after warfare, there can be no more nationalistic enterprise than the Olympics or the World Cup. Oddly, however, for all the assessment of the term nationalism, there are remarkably few sport case studies that explore it in detail. Those that do so tend to be macro-analyses (rather than studies of particular instances) or case studies employing conventional autonational definitions.[84] *Baseball on the Border* departs from these trends in favor of a micro-analysis in which structural relations provides us with a greater range of definitions of nationalism.

In terms of sport sociology, the present study has sought to methodologically direct examinations of nationalism and sport toward the use of ethnography and history, and away from trendy but overly simplistic methods such as media analysis. The latter has a role in social analysis, of course, but there is an increasing reliance on cultural studies or media analysis in place of more field-oriented or social historical analysis. This style of social examination has become the favorite beverage of the postmodern sport analyst. As Foley has demonstrated, postmodern analysis certainly has a role in the study of sport. Nevertheless, those who eschew conventional methods in favor only of literary interpretation (i.e. "reading" their subject from a distance) often pauperize explanation and theory.[85] For someone to examine, for instance, the Olympics *only* through the way the media handles it may give us insights into mass communications, but tells us virtually nothing about the "emics" of Olympics—the insider's perspective, as anthropologists use the term—or structural relations. There are postmodern sociologists who study, in this instance, sport, and systematically confuse the Olympics as a sociological event with the media's representation of the Olympics as an event. Worse still, there are scholars who perceive the media's depiction of the sporting event as the way that event is perceived by those reading or watching their description. This is a "poor man's" (sic) social science. Better to wade into the quagmire of data collection and risk all the hazards (including being wrong) than to sit and interpret at a distance and almost certainly be wrong. This disturbing trend has found its way into the sport sociology (as elsewhere) and particularly into the study of sport and nationalism. None other than the renowned British historian E. J. Hobsbawm has cautioned against the facile use of distanced views to explain nationalism. In speaking of the difficulty attendant to ascertaining views of nationalism held by "ordinary persons," Hobsbawm says: "Fortunately social historians have learned how to investigate the history of ideas, opinions, and feelings at the sub-literary level, so that we are today less likely to confuse, as historians once habitually did, editorials in select newspapers with public opinion. . . . official ideologies of states and movements are not guides to what it is in the minds of even the most loyal citizens or supporters."[86]

Ironically, having tried to cast suspicion on the exclusive use of postmodern discursive methods in which everything is reduced to a "text" and given "readings," I now use a proponent of this method who, rather than impoverishing the study of sport and nationalism, has enriched it. In the field of sport sociology, Joseph Maguire has done more to direct attention to the study of national identity and sport and keep it there than has anyone over the past decade.[87] Rather than assume a simple mirroring between nationalism and sport, Maguire has brought into the discussion intriguing concepts from other disciplines and fused them with a content analysis of the media, primarily in Great Britain. Whether borrowing for his analysis the concepts of "willful nostalgia" or "invented traditions," Maguire has managed to blend his method with interdisciplinary trends that have consistently forced sports scholars in sociology, anthropology, and history to rethink their paradigms. Unfortunately Maguire turns out to be the exception that proves the rule, and most attempts to explain nationalism and sport in this fashion have tended to pale by comparison.

When we turn to the study of Latin American sport we find so little that virtually any interpretation is welcome. Still, the region has produced works of note. Janet Lever's book on Brazilian soccer represented the first lengthy examination of sport in South America by a sport sociologist.[88] Several others have looked at sport with good, but shorter efforts.[89] The Caribbean has succeeded in attracting a certain amount of attention, mostly in the English-speaking half,[90] where the legacy of C.L.R. James plays a role in drawing attention to the role of cricket in British cultural imperialism.[91] Looking at James's homeland, the Mandels have written extensively about the structural relations of basketball in Trinidad and To-bago,[92] and most recently Michael Malec has edited a volume on sport in the Caribbean that contains new contributions to cricket analysis.[93] In the Spanish Caribbean two serious works by Ruck[94] and Klein[95] on baseball in the Dominican Republic represent the totality of scholarly efforts, in a field that spawns as many as sixty-five new books a year.

The paucity of scholarly work in Latin America has continued despite the persistent efforts of historians William Beezley and Joseph Arbena to turn attention to this area. Beezley's pioneering efforts to study the diffusion of sport into Mexico ranks as one of the first book-length treatments of sport in Latin America.[96] His scholarly studies preceded even this, and it was his 1985 article in *Studies in Latin American Popular Culture* on the rise of baseball in Mexico that is read by all serious students of baseball in Latin America.[97] Beezley's efforts were carried forward in the work of Arbena, who has, since 1988, become the standard bearer for scholarly studies of sport in Latin America. More importantly, several of his pieces have dealt directly with the study of nationalism and sport.[98]

Narrowing the focus down to Mexican baseball is relatively easy, considering the small body of literature one has to work with in Latin American sports. If Beezley's work represents a starting point for the study of Mexican baseball, then fellow historian David LaFrance's work on the cultural and political significance Fernando Valenzuela's astounding success in major league baseball in the early 1980s, and a political history of the Mexican League's only serious labor challenge, the ANABE strike of 1980, is the latest word on the subject.[99] Straddling the academic-journalistic fence is the work of Milton Jamail, whose articles range all over the Latin American baseball scene, including several very provocative pieces on the U.S. Labor Department's visa policy on Latin players, and a response to the racist perceptions of Mexicans that exist within organized baseball.[100]

The present study has attempted to illustrate the need for case studies of sport, situated in time and place, and attended to by the investigator in a methodologically quasi-traditional way. In this instance the subject matter was nationalism on the U.S.-Mexican border, but it could have just as easily been the construction of masculinity or the loss of local autonomy in an age of professionalism. What is essential is that we provide our readers and students with a sufficient range of case studies to enable them to develop and eventually test some of our arguments. Furthermore, the subject of nationalism has, hopefully, been made to bow to the local and regional way in which people think of it rather than some centralized construct. And finally, the Tecos have shown us that popular culture can provide as rich an area for the study of society and/or politics as any political institution or happening that one encounters.

# B

## Methods and Perspective

I MADE seven field trips, spanning four different baseball seasons. Each visit ranged in duration from one to five weeks, but five of these trips covered the 1993 and 1994 seasons. These two years formed the heart of the study. There is a reason for my repeated trips of shorter duration rather than a few for longer periods. I have long believed that with repeated visits the people being studied perceive the ethnographer as somehow more real, a person who will return continually. With that perception comes a greater degree of trust and access to more information. Also, with the repeat-visit pattern, people grow less tired of ethnographers and look forward to their presence.

Since I was unable to spend the entire season with the team, I made certain to be with them at every phase of the season—from spring training through the postseason championship series. I was with them both at home and on the road; before, during, and after games.

I covered every layer of the team's composition, from rookies to the owner. This involved an array of methods. To be sure, my ability to include every member of the Tecos was limited by a range of things, from my attempting to do this by myself, to my status as a white Anglo male, but I did gain a good deal of access to people and managed to breakdown many of the barriers. At the onset I only observed the players rather than interact with them. I described the surroundings and noted first impressions, which filled the pages of my field journals early on. Anthropologists often refer to the work in these early days as "counting teepees," a time when both ethnographer and subject size each other up. These early encounters often yield false impressions that come to light later on, but underscore the need for prolonged times in the field. As qualitative researchers, ethnographers have one substantial string to their bows—they stay long enough to discover and correct their mistakes. In looking over my notes and seeing how inaccurately I initially judged certain Tecos like Alejandro Ortiz or Jay Baller or Marco Antonio Romero—even if I was on the mark with Ernesto Barraza or Enrique Couoh—I no longer mind the expense and feverish struggle to find the time for subsequent fieldtrips.

I began formal interviewing immediately, not with the players, but with the gatekeepers (administrators) who had already come to know me a bit and approved of my project. Formal interviews were carried out with the express purpose of completing a set of life histories. These oral histories consisted of one-hour taped interviews, with subsequent shorter sessions covering areas in need of completion. Interviews were in Spanish or English, most in the former. My command of Spanish was serviceable, able to handle straightforward interviews, or day-to-day conversation. All these exchanges were taped so that I could go back and better translate and transcribe. In areas that involved detailed subtleties or areas of multiple levels of meaning, I would ask the interviewee to simply talk away and I would translate later, coming back to him for subsequent questions. In that way these histories grew. After several weeks I began to conduct similar formal interviews with players. Of the twenty-five regular players on the team, I recorded fourteen complete life histories and seven partial histories. I collected over thirty-eight hours of formal interviews.

I also conducted field interviews, which were shorter and more informal, ranging from a brief question and answer to half-hour conversations on various topics. These interviews were carried out in various places, such as the dugout, hotel lobbies, or the bus. Field interviews were in either Spanish or English. Players actually grew to enjoy using these sessions to practice their English. At least a half dozen Tecos were trying to learn English and we would often wind up our sessions by teaching each other. In most cases my command of Spanish was greater than their knowledge of English, so I benefited by probing the use of idioms and other linguistic subtleties more than they did.

I also felt that their ability to teach coupled with my eagerness to improve my Spanish cut down sociocultural distance. This ease and accessibility eventually filtered down to my observations. When I encountered things that I did not completely grasp, I was made comfortable enough to ask. The idea of a gringo who approached their culture with deference and willingness was not lost on these men. Because baseball remained the express goal of our relationship—the point of departure for nonbaseball topics and the home to come back to—interactions were somewhat comfortably bounded.[1]

## Fan Survey

I also attempted to get data on larger numbers of people in both cities. A bilingual fan questionnaire was created and administered to 200 people in each city. In particular, I was attempting to get some insight into how fans perceived the team's 1994 fall from grace, as well as uncovering any residual autonationalist antagonism in patterned responses to certain questions. The questionnaire was prepared in Spanish and English:

1. Are you a Teco fan?
2. If you are, how many games have you attended this year?
3. How many of those games did you go over to the other side for?

4. Are you aware that attendance at the Tecos games has declined?
5. Choose the most correct reason for this decline:
    a. Need a better stadium.
    b. The owner doesn't run the team well.
    c. Tecos traded or sold off key players.
    d. Other reasons.
6. What would it take to get more fans to attend?
7. Would you be upset if the Tecos moved away from the border?
    Very upset    Somewhat upset    Not at all
8. Would you be upset if the Tecos were bought by North Americans [sic] and played most of their games in Laredo?
    Very upset    Somewhat upset    Not at all
9. Sex and Age: 15–25   26–40   41–55   56 and older
10. Occupation:
11. Neighborhood of residence:

Question 5, on reasons for the decline in attendance, was particularly interesting. As noted in Chapter 7, the selling of players (Ortiz and Barraza, and subsequently others) and the direct sense that owners were mismanaging the franchise were two variations of a single "owner is to blame" category. Hence, there were really only three separate categories: owners, facility and operations, and a category marked "other." The people of the two Laredos differed in their perception of the problem.

|                | Nuevo Laredo | Laredo |
|----------------|--------------|--------|
| Better Stadium | 12%          | 43%    |
| Owners' Fault  | 88%          | 45%    |
| Other          | 0%           | 12%    |

Questions 7 and 8 attempted to get at autonationalist tendencies by seeing if Nuevo Laredoans would become more upset if the team moved to Laredo than if it left the border. In short, would Nuevo Laredoans rather see the team go than play second fiddle to their neighbors across the river?

Degree of Upset if Tecos Left the Border

|                  | Nuevo Laredo | Laredo |
|------------------|--------------|--------|
| Very Upset       | 87%          | 42%    |
| Somewhat Upset   | 11%          | 38%    |
| Not At All Upset | 2%           | 20%    |

Degree of Upset if Tecos Became Property of Laredo

|                  | Nuevo Laredo | Laredo |
|------------------|--------------|--------|
| Very Upset       | 63%          | 22%    |
| Somewhat Upset   | 35%          | 40%    |
| Not at all Upset | 2%           | 38%    |

Nuevo Laredoans were revealed as the more committed fans, even if they were outdrawn by Laredo during the 1994 season. Nevertheless it seems apparent that the people of both Laredos continue to see the team as the cultural and economic property of Nuevo Laredo.


## Archival Research

It was my intention to make a modest contribution to the history of the people in the two Laredos; hence a good deal of the study consisted of archival work that would chronicle the origins of the sport in this region. Primarily using newspaper accounts dating back to the beginnings of the game, I was able to clear up some of the myth that collected around the game's beginnings. The *Laredo Times*, begun in 1881, dated back to the introduction of baseball in the region, and was available in its entirety. This was not the case with the newspapers of Nuevo Laredo. However, Nuevo Laredo gave us the work of Fiacro Díaz Corpuz (see Chapter 2), who collected valuable oral histories dating back to the last decade of the nineteenth century, and so assured a Mexican perspective in writing the history of the sport. I was also fortunate enough to encounter several men who were stars of the 1930s, a transitional period for the game. In a series of long formal interviews I took their oral accounts and spent several afternoons pouring over old photos of their days with the first La Junta team.

I mixed and matched methods depending on the question asked. In trying to represent historical events crossing cultural and national lines, one must utilize anything and everything available: ethnography, archival research, oral histories, or quantitative surveys. Interpreting the results also calls for a blend of positivist analysis and more modern, creative forms that injects the anthropologist into the analysis.


## Interpretation

In the end, the methodological and philosophical direction of this ethnography is close to another south Texas ethnography, Douglas Foley's *Learning Capitalist Culture*.[2] While the shared perspectives were not intentional, becoming apparent to me only in the final stages of writing, I welcomed this affinity since our works are concerned with southern Texas, popular culture, Anglo-Latino relations, and ethnography.

Like Foley, I consider my work as falling between "realist ethnography" and the new, more critical ethnography.[3] I share objections to the idea that scientific realism, with its claim for pure objectivity, omnipresent ethnographer, presentation of subjects as generic (typical), and a heavy reliance upon jargon, is an impediment to interpretation. Consequently, I attempted to put something of myself into the ethnography, and eschewed the notion that I might be fully objective and able to represent all actors at all times. Like Foley, I also have tended to look to the writings of the "new journalists," such as Hunter S. Thompson, George Plimpton, Jimmy Breslin, and Tom Wolfe. These writers maximize the use of intimate, first-person styles of writing in the course of their investigative forays into slightly exotic areas. The result is an attempt to get at the drama in every story.

While I wanted to write my account from a critical perspective, as I attempted to deal with the "crisis of representation" issue, I had no intention of making it central to my work. Admittedly, I read most of the valuable writings by Clifford,[4] Marcus and Fischer,[5] and Rosaldo[6] after I had developed my style of doing ethnography, and long after I should have. I have benefited from these works, but my sense of critical ethnography came originally from the work of philosopher Paul Feyerabend[7] and anthropologist Stanley Diamond[8]. While I share a sense of the flaws embedded in our research agendas, I am, nevertheless, committed to using a wide range of approved methods in carrying out my research. If I eschew the idea of the ethnographer as omniscient, I nevertheless still see myself as authoritative as a result of the research I carried out.

Similarly, I adhere to the new ethnography in declining to separate author and subject of study, as I do to the view of ethnographer as limited by his/her social qualities. True, my race, ethnicity, and age all served to distinguish me from the community I was studying, prompting a problem with accurately representing their reality. These barriers being acknowledged do not disqualify me from carrying out the investigation, however. The crisis of representation of cultural matter is based upon differences that exist between researcher and subjects, but these differences can be reduced and/or prove methodologically advantageous. I have even come to realize that, if trust is gained, my "foreignness" can be used to advance my work. Despite being an older Anglo, I could build bridges along lines of gender and baseball that would link ethnographer and subjects. Obviously my baseball background in high school and junior college provided us a common orientation and set of concerns and appreciations. But it was the little things that really fostered a sense of familiarity and ease between this old gringo and the others. For instance, going on long bus trips and sharing life on the road helped bring us together. A gringo nonplayer sharing this dimension of their lives made an impression on the Tecos. They began to joke with me, and at my expense, but most importantly openly, thus including me in their jokes. Coming to share jokes and joking represents a treasured portal of fieldwork.

In another instance, the players were impressed with my willingness to share the conditioning demands made of them. Despite the fact that I was twenty to twenty-five years older than most Tecos, a lifetime of weight training allowed me to outlift most of them in the gym. As a runner I was also able to run with the pitchers, who always prided themselves on their distance running. This was a respect along basic machismo-hypermasculine lines that I gladly, if politically incorrectly, took since it enabled a basis of sharing (male) culture.

After a time even my differences became material used to close the gaps between us. My antiwar activity in the military during the Vietnam "conflict," for instance, was of great interest to some. On several occasions they queried me over beers until late into the night. In the end, the study wound up resting, though not complacently, between traditional and newer forms of ethnography. When all is said and done I still believe that a good ethnography has to be able to recount a people's story, one that is intrinsically interesting and able to capture much of what the storytellers had in mind. If I as ethnographer was further enriched by it, so much the better; but my first responsibility was to the good people of the two Laredos, who have been ignored for too long.

# Notes

## Introduction

1. Alan M. Klein, *Sugarball: The American Game, The Dominican Dream* (New Haven: Yale University Press, 1991).

2. Gilbert M. Joseph, "Forging the Regional Pastime: Baseball and Class in Yucatan," in *Sport and Society in Latin America*, ed. Joseph Arbena (Westport: Greenwood, 1988), 29–63.

3. A. J. Spalding, *Baseball: America's National Game* (1911; reprint, San Francisco: Halo Books, 1991), 9.

4. See, for instance, Oscar Martínez, *Border People: Life and Society in the U.S.-Mexico Borderlands* (Tucson: University of Arizona Press, 1994), 310.

5. *Borderlands: La Frontera*, (San Francisco: Spinsters/Aunt Lute, 1987), 62.

6. E. J. Hobsbawm and Terrence Ranger, eds., *The Invention of Tradition* (Cambridge: Cambridge University Press, 1983).

7. See for instance Joseph Maguire, "Globalization, Sport, and National Identities: The Empire Strikes Back," *Society and Leisure* 16 (1993): 293–322; Grant Jarvie and Graham Walker, "Ninety Minute Patriots? Scottish Sport and the Making of the Nation," In *Scottish Sport in the Making of the Nation*, ed. G. Jarvie and G. Walker (Leicester: Leicester University Press, 1994), 1–8.

8. Benedict Anderson, *Imagined Communities: Reflections on the Origin and Spread of Nationalism* (London: Verso, 1983).

9. Ernest Gellner, *Nations and Nationalism* (Ithaca: Cornell University Press, 1983).

10. Robert Whiting, *You Gotta Have Wa: When Two Cultures Collide on the Baseball Diamond* (New York: Macmillan, 1989); Milton Jamail, "Will There Be Free Trade for Baseball?" *Washington Post*, October 26, 1991.

11. Anderson, *Imagined Communities*, 2.

12. Gellner, *Nations and Nationalism*, 26.

13. Martínez, *Border People*.

14. John Breuilly, *Nationalism and the State*, 2nd ed., (Chicago: University of Chicago Press, 1993), 64.

15. See the classic study of ethnocentrism by T. Adorno, E. Frankel-Brunswick, E. Levinson, and D. Sanford, *The Authoritarian Personality* (New York: W. W. Norton, 1950), which links ethnocentric hatred of others with building national identity. See also Tom Nairn, *The Breakup of Britain* (London: New Left Books, 1977).

16. Thomas Patterson, and Christine Gailey, eds., *Power Relations and State Formation* (Salem, Wisc.: Sheffield Publishing Company, 1987).

17. Michael Meyer and William Sherman, *The Course of Mexican History* (London: Oxford University Press, 1991), 449.

18. Ibid., 449.

19. Ibid., 532.

20. Daniel Arreola and James Curtis, *The Mexican Border Cities: Landscape Anatomy and Place Personality* (Tucson: University of Arizona Press, 1993), 77–110.

21. Ibid., 77.

22. Ibid.

23. Milton Jamail, personal communication.

24. Franz Fanon, *Black Skins, White Masks* (New York: Grove, 1963); C.L.R. James, *Beyond a Boundary* (New York: Pantheon, 1983).

25. *Laredo Morning Times* (hereafter cited as LMT), June 3, 1994. (Note that the paper was called the *Laredo Times* until 1977.)

26. LMT, May 11, 1993.

27. LMT, August 8, 1994.

28. Lawrence Herzog, *Where North Meets South: Cities, Space, and Politics on the U.S.–Mexican Border* (Austin: University of Texas Press, 1990).

29. LMT, August 9, 1994.

30. LMT, April 27, 1994.

## Chapter One

1. LMT, August 18, 1994.

2. Stanley Green, *A History of the Washington Birthday Celebration* (Laredo: Border Studies Publishing, 1992).

3. Gilberto Hinojosa, *A Borderland Town in Transition* (College Station: Texas A&M Press, 1983).

4. Green, *Washington Birthday Celebration*, 17–18.

5. José Limón, *Dancing with the Devil: Society and Cultural Poetics in Mexican-American South Texas* (Madison: University of Wisconsin Press, 1994), 41.

6. Green, *Washington Birthday Celebration*, 11.

7. Stanley Green, *Laredo, 1755–1920: An Overview* (Laredo: Border Studies Publishing, 1990), 4.

8. Ibid.

9. Stanley Green, *The Story of Laredo* (Laredo: Border Studies Publishing, 1991), 2:137.

10. One of the most famous factional disputes on the border was that between the town of Laredo's two political parties, the "botas" and the "huaraches" of 1886. In that political battle, the factionalism turned deadly when the two sides confronted each other in the town plaza with guns and cannon. See Jerry Thompson, *Hard Times and Bad Whiskey: The Laredo Election Riot of 1886* (El Paso: Western Texas University Press, 1991).

11. James Dunn, ed., *The Two Laredos* (New York: Manus, 1944), 23.

12. Ismael, Villarreal Peña *Seis Villas del Norte: antecedentes históricos de Nuevo Laredo, Dolores, Guerrero, Mier, Camargo, y Reynosa* (Ciudad Victoria: Universidad Autónoma de Tamaulipas, 1986), 11.

13. Ibid.

14. Dunn, *Two Laredos*, 23.

15. Green, *Laredo, 1755–1920*, 12.

16. Ibid., 8.

17. Green, *Story of Laredo*, 1:10.

18. Victoria Mudd and Thom Tyson, directors, *Broken Rainbow* (documentary film), 1986.

19. Walter Prescott Webb, *The Great Plains* (Boston: Ginn and Co., 1931).

20. Américo Paredes, *With His Pistol in His Hand* (Austin: University of Texas Press, 1958).

21. Américo Paredes, *Folklore and Culture on the Texas-Mexican Border* (Austin: University of Texas Press, 1993), 23.

22. Oscar Martínez, *Troublesome Border* (Tucson: University of Arizona Press, 1988), 107.

23. S. S. Wilcox, "Laredo During the Texas Republic," *Southwestern Historical Quarterly* 42 (1938): 76–91.

24. Oscar Martínez (1988) stands out for his inclusion of the Native American groups as part of the borderland's overall sociocultural equation.

25. Edward Dozier, *The Pueblos of North America* (New York: Holt, Rinehart, and Winston, 1970).

26. Edward Spicer, *Pasqua: A Yaqui Village* (Chicago: University of Chicago Press, 1940); W. W. Newcomb, *Indians of Texas* (Austin: University of Texas Press, 1961).

27. Martínez, *Troublesome Border*, 56.

28. Newcomb, *Indians of Texas*, 333–383.

29. Walter Prescott Webb, *The Texas Rangers: A Century of Frontier Defense* (Austin: University of Texas Press, 1965).

30. Newcomb, *Indians of Texas*, 343.

31. Rupert Richardson, *The Comanche Barrier to South Plains Settlement* (Glendale, Calif.: 1933), 103.

32. Newcomb, *Indians of Texas*, 29.

33. Stanley Green, *The Rise and Fall of the Rio Grande Settlements: A History of Webb County* (Laredo: Border Studies Publishing, 1991), 53.

34. Ibid.

35. Ibid.

36. Ibid.

37. Green, *Rise and Fall of Rio Grande Settlements*, 14.

38. Ibid.

39. Ibid., 11.

40. Ibid., 15.

41. Ibid., 24.

42. Green, *Laredo, 1755–1920*.

43. Wilcox, *Laredo During the Texas Republic*, 48.

44. Green, *Washington Birthday Celebration*, 125.

45. Ibid., 136.

46. Martínez, *Troublesome Border*, 81.

47. Montejano, *Anglos and Mexicans*, 24.

48. Ibid., 26.

49. Ibid., 28; Martínez, *Troublesome Border*, 88.

50. Martínez, *Troublesome Border*, 91.

51. Ibid., 37; Manuel Ignacio Salinas Domínguez, *Orígenes de Nuevo Laredo* (Ciudad Victoria: Universidad Autónoma de Tamaulipas, 1981).

270

52. Green, *Washington Birthday Celebration*, 97.
53. Green, *Story of Laredo*, 1:70.
54. Ibid., 83.
55. Larry Dovalina, personal communication.
56. Salinas Domínguez, *Orígenes de Nuevo Laredo*; Villarreal, *Seis Villas del Norte*.
57. Salinas Domínguez, *Orígenes de Nuevo Laredo*.
58. Manuel Ceballos-Ramírez, "The Epic Tradition of the Founding of Nuevo Laredo," in *Festival of American Folklife*, ed. Peter Seitel (Washington D.C.: Smithsonian Institution, 1993), 42–43.
59. Michael Meyer and William Sherman, *The Course of Mexican History*, 4th ed. (London: Oxford University Press, 1991).
60. Ceballos-Ramírez, "The Epic Tradition," 42.
61. Oscar Martínez, *Border Boomtown: Ciudad Juarez Since 1848* (Austin: University of Texas Press, 1978).
62. Ibid.
63. Ibid., 15.
64. Salinas Domínguez, *Orígenes de Nuevo Laredo*, 27.
65. Green, *Story of Laredo*, 2:121.
66. Ibid., 47.
67. Ibid., 115.
68. Ibid.
69. Ibid., 116.
70. Paredes, *Folklore and Culture*, 26.
71. Manufacturing plants were owned by foreign, typically American, companies and located just across the border in Mexico where they receive generous grants from the Mexican government. These companies are also exempt from U.S. regulations and law.
72. LMT, May 19, 1995.
73. LMT, June 6, 1994.
74. Paredes, *Folklore and Culture*, 26.
75. Rodolfo Gonzáles de la Garza, *Los Laredos historia*, 2 vols. (N.p.: Nuevo Laredo, 1989).
76. Meyer and Sherman, *Course of Mexican History*, 440.
77. See William Beezley, *Judas at the Jockey Club and Other Episodes of Porfirian Mexico* (Lincoln: University of Nebraska Press, 1987).
78. Meyer and Sherman, *Course of Mexican History*, 449.
79. Stanley Green, *History of the Tex-Mex Railroad* (Laredo: Border Studies Publishing, 1993), 9.
80. Montejano, *Anglos and Mexicans*, 98.
81. Gonzáles de la Garza, *Los Laredos historia*; Green, *History of the Tex-Mex Railroad*.
82. Richard O'Conner, *Iron Wheels and Broken Men: The Railroad Barons and the Plunder of the West* (New York: G. P. Putnam and Sons, 1987.).
83. Montejano, *Anglos and Mexicans*; Limon, *Dancing with the Devil*.
84. Gonzáles de la Garza, *Los Laredos historia*; Green, *History of the Tex-Mex Railroad*.
85. Beezley, *Judas at the Jockey Club*.

## Chapter Two

1. Eric Wagner, "Baseball in Cuba," *Journal of Popular Culture* 18 (1984): 113–120.

2. Louis Pérez, "Between Baseball and Bullfighting: The Quest for Nationalism in Cuba, 1868–1898," *Journal of American History* 81 (1994): 493–517.

3. Tomás Morales, "El beisbol mexicano a traves de las decadas," *Enciclopédia del beisbol mexicano* (Monterrey: Revistas Deportivas, S.A., 1994), 6–9.

4. Ibid., 6.

5. Ibid., 7.

6. Joseph, "Forging the Regional Pastime," 34.

7. William Beezley, "The Rise of Baseball in Mexico and the First Valenzuela," *Studies in Latin American Popular Culture* 2 (1985): 3–13.

8. Ibid., 8.

9. Morales, *El beisbol mexicano*, 6.

10. Fiacro Díaz Corpuz, *Historia del beisbol neolaredense* (Nuevo Laredo: Tamaulipas, 1955).

11. Fiacro Díaz Corpuz, *Por donde entro el beisbol a Mexico?* (Saltillo: Coahuila, 1979).

12. Díaz Corpuz, *Historia del beisbol*, 17.

13. Ibid., 22.

14. Green, *History of the Tex-Mex Railroad*, 10.

15. *Laredo Times* (hereafter LT), September 23, 1884. (The paper assumed its present name, the *Laredo Morning Times*, in 1977.)

16. I use the term *mexicano* for Mexican American here because the men of that day referred to themselves by this term.

17. LT, June 8, 1888.

18. LT, June 10, 1888.

19. LT, July 3, 1888.

20. Bill Walraven, "Yachts Raced Here in 1888," *Corpus Christi Caller Times*, May 11, 1988.

21. LT, June 21, 1889.

22. LT, July 3, 1889.

23. Hernández and Ramos are mentioned as playing for Laredo against Nuevo Laredo in 1909 (Gonzáles de la Garza, *Los Laredos historia*, 330).

24. LT, July 20, 1903.

25. LT, July 11, 1915.

26. Montejano, *Anglos and Mexicans*.

27. Límon, *Dancing with the Devil*.

28. LT, June 10, 1887.

29. Beezley, *Judas at the Jockey Club*.

30. Díaz Corpuz, *Historia del beisbol*, 19.

31. Ibid., 22.

32. Ibid., 17.

33. Ibid., 22.

34. Gonzáles, *Los Laredos historia*, 333.

35. Díaz Corpuz, *Historia del beisbol*, 18.

36. Gonzáles, *Los Laredos historia*, 502.
37. Díaz Corpuz, *Historia del beisbol*, 25.
38. Ibid., 26.
39. Beezley, *Rise of Baseball*, 8.
40. Díaz Corpuz, *Historia del beisbol*, 32.
41. Ibid., 30.
42. Ibid., 28–29.
43. Ibid., 31–32.
44. Ibid., 32.
45. Ibid., 17.
46. Díaz Corpuz, *Por dentro entro el beisbol*, 41.
47. Díaz Corpuz, *Historia del beisbol*, 21.
48. Díaz Corpuz, *Por dentro entro el beisbol*, 52.
49. LT, July 4, 1903.
50. Díaz Corpuz, *Historia del beisbol*, 30.
51. LT, July 19, 1929.
52. LT, July 11, 1929.
53. Rudolfo Gonzáles Castillo, "Los pioneros de la Liga mexicana," *Enciclopédia del beisbol mexicano*, 27.
54. Ibid., 28.
55. Ibid.
56. LT, February 6, 1934.
57. LT, February 18, 1934.
58. LT, March 15, 1934.
59. LT, March 16, 1934.
60. LT, July 31, 1934.
61. LT, August 3, 1934.
62. LT, August 4, 1934.
63. LT, September 14, 1934.
64. LT, September 22, 1934.
65. LT October 6, 1934.
66. Richard Derby, Jr., and Jim Coleman, "House of David Baseball," *A Review of Baseball History* 14 (1994): 7.
67. LT, October 6, 1934.
68. LT, September 26, 1934.
69. Derby and Coleman, "House of David," 9.
70. LT, February 20, 1935.
71. Montalvo interview, July 28, 1993.
72. Dovalina interview, March 19, 1993.
73. LT, May 6, 1935.
74. Klein, *Sugarball*.
75. Milton Jamail, personal communication.
76. Dovalina interview, March 19, 1993.
77. Montalvo interview, April 3, 1994.
78. Dovalina interview, March 19, 1993.
79. Lázaro Dovalina interview, March 20, 1993.
80. Montalvo interview, July 28, 1993.
81. Dovalina interview, May 2, 1994.

82. Ibid.
83. Montalvo interview, July 28, 1993.
84. Ibid.
85. Dovalina interview, May 2, 1994.
86. Montalvo interview, April 29, 1994.
87. Ibid.
88. Dovalina interview, May 2, 1994.
89. Scott Roper, "Satchel Paige's 1935 Season in North Dakota," *Baseball Research Journal* 23 (1994): 53.
90. Ramon Dovalina, *El Noticario Nacional*, May 1993, 2.
91. Dovalina interview, March 19, 1993.
92. Dovalina interview, May 2, 1994.
93. LT, June 18, 1935.
94. Montalvo interview, July 1993.
95. Dovalina interview, March 30, 1995.
96. Dovalina interview, March 19, 1993.
97. LT, August 18, 1935.
98. Roper, "Satchel Paige," 51.
99. Ibid.
100. Ibid.
101. Montalvo interview, July 29, 1993.
102. Dovalina interview, March 19, 1993.
103. Roper, "Satchel Paige," 54.
104. LT, July 29, 1935.
105. LT, August 4, 1935.
106. Gonzáles de la Garza, *Los Laredos historia*, 339.
107. LT, October 7, 1935.
108. Ibid.
109. Montalvo interview, April 2, 1994.
110. Montalvo interview, July 28, 1993.
111. Allen Guttmann, *From Ritual to Record: The Nature of Modern Sports* (New York: Columbia University Press, 1978).

## Chapter Three

1. Many thanks to Gerald Vaughn, whose articles on the Mexican League and Jorge Pasquel served as the foundation of this chapter, for his generous support of this project.
2. Tom Gorman, with Jerome Holtzman, *Three and Two* (New York: Scribner and Sons, 1979).
3. Ibid., 25.
4. Morales, "El beisbol mexicano," 6.
5. Montalvo interview, April 2, 1993.
6. Montalvo interview, July 28, 1994.
7. The court ruled that since baseball did not traffic between states it was exempt from antitrust regulations that applied to other industries. This ruling has continued to be held up over several subsequent challenges.
8. LT, February 22, 1946.

9. *Current Biography 1946*, 459.

10. Ibid.

11. Gerald Vaughn, "Jorge Pasquel and the Evolution of the Mexican League," *Review of Baseball History* 12 (1992): 10.

12. Klein, *Sugarball*.

13. Bruce Calder, *The Impact of Intervention: Dominican Republic During the U.S. Occupation of 1916–1924* (Austin: University of Texas Press, 1984).

14. Vaughn, "Jorge Pasquel," 10.

15. Cuauhtémoc Rodríguez, personal communication.

16. Gorman, *Three and Two*, 24–27.

17. Montalvo interview, July 1993.

18. Montalvo interview, April 2, 1994.

19. Rogosin, *Invisible Men*, 169; Díaz Corpuz, *Historia del beisbol*, 43.

20. Satchel Paige, with David Lipman, *Maybe I'll Pitch Forever* (Lincoln: University of Nebraska Press, 1993), 122.

21. John Holway, ed., *Black Diamonds: Life in the Negro Leagues From the Men Who Lived It* (New York: Stadium Books, 1991), 81.

22. John Holway, *Blackball Stars: Negro League Pioneers* (New York: Carroll and Graff, 1988), 363.

23. Rogosin, *Invisible Men*, 172.

24. Ibid., 173.

25. Holway, *Blackball Stars*, 364.

26. Rogosin, *Invisible Men*, 174.

27. Montalvo interview, March 11, 1993. Laughingly referring to Gibson as a "black son-of-a-whore" was not interpreted as racist by those in the room, including, according to Montalvo, Gibson himself. In the wake of Pasquel's personal style and his respectful treatment of black players, the comment is thought of as more of a macho reference. Mexicans often refer to race and nationality in talking of someone. Various Tecos were called "Indio" or "Chino."

28. Rogosin, *Invisible Men*; Vaughn, "Jorge Pasquel."

29. Vaughn, "Jorge Pasquel."

30. Gorman, *Three and Two*, 24.

31. LT, January 26, 1946.

32. *Current Biography 1946*, 459.

33. LT, January 26, 1946.

34. LT, April 10, 1946.

35. LT, April 2, 1946.

36. LT, May 3, 1946.

37. Vaughn, "Jorge Pasquel," 11.

38. Ibid.

39. *New York Times*, April 10, 1946.

40. *Current Biography 1946*, 460.

41. Donald Rhoden, "Baseball and the Quest for National Identity in Meiji Japan," *American Historical Review* 85 (1980): 511–34. The summary of the Ichiko team's victory is based on Rhoden's article.

42. Spalding, *Baseball*, 3.

43. Rhoden, "*Baseball and the Quest*," 511.

44. Ibid., 534.
45. Calder, *Impact of Intervention*, 27.
46. The following summary is taken from Klein, *Sugarball*, chapter one.
47. Rogosin, *Invisible Men*, 115.
48. Cordova interview, April 1989, in Klein, *Sugarball*, 23.
49. *New York Times*, April 9, 1946.
50. LT, February 8, 1946.
51. LT, February 2, 1946.
52. LT, February 7, 1946.
53. Ibid.
54. LT, February 8, 1946.
55. Ibid.
56. LT, February 17, 1946.
57. LT, February 22, 1946.
58. LT, March 21, 1946.
59. LT, February 28, 1946.
60. LT, March 5, 1946.
61. LT, March 7, 1946.
62. Ibid.
63. LT, March 8, 1946.
64. LT, March 12, 1946.
65. Ibid.
66. LT, March 15, 1946.
67. LT, April 8, 1946.
68. *New York Times*, April 13, 1946.
69. LT, April 16, 1946.
70. LT, April 17, 1946.
71. *New York Times*, April 18, 1946.
72. *New York Times*, April 6, 1946.
73. *New York Times*, April 10, 1946.
74. LT, April 8, 1946.
75. *New York Times*, April 13, 1946.
76. Ibid.
77. *New York Times*, April 9, 1946.
78. *New York Times*, April 13, 1946.
79. LT, March 20, 1946.
80. LT, April 4, 1946.
81. Vaughn, "Jorge Pasquel"; and David LaFrance, "Sport or Work: Professional Baseball in Mexico, 1980–1989," *Journal of Sport History* 14, no. 2 (1995): 111–35.
82. LT, April 18, 1946.
83. Ibid.
84. LT, May 25, 1946.
85. LT, May 4, 1946.
86. LT, May 21, 1946.
87. LT, May 17, 1946.
88. Ibid.

89. LT, June 6, 1946.
90. LT, July 19, 1946.
91. LT, June 11, 1946.
92. LT, May 19, 1946.
93. Ibid.
94. Andrew Zimbalist, *Baseball and Billions* (New York: Basic Books, 1992), 12.
95. LT, March 7, 1946.
96. LT, March 12, 1946.
97. *New York Times*, April 10, 1946.
98. LT, April 6, 1946; LT, April 10, 1946.
99. LT, May 18, 1946.
100. *New York Times*, April 7, 1946.
101. *New York Times*, April 6, 1946.
102. Ibid.
103. Spalding, *Baseball*, 9.
104. *New York Times*, April 12, 1946.
105. Ibid.
106. Ibid.
107. LT, April 16, 1946.
108. LT, April 25, 1946.
109. LT, June 21, 1946.
110. Ibid.
111. LT, June 22, 1946.
112. *New York Times*, June 22, 1946.
113. LT, June 29, 1946.
114. Ibid.
115. *New York Times*, April 12, 1946.
116. *New York Times*, April 13, 1946.
117. In June 1946, Commissioner Chandler instituted a ban of five years on any player signing with a Mexican League team. The ban was lifted in June 1949.
118. LT, March 12, 1946.
119. LT, August 14, 1946.
120. LT, May 19, 1946.
121. LT, June 1, 1946.
122. Ibid.
123. Ibid.
124. Ibid.
125. LT, April 6, 1946.
126. Ibid.
127. *New York Times*, April 3, 1946.
128. LT, February 4, 1946.
129. Ibid.
130. February 26, 1946.
131. LT, April 3, 1946.
132. LT, April 2, 1946.
133. LT, May 19, 1946.
134. *New York Times*, April 10, 1946.
135. *New York Times*, April 13, 1946.

136. LT, April 11, 1946.

137. The reporting of this entire drama by the *Laredo Times* constitutes something of a treasure trove of material. Not only did the newspaper regularly carry AP and UP stories out of cities such as New York, it also carried Mexican reports from Mexico City as well as the locally oriented stories because of its proximity to Nuevo Laredo. As such, the *Laredo Times* offers researchers of this "baseball war" a rare and full body of data for which I am grateful.

138. Bracker's quote appeared in Vaughn, "Jorge Pasquel," 13.

139. *Personalismo* connotes the individualistic style of the *patrón*.

140. Vaughn, "Jorge Pasquel."

141. LT, February 17, 1946.

142. LT, March 12, 1946.

143. LT, April 15, 1946.

144. LT, June 29, 1946.

145. Gerald Vaughn, "George Hausmann Recalls the Mexican League of 1946–47," *Baseball Research Journal* 19 (1990): 50–63.

146. Vaughn, "Jorge Pasquel."

147. Luís Suárez Fernández, *Alejo Peralta: Un patrón, sin patrones* (Mexico City: Editorial Grijalbo, 1992), 75.

148. Cuauhtemoc Rodríguez, personal communication.

149. Readers wishing to learn more about the politics of Peralta should read David LaFrance, "Labor, the State, and Professional Baseball in Mexico in the 1980s," *Journal of Sport History* 22 (1995): 111–34.

150. LT, April 21, 1949.

151. Montalvo interview, April 2, 1994.

152. The Tecos history from the 1950s through the 1980s is statistically summarized in Homero Solís Ramos, *Los Tecolotes de los dos Laredos: Una historia de un gran equipo* (Mexico City: Revistas Deportivas, 1994).

153. Luque was the first Latin American (Cuban) to play major league baseball. He played from 1914 to 1935, pitching for a variety of teams. His best season came in 1923 when he compiled a 27–8 record, while leading the league in ERA, shutouts, and wins.

154. Solís Ramos, *Los tecolotes*, 82.

155. Rodríguez interview, February 7, 1995.

156. Ibid.

157. LMT, March 16, 1985.

158. Ibid.

159. Rodríguez interview, February 7, 1995.

160. LMT, March 15, 1985.

161. Rodríguez interview, February 7, 1995.

162. Rodríguez interview, February 10, 1995.

163. Couoh interview, July 27, 1994.

## Chapter Four

1. Martínez, *Border People*.

2. *Forbes*, July 15, 1996, 184.

3. LMT, September 3, 1994.

4. Dovalina interview, April 3, 1995.

5. Ibid.

6. Dovalina interview, July 29, 1992.

7. Esther Firova interview, June 16, 1993.

8. Firvoa was hired to manage the Mexico City Tigres in 1995 by his old boss "Chito" Rodríguez, who had become the team's general manager.

9. Barraza interview, May 11, 1993.

10. Ibid.

11. Ibid.

12. Ibid.

13. Fieldnotes, May 7, 1993.

14. Ibid.

15. Couoh interview, August 1, 1994.

16. Barraza interview, May 11, 1993.

17. Barraza was sold to the Mexico City Tigres, for whom he currently pitches.

18. Fieldnotes, April 3, 1994.

19. Mora interview, March 14, 1993.

20. Milton Jamail, "Scouts Showed Ignorance," *Baseball Weekly*, February 24, 1993, 11; idem, "Furor Over Fernando Misdirected," *Baseball Weekly*, May 10, 1991, 20.

21. Ortiz interview, May 12, 1993.

22. Fieldnotes, May 4, 1994.

23. Fieldnotes, March 3, 1993.

24. Ortiz was sold to the Mexico City Tigres in 1994. Andrés Mora was named manager of the Tecos in 1995.

25. Alvarez interview, July 30, 1994.

26. Ibid.

27. Ibid.

28. Ibid.

29. Ibid.

30. Ibid.

31. Alvarez was traded to the Mexico City Tigres in 1995.

32. Couoh interview, May 13, 1993.

33. Fieldnotes, July 28, 1994.

34. Couoh interview, July 20, 1994.

35. Couoh was traded to the Mexico City Tigres in 1995.

36. Meré interview, July 28, 1994.

37. Luis Meré pitched very effectively for three teams in the Mexican League from 1967 to 1980. His lifetime ERA was 2.97.

38. Meré interview, April 4, 1994.

39. Ibid.

40. Meré interview, July 28, 1994.

41. Meré was traded to the Mexico City Tigres in 1995.

42. Fieldnotes, April 6, 1993.

43. Baller interview, July 22, 1993.

44. Baller interview, July 25, 1993.

45. Ibid.

46. Ibid.

47. Barraza interview, May 13, 1993.

48. LaFrance, "Labor, the State and Professional Baseball."

49. Romero interview, August 1, 1994.

50. Although one can always find examples to the contrary, as a rule Americans playing in other countries tend to experience adjustment problems (see Robert Whiting, *You Gotta Have Wa* [New York: Macmillan, 1989]). The difference between Latinos experiencing problems here and Americans encountering problems abroad is due to the arrogance of the latter group.

51. Jamail, "Scouts Showed Ignorance"; idem, "Furor Over Fernando Misdirected."

52. I am not identifying the following three players at their requests.

53. The player asked not to be identified.

54. The player asked not to be identified.

55. Rodríguez interview, May 11, 1993.

56. Barraza interview, March 28, 1994.

57. Milton Jamail, personal communication.

58. James Scott, *Weapons of the Weak: Everyday Forms of Peasant Resistance* (New Haven: Yale University Press, 1985).

59. The player asked not to be identified.

**Chapter Five**

1. An abbreviated version of this chapter appeared in *Sport Sociology Journal* 12 (1995): 370–389.

2. Paredes, *Folklore and Culture*, 217–237.

3. Ibid., 217.

4. Ibid., 218.

5. Ibid., 219.

6. Octavio Paz, *Labyrinth of Solitude* (New York: Grove Press, 1962), 81.

7. Interview with Teco wife (who asked not to be identified), July 22, 1994.

8. See Maxine Baca-Zinn, "Chicano Men and Masculinity," *Journal of Ethnic Studies* 10 (1982): 2944; and Alfredo Mirandé, "Machismos: Rucas, chingasos, y chingaderas," *De Colores* 6 (1982): 17–47.

9. Alfredo Mirandé, "Que gacho es ser macho: It's a drag to be a macho man," *Aztlan* 17 (1988): 81.

10. Interview with Teco wife, July 12, 1994.

11. Paredes, *Folklore and Culture*; Kathleen Sands, *Charrería Mexicana: An Equestrian Folk Tradition* (Tucson: University of Arizona Press, 1993).

12. Matthew Gutmann, "The Meanings of Macho: Changing Mexican Male Identities," *Masculinities* 2 (1994): 21–33.

13. Robert Bly, *Iron John* (Reading, Mass.: Addison-Wesley, 1990).

14. Sam Keen, *Fire in the Belly* (New York: Bantam, 1991).

15. Jose Limón, "Carne, Carnales, and Carnivalesque: Bakhtinian Batos, Discourse, and Narrative Discourse,' *American Ethnologist* 16 (1989): 471–486.

16. Roger Lancaster, *Life is Hard: Machismo, Danger, and the Intimacy of Power in Nicaragua* (Berkeley: University of California Press, 1992).

17. Stanley Brandes, *Metaphors of Masculinity: Sex and Status in Andalusian Folklore* (Philadelphia: University of Pennsylvania Press, 1980); Matthew Gutmann, "Machismo and Lo Mexicano: An Ethnohistorical Appraisal," paper delivered at the Latin American Studies Association Meeting, Atlanta, December 1994.

18. Paz, *Labyrinths of Solitude*, 77.

19. Lancaster, *Life is Hard*, 19.

20. Vicente Mendoza, "El machismo en Mexico a través de las canciones, corridos, y cantares," in *Cuadernos del Instituto Nacional de Antropologia III* (Buenos Aires: Ministerio de Educacíon y Justica, 1962).

21. Paredes, *Folklore and Culture*.

22. Mirandé, "Que gacho es ser macho."

23. Mendoza, "El machismo en Mexico."

24. Paz, *Labyrinth of Solitude*, 81.

25. This account is taken from fieldnotes, July 20, 1992.

26. Fieldnotes, March 12, 1993.

27. Fieldnotes, March 7, 1993.

28. Esther Firova interview, July 22, 1994.

29. Interview (anonymous), July 30, 1994.

30. Interview (anonymous), May 15, 1994.

31. Interview (anonymous), July 30, 1994.

32. Ibid.

33. Mendoza, "El machismo en Mexico."

34. Paredes, *Folklore and Culture*.

35. Mirandé, "Que gacho es ser macho."

36. Couoh interview, July 29, 1994.

37. Cynthia Nelson, *The Waiting Village: Social Change in Rural Mexico* (Boston: Little, Brown, 1971).

38. Hyman Rodman, "The Lower Class Value Stretch," in *Poverty in America*, ed. L. Ferman (Ann Arbor: University of Michigan Press, 1965).

39. Irving Goffman, *Presentation of Self in Everyday Life* (Garden City, N.Y.: Doubleday, 1959).

40. Paredes, *Folklore and Culture*.

41. Interview, July 22, 1994.

42. Fieldnotes, April 4, 1994.

43. Fieldnotes, July 24, 1994.

44. A. Hochschild, "Emotion Work, Feeling Rules, and Social Structure," *American Journal of Sociology* 85 (1979): 551–575; idem, *The Managed Heart: Commercialization of Human Feeling* (Berkeley: University of California Press, 1983).

45. Interview, September 4, 1994.

46. Fieldnotes, April 3, 1994.

47. Interview, March 29, 1994.

48. Fieldnotes, April 6, 1993.

49. Fieldnotes, July 28, 1994.

50. R. W. Connell, "An Iron Man: The Body and Some Contradictions of Hegemonic Masculinity," in *Sport, Men, and the Gender Order*, ed. M. Messner and D. Sabo (Champaign, Ill.: Human Kinetics Press, 1991), 83–96; Michael Messner, *Power at Play: Sport and the Problem of Masculinity* (Boston: Beacon Press, 1992).

51. Earvin "Magic" Johnson (with William Novak), *My Life* (New York: Fawcett, 1992).

52. *Parade Magazine*, August 14, 1994.

53. Timothy Curry, "Fraternal Bonding in the Lockerroom: A Profeminist Analysis of Talk About Competition and Women," *Sociology of Sport Journal* 8 (1991): 130.

54. Phillip G. White and Ann B. Vagi, "Rugby in the 19th Century British Boarding-School System: A Feminist Psychoanalytic Perspective," in *Sport, Men, and the Gender Order*, ed. M. Messner and D. Sabo (Champaign, Ill.: Human Kinetics Press, 1991), 79.

55. Fieldnotes, April 2, 1994.

56. Over the years that I have observed and studied baseball players, I have, of course, witnessed many instances of American men showing signs of physical affection, but by comparison with their Mexican counterparts the former seemed more physically tentative, more self-conscious of their behavior.

57. Fieldnotes, July 29, 1994.

58. Fieldnotes, August 2, 1994.

59. See Michael Messner and Michael Kimmel, eds., *Men's Lives* (Boston: Allyn and Bacon, 1985).

60. Bruce Kidd, "The Men's Cultural Center: Sports and the Dynamic of Women's Oppression/Men's Repression," in *Sport, Men, and the Gender Order*, ed. M. Messner and D. Sabo (Champaign, Ill.: Human Kinetics Press, 1991), 31–45.

61. Don Sabo, "Pigskin, Patriarchy, and Pain," *Changing Men: Issues in Gender, Sex, and Politics* 16 (1986): 20–24.

62. See for instance Rob Connell, *Masculinities* (Berkeley: University of California Press, 1994); Alan M. Klein, *Little Big Men: Bodybuilding Subculture and Gender Construction* (Albany: State University of New York Press, 1993).

63. Interview, July 22, 1994.

64. Lee Upshaw was somewhat unusual in that he had already played with the Tecos, then gone away for a few seasons before being signed again. Upshaw was seen to some extent as a returnee, hence treated more familiarly. More importantly, Upshaw liked playing on the team and enjoyed his experiences in Mexico, a point not lost on his Mexican teammates.

65. Klein, *Little Big Men*; Robert Harlow, "Masculine Inadequacy and Compensatory Development of Physique," *Journal of Personality* 19 (1951): 312–333; Mirandé, "Que gacho es ser macho."

66. Baca-Zinn, "Chicano Men and Masculinity."

67. Gutmann, "The Meaning of Macho."

## Chapter Six

1. Donald Hall, *Fathers Playing Catch with Sons* (San Francisco: North Point Press, 1985), 48.

2. Thomas Boswell, *Why Time Begins On Opening Day* (New York: Penguin, 1987).

3. Fieldnotes, March 1, 1993 (all subsequent quotes by Neiman are from March 1–7, 1993).

4. Jamail, "Scouts Showed Ignorance."

5. Fieldnotes, March 4, 1993 (all subsequent quotes by Roberts are from March 1–7, 1993).

6. George Gmelch, "Baseball Magic," *Transaction* 8 (1971): 234–240.

7. For instance, see Charles Gallmeier, "Putting on the Game Face: The Staging of Emotions in Professional Hockey," *Sport Sociology Journal* 4 (1987): 347–362; Limón, "Carne, Carnales, and Carnivalisque"; Klein, *Sugarball*, Chapter 3.

8. See Philip Newman, "'Wild Man' Behavior in a New Guinea Highlands Community," *American Anthropologist* 66 (1962): 1–19.

9. Fieldnotes, July 12, 1993.

10. Ibid.

11. Fieldnotes, July 27, 1993.

12. Ibid.

13. *El Diario*, July 14, 1993.

14. Rodríguez interview, September 9, 1993.

15. Firova interview, August 26, 1993.

16. Baller interview, August 26, 1993.

17. Firova interview, September 2, 1993.

18. Rodríguez interview, September 9, 1993.

19. Sánchez interview, September 9, 1993.

## Chapter Seven

1. Larry Rhoter, *New York Times*, June 3, 1988.

2. *Dallas Life Magazine*, July 25, 1993.

3. Daniel Arrieola and James Curtis, *The Mexican Border Cities: Landscape Anatomy and Place Personality* (Tucson: University of Arizona Press, 1993), 77–97.

4. Gary Cartwright, "Chasing the Red Eagle,"*Texas Monthly Magazine*, August 1993: 92.

5. Ibid., 124.

6. Jamail, "Scouts Showed Ignorance"; Rod Beaton and Jim Myers, "Scouts Say Players Lack Speed, Power," *USA Today*, February 25, 1993.

7. Peter Gammons, "Plei Bol," *Sport Illustrated*, February 20, 1989.

8. The McAllen-Reynosa ties cannot work as well as those between the two Laredos, because not only are the towns not historically linked in the same way as the Laredos, but McAllen is six miles from the border and the stadium is at Edinburg, several miles further away from the border. Because the stadium is located on the campus of the University of Texas–Pan American, beer cannot be served, further dampening the possibility of baseball as entertainment in a binational format.

9. See for instance Chapter 4's biographical sketches of Pedro Meré or Juan Jesús Alvarez.

10. James Scott, *Domination and the Arts of Resistance* (New Haven: Yale University Press, 1990).

11. Cuevas interview, July 29, 1993.

12. Firova interview, July 29, 1993.

13. Barraza interview, June 1, 1993.

14. Moreno interview, June 1, 1993.

15. With his thirty saves, Baller would come within five saves of breaking the single-season save record for the team. Parenthetically, had Baller been allowed to play the entire season (instead he was assigned to the Tecos three weeks into the season), this mark might have easily been eclipsed.

16. Fieldnotes, July 13, 1993.

17. Firova interview, July 30, 1993.

18. Ibid.

19. *El Mañana*, May 6, 1993.

20. *El Diario*, May 8, 1993.

21. Otero interview, April 5, 1994.

22. LMT, March 17, 1994.

23. *Baseball America's* almanac for 1993 listed the attendance at 181,392.

24. Interview (anonymous), September 14, 1994.

25. Interview (anonymous), August 2, 1994.

26. Interview (anonymous), August 2, 1994.

27. Interview (anonymous), July 30, 1994.

28. LMT, June 16, 1994.

29. Fieldnotes, July 25, 1994.

30. Ibid.

31. See LaFrance, "Labor, the State, and Professional Baseball."

32. After the binational agreement ruptured and the Tecos became the sole concern of Nuevo Laredo in 1995, Samuel Lozano and the new owners paid a great deal more attention to winning their constituency back with promotions and a full slate of entertainment.

33. Dovalina interview, May 19, 1994.

34. LMT, October 28, 1994.

35. Rodríguez interview, October 22, 1994.

36. In an attempt to curb illegal immigration, the state of California passed Proposition 187, which severely restricts public assistance to those who enter the state illegally. Although the law (later overturned in court) had no legal bearing in Texas, it was considered by many Mexicans to be the product of anti-Mexican sentiment common among Americans, as well as to resident aliens.

37. Rodríguez interview, October 22, 1994.

38. Dovalina interview, January 14, 1995.

39. Anderson, *Imagined Community*, 6.

40. Ibid.

41. Robert Redfield, *The Little Community* (Chicago: University of Chicago Press, 1955).

42. Hobsbawm and Ranger, *Invention of Tradition*, 177.

43. Ibid.

44. LT, July 4, 1912.

45. LT, July 5, 1924.

46. Leistra interview, February 22, 1995.

47. LMT, July 14, 1995.

48. LMT, July 21, 1995.

49. LMT, August 2, 1995.

50. Malcolm Chapman, M. McDonald, and E. Tonkin, eds., *History and Ethnicity* (London: Routledge, 1989).
51. Interview (anonymous), July 22, 1994.
52. Van Brant interview, December 10, 1994.
53. Ibid.
54. *Baseball America*, March 3, 1993, 12.
55. Ibid., 14.
56. Ibid.
57. Mike Wagner, "Badlands of Border Baseball," LMT, February 4, 1991, 2B.
58. Goffman, *Presentation of Self in Everyday Life*.
59. LMT, March 28, 1985.
60. Firova interview, March 30, 1995.
61. Ibid.

**Appendix A**

1. Peter Alter, *Nationalism* (London: Edward Arnold, 1989), 4.
2. Anderson, *Imagined Communities*, 5.
3. John Breuilly, *Nationalism and the State*, 2nd ed. (Chicago: University of Chicago Press, 1993).
4. Ibid., 404.
5. Ibid.
6. Terry Eagleton, "Nationalism: Irony and Commitment," in *Nationalism, Colonialism, and Literature*, ed. Terry Eagleton, Fredric Jameson, and Edward Said (Minneapolis: University of Minnesota Press, 1990), 23.
7. Raymond Williams, *The Second Generation* (London: Cass, 1964).
8. Gellner, *Nations and Nationalism*.
9. Max Weber, *Economy and Society: An Outline of Interpretive Sociology*, ed. J. Roth and R. Wittich (Berkeley: University of California, 1978).
10. Anderson, *Imagined Communities*.
11. Weber, *Economy and Society*, 122.
12. I concur with Breuilly that whether or not a group actually manages to realize their collective identity is of secondary importance to the promotion of nationalism. It is more critical that a minority is in a position of projecting a sense of collective identity to which the nation only imperfectly and parially adheres. Still, the overall effect is to promote nationalism as an ideology passively tolerated by most, and actively pursued by some (Breuilly, *Nations and Nationalism*, 66–69).
13. Alter, *Nationalism*, 28.
14. V. I. Lenin, *On the National and Colonial Questions* (Peking: Foreign Languages Press, 1970).
15. Immanuel Wallerstein, *The Modern World System* (London: Academic Press, 1974).
16. Andre Gunder Frank, *Capitalism and Underdevelopment in Latin America* (New York: Monthly Review Press, 1969).
17. Ernest Mandel, *Late Capitalism* (New York: Vintage, 1970).
18. Michael Kearney, "Borders and Boundaries of the State and Self at the End of the Empire," *Journal of Historical Sociology* 4 (1991): 52–71.

19. C.L.R. James, *Beyond a Boundary*.

20. Franz Fanon, *Black Skins, White Masks*.

21. Ashis Nandy, *The Intimate Enemy: The Loss and Recovery of Self Under Colonialism* (Delhi: Oxford University Press, 1983).

22. Klein, *Sugarball*.

23. Partha Chatterjee, *The Nation and its Fragments* (Princeton: Princeton University Press, 1993).

24. Herzog, *Where North Meets South*.

25. Ibid., 136.

26. Arreola and Curtis, *The Mexican Border Cities*, 219.

27. Ibid., 221.

28. Ibid.

29. The Tijuana–San Diego studies are, I believe, somewhat less representative of border city couplings. Tijuana and San Diego reflect the greatest disparity in economic development of any of the border couplings, certainly much greater than any of those on the Texas-Mexico border. This translates into less perceived common ground between the residents of Tijuana and San Diego than along the Laredos border, where economic disparity is less striking and mutual assistance more encouraged.

30. Arreola and Curtis, *The Mexican Border Cities*, 203.

31. Ibid.

32. Kearney, "Border and Boundaries of the State and Self."

33. Herzog, *Where North Meets South*, 39; Martínez, *Border People*, 125.

34. Arreola and Curtis, *The Mexican Border Cities*, 25–26.

35. Herzog, *Where North Meets South*, 50.

36. Ibid., 58.

37. Avelardo Valdez, "An Interpretation of the Underclass: The US-Mexican Border Region," paper presented to Border Scholars Meeting, El Paso, April 1992.

38. Salo Otero, personal communication.

39. LMT, July 2, 1994.

40. Herzog, *Where North Meets South*, 44.

41. Ibid., 46–47.

42. Raúl Fernández, *The Mexican-American Border Region: Issues and Trends* (South Bend: Notre Dame University Press, 1989).

43. Ibid., 31.

44. Ibid., 32.

45. Certainly in the lower Rio Grande region of Texas this has been documented: see Dianne Betts, David Slottje, and Jesús Vargas García, *Crisis on the Rio Grande: Poverty, Unemployment, and Economic Development on the Texas-Mexican Border* (Boulder: Westview, 1994); Herzog, *Where North Meets South*, 46.

46. Herzog, *Where North Meets South*, 107.

47. Martínez, *Border Boom Town*; idem, *Troublesome Border*; idem, *Border People*.

48. Martínez, *Troublesome Border*, 106.

49. Ibid., 2.

50. Montejano, *Anglo and Mexicans*.

51. Wilcox, "Laredo During the Texas Republic."

52. Montejano, *Anglo and Mexicans*, 89.

53. Ibid., 47, 80.

54. Ibid., 37.

55. Paredes, *Folklore and Culture*, 27.

56. Cortez was a Mexican American border dweller, an ordinary citizen who, in response to the shooting of his brother by two Texas sheriffs, exacted revenge by killing them both. This act led to an epic hunt for Cortez by scores of Texas Rangers.

57. Limón, "Carne, Carnales, and Carnivalesque"; idem, *Dancing with the Devil.*

58. Kearney, "Borders and Boundaries of the State and the Self."

59. Guillermo Hernández, *Chicano Satire: A Study in Literary Culture* (Austin: University of Texas Press, 1991).

60. Guillermo Gómez Peña, "Binational Performance Pilgramage," in *Artes pasticas en la frontera Mexico-Estados Unidos*, ed. H. Polkinhorn, R. Reyes, G. Muños, and T. DiBella (Calexico, Calif.: Binational Press, 1980), 51, 60.

61. Martínez, *Border People*, 112; Montejano, *Anglos and Mexicans*, chapter 2.

62. Wilcox, "Laredo During the Texas Republic."

63. Mexicans outside of Mexico City refer to people from the capital by this slightly derogatory term.

64. Limón, *Dancing with the Devil*, 41.

65. LT, June 8, 1888.

66. LT, July 4, 1912.

67. LT, July 5, 1925.

68. Ibid.

69. Kearney, "Borders and Boundaries of the State and the Self."

70. Jorge Bustamante, "Commodity Migrants: Structural Analysis of Mexican Immigration to the United States," in *Views Across the Border*, ed. S. Ross (Albuquerque: University of New Mexico Press, 1978), 183–203.

71. Niles Hansen, *Border Economy* (Austin: University of Texas Press, 1980).

72. LMT, June 8, 1994.

73. Valdez, "An Interpretation of the Underclass," 10.

74. Paredes, *Folklore and Culture*, 26.

75. Green, *History of the Washington Birthday Celebration.*

76. Montejano, *Anglos and Mexicans*, 47.

77. Fred Rippy, "Border Troubles along the Rio Grande, 1848–1860," *Southwestern Historical Quarterly* 23 (1919): 91–111.

78. Ibid.

79. Martínez, *Border Boomtown*, 15; LT, August 24, 1881.

80. Valdez, "An Interpretation of the Underclass."

81. LMT, June 29, 1994.

82. Hernández, *Mexican-American Border Region*, 22; Valdez, "An Interpretation of the Underclass," 8–15.

83. Arreola and Curtis, *Mexican Border Cities*, 91–94.

84. Cases in point include several excellent books on the Olympics, such as Richard Mandell, *The Nazi Olympics* (Urbana: University of Illinois Press, 1987); John MacAloon, *This Great Symbol: Pierre de Coubertin and the Origins of the Modern Olympic Games* (Chicago: University of Chicago Press, 1981); and Michael Real, *Global Ritual: Olympic Media Coverage and International Understanding* (San Diego:

San Diego State University Press, 1986), all of which treat the concept of nationalism conventionally. Others, such as James Riordan, *Sport in the Soviet Union* (Cambridge: Cambridge University Press, 1977); John Sugden and Alan Tomlinson, *Soccer Culture, National Identity, and the USA World Cup* (London: Routledge, 1994); and Richard S. Gruneau and David Whiten, *Hockey Night in Canada: Sport, Identities and Cultural Politics* (Toronto: Garamond Press, 1993), while providing us fine case studies, also wind up discussing nationalism as a concept defined by the state.

85. Douglas Foley represents the successful merger of conventional and postmodern interpretations in sport sociology. See "The Great American Football Ritual: Reproducing Race, Class, and Gender Inequality," *Sociology of Sport Journal* 7 (1990): 111–135; and "Making the Familiar Strange: Writing Critical Sports Narratives," *Sociology of Sport Journal* 9 (1992): 36–47.

86. E. J. Hobsbawm, *Nations and Nationalism Since 1780* (Cambridge: Cambridge University Press, 1990), 11.

87. Joseph Maguire, "More Than A Sporting Touchdown: The Making of American Football in Britain," *Sociology of Sport Journal* 7 (1990): 213–237; idem, "Globalization, Sport, and National Identities: The Empire Strikes Back," *Society and Leisure* 16 (1993): 293–322; idem, "Sport, Identity Politics, and Globalization: Diminishing Contrasts and Increasing Varieties," *Sociology of Sport Journal*, 11 (1994): 398–427.

88. Janet Lever, *Soccer Madness* (Chicago: University of Chicago Press, 1983).

89. See, for instance, the Joseph Arbena anthology, *Sport and Society in Latin America* (Westport, Conn.: Greenwood, 1987). This anthology includes some of the best work done on Latin American sport, such as Gilbert Joseph, "Forging the Regional Pastime"; Matthew Shirts, "Socrates, Corinthians, and Questions of Democracy and Citizenship"; and Steve Stein, "The Case of Soccer in Early Twentieth-Century Lima."

90. Brian Stoddard, "Cricket and Colonialism in the English Speaking Caribbean to 1914: Step Toward Cultural Analysis," University of the West Indies Seminar Series, 1985.

91. James, *Beyond a Boundary*.

92. Jay Mandel and Joan Mandel, *Grass Roots Commitment: Basketball and Society in Trinidad and Tobago* (Parkersburg, Ia.: Caribbean Books, 1988).

93. Michael Malec, ed., *The Social Role of Sport in the Caribbean* (Luxembourg: Gordon and Breach Publishers, 1995). See Maurice St. Pierre, "West Indian Cricket as Cultural Resistance," in Malec, *Social Role of Sport*, 53–83.

94. Rob Ruck, *The Tropic of Baseball* (Westport, Conn.: Meckler, 1991).

95. Klein, *Sugarball*.

96. William Beezley, *Judas at the Jockey Club*.

97. William Beezley, "The Rise of Baseball in Mexico."

98. Joseph Arbena, "Generals and 'Goles': Assessing the Connection Between the Military and Soccer in Argentina," *The International Journal of Sport History* 7 (1990): 120–130; idem, "Sport, Development, and Mexican Nationalism, 1920–1970," *Journal of Sport History* 18 (1991): 340–354; idem, "Sport and Nationalism in Latin America, 1880–1970: The Paradox of Promoting and Performing 'European' Sports," *History of European Ideas* 16 (1993): 837–844.

99. David LaFrance, "A Mexican Popular Image of the United States Through the Baseball Hero, Fernando Valenzuela," *Studies in Latin American Popular Culture* 2 (1983): 14–21; idem, "Labor, the State, and Professional Baseball."

100. Milton Jamail, "Scouts Showed Ignorance"; idem, "Will There Be Free Trade for Baseball?"; idem, "Furor Over Fernando Misdirected."

**Appendix B**

1. I made every effort not to venture into areas that exceeded my linguistic or cultural grasp, keeping in mind Paredes's chiding of fieldworkers who overstepped their linguistic bounds (Paredes, *Folklore and Culture*, 73–110).

2. Douglas E. Foley, *Learning Capitalist Culture: Deep in the Heart of Tejas* (Philadelphia: University of Pennsylvania Press, 1990).

3. George Marcus and Michael Fischer, *Anthropology as Cultural Critique: An Experimental Moment in the Human Sciences* (Chicago: University of Chicago Press, 1986).

4. James Clifford, *The Predicament of Culture: Twentieth Century Ethnography, Literature and Art* (Cambridge, Mass.: Harvard Univesity Press, 1988).

5. Marcus and Fischer, *Anthropology as Cultural Critique.*

6. Renato Rosaldo, *Culture and Truth: The Remaking of Social Analysis* (Boston: Beacon, 1989).

7. Paul Feyerabend, "Against Method: An Anarchistic Theory of Knowledge," in *Minnesota Studies in the Philosophy of Science*, ed. R. Rodman and P. Wanaker (Minneapolis: University of Minnesota Press, 1972), 102–150.

8. Stanley Diamond, *In Search of the Primitive: A Critique of Civilization* (New Brunswick, N.J.: E. P. Dutton/Transaction, 1974); idem, *Totems* (Barrytown, N.Y.: Open Book/Station Hill, 1982).

# Index

About the Author

**Alan M. Klein** is Professor of Sociology and Anthropology at Northeastern University. He is the author of *Sugarball: The American Game, the Dominican Dream* and *Little Big Men: Bodybuilding Subculture and Gender Construction.*